THEMES IN HISTORY

PROPAGANDA

POLITICAL RHETORIC AND IDENTITY
1300–2000

EDITED BY
BERTRAND TAITHE
& TIM THORNTON

SUTTON PUBLISHING

*We dedicate this book to Carys, Louis
and Emily*

First published in the United Kingdom in 1999 by
Sutton Publishing Limited · Phoenix Mill
Thrupp · Stroud · Gloucestershire · GL5 2BU

British Library Cataloguing in Publication Data
A catalogue record for this book is available from the British Library

ISBN 0 7509 2028 9 (cased)
ISBN 0 7509 2029 7 (paperback)

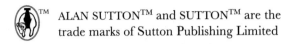
ALAN SUTTON™ and SUTTON™ are the
trade marks of Sutton Publishing Limited

Typeset in 10/12pt Baskerville.
Typesetting and origination by
Sutton Publishing Limited.
Printed in Great Britain by
Biddles, Guildford, Surrey.

PROPAGANDA

POLITICAL RHETORIC AND IDENTITY
1300–2000

CONTENTS

THEMES IN HISTORY
General Editors:

BERTRAND TAITHE AND TIM THORNTON
UNIVERSITY OF HUDDERSFIELD

Themes in History is a new academic series, suitable for students and the general reader. Each volume deals with a particular historical theme, including a methodological and historiographical introduction, essays dealing with the subject in different historical periods, and a concluding bibliographical essay. The essays are accessible to an undergraduate readership without assuming previous specific knowledge, while at the same time offering innovative research and approaches to appeal to all scholars. The time span covered is itself an innovation and enables unprecedented scope for contrasts and parallels. Gender, ethnicity, political and social history are continuous themes throughout the series.

EDITORS AND SERIES EDITORS

Bertrand Taithe read history at Montpellier, the Sorbonne and Manchester University where he completed a thesis on the Contagious Diseases Acts and Victorian society. He has published *The Essential Mayhew: Representing and Communicating the Poor* (1996) and has written a number of articles and a monograph on the Franco-Prussian war: *Defeated Flesh: Welfare, Warfare and the Making of Modern France*, published by Manchester University Press in 1999. He is a member of the French Commission Nationale d'Histoire Militaire, a fellow of the Royal Historical Society and is currently a senior lecturer in modern French and British history at the University of Huddersfield. He is an editor of *European Review of History/Revue Européenne d'Histoire*.

Tim Thornton read history at New College, Oxford and completed a thesis on political society in early Tudor Cheshire. He has recently completed the manuscript of a monograph entitled *Political Society in Early Tudor Cheshire, 1480 to 1560* and has published a number of articles on aspects of community and identity in the late medieval and early modern period. He was awarded the Royal Historical Society's David Berry Prize for 1997. He is currently a senior lecturer in late medieval and early modern history at the University of Huddersfield.

LIST OF CONTRIBUTORS

Graham Barnfield is a lecturer in American studies at Brunel University. His Ph.D. thesis was a study of responses to the Great Depression in the sphere of cultural patronage. He is series editor of *Culture Matters: Communications, Media and Communities*, for Sheffield Hallam University Press.

Peter Beck is professor of international history at Kingston University. Educated at LSE, he did his doctorate on Britain and League peacekeeping, 1924–29, under the supervision of James Joll. His books include *The Falkland Islands as an International Problem* (1988), while *Scoring for Britain: International Football and International Politics, 1900–39* is in press. He served on the history panel for the 1992 and 1996 RAEs, and on the history postgraduate awards panel for the Humanities Research Board, British Academy 1994–97.

Tim Bowman graduated from the Queen's University of Belfast in 1995. He is currently completing a Ph.D. thesis, under the supervision of Professor Ian Beckett, at the University of Luton. His postgraduate research relates to disciplinary problems in the Irish regiments during the First World War.

Máire F. Cross is a senior lecturer in the French department at the University of Sheffield. She has co-authored works on nineteenth-century French feminism including *The Feminism of Flora Tristan* (Berg, 1992) and *Early French Feminism: A Passion for Liberty* (Edward Elgar, 1996), and has published extensively elsewhere on French politics. She is on the editorial board of *Modern and Contemporary France*.

Nicholas J. Cull is professor of American studies at the University of Leicester. He studied under Philip M. Taylor at the University of Leeds. His first book, *Selling War: British Propaganda and American 'Neutrality' in World War II* was published in 1995. He has written numerous articles on film and propaganda, and is currently working on a history of the United States Information Agency since 1953.

Kate Currey was awarded her doctorate, 'The Political and Social Context of Court Festivals in Lorraine 1563–1624', in 1997. She holds two visiting lectureships at the University of the West of England and the University of Plymouth.

Roger Davidson is reader in economic and social history at the University of Edinburgh. He has published widely on the social history of VD and its significance for the regulation of sexuality by central and local government. He is currently completing a book on *Dangerous Liaisons: The Social History of VD in Twentieth-Century Scotland*.

Sarah Gaunt is a postgraduate student and research assistant at the University of Huddersfield. She graduated in social and economic history from the University of Leeds and is now working on aspects of political communication in late medieval England.

June Hannam is a principal lecturer in history at the University of the West of England. Her publications include *Isabella Ford, 1855–1924* (Blackwell, 1989) and several articles on women and the ILP and women and politics. She is writing a book with Karen Hunt, *Debating Socialist Women*, for Routledge.

Karen Hunt is a senior lecturer in the department of history and economic history at Manchester Metropolitan University. Her *Equivocal Feminists: The Social Democratic Federation and the Woman Question, 1884–1911* was published by Cambridge University Press in 1996, and she is currently working with June Hannam on a book on women and British Socialism for Routledge.

Margaretta Jolly is a research fellow at the Mass Observation Archive, University of Sussex. She has published *Dear Laughing Motorbyke: Letters from Women Welders of the Second World War* (Scarlet Press, 1997).

László Kontler is a historian born and educated in Budapest, who currently lectures at Eötvös Lorand University and is also associate professor at the Central European University (both in Budapest). He published the first Hungarian edition of Burke's *Reflections on the Revolution in France* (1990) and a monograph in Hungarian about British conservatism and the early modern languages of politics. His publications in English include a number of articles on the reception of Burke and William Robertson in Germany.

Steve Murdoch has been project manager of the Aberdeen University Mapping Project (GIS) since the summer of 1997. Since March 1998 he has also been employed at the Roehampton Institute (London) as a researcher on the Arms Imports to Britain, 1638–1651 Project.

Michael Rowe is a prize research fellow of Nuffield College, Oxford. After studying at King's College, London, he completed his doctoral dissertation on the Napoleonic Rhineland at Cambridge in 1996. He has recently published articles on the impact of Napoleon on Germany, and on the early development of concepts of citizenship and nationality law, and is currently working on a history of the Rhineland from 1780 to 1830.

Philip Taylor is professor of international communications and director of the Institute of Communications at the University of Leeds. He is associate editor of the *Historical Journal of Radio, Film and Television*, chair of the InterUniversity History Film Consortium and a fellow of the Royal Historical Society. His latest book is *Global Communications, International Affairs and the Media since 1945* (Routledge, 1997).

Geoff Watkins is principal lecturer in European history at the University of Teesside. He has written on several aspects of French cultural history in the nineteenth century, and he is currently working on a book on the Napoleonic Legend and its impact on France.

ACKNOWLEDGEMENTS

E diting a collective work like this one is not an easy task and we thank the contributors first of all for putting up with our tight deadlines, our suggestions and amendments. We also have to thank the history department of the University of Huddersfield which encouraged us and helped finance the workshop preliminary to this volume. The various good libraries our central location enabled us to use made our work more straightforward, and we are grateful for the assistance of their staff. We would like to thank Jane Crompton at Sutton Publishing for her continuing support for the series and the book.

PROPAGANDA: A MISNOMER OF RHETORIC AND PERSUASION?

Bertrand Taithe and Tim Thornton

P ropaganda is one of the many words whose origin stands in sharp contrast to their current meaning. In its strictest terms, propaganda referred to the activities of the papal body the *Sacra Congregatio de Propaganda Fide*.[1] This body, which was established in 1622, was entrusted with promoting adherence to the key tenets of the Counter Reformation Papacy in the context of the reforms and decisions of the Council of Trent. This religious element will be seen as crucial to the practice and perception of propaganda in much of the following discussion, at least in periods up to the later eighteenth century.

The real paradox about propaganda arises from the fact that most readers will assume that it is largely composed of lies and deceits and that propagandists are ultimately manipulators and corrupt. In twentieth-century Western Europe the popular perception of propaganda focuses on the activities of governments and the state; thus propaganda has become a misnomer and its image has been perverted by the developments of German and Russian totalitarianism or by its close links with advertising. While advertising has become almost an artform with its own aesthetics and critical studies, propaganda has ended in the dustbin of historical analysis and practice along with the Gestapo, the Stasi and the KGB. Even the Nazi propaganda ministry's name was debated and left a 'bitter aftertaste' for Goebbels, who had to accept Hitler's choice of the term propaganda.[2] Less well-known is the fact that the second Blum radical Socialist government of 1938 still had a ministry of propaganda. Significantly, as war approached, the Daladier government of July 1939 chose to name the service 'commissariat de l'information'.[3] This evolution of the term in a democracy facing a totalitarian enemy provides an excellent illustration of the fate of the concept.

Propaganda is often most fully discussed in counter-propaganda. Denouncing the other's devious techniques and lack of credibility, while displaying similar methods, makes this a paradoxical and in some ways self-undermining process. For instance, Peter de Mendelssohn [*sic*] wrote in 1944 of 'that vast and monstrous conspiracy against the free mind of the world far more devilish than anything Hitler ever attempted – the Nippon Thought War'.[4] One is tempted to say that in our age of conspiracy theories 'Nippon' could be replaced by any nationality or even the name of some Australian media magnate. Over 200 years ago, it was rapidly realised that the list of banned passages shown in the *Index* provided an easy finding-aid to the key ideas of Protestant thinkers.[5]

Propaganda has been marginalised as a practice to such an extent that practitioners of propaganda now choose not to be labelled as such. The multiplication of cryptic euphemisms, 'image consultants', 'public relations officers', 'spin doctors', etc., reveals the extent of this demonisation of propaganda.[6] As a form of political language, however, propaganda is always articulated around a system of truths and expresses a logic of exclusive representation. It is the purpose of propaganda to convince, to win over and to convert; it has therefore to be convincing, viable and truthful within its own remit. The second major argument developed by theoreticians of propaganda from Jacques Ellul to Philip Taylor is that propaganda is a social phenomenon and therefore operates in several directions,[7] that it is not simply a message communicated from the powers to the public but also a reciprocal message, self-reinforcing and flexible, which must contain the logic and elements of truth, which must explain and make sense of political and social reality to the point that the propaganda message will become significant of a whole political cosmology. This deeper meaning in the term propaganda does not imply that cynicism is not to be found in specialists of so-called crowd behaviour or mass instincts. That some or even most propagandists were self-consciously striking a balance between downright lying and truth telling is obvious. The more intellectual minds had to decide whether they chose to serve society or what they believed to be society or more idealistic values of truth.[8] This tension can be superficially construed as hypocrisy but, on reflection, it lies at the heart of all human actions. The more bizarre or atrocious systems of representations allow themselves to be easily decoded and cynically exposed, but historians should not be smug. The values that inhabit our own writings and which move us to write are not neutral, and we must accept that at the root of all propaganda is a historical perception, a historiographical understanding of the past and of our destiny. Further analysis of propaganda has expanded on techniques and methods, decoding what could be summarised and taught in either specialised propaganda centres or in the media. Even though one needs to consider much more carefully the chronological spread over which propaganda has been referenced and construed, one can perceive a long tradition of the art of pleading and convincing. Western culture and literature thus entirely rests on the art of communicating orally and in written form, which takes such a vital role in all forms of politics and public spheres from the ancient world to the modern age. Rhetoric is the ancient name of that art, and it is significant that this term is now also largely negatively used:[9] 'let Rhetoric be defined as the faculty of discovering in the particular case what are the available means of persuasion'.[10] From the critiques of the Greek Sophists by Plato, who opposed philosophy to rhetoric,[11] to the modern routine denunciation of wooden politics and ready-made phrases, many have lost the real purpose of rhetoric which is to convince and persuade, in effect to end disputes and iron out dissent through a reasoned argument in which language will matter as much as ideas. This latter point has over the last two decades been analysed by historians as the linguistic turn[12] which challenged earlier readings of class language and representations of the world.[13] One of the key aspects of this postmodern rediscovery of the centrality of language was the new emphasis on the linguistic limits of knowledge and perceptions of the world. Also important was the newly found certitude that a class language could be a self-standing element of identity and be both conscious and unconscious.[14]

Rhetoric long remained a cornerstone of university and scholastic education, shaped by its conflict with and its similarities to philosophy, to the point of being formally defined and taught using increasingly refined and esoteric rules which then led to its marginalisation in the curriculum.[15] This relationship between language and quasi-theological values is of course part of Judaeo-Christian traditions and it informs propaganda which can be defined, at least for the time being, as a secular branch of rhetoric. Rhetoric and propaganda are thus closely related but not totally interchangeable; for the purpose of this book and in the context of this series we wish to narrow the definition of propaganda as the expression of a secular cosmology, a political grammar of the conscious and unconscious. Some might indeed say that so clearly pejorative was the term that it had become useless for historical analysis. It remains, however, extremely important in the study of themes which we have pursued before in this series, such as identity, community and rhetoric, and of the themes of citizenship and state in the forthcoming volumes. It allows an approach to several key topics in political and social history. First, propaganda allows an examination of the means of communication and persuasion in the political societies of Western Europe in the period from the late Middle Ages when a combination of growing literacy and increasing incentives to involve and consult the wider population revolutionised the need to transmit ideas and information. Second, it gives us the chance to look at the way that such communication in itself was viewed by participants in the political process and those outside it. The shaping of the term propaganda is also an indication of the way the political nation judges the manner in which political messages are communicated. One must agree that propaganda is not evil or avoidable, and that it can be both a conscious trait and an unconscious, instinctive, reinforcement of self-identity and the promotion of a form of knowledge held as truth.[16] The moral values that are promoted by perhaps a handful of individuals will thus only work if the audience agrees or finds enough points of congruence to accept the new elements of the message. The language of propaganda often touches on nostalgia and sentimentalism,[17] leading collectors to value its iconic and naive representations of what is worth defending.[18] Propaganda promotes the ways of a community as well as defining them; in this sense at least, it is a two-way process which reaches out for unanimity within a group it often helps to define. This defining purpose is central to propaganda, and propaganda is a tool of exclusion as well as inclusion, as most of the papers of this book will show. In some ways propaganda has an almost autonomous existence in the public sphere beyond the intervention of the ruling powers. It is perhaps the principal problem of Ellul's theories of propaganda, or of much history of propaganda before him and since, that they postulate a very clear-cut chasm between the state and public opinion which ignores the historical debates and processes at the heart of their definitions.[19] Ellul's insistence on effectiveness which ties all propaganda to the development of mass production and technological drives thus neglects the earlier uses of the term and the issue of where propaganda fitted in the early societies and states which did not enjoy modern mass media or could not conceive similar concerns about opinion and control. On the other side of the historical perspective, Philip Taylor pursued a genealogy of propaganda from the earliest days to the most recent instances which is perhaps more narrowly focused on state-led initiatives than the following pages.

As the origins of the term strongly imply, propaganda was something essentially religious in form until the eighteenth century, and, in the colonial and neo-colonial world, arguably down to the present day.[20] The very idea of communication of ideas was something over which the Church had achieved a very strong grip by the high Middle Ages, thanks to its technical control of writing, its control of the forms of rhetoric through the universities, and its ideological control of the mechanisms to identify and attack heresy. By contrast, the royal state was slow to create the mechanisms to deal with ideas, as the history of the law of treason suggests. In England at least, physical force and action against the person of the king was the prime indication of treason until the sixteenth century, when the complex issue of treason by words was first legislated upon. Even the codes of honour which represented lay society *par excellence* were treated by the crown only in so far as they impinged upon its prime responsibilities of maintaining defence and war against the king's enemies, and putting down evil-doers at home. Such a fundamental element to the honour of society as heraldry, which expressed in symbolic form what members of lay society stood for in their heritage and persons, was not touched upon by the crown until the 1480s with the incorporation of the College of Arms, and even then acceptance by the crown and population of a regulated language of arms was very slow to develop.

This has led some to view propaganda as impossible where there are no two competing ideologies, and perhaps even to argue that propaganda is something created by and possible only in the context of the religious controversy of the Reformation.[21] On the other hand, it is hard to find any pre-Reformation society where there were not controversies of some nature and in which ideas, even if consensually held, supported a debate about political or social questions. In these circumstances, it is useful to retain propaganda as a concept to allow for the discussion of the rhetorical means of these debates, and the way in which value judgements were placed upon them: as Sarah Gaunt shows in her contribution to this volume, a very wide range of media could be used in fifteenth-century England to convey messages about political and social issues. One example from the mid-fifteenth century suggests the potential for this debate. Preaching at the court of Henry VI in the 1440s was a major means to raise issues of concern at a time of setbacks in foreign war, economic recession and government fiscal weakness; those to whom sermons were directed included not only the king but his court and those involved in the chains of communication, written and especially verbal, that spread out from there. The denial of this communication to some, and the perceived distortion perpetrated by those who either preached, or had control over the choice of preacher, was a major political issue. Lord Saye and Sele, denounced in part for his corruption and support of political violence, was also attacked for preventing dissenting voices being heard before the king; and those attacks were made through a variety of media which in fact echoed the rhetoric of the men being denounced.[22]

Michel de Certeau's notion of heterology, knowledge of otherness, plays an important part in the chronological developments of propaganda.[23] In the Middle Ages the other was the alien. In the representations of the confrontation between Christians and non-Christians (Muslims, Baltic Pagans, and, more indirectly, Hindus, Buddhists and Confucians) the other was external to society and even humankind in the metaphorical cosmology locating Christians between heaven and hell. Even heretics at home could be placed in this scheme. Dissensions within Christendom always existed but were conducted within an assumption of unity implicit in all pre-Reformation rhetoric.[24] The well-charted process of state formation in Europe, however, supported the emergence of religious difference, schisms and the struggle for supremacy between religious and secular hierarchies. It is in this sort of political and social order that rhetoric found its place in debate and discussion within accepted boundaries of knowledge, a deliberative role which conditioned a course of action of the state and a forensic role defending the course of action in legal and judicial systems. This pivotal role which structured all university teaching and much of the public sphere began to fragment and to take a new role during the Reformation. One reformer, Talaeus, explained how he and Pierre Ramus had removed the theories of invention and memory from rhetoric and returned them to logic. Rhetoric then concentrated upon style and delivery as Platonist notions were revived to renew a fundamentally Aristotelian practice.[25] The old idea that rhetoric could bring unity no longer held its sway; instead it began to give formal structures to the expression of dissent and radical division.[26] Early Reformation debates and discussions broke down on the most basic points of rules and authority.[27] While the mission of rhetoric lost some of its importance, the forms of rhetoric carried on being taught and eventually evolved into the purely formal and perhaps sterile rules of classical writing.[28] The original meaning of rhetoric as the art of persuasion remained attached to the classical training while the Renaissance used the term to describe decoration and the modern age understands rhetoric as an art of formal composition.[29] One should not assume, however, that formality carries no meaning: McGinness's work shows the relevance and importance of formal demonstrations as found in counter-Reformation liturgy.[30]

These changes in the style and meaning of rhetoric coincided with technological changes, notably the diffusion of printing techniques and the greater availability of printed matter which was often publicly displayed in pictorial or textual form.[31] The relationship between technology and the explosion of forms of discourse is not deterministic in a simple way.[32] Printed matter could be construed as propaganda and often was another way of prolonging open debates, but the use of print and the type of exchange it implied also had propaganda meanings. The fact that printing expresses power can be understood in several ways and it perhaps matters less that books are read and understood than that they exist. The physical presence of books in gestual propaganda inspires and stimulates the expression of authority. Autodafé, book-burning, from the inspired gesture of Savonarola to the seizure of printers' stock and equipment, reflects the power of the objects as well of the texts.[33] What is new perhaps is that printed texts have enabled historians to comprehend better the great fluidity and the wealth of exchanges which existed throughout Europe. In terms of state building this fluidity of the market prevented exclusive control, sponsoring and censorship.[34] From the fifteenth century onwards presses printing in Latin, Greek and many more forms of Italian, German, French, Dutch, Flemish, Spanish and English vernaculars[35] would exist on a pan-European scale and print indifferently for the home and foreign market, if one can use such terms.[36] The role of the early-modern state could only be to foster home production, however hard it tried to control printed matter. It is an indictment of post-Weberian generations that the assumption that literacy and printed debates reflect a healthy society has long served to demonstrate the intellectual superiority of northern Europe over less literate and less 'free' Catholic, obscurantist, environments.

Comparable assumptions about 'high' and 'low' cultures led to a view of propaganda which implied projection and transfer of ideas and attitudes. That historiography has now been challenged by another which sees the considerable potential for the masses to influence their cultural environment. First, the mechanisms for propaganda in the conventional sense were relatively limited, flawed, and perhaps most importantly never used with determination and system. Second, the broader cultural environment, in which the printing press plays for most of this period a predominant role, is censored but never consistently managed, and at most periods it is the market for print which determines what is printed and sold. Third, the growing appreciation of the complexity of the process of reception means we can no longer simply assume that messages promulgated by the elite, even if they reached the villager or townsperson in any recognisable form, were received by their audience in any way that would have satisfied their authors.[37]

Even given the considerable potential that lay behind communication in manuscript or through oral proclamation, the development of printing had a very important role in expanding the political nation at its broadest definition, in the sense of those who made some contact with the political affairs of entities larger than their own immediate community. Superficially, the earliest printing technology in its complexity, novelty and cost might have assisted the state in communicating its messages to its subjects and others elsewhere. What is striking, however, is the relative reluctance with which elites approached the press as a tool of propaganda, a point developed in Tim Thornton's chapter in this volume.[38] The use of placards in the French wars of religion from the early instances pasted on the king's door itself to the Fronde a hundred years later show how messages composed of text and images came to be taken on by French governments late and mostly to reply to opposing Protestant, Catholic or aristocratic factions.[39] The predominant concern in most of Europe was not the positive promotional benefits of the press but its potential dangers. When ecclesiastical authorities struggled to control and censor they generated a huge growth in clandestine publications. As a result they then led in the use of the press to promote their aims; civil authorities on the other hand lagged far behind, with limited objectives of discouraging rebellion and enjoining obedience their prime motives.[40]

This argument should not be allowed to obscure the fact that ministers were aware of the need to use print to influence attitudes,[41] and the involvement of the Tudor printers in such projects as the publication of editions of Geoffrey Chaucer has been used to argue that they were aware of the need to support the growth of an English national consciousness through the provision of a recognisably English body of literature.[42] On the other hand, it is clear that small interest groups, albeit with an important role in the state, were far more important in promoting, for example, the transfer of romance literature into printed form in England. Edward, duke of Buckingham, was probably the key patron in this development, whatever the commitment of Henry VIII to a chivalric culture at his court and in the projection of his image.[43] The courtier's role was that of persuasion as expressed in Castiglioni's *The Courtier*.[44] Literature here enters the picture as a form of identification, from the authors of the *Plëiade* movement writing in and promoting French as a language of culture to Sydney and other national examples who both reinforced the crucial role of language in acting as a bond for a nation and challenged the relevance of scholastic divagations.[45] The work of

Roger Chartier, following in the footsteps of Norbert Elias, demonstrates the wider relevance of court mores and how a propaganda of gestures and behaviour could help structure society and politics.

The paradox of printed matter is both its immediacy and its intemporality: a debased version of manuals of court behaviour could thus be promoted a century or more after the original appeared, chivalric romance might also be read by an eighteenth-century merchant, and apparently redundant self-help and didactic texts have had extraordinarily long imprints.[46] The immediacy of print is to be found in self-promoted ephemera. Printed matter had to conquer the psychological barrier that manuscript represented the most immediate form of communication, that print in other words remained a cumbersome and unwieldy tool. The cost of typesetting and selling meant that news material was not naturally suited to print. News-reading and news-writing entertained a symbiotic development where the market seems to have been created by the medium while demand could be stimulated to accept new formats and new information provisions. This complex process which expanded the public sphere was only stimulated by governmental propaganda.[47] Renaudot's *Gazette de France*, printed on orders from Cardinal de Richelieu, enjoyed the official status found in modern state papers.[48] The French *Moniteur* of the nineteenth century became a voice of the government and was widely read as the officially sanctioned account of news and public developments. The agents of the government could then ensure that the right 'spin' was given to the events. There could be tensions in this process of communication and between the lines of official printing it was possible to read the dissensions within a regime. What matters perhaps more at this stage is the invention of events and news which builds a chronology later compiled by state-sponsored historians. Annals, compendiums, almanacks can often be the compilation of news items which can themselves be either fictional, symbolic or metaphorical.[49] History as a branch of rhetoric[50] developed as unreconstructed propaganda sponsored by and dedicated to a state, a patron, a monarch or a government.[51] Even opposition material employed it, such as Voltaire's history of the *Siècle de Louis XIV* which expressed his opposition to Louis XV through historical and moral comparisons to the disadvantage of the latter king.[52]

When falling printing costs meant print could be within the reach of the vast majority of the population, as happened in Western Europe in the seventeenth century, the stage was set for a massive growth in the print media, especially when political conditions encouraged this.[53] The consequence was that governments and elites had to contend with communications that had become massively eased, without the means either to control or significantly to influence them except through abrupt and iniquitous censorship or closure.[54] The result in the religious literature of the English, for example, was that while the government and Anglican Church of the late seventeenth century were attempting to reassert a ceremonialist, anti-Calvinist Church, the vast majority of religious work in circulation was supported and controlled by the printing and publishing industry and by their need to respond to the market they served. The mass of the population was therefore provided with tracts that enjoined a simple, prayer-book based religion.[55]

The complexities of dissent and dissemination mean that for a message to permeate society it will need a diversity of entry points in the public sphere. In some respects any attempt to control the public sphere is doomed and will be effectively challenged and undermined from within and without. Even though historians criticise the exact chronology at the heart of Habermas' work on the development and growth of a public sphere,[56] many agree that a healthy public sphere guarantees a healthy public debate and a greater level of freedom.[57] Perhaps we should read in this a striking example of successful liberal propaganda. The weakness of a 'rise of the public sphere narrative' is its insistence that to be effective the public sphere should be all-inclusive and fundamentally united. The nineteenth century seems to demonstrate a fragmentation of the public sphere which may lead to a contemporary state where commercial interests dominate it to the point of making the concept of public sphere a mockery.[58] Packaged politics and campaigns based on slogans and advertising further undermine idealistic views of capitalist democracies as the best instance of healthy public spheres.[59]

The rapidly advancing commercialisation of society added another element to this equation. The vast print circulation of the late eighteenth and nineteenth centuries began to support the development of propaganda on behalf of capitalist enterprise.[60] Newspaper advertising, the use of promotional cards and other items, promotional stunts and displays, and the development of posters and billboards permitted enterprises at first to announce their existence and intentions to the public and then later to try to manage perceptions of their products and services in more and more sophisticated ways.[61] This use of a diversity of media to communicate a political, social or historical message was harnessed in some instances by commercial interests which promoted a story as a way of selling the propagandistic material. In his chapter, Geoff Watkins analyses the commerical forces which promoted the reappearance of Napoleon I in popular almanacks in the 1830s, well before Bonapartist restoration could even be contemplated. Indeed, he argues that the political hijacked the commercial. In a sense the media sold the message to sell itself: Nancy Fitch has shown that the Dreyfus affair helped fuel the circulation of the press in rural France.[62] The state was a relatively late convert to this process: as the contribution in this volume from Tim Bowman shows, as late as the First World War, propaganda campaigns could be crude, ill thought-out and even counterproductive. If we might call propaganda which attempted to influence attitudes and ideas on all levels 'thick' propaganda, the state's efforts even in the early twentieth century were relatively weak. It was only from the 1910s that states began to use a broad range of cultural media to attempt to secure the desired attitudes and actions from their peoples. This process was partly stimulated and considerably hastened by the development of new media, such as the telegraph or cinema which extended considerably the range of propaganda techniques available.[63] Cinema has attracted greater attention not only for its obvious aesthetic dimensions but also because the circumstances of the projections (the dark room, the bright image on the wall) and the concept of a captive cinema audience corresponded to some of the wishes of mass-theorists and crowd manipulators. The reaction of the crowd could be measured and thus help test directly the effectiveness of the propaganda. Cinema also merged two genres when newsreel and fiction blurred; later on, in the age of television,[64] historical documentaries tend to use fiction and newsreel footage indiscriminately, the latter only slightly more explicitly conveying a propagandist message.[65] Expenditure on propaganda and the complexity of the effort grew dramatically, and it has been argued convincingly that it helped maintain relative social peace in the British interwar period.[66] For the postwar period the same argument has been developed by William Crofts who shows how state propaganda was redirected towards productivity with mixed results.[67] The message may seem crude but it mobilised all the means that had been at the disposal of the government since the First World War.[68] On the national and international stage it is worth looking for propaganda beyond the most obvious instances of posters and films. Propaganda also encompassed the popularisation and internationalisation of older fields of cultural endeavour, such as sport, as illustrated by Peter Beck in Chapter 15.[69]

If we agree that an autonomous public sphere existed then it appears that the state depended on its vitality rather than fostering or controlling it. A real problem with this so far is the definition of the state. If the state is taken as a closely defined, coherent and powerful group of individuals and institutions focused at a metropolitan centre, with a directive and even repressive aim, propaganda is singularly absent from its armoury. Even given a more Gramscian emphasis on the state using instruments such as propaganda to maintain a consensus in its favour, the evidence for propagandistic effort, especially propaganda which might manipulate opinions to sustain the power of ruling elites, is very limited. Even during periods of war notoriously centralist states demonstrate their frailty. Bertrand Taithe's paper on the propaganda efforts of the republican regime of 1870, struggling against internal challenges and invasion, demonstrates that state-controlled propaganda was often inane and ineffective while the propaganda material sponsored by other groups and classes had more enduring qualities. In this instance the state belongs to those who wish to have a stake or whose identity depends on the existence of the state. Professional groups such as lawyers and medical experts thus played an important role in 1870 France even though their professions did not make them civil servants. An interpretation of the state which allows it to be seen as a loose and shifting coalition of various interests, and in particular allows the recruitment to the state of a whole variety of local elites, potentially weakens the whole purpose of the discussion of propaganda. In many cases, such an analysis allows us to see 'propaganda' as a means of persuasion among competing groups within the state. Such a conclusion might emerge from study of events such as the ceremonial entries and festival described in Chapter 4 by Kate Currey.[70] The prince entering the city in Lorraine was as much if not more the target of the messages represented by the speeches and tableaux as the mass of the people who may have stood by to watch. In the same way, the Protestant city fathers of London in 1558 sought to articulate an image of Elizabeth I[71] as Deborah, saviour of the true faith, in the pageants they laid on for their new monarch, as pointed out by Ann McLaren in the first volume of this series.[72] In doing so, they not only communicated to the masses in the city but also put forward a persuasive vision of what the new queen's regime might be, at a time when its formation was still highly problematic.[73] Modifying the urban landscape and imposing the monarch's image can be a double-edged weapon of course, and buildings and statues stand there to be defaced or subverted. In 1772 a stick placed in the hand of the statue of Louis XV at Reims thus transformed his benevolent image into that of a tyrant.[74]

Propaganda then becomes in a way the very substance of the state, for it is only this superficially externally oriented communication which articulates the bonds that hold the elites together. On the other hand, there are considerable dangers in this approach that the state will be rendered such a large and amorphous entity that its usefulness for the study of other aspects of political and social action will be diminished. If the poor yeoman in seventeenth-century England, who spared a few pence every month to afford a cheap chapbook and who thereby influenced the market and the content of the work he bought, is to become a powerful and active agent of the state, the problem we face of looking for the propagandist in society has become increasingly complicated. On the other hand, from the nineteenth century onwards the theory seems to be increasingly well-grounded in the more unified and state worshipping nations like France after the Revolution. Even though the French Revolution shaped anew the state throughout Europe and did away with a society structured around orders or aristocratic elites, the powers of the state cannot be too cautiously ascertained. Even in centralist countries the state gravitates around an often minimal centre and its benign neglect and inertia challenge our more interventionist modern perspectives. In this sense the state was often inert and remained a drum which many might beat.

Even if there appears to be a central agenda it remained easy for local forces, administrators and authorities to influence or even silence the message. Reception here was vital and crucially in the hands of individuals who might or might not subscribe, obey, oppose or passively resist. The way citizens approach state propaganda is a demonstration of the quality of the propagandist message and of the vitality of values of citizenship, an argument which tends to send us back to the public sphere issue. This sort of argument has been propounded by the likes of Goldhagen in *Hitler's Willing Executioners* and we ought to be more than careful with such comforting smugness.[75] Propaganda works not by being simple or deceitful but in being credible and complex, and indeed, in the democratic powers of the twentieth century, definitions of citizenship were often at the heart of the propagandist's message.[76] Philip Taylor's work demonstrates how propaganda needs to attain a higher level of sophistication to win over the audience. In many ways the recipients need to be able to engage in a constructive manner with the propaganda they are subjected to or eventually end up producing themselves.[77] A simple example would be letter writing following governmental guidelines, as discussed in this collection by Margaretta Jolly, or even, more perversely, the simple discussion of news items or texts, teaching and lessons learnt from parents and school. It is not irrelevant that anti-Nazi re-education of prisoners of war during the Second World War was often entrusted to the hands of teachers.[78] The German postwar press and all educative materials were thus directed to this most thorough of propagandistic aims.[79] Schooling, which is about the making of a mindset, the learning of a logic and the articulation of one's identity within socially compatible parameters, is the best example of consensually applied propaganda.[80] On a more sinister note, rumour can be deliberately orchestrated or backfire tragically as it did during the siege of Paris in 1870. Controlling propaganda can be more dangerous than initiating it. State censorship only gives greater credibility to subversive propaganda in a pluralist environment.

The challenge to this evolutionary chronology came from the ideological turmoil of the later eighteenth century when, for a handful of years, French revolutionaries intended to wipe the slate clean. The redefinition of the other then took place in historiographical terms. Burke and his followers abhorred the French Revolution for its epistemological break with history. At this level it is interesting that the French Revolution reverted to republican rhetoric and classical style and language to find the purest expression of universal values. The rhetoric and its dogmatic ordering of the universe flew against two thousand years of Christianity and expressly opposed religion in most organised forms, replacing it with vague philosophical theism. From 1789 onwards the religious content of propaganda leaked away to be replaced with radically opposing ideological views. In his chapter László Kontler charts the early uses of the negative understanding of propaganda as the attempted supremacy of an overpowering ideology. There is therefore an interesting tension created by the revolutionary age of the long nineteenth century (1789–1917) between Utopian social unity and ideals based around equality, liberty and fraternity on the one hand and the fragmentation of politics and even propaganda on the other.

*

Rhetoric came to the end of its sterile evolution in the nineteenth century when history and literature[81] (and indeed literary criticism)[82] sprang into existence in universities and on the printing market. While rhetoric acquired many of its current negative connotations, history aligned itself with physical sciences to acquire an aura of neutrality and objectivity while literature freed itself from courtly patronage to fall into the hands of the market.[83] The change in modes of production cannot hide the fact that, if one takes propaganda in its wider sense, both history and literature carried on with their national and identity-strengthening missions independently from the state's intervention.[84] Some historical sub-disciplines like international history had great importance. State-sponsored commissions and printed edited texts, through selection and interpretation, vindicated the state's role in the recent past. This propaganda used university staff to create historical proofs of the state's legitimacy. The First World War allies and the Germans competed in producing a historical literature which redistributed or concentrated the responsibility for what now appeared a senseless tragedy. The defeated powers were most successful in proving that the warmongering often attributed to Germany[85] was more diffuse and complex.[86] This fragmentation in means of propaganda was also associated with a fragmentation of the political sphere where overarching concepts such as 'the people' or the nation were challenged by languages of class and gender.

The emphasis so far, on the diversity of the elements within the state which may be involved in the production of propaganda, has taken the focus away from other groups that might be involved. Groups and individuals who defined themselves as external to the *status quo ante* in state or church frequently aimed to project their message to others. This might be explicitly evangelistic; it might be self-justificatory or even defensive; or it might simply be a way of articulating their own identity. The rhetoric employed here depended crucially on definitions of the 'other' which the group were rejecting, campaigning against or simply defining themselves against. Two such examples appear in this book, and they both crucially turn on the issue of gender in politics. A key issue for socialist women of early twentieth-century Britain and for Flora Tristan in nineteenth-century France was whether they should adopt the propaganda techniques of those against whom they were working. On balance, significantly, they did. Flora Tristan, discussed in this volume by Máire Cross, came closest to rejecting the methods of the day, with her emphasis on the personal, and the importance of her own individual witness to the ideas which she espoused. The socialist women of twentieth-century Britain, on the other hand, who form the subject of the chapter by Karen Hunt and June Hannam, were generally happy to write women's pages and columns in the socialist press of the time, conscious though so many of them were that this risked ghettoising their audience in the world of housework, childcare and cooking.[87] In this sense, the rhetorical forms and techniques of propaganda acted as an inclusive force, ensuring that these oppositional groups and individuals never departed from a debate anchored firmly within the terms of the hegemonies they sought to challenge.[88] A similar story could be constructed in the colonial and neo-colonial environment around ethnicity.

All such alternative forms of propaganda were opposed to the great quest for absolutes which would eventually make ethnicity, gender and class irrelevant categories of social analysis. Totalitarianism, which was more than a political system because it represented the expression of ideals taken to their extreme development of unity, has made great use of propaganda[89] to erase the right to differ and, in a perverse manner, revert to idealised views of the past and organic metaphors of unity.[90] The manner in which propaganda permeated every organisation, club or authorised social activity turned each citizen into both a recipient and a disseminator of propaganda.[91] The emphasis was mainly on productivity rather than individuality. Some of the manufacturing nightmares explored in Rabinbach's work provided an example of a productive society orchestrated by one mind and feeding the world one product.[92] Fordism and Taylorite Brave New Worlds may never have existed beyond the confines of autocratic manufacturing plants but the attraction of standardised products endured in the early days of consumerism. Here again the state seemed to lag behind industrial techniques and models of division of labour. The First World War which witnessed the sudden expansion of the remits of state intervention led the state to take on forms of censorship[93] and propaganda it had never used before to recruit, undermine the enemy or even struggle against diseases.[94] Roger Davidson's paper shows how the commercial methods of early cinema, posters and mass media could be harnessed in a moral crusade against venereal disease or any major plagues.[95] A caveat ought to be added here, and it appears from recent research that state organs were not unanimous in endorsing the use of new media.[96] The social control of the medical hygiene campaigns dreamed of in the nineteenth century and applied in the twentieth implied a much finer and diverse range of methods of communication.[97] There is, in fact, a danger of over-reading propaganda, perhaps a feature of the construction of totalitarianism as part of a hostile propagandist viewpoint. Graham Barnfield, in his contribution to this volume, examines the way in which much American literature was read as part of a sustained communist campaign, when the evidence suggests no such organisation existed. In propaganda terms the world wars have often been defined as the apex of state-led activity. The great innovations of the First World War in the use of cinema, press, cartoons and other media led to a more centralised monopoly on information and propaganda than ever before.[98] The Second World War was a period of immense propaganda and innovation.[99] The war also came after twenty years of reflection on the earlier world conflict and on the role that propaganda played at that time.[100] The political aims of the various powers of Europe were the same as in 1917, to drag the United States into the war or to keep it out.[101] As in 1917 the British were more successful but they had to innovate and use many new techniques which, contrasted with some of the cruder attempts, reveal great ingenuity and manipulation.[102] Margaretta Jolly's chapter in this volume shows how gender stereotypes and feminine tropes could be mobilised for the war effort through discreet yet effective individual letter writing and propaganda. Between the wars the role of veterans, in either defending the fragile peace or promoting a warmongering party, turned individuals and social clubs into instruments, willing or not, of propaganda. Propaganda thus assumed an ever wider range of formulations and touched areas of life which a simple campaign of posters could never approach.[103]

Within Europe the role of propaganda was as important as it had been in the last few years of the First World War in trying to undermine the confidence of the enemy's population.[104] Lord Haw-Haw and Goebbels' early techniques in Britain and France proved only partially effective,[105] but the allied campaigns of mass leafleting and broadcasting certainly proved successful in further undermining a German army in decline.[106] This propaganda could appear crude and simplistic if one considers only the most obvious state production but total war implied total propaganda which could emanate from many sources and consequently be more discreet and effective.

We earlier mentioned the concept of 'thick' propaganda, multi-layered and emanating from various outlets which may or may not belong formally to the state; another equivalent might be 'thick' advertising. Advertising, which on the face of it predates even the French Revolution, only became a specialised professional activity distinguished from the act of selling one's own products in the twentieth century.[107] Even within totalitarian societies of a non-collectivist sort, the diversity of brands challenged the uniformity of the political ideal. There are many paradoxes in advertising which betray its rhetorical origins and some of its ideological underpinning such as the notion of customer loyalty. While many current propagandists talk about rebranding a country or a government there are fundamental differences in the manner in which propaganda can reach beyond the hedonistic values of consumerism. While one cannot reject out of hand the crucial role of consumption in the shaping of national identity,[108] the means of encouraging consumption are not synonymous with propaganda.[109] Propaganda is about life and death and this choice is never better exemplified than in time of war when the choice is indeed between staying at home and going to the front. Any comparison between this sort of message and selling a tub of margarine seriously overstates the powers of advertising.[110] Even though advertising now enjoys a central role in consumer societies and can even have a ludic dimension it does not shape culture in the way propaganda has.[111]

This parallel development of modern, liberal consumer advertising has meant, however, that propaganda and state-sponsored communication has tended to be redefined less as history-making and more as thick advertising. Nick Cull's chapter on the promotion of US values and government at the height of the Cold War makes the point clearly. Jackie Kennedy paraded her handshake and style across the screens of millions of Americans and non-Americans, making news and selling a product centred on care and love. This sort of documentary newsreel played in many different ways and was as much a product of specific propaganda agencies as Radio Liberty or Radio Free Europe were.[112] The irony, of course, is that this campaign roughly coincided with the early involvement in Vietnam.[113] The powers of soap operas, lifestyle propaganda, Western values and moral tales can only be successfully exploited in liberal societies where spontaneous propaganda can harness commercial forces and answer a need for reassurance in pluralistic values which, on the face of it, appear weak and feeble compared with totalitarian unanimity.[114]

The warfare of large masses required some consensus and after centuries of internal divisions propaganda managed to move people and ideas throughout the twentieth century. The ministers of information, state-controlled mass media, television and even subtly censored newspapers or radio have given a false impression of the power of state propaganda.[115] The false dichotomy between truth and propaganda and the absurd opposition between propaganda and the propagation of democracy need to be seriously challenged as shown by many authors in this volume.[116] The truth is elsewhere, especially when one considers the need for propaganda which is defended by Philip Taylor in the conclusion of this volume. In an era of new technologies and information warfare and rampant misinformation,[117] Taylor calls for more propaganda to counter the nihilism born of conspiracy theories and news saturation.[118] How the history of these late years will come to be written in the absence of guiding rules of propaganda is anyone's guess.

Notes

1   John K. Thornton, 'A Note on the Archives of the Propaganda Fide and Capuchin Archives', *History in Africa*, 6 (1979), 341–4.

2   The sinister career of Joseph Goebbels made Germany one of the most important instances of modern mass-manipulations. Ralf Georg Reuth, *Goebbels* (London, Constable, 1993), pp. 172–3. For a contemporary account, see H.B. Summers, *Radio Censorship*, The Reference Shelf (New York, The H.W. Wilson Co., 1939), pp. 22–3.

3   Marc Martin, *Trois Siècles de Publicité en France* (Paris, Odile Jacob, 1992), p. 20.

4   Peter de Mendelssohn, *Japan's Political War* (London, George Allen and Unwin, 1944), p. 177.

5   Elizabeth L. Eisenstein, *The Printing Press as an Agent of Change: Communications and Cultural Transformations in Early Modern Europe* (2 vols, Cambridge University Press, 1979), vol. 1, p. 416; cf. the protest movements of the 1960s, among whom it was possible to reproduce without comment the leaflets of their opponents, which they considered sufficiently damning: Wayne C. Booth, *Modern Dogma and the Rhetoric of Assent* (University of Chicago Press, 1974), p. 9.

6   The British army had a director of public relations in 1938: Anthony James, *Informing the People: How the Government Won Hearts and Minds to Win WW2* (London, HMSO, 1996), p. 41. This book is in itself an example of propaganda about propaganda. Richard S. Tedlow, *Keeping the Corporate Image: Public Relations and Business, 1900–1950* (Greenwich, CN, JAI Press, 1979).

7   Jacques Ellul, *Propaganda: The Formation of Men's Attitudes* (New York, Vintage Books, 1973).

8   Gary S. Messinger, *British Propaganda and the State in the First World War* (Manchester University Press, 1992), pp. 24–52; the portrayal of Charles Masterman is a good example. Darwin's resolution of this problem involved systematically orchestrating propaganda for his theories from the background, while himself only addressing his scientific questions: John Angus Campbell, 'The Invisible Rhetorician: Charles Darwin's "Third Party" Strategy', *Rhetorica*, 7 (1989), 55–85.

9   Cf. the collapse of interest in rhetoric in study of the ancient world, Brian Vickers, *In Defence of Rhetoric* (Oxford, Clarendon Press, 1988), pp. 435–6: *The Cambridge History of Classical Literature* in neither volume (1982–5) treated rhetoric as a subject in its own right, with a continuous history.

10   Dudley Bailey (ed.), *Essays on Rhetoric* (New York, Oxford University Press, 1965), p. 59.

11   Cf. the comments of Roger Moss, 'The Case for Sophistry', in Brian Vickers (ed.), *Rhetoric Revalued: Papers from the International Society for the History of Rhetoric* (Binghampton, NY, Center for Medieval and Early Renaissance Studies, 1982), pp. 207–24; and John Poulakos, 'Terms for Sophistical Rhetoric', in Takis Poulakos (ed.), *Rethinking the History of Rhetoric: Multidisciplinary Essays on the Rhetorical Tradition* (Boulder, CO, Westview Press, 1993), pp. 53–74.

12   The linguistic turn as an alternative to older theoretical frameworks is now a minor industry. See recent instances: Gareth Stedman Jones, *The Languages of Class: Studies of English Working Class History, 1832–1982* (Cambridge University Press, 1983); Patrick Joyce, *Visions of the People: Industrial England and the Questions of Class, 1848–1914* (Cambridge University Press, 1991); Patrick Joyce, *Democratic Subjects: The Self and the Social in Nineteenth-Century England* (Cambridge University Press, 1994); Dror Wahrman, *Imagining the Middle Class: The Political Representation of Class in Britain*, c. *1780–1840* (Cambridge University Press, 1995).

13   See Hayden White, *Topics of Discourse: Essays in Cultural Criticism* (Baltimore, The Johns Hopkins University Press, 1978); for a recent critique see Vickers, *In Defence of Rhetoric*, pp. 444, 468–72.

14   For a critique of Foucault, in particular focusing on his use of the rhetoric of experience, see James A. Berlin, 'Revisionary History: The Dialectical Method', in Poulakos (ed.), *Rethinking the History of Rhetoric*, pp. 135–51.

15   James J. Murphy, *Rhetoric in the Middle Ages: A History of Rhetorical Theory from Saint Augustine to the Renaissance* (Berkeley, CA, University of California, 1974); James J. Murphy (ed.), *Medieval Eloquence: Studies in the Theory and Practice of Medieval Rhetoric* (Berkeley, CA, University of California, 1978); J.M. Fletcher, 'The Faculty of Arts', in James McConica, *The Collegiate University*, The History of the University of Oxford, 3 (Oxford, Clarendon Press, 1986), pp. 157–99.

16   Kenneth Burke, *A Rhetoric of Motives* (New York, Prentice-Hall, 1950), p. 55.

17   David J. Denby, *Sentimental Narrative and the Social Order in France, 1760–1820*, Cambridge Studies in French, 47 (Cambridge University Press, 1994), pp. 139–65.

18   James, *Informing the People*, pp. 130–1. The term 'ethos' can be used to express the attitude

towards a source of communication held at a given time by the receiver: James C. McCrosky, *An Introduction to Rhetorical Communication* (1968; 4th edn, Englewood Cliffs, NJ, Prentice-Hall, 1982), ch. 4; Lawrence J. Prelli, 'The Rhetorical Construction of Scientific Ethos', in Herbert W. Simons (ed.), *Rhetoric in the Human Sciences* (London, Sage, 1989), pp. 48–68.

19   Ellul, *Propaganda*, pp. 132–3.

20   Nicholas Thomas, 'Colonial Conversions: Difference, Hierarchy, and History in Early Twentieth-Century Evangelical Propaganda', *Comparative Studies in Society and History*, 34 (1992), 366–89.

21   Robert W. Scribner, *For the Sake of Simple Folk: Popular Propaganda for the German Reformation*, Cambridge Studies in Oral and Literate Culture, 2 (Cambridge University Press, 1981).

22   Thomas Gascoigne, *Loci e Libro Veritatum* (ed.) James L. Thorold Rogers (Oxford, Clarendon Press, 1881), p. 91.

23   Michel de Certeau, 'Heterologies: Discourse on the Other', *Theory and History of Literature*, 17 (Manchester University Press, 1986), pp. 67–79.

24   Nancy S. Struever, *The Language of History in the Renaissance: Rhetoric and Historical Consciousness in Florentine Humanism* (Princeton University Press, 1970), p. 9; cf. the concern of Socrates and Plato, that if rhetoric is not grounded in truth it becomes a pure technique that can be used for good or ill, emphasised by Paul Cantor, 'Rhetoric in Plato's Phaedrus', in Kenneth W. Thompson (ed.), *The History and Philosophy of Rhetoric and Political Discourse* (2 vols, Lanham, MD, University Press of America, 1987), p. 19.

25   George A. Kennedy, *Classical Rhetoric and its Christian and Secular Tradition from Ancient to Modern Times* (Chapel Hill, University of North Carolina Press, 1980); Wilbur Samuel Howell, *Logic and Rhetoric in England, 1500–1700* (Princeton University Press, 1956), pp. 148–9; Ch. Perelman, 'Rhétorique, dialectique, et philosophie', in Vickers (ed.), *Rhetoric Revalued*, pp. 277–81; Walter J. Ong, *Ramus: Method, and the Decay of Dialogue: From the Art of Discourse to the Art of Reason* (Cambridge, MA, Harvard University Press, 1958); Wilbur Samuel Howell, *Eighteenth-Century British Logic and Rhetoric* (Princeton University Press, 1971); Richard Marback, 'The Phoenix of Hermes, or the Rebirth of Plato in the Eighteenth Century', *Rhetorica*, 13 (1995), 61–86.

26   Frederick J. McGinness, *Right Thinking and Sacred Oratory in Counter-Reformation Rome* (Princeton University Press, 1995), p. 13.

27   Norman L. Jones, *Faith by Statute: Parliament and the Settlement of Religion 1559* (London, Royal Historical Society, 1982), pp. 123–7.

28   In French education, A. Ed. Chaignet, *La Rhétorique et son histoire* (Paris, Bouillon et Vieweg, 1888). The final year of secondary education lost its name and its teaching of rhetoric only in 1885: p. vii.

29   Leo Rockas, *Modes of Rhetoric* (New York, St Martin's Press, 1964), p. ix; Catherine Hobbs Peaden, 'Condillac and the History of Rhetoric', *Rhetorica*, 11 (1993), 135–56.

30   McGinness, *Right Thinking*, pp. 87–108.

31   Elizabeth L. Eisenstein, *The Printing Revolution in Early Modern Europe* (Cambridge University Press, 1983, Canto edition 1993), p. 36.

32   Miriam Usher Chrisman, *Lay Culture, Learned Culture: Books and Social Changes in Strasburg 1480–1599* (New Haven, Yale University Press, 1982), pp. 284–6.

33   D. Weinstein, *Savonarola and Florence: Prophecy and Patriotism in the Renaissance* (Princeton University Press, 1970).

34   Many instances of trading in forbidden books prove how ineffectual or even counterproductive authoritarian measures were: J.P. Belin, *Le Commerce des livres prohibés à Paris de 1750 à 1789* (New York, Burt Franklin, 1962).

35   Rudolf Hirsch, *Printing, Selling and Reading, 1450–1550* (Wiesbaden, Otto Harrassowitz, 1967), p. 133.

36   Lucien Febvre and Jean-Henri Martin, *L'Apparition du livre* (Paris, Albin Michel, 1958), pp. 162–92, 326–75.

37   See Roger Chartier and Hans-Jürgen Lüsebrink (eds), *Colportage et lecture populaire, imprimés de large circulation en Europe XVIe–XIXe siècles* (Paris, Imec Editions, Editions de la maison des sciences de l'homme, 1996).

38   For instances of an unwillingness to control the press, see Colin Clair, *A History of Printing in Britain* (London, Cassell, 1965), pp. 104–5 (the exemption of printers from controls on alien merchants in a statute of Richard III). John Feather, *A History of British Publishing* (London, Croom Helm, 1988), pp. 43–9, 67–83, describes the effects of two periods of press freedom in seventeenth-century England.

39   Christian Jouhaud, 'Lisibilité et persuasion, les placards politiques', in R. Chartier (ed.), *Les usages de l'imprimé (XVe–XXe siècle)* (Paris, Fayard, 1987), pp. 309–42, esp. p. 323.

40   Thomas Cogswell, 'The Politics of Propaganda: Charles I and the People in the 1620s', *Journal of British Studies*, 29 (1990), 187–215.

41   G.R. Elton, *Policy and Police: The Enforcement of the Reformation in the Age of Thomas Cromwell*, (Cambridge University Press, 1972), esp. Ch. 4. The emphasis here is on Thomas Cromwell, but equal importance was clearly attached to printed propaganda by others, including Henry VIII himself, as over the issue of *The Glasse of Truthe*, in Henry Ellis (ed.), *Original Letters, Illustrative of English History, Third Series* (4 vols, London, Richard Bentley, 1846), vol. II, pp. 194–9.

42   *The Workes of Geoffray Chaucer Newly Printed, with Dyuers Workes Neuer in Print Before* (London, T. Godfray, 1532; STC 5068).

43   Carol M. Meale, 'Caxton, de Worde, and the Publication of Romance in Late Medieval England', *The Library*, 6th series, XIV (1992), 283–98; Steven Gunn, 'Chivalry and the Politics of the Early Tudor Court', in Sydney Anglo (ed.) *Chivalry in the Renaissance*, (Woodbridge, Boydell, 1990) pp. 106–28.

44   Mark D. Johnston, 'The Treatment of Speech in Medieval Ethical and Courtesy Literature', *Rhetorica*, 4 (1986), 21–46, suggests that even in less formal environments than the royal court there were attempts to control and order speech.

45   Burke, *Rhetoric of Motives*, pp. 221–33; Kenneth J.E. Graham, *The Performance of Conviction: Plainness and Rhetoric in the Early English Renaissance* (Ithaca, Cornell University Press, 1994), p. 17

46   See Jean Hébrard, 'Les livres scolaires de la Bibliothèque bleue: Archaisme ou modernité?', in Chartier and Lüsebrink (eds), *Colportage et lecture populaire*, pp. 109–36.

47   See Michael Harris, 'The Structure, Ownership and Control of the Press, 1620–1780', in George Boyce, James Curran and Pauline Wingate (eds), *Newspaper History from the Seventeenth Century to the Present Day* (London, Constable, 1978), pp. 83–97.

48   Gilles Feyel, 'Réimpressions et diffusion de la "Gazette" dans les provinces', in Pierre Retat (ed.), *Le Journalisme d'Ancien Régime*, Centre d'Études du XVIIIe siècle Université Lyon II (Lyons, Presses Universitaires de Lyon, 1982), pp. 69–86; Blanche B. Elliott, *A History of English Advertising* (London, Batsford, 1962), pp. 17–19. For a synthesis, see Bob Harris, *Politics and the Rise of the Press: Britain and France, 1620–1800* (London, Routledge, 1996), pp. 29–52.

49   News and truths are not necessarily the same: what is newsworthy can be more symbolic than real or its importance can be blown out of proportion to serve a political or social purpose. Martin Mayer, *Making News* (New York, Doubleday, 1987), pp. 2–44.

50   Struever, *Language of History*, pp. 63–81.

51   Gary Ianziti, *Humanistic Historiography under the Sforzas: Politics and Propaganda in Fifteenth-Century Milan* (Oxford, Clarendon Press, 1988), pp. xii, 49–60; see also Joan Davies, 'History, Biography, Propaganda and Patronage in Early Seventeenth-Century France', *Seventeenth-Century French Studies*, 13 (1991), 5–17.

52   Voltaire, *Le Siècle de Louis XIV* (Paris, 1751).

53   On the economics of the print market, see Margaret Spufford, *Small Books and Pleasant Histories: Popular Fiction and its Readership in Seventeenth-Century England* (London, Methuen, 1981); Tessa Watt, *Cheap Print and Popular Piety, 1550–1640* (Cambridge University Press, 1991). The most obvious example of such political circumstances is provided by the collapse of control on printing in England in the early 1640s: Joan Raymond, *The Invention of the Newspaper: English Newsbooks, 1641–1649* (Oxford, Clarendon Press, 1996).

54   Jeremy Black, 'A Short-Lived Jacobite Newspaper: The National Journal of 1746', *Journal of History and Politics*, 7 (1989), 77–88; also see Simon Targett, 'A Pro-Government Newspaper during the Whig Ascendancy: Walpole's London Journal, 1722–1738', *Journal of History and Politics*, 7 (1989), 1–32.

55   Watt, *Cheap Print and Popular Piety*.

56   Jürgen Habermas, *L'Espace public: Archéologie de la publicité comme dimension constitutive de la société bourgeoise* (Paris, Payot, 1978), pp. 212–19.

57   N.B. especially in this connection the liberal views of W. Ross Winterowd, *Rhetoric: A Synthesis* (New York, Holt, Rinehart and Winston, 1968), p. 85: 'the rhetorician has always been a citizen of the agora, in most senses a real democrat'.

58   This is of course a point made by Habermas who opposed manipulated opinion and public opinion, stressing the fictional dimension of both. Habermas, *L'Espace public*, pp. 246–60.

59   See Joanne Morreale, *The Presidential Campaign Film: A Critical History*, Praeger Series in Political Communication (Westport, CN, Praeger, 1993), pp. 26–43 which briefly surveys the meshing of old and new propaganda techniques in the nineteenth- and twentieth-century United States. Kathleen Hall Jamieson, *Packaging the Presidency: A History and Criticism of Presidential Campaign Advertising* (New York, Oxford University Press, 1984), pp. 3–38.

60   Martha L. Olney, *Buy Now, Pay Later: Advertising, Credit and Consumer Durables in the 1920s* (Chapel Hill, University of North Carolina Press, 1991), pp. 135–81.

61   Elliott, *History of English Advertising*, pp. 164–71.

62   Nancy Fitch, 'Mass Culture, Mass Parliamentary Politics, and Modern Anti-Semitism: The Dreyfus Affair in Rural France', *American Historical Review*, 97 (1992), 55–95.

63   See for instance: Philip M. Taylor, *Britain and the Cinema in the Second World War* (Basingstoke,

Macmillan, 1988); Nicholas Reeves, *Official British Film Propaganda During the First World War* (London, Croom Helm, 1986).

64   The history of television is a whole industry in itself.

65   Larry Wayne Ward, *The Motion Picture Goes to War: The U.S. Government Film Effort during World War I* (Ann Arbor, UMI, 1985), pp. 27–9 on the German effort to introduce more structured propaganda material in the USA. Marshal Joffre even stated in 1915 his intention to create a film-based historical source for future generations of historians, p. 31.

66   Nicholas Pronay and D.W. Spring, *Propaganda, Politics and Film, 1918–45* (Basingstoke, Macmillan Press, 1982).

67   S.W. Crofts, 'The Attlee Government's Economic Information Propaganda', *Journal of Contemporary History*, 21 (1986), 453–71.

68   William Crofts, *Coercion or Persuasion? Propaganda in Britain after 1945* (London, Routledge, 1989); Susan L. Carruthers, '"Manning the Factories": Propaganda and Policy on the Employment of Women, 1939-1947', *History*, 75 (1990), 232–56.

69   Cf. the development of 'tourist propaganda', promoting images of a country and ideas about its society and culture: e.g. Taina Syrjämaa, *Visitez L'Italie: Italian State Tourist Propaganda Abroad, 1919–1943: Administrative Structure and Political Realization* (Turku, Turun Yliopisto, 1997).

70   For French instances of entries and ceremonial propaganda, see Peter Burke, *The Fabrication of Louis XIV* (New Haven, Yale University Press, 1992), pp. 19, 87–105, 151–79. Also see Helen Watanabe-O'Kelly, 'Festival Books in Europe from Renaissance to Rococo', *Seventeenth Century*, 3 (1988), 181–201.

71   Peter McClure and Robin Headlam Wells, 'Elizabeth I as a Second Virgin Mary', *Renaissance Studies*, 4 (1990), 38–70.

72   A.N. McLaren, 'Prophecy and Providentialism in the Reign of Elizabeth I', in B. Taithe and T. Thornton (eds), *Prophecy: The Power of Inspired Language in History, 1300–2000*, Themes in History, 1 (Stroud, Sutton, 1997), pp. 31–50.

73   John Guy, *Tudor England* (Oxford University Press, paperback edn, 1990), pp. 250–1; William P. Haugaard, *Elizabeth and the English Reformation: The Struggle for a Stable Settlement of Religion* (Cambridge University Press, 1968), esp. Ch. 3.

74   Jeffrey Merrick, 'Politics on Pedestals: Royal Monuments in Eighteenth-Century France', *French History*, 5 (1991), 234–64, esp., p. 249.

75   Robert R. Shandley (ed.), *Unwilling Germans? The Goldhagen Debate* (University of Minnesota Press, 1998).

76   Arthur L. Smith, jnr, *The War for the German Mind: Re-educating Hitler's Soldiers* (Providence, Berghahn Books, 1996), pp. 80–1.

77   The discrepancy between captive audience and sceptical audience is best illustrated in Sarah Fishman, 'Grand Delusions: The Unintended Consequences of Vichy France's Prisoner of War Propaganda', *Journal of Contemporary History*, 26 (1991), 229–54.

78   Smith, *War for the German Mind*, p. 30.

79   Peter J. Humphreys, *Media and Media Policy in West Germany: The Press and Broadcasting since 1945* (Oxford, Berg, 1990), pp. 24–43; Isa Van Eeghen, '*Lieux de mémoire* Recycled: The Denazification of German Feature Films with a Historical Subject', *European Review of History*, 4 (1997), 45–72.

80   C. John Somerville, 'The Distinction between Indoctrination and Education in England, 1549–1719', *Journal of the History of Ideas*, 44 (1983), 387–406.

81   Which might be seen to include, at least until the 1920s, advertising: Jennifer Wicke, *Advertising Fictions: Literature, Advertisement, and Social Reading* (New York, Columbia University Press, 1988).

82   For literary criticism springing from the 'Belletristic Rhetorics': Stephen H. Browne, 'Edmund Burke', H. Lewis Ulman, 'Adam Smith', Christy Desmet, 'Henry Home, Lord Kames', and Linda Ferreira-Buckley, 'Hugh Blair (1718–1800)', in Michael G. Moran (ed.), *Eighteenth-Century British and American Rhetorics and Rhetoricians: Critical Studies and Sources* (Greenwood Press, Westport, CN, 1984), pp. 42–51, 207–18, 132–41, 21–35 (respectively). Cf. the idea that double-entry book-keeping, in origin at least, was a form of justificatory rhetoric, not a tool for profit-maximisation: James A. Aho, 'Rhetoric and the Invention of Double Entry Bookkeeping', *Rhetorica*, 3 (1985), 21–43.

83   Suzanne L. Marchand, 'The Rhetoric of Artifacts and the Decline of Classical Humanism: The Case of Josef Strzygowski', *History and Theory*, 33 (1994),106–30.

84   Stuart Wallace, *War and the Image of Germany: British Academics, 1914–1918* (Edinburgh, John Donald Publishers, 1988), pp. 58–73, 167–90. Stephen Vaughn, *Holding Fast the Inner Lines: Democracy, Nationalism and the Committee on Public Information* (Chapel Hill, University of North Carolina Press, 1980), pp. 65–7. Romke Visser, 'Fascist Doctrine and the Cult of the Romanità', *Journal of Contemporary History*, 27 (1992), 5–22.

85   *J'accuse by a German*, trans. Alexander Gray (London, Hodder & Stoughton, 1915).

86   Keith Hamilton, 'The Historical Diplomacy of the Third Republic', in Keith Wilson (ed.), *Forging the Collective Memory: Government and International Historians Through Two World Wars* (Providence, Berghahn Books, 1996), pp. 29–63; Catherine Ann Cline, 'British Historians and the Treaty of Versailles', *Albion*, 20 (1988), 43–58; Herman J. Wittgens, 'War Guilt Propaganda Conducted by the German Foreign Ministry during the 1920s', *Historical Papers, Communications historiques* (Canadian Historical Association) (1980), 228–47.

87   Lori Anne Loeb, *Consuming Angels: Advertising and Victorian Women* (New York, Oxford University Press, 1994) reads systematically how women could be portrayed and targeted in Victorian and Edwardian society; also see Katrina Rolley, 'Fashion, Femininity and the Fight for the Vote', *Art History*, 13 (1990), 47–71.

88   See, for Russia, Françoise Navailh, 'The Emancipated Woman: Stalinist Propaganda in Soviet Feature Film 1930–1950', *Historical Journal of Film, Radio and Television*, 12 (1992), 203–15.

89   Richard Taylor, 'The Spark that Became a Flame: The Bolsheviks, Propaganda and the Cinema', in T. H. Rigby, Archie Brown and Peter Reddaway (eds), *Authority, Power and Policy in the USSR: Essays Dedicated to Leonard Schapiro* (New York, St Martin's Press, 1980), pp. 57–76.

90   For the systematic attempts to indoctrinate children in Vichy France, see Judith K. Proud, *Children and Propaganda: Il était une fois . . . : Fiction and Fairy Tale in Vichy France* (Oxford, Intellect, 1995); Dominique Rossignol, *Histoire de la propagande en France de 1940 à 1944* (Paris, Presses Universitaires de France, 1991), pp. 113–76; Margaret Atack, *Literature and the French Resistance: Cultural Politics and Narrative Forms, 1940–1950* (Manchester University Press, 1989), pp. 16–29.

91   Peter Kenez, *The Birth of the Propaganda State: Soviet Methods and Mass Mobilization, 1917–29* (Cambridge University Press, 1985), pp. 254–5. Cf. the hugely successful campaign to mobilise the USA through volunteers speaking during cinema intervals: Alfred E. Cornebise, *War as Advertised: The*

Four Minute Men and America's Crusade 1917–1918 (Philadelphia, The American Philosophical Society, 1984): audiences addressed numbered more than 314 million people (p. 158).

92 A. Rabinbach, *The Human Motor* (New York, Basic Books, 1991).

93 Ross F. Collins, 'The Development of Censorship in World War I France', *Journalism Monographs*, 131 (1992), 1–25.

94 Harold D. Lasswell, *Propaganda Technique in World War I* (Cambridge MA, MIT Press, 1971); James Morgan Read, *Atrocity and Propaganda, 1914–1919* (New Haven, Yale University Press, 1941); George G. Bruntz, *Allied Propaganda and the Collapse of the German Empire in 1918*, Hoover War Library Publications, 13 (Stanford University Press, 1938).

95 Another example is Edwina Palmer and Geoffrey W. Rice, '"Divine Wind Versus Devil Wind": Popular Responses to Pandemic Influenza in Japan, 1918–1919', *Japan Forum*, 4 (1992), 317–28.

96 David A. Welch, 'Cinema and Society in Imperial Germany 1905–1918', *German History*, 8 (1990), 28–45, esp. pp. 34–5. Also see Mark Cornwall, 'News, Rumour and the Control of Information in Austria-Hungary, 1914–1918', *History*, 77 (1992), 50–64.

97 All campaigns were not state sponsored; see for instance John Macnicol, 'Eugenics and the Campaign for Voluntary Sterilization in Britain between the Wars', *Social History of Medicine*, 2 (1989), 147–69.

98 Eberhard Demm, 'Propaganda and Caricature in the First World War', *Journal of Contemporary History*, 28 (1993), 163–92.

99 To reassess the importance of the Second World War see the general survey of propaganda through history in Philip M. Taylor, *Munitions of the Mind: A History of Propaganda from the Ancient World to the Present Day* (Manchester University Press, 1995); on the phoney war see Robert Cole, 'The Other "Phoney War": British Propaganda in Neutral Europe, September–December 1939', *Journal of Contemporary History*, 22 (1987), 455–79.

100 Read, *Atrocity and Propaganda*. Also see George G. Bruntz, *Allied Propaganda and the Collapse of the German Empire in 1918*, Hoover War Library Publications, 13 (Stanford University Press, 1938).

101 See the most comprehensive survey of the British action in the United States: Nicholas John Cull, *Selling War: British Propaganda Campaign against American 'Neutrality' in World War II* (New York, Oxford University Press, 1995).

102 Nicholas J. Cull, 'Overture to an Alliance: British Propaganda at the New York World's Fair, 1939–1940', *Journal of British Studies*, 36 (1997), 325–54. The British promoted Britain as the mother of all democracies by distributing copies of the Magna Carta; Philip M. Taylor, '"If War Should Come": Preparing the Fifth Arm for Total War 1935–1939', *Journal of Contemporary History*, 16 (1981), 27–51.

103 James M. Diehl, 'Victors or Victims? Disabled Veterans in the Third Reich', *Journal of Modern History*, 59 (1987), 705–36.

104 David Welch, *Propaganda and the German Cinema, 1933–1945* (Oxford University Press, 1983); on the other side, see Frederic James Krome, '"A Weapon of War Second to None": Anglo-American Film Propaganda during World War II' (unpublished Ph.D. thesis, University of Cincinnati, 1992).

105 For France see Christian Brochand, *Histoire générale de la radio et de la télévision en France* (2 vols, La Documentation Française, 1994), Ch. 6; David Welch, 'Propaganda and Indoctrination in the Third Reich: Success or Failure?', *European History Quarterly*, 17 (1987), 403–22.

106 Gerald Kirwin, 'Allied Bombing and Nazi Domestic Propaganda', *European History Quarterly*, 15 (1985), 341–62.

107 Martin, *Trois siècles de publicité*, pp. 21–50, 122–214.

108 Consumerism defined class and national identities jointly. See Whitney Walton, *France at the Crystal Palace: Bourgeois Taste and Artisan Manufacture in the Nineteenth Century* (Berkeley, University of California Press, 1992); Thomas Richard, *The Commodity Culture of Victorian England: Advertising and Spectacle* (London, Verso, 1991), pp. 119–63; Cary Carson, Ronald Hoffman and Peter J. Albert, *Of Consuming Interests: The Style of Life in the Eighteenth Century* (Charlottesville, University Press of Virginia, 1994).

109 John Benson, *The Rise of Consumer Society in Britain 1850–1890*, Themes in British Social History (London, Longman, 1994), pp. 143–63.

110 Ralph K. Winter, 'Advertising and Legal Theory', in David G. Tuerck (ed.), *Issues in Advertising: The Economics of Persuasion* (Washington, AEIPPR, 1978), pp. 15–27, esp. p. 17.

111 See Frank Mort, *Cultures of Consumption: Masculinities and Social Space in Late Twentieth-Century Britain* (London, Routledge, 1996), pp. 91–8; Gary Cross, *Time and Money: The Making of Consumer Culture* (London, Routledge, 1993), pp. 184–212.

112 Jon Lodeesen, 'Radio Liberty (Munich): Foundations for a History', *Historical Journal of Film, Radio and Television*, 6 (1986), 197–210.

113 See J. Walsh and James Aulich, *Vietnam Images: War and Representation* (Basingstoke, Macmillan, 1989); Robert W. Chandler, *War of Ideas: The US Propaganda Campaign in Vietnam* (Boulder, CO, Westview Press, 1981).

114 Roland Marchand, *Advertising the American Dream: Making Way for Modernity, 1920–1940* (Berkeley, University of California Press, 1985).

115 Television entertains ambiguous relations with democracy, particularly in the age of commercial satellite media which enable the audience to hear an uncensored message which may not even originate from their own country, when it thus becomes a power to be reckoned with. For a pessimistic assessment of television in the age of world capitalism and the Internet see Douglas Kellner, *Television and the Crisis of Democracy* (Boulder, Westview Press, 1990), pp. 214–24. More optimistic is John Keane, *The Media and Democracy* (Cambridge, Polity Press, 1991), pp. 182–93; Colin Seymour-Ure, *The British Press and Broadcasting since 1945* (Oxford, Blackwell, 1996), pp. 225–70; Peter J. Humphreys, *Mass Media and Media Policy in Western Europe* (Manchester University Press, 1996), pp. 199–228.

116 A typical example is to be found in Bob Franklin, *Packaging Politics: Political Communications in Britain's Media Democracy* (London, Edward Arnold, 1994), pp. 112–18.

117 It seems that the usual propaganda machines, such as American cinema, have harnessed some of the technological mutations and will carry on serving global propagandistic campaigns of lifestyle and soft ideology; Janet Wasko, *Hollywood in the Information Age* (Cambridge, Polity Press, 1994).

118 Philip M. Taylor, *Global Communications, International Affairs and the Media since 1945* (London, Routledge, 1997).

Part One

STATE BUILDING AND PROPAGANDA

One of the key themes of this book is the relationship between the state and propaganda. In this section, three chapters discuss the use of a variety of means of propaganda against the background of the emergence of nation states in Western Europe. Sarah Gaunt first argues that in England in the fifteenth century a highly complex political and social debate was conducted through a variety of media: religious division was not necessary for elites to develop propagandistic techniques. Tim Thornton carries some similar themes into a discussion of the subsequent fifty years: examining the way that printed material was used by English governments in the half century after print technology was introduced into the country, he shows how tentative was its adoption of the opportunities which arose thereby. Finally Kate Currey's contribution outlines the way small European courts used ceremonial entries and literature to reinforce their power. This section shows how propaganda in this earlier period came increasingly to define the state and reinforce its existence.

2

VISUAL PROPAGANDA IN ENGLAND IN THE LATER MIDDLE AGES

Sarah Gaunt

'an historical painting is, in a sense, a vehicle of communication'[1]

As Panofsky suggested, art had a purpose other than merely to appeal to the observer at a decorative level. It was a means to convey certain messages, whether political, social or religious. In the medieval period when literacy was restricted to the privileged classes the need to communicate with the public at large had to be met by other methods. We have, however, to ask the question of how messages were conveyed before there was a significant rise in literacy. An inability to read or write did not mean an inability to understand other symbols or images. Medieval people were used to being informed through pictures – they were educated in visual symbolism. The thirteenth-century Franciscan St Bonaventure wrote of the use of images for religious instruction: 'They were introduced on account of the transitory nature of memory, because those things which are only heard fall into oblivion more easily than those things which are seen.'[2] This statement is as readily applicable to politics as religion. In identifying the shortcomings of many of the literary sources, historians have looked towards the visual arts as a less corrupted source.

The problem with treatment of the genre of visual propaganda is that it can be highly subjective. When does a livery badge become political rather than familial – is it only during times of war? Or is it only with a historian's desire to make sense of the past with the use of hindsight? Francis Haskell warns against too much reliance on this approach: 'Many investigations . . . have sought to demonstrate that even images formerly assumed to depict only what could have been seen by an innocent eye . . . were in fact the products of conscious or unconscious manipulation.'[3] We must not be too eager to ascribe propagandist traits to something in order to make it fit in with a theory or certain perceptions that we are trying to convey. Sydney Anglo, in examining the Tudor period, has argued that too much is read into the symbolism of the past using the methodology of the twentieth century and thus we are in danger of incorrectly interpreting signs as portentous when in contemporary eyes they were innocent.[4]

On the other hand there is the danger of denying the presence of a visually literate and intelligent society by pursuing Anglo's argument too far. Medieval society was educated and ambitious enough to be able both to employ and interpret the subtle and less subtle aspects of visual propaganda that were used. To quote M.V. Clarke, 'it must be remembered that Richard [II]'s subjects could read a coat more easily than they could read a letter'.[5] M. Michael sees the use of badges as political as there must have been a consensus of opinion about the significance of the gesture: it was universally recognised as having more than a purely familial meaning.[6] In particular, attention should be drawn to the frequency of visual references within many of the chronicles. As the chronicles tended to refer only to important issues these visual references must have had significance to contemporaries for them to have been recorded. The medieval population were able to assimilate knowledge from a visual source; they could, therefore, also be manipulated via the visual medium. The political turbulence of the medieval period ensured that all possible methods of communication would be utilised and within this framework visual propaganda had an important role to play.

Although Sydney Anglo warns against the use of twentieth-century criteria, the term propaganda must be clarified before embarking on an undertaking such as this. A useful theoretical framework has been provided by Jacques Ellul in his book *Propaganda: The Formation of Men's Attitudes*.[7] Briefly, Ellul declines to define propaganda but rather establishes a set of circumstances under which it may exist. He divides it into agitation and integration propaganda. The former he sees as leading people into action or rebellion. The latter is meant to make them adjust to desired patterns. The differentiation between agitation and integration propaganda may be taken to another stage with regard to the visual medium. Intimidation propaganda, such as the massing of a well dressed and armed retinue to meet a foreign embassy could have a powerful impact upon one's enemies. These categories enable the historian not only to identify incidences of propaganda but to assess their impact. Visual propaganda may be divided into two further categories, 'artistic' and 'physical'. The former is represented by portraits, architecture and the decorative arts – essentially the conventional image of 'visual' propaganda. It is also found in combination with the literary genre, for example in the case of genealogies. The latter is manifested via the use of processions, military displays and public executions.

The question of what is the purpose of the propaganda – integration or agitation, the promotion of kingship, political allegiance or war – raises another important historiographical point. Colin Richmond regards the promotion of kingship as publicity; propaganda he regards as the deliberate manipulation of information by the government.[8] Richmond's dichotomy is not convincing: kingship was such an integral yet potentially divisive part of medieval politics that such a distinction serves only to cloud the issue. This reflects, in part, Ellul's definition of propaganda, which is broader in compass than Richmond's. The latter assumes a more negative view of propaganda as deliberate deception and manipulation, an assumption which itself relies on a belief that the medieval period was one without deep ideological or cultural divisions and tensions, unlike, for example, the period of the Reformation. An assessment of visual propaganda allows us to see controversy – involving a need both for agitation and for integration – in media that might immediately seem more suited to publicity than propaganda.[9]

There is much visual evidence to be found in illuminated manuscripts; however, these were for such a limited and privileged audience that we have to question their value in the politics of the day. As Evelyn Welch has argued of Italy, 'for the majority of citizens simpler and more ubiquitous objects, such as . . . pennants, banners and coats of arms, acted as the most overt expression of political authority'.[10] The strongest tradition at that time was to be found in heraldry. Since the beginning of the thirteenth century the art of heraldry had developed into a pictorial language that was universally recognisable, and this system of armorial bearings had been fully established by the fourteenth century. Heraldry had gradually become integrated into the decorative arts. Heraldic decoration could be found on buildings, ships, horse harnesses, clothing and domestic plate. Out of the heraldic tradition developed the badge which often had political overtones rather than familial ones. The use of badges increased as coats became more complex and thus harder to immediately identify.[11] As David Starkey has written, '[t]o fulfil its function the badge had to be, of necessity, a simple, easily remembered and recognisable emblem.'[12] An extremely famous example of the problem of mistaken identity at the vital battle of Barnet in 1471, where 'the Erle of Oxenfordes men hadde uppon them ther lordes lyvery, both before and behynde, which was a sterre withe stremys, wiche [was] myche lyke kynge Edwardes lyvery, the sunne with stremys',[13] led to the killing of the earl of Oxford's men by the earl of Warwick's men in error and to Edward IV's victory. The initial choice of badge, Starkey notes, was diverse. Some commemorated events, such as Henry VII's crown in a hawthorn bush; others were visual puns, such as the bray of Sir Reginald Bray.[14] Strong reactions could be provoked by the mere sight of a badge. On the morning before the battle of Poitiers, Sir John Chandos reconnoitred the French positions, and Marshal Jean de Clermont did the same for those of the English. Each noticed that the other employed the same badge as himself, 'une bleue dame ouvrée de broudre ou ray d'un soleil'.[15] The meeting resulted in an argument over the badge and proves that heraldic devices and badges were not just decorative, but could arouse strong emotions: such was their visual power.

Given that badges were so instantly recognisable, it is unsurprising that they carried a very powerful political message. According to the Dieulacres chronicler it was through badges that in 1399 Henry Bolingbroke's political motives became apparent once he had left Wales on his way to overthrow Richard II:

Then indeed, were those royal badges both of the hart and of the crown hidden away, so that some said that the esquires of the duke of lancaster, wearing their collars, had been preordained by a prophecy to subdue like greyhounds in this year the pride of that hated beast the white hart.[16]

The livery of Richard II was the white hart as famously portrayed in the Wilton Diptych. Bolingbroke also ordered a more violent suppression of his opponent's royal livery. According to John Catesby 'above the gates of Warwick castle [was] a crowned hart of stone, which at that time was the said King Richard's livery[;] . . . the duke of Lancaster ordered them to be knocked down, which was done.'[17] If these had not been powerful images then there would not have been a need for Bolingbroke to destroy evidence of their presence. These actions showed that he no longer recognised the king's badge or his authority. Throughout his subsequent reign, Henry IV was plagued by the ghost of Richard II. He had to contend with the various rumours of Richard's survival and flight to Scotland. Bolingbroke's opponents used badges as a talisman of Richard's cause even after his death. In a case before the King's Bench in Essex in 1405 certain people were accused of treason for promoting the story that Richard II was still alive. One of those involved was Maude, countess of Oxford, who had apparently 'set down as pledge to Neil Goldsmith a censer of silver-gilt to pay for the harts that were of king Richard's livery'.[18] It is likely that these were for distribution, probably to a select few but nevertheless this reveals the power that was associated with a badge as a political tool. The importance of the badge as a weapon in the propagandist's war may be seen by Henry Percy's adoption of the white hart in 1403 at Lichfield, as the English Chronicle describes: 'And the said ser Henri Percy and alle his men wered and were araid in the liverey of the hertis, the whiche was king Richard's liverey.'[19] The significance of this may be seen in the fact that Percy was wearing not a familial badge but that of a dead king, which suggests a political statement, especially as the Percys had helped Henry take the throne from Richard II. They believed that they had been unfairly treated, particularly with regard to payment from Henry, and they saw that the only way to revive their position was to try and raise support for Richard II, despite the fact that it was known that he was already dead. Unfortunately the hart proved as unlucky for Henry Percy as it had for Richard II as he was defeated at Shrewsbury, and his 'hed was smyte of and set up at York, lest his men wolde have saide that he hadde be alive'.[20]

Such badges might also be important in a period of relative domestic peace and of the assertion of English power on the continent of Europe. Henry V was a far more astute politician than his father had been. His campaign to conquer France was his sole ambition and all his energies were thus directed. Perhaps Henry's greatest political coup was his courtship of the emperor Sigismund in an attempt to gain more universal support for his French campaign. He wined and dined Sigismund lavishly, but more importantly he made Sigismund a knight of the Garter and gave him a collar with the Lancastrian SS symbol. In

1417 when Sigismund returned to Constance it was reported that he wore the robes of the Order of the Garter and the collar at high mass.[21] It was the visual impact of Sigismund wearing the collar of the king of England which depressed French morale and buoyed that of Henry's allies. In an age when visual symbolism, whether paintings on church walls, comets or other phenomena, was respected and understood, the possibilities for manipulation were quite extensive. The use of a badge had broad political implications. It could be used for agitation propaganda as in the case of Henry Percy and the hart livery or for intimidation purposes as Sigismund's wearing of the Lancastrian collar suggests.

Conflict might in fact be expressed through a jockeying for position, not between men but between badges and what they represented. Bale's chronicle provides us with a particularly stark example of the use of badges for propagandist purposes in 1450. 'Item the ffriday the xxx of Octobr wer drawe doun in divers places of the citie and aboute in the subarbes the armes of the seid duk of york a bage of the ffetherlok and the kings armes set up.'[22] And on the following day 'upon all halowen eve the seid armes of the duk of york wer set up agein'.[23] This is indicative of an organised and concerted propaganda campaign by both supporters and opponents of the duke of York.

The importance of being correctly identified with the predominant political power was paramount during the crisis years of 1469–71, when the wearing of the wrong badge may have been literally fatal. As Commines noticed upon the news of the flight of Edward IV from England, the immediate sign of changed allegiance was visual, the badge: 'They told me at this dinner that after the news had arrived from England, within less than a quarter of an hour everyone was wearing that livery', the ragged staff, the badge of the earl of Warwick who was trying to reinstate Henry VI as king.[24] Commines, writing again of events in 1470, attended a dinner with Lord Wenlock who 'had on his hat the emblem of a golden ragged staff, which was the earl's token'.[25] Commines was obviously acutely aware of the significance of the open wearing of these badges to record both these examples during a time of political crisis in England. It is interesting to note that it was the badge of Warwick that was worn and not that of the king. Warwick was a popular and powerful figure and perhaps it had been realised that his badge would elicit more support for their cause, ironically more than that of a king who was not held in such high popular esteem. Such incidents illustrate the demand for badges which must have existed at such times of tension. The issuing of badges at times of crisis was a method used by kings in order to try and gain support. In 1483 Richard III ordered 13,000 livery badges bearing the white boar to be distributed while he travelled north.[26]

The increasing use and abuse of badges by the leading families was associated with maintenance and other abuses of the legal system, so when Henry IV came to the throne he took actions to limit their use, as Adam of Usk records:

It was also ordained that the lords of the realm henceforth give not their suit or livery of clothes or badges, or more especially of hoods, to any man, except their own servants who are always with them, by reason of the many straifes which had been thereby caused in the realm.[27]

What monarchs sought was, however, not the outlawry of the badge but its control. Henry was able to preserve his own livery as it was a major factor in controlling the potential raising of support by rival factions within the aristocracy, which of course had served Henry well when he challenged Richard II for the throne.

Contemporary portraits of this period in England are quite rare. A couple, however, merit discussion in this connection. In the Donne triptych by Memling, dated approximately 1479/80, both Sir John and his wife Elizabeth are clearly seen wearing the Yorkist collar of suns and roses with Edward IV's personal badge, the lion of March, as a pendant. Donne was in the service of Edward and had also supported his father. It is believed that Donne and his wife were both in the wedding party that went to Burgundy in 1468 for the marriage of Margaret to Charles of Burgundy; thus we can ascribe the wearing of the collar to 'official' business. What is interesting, however, is that the personal arms of John and Elizabeth are to be found only on the capitals of the columns in the painting and they are not wearing a token. They were obviously proud to wear their king's livery, but when we consider that the triptych would have been for family use any propagandist value becomes slight. Conversely, it is quite rare to find royal portraits of kings wearing their own livery, apart from Richard II in the Wilton diptych. Does this suggest that it was more important as a political tool to be worn by the public rather than by the king? Badges were about the assertion not of individual identity but of the identity of the individual with a group and its aims, which had political connotations.

Second, as regent of France for Henry VI the duke of Bedford vigorously sought to legitimise the English claim to the French throne that his brother Henry V had fought so hard to attain. He commissioned both a poem and a picture to this end, mainly to be seen by the French public.[28] It is essentially a genealogical tree showing the descent of Henry from Saint Louis. The picture and the poem were hung side by side in Notre Dame. Bedford obviously meant that they should be seen by as many of the French public as possible; he was imposing a Lancastrian presence within the French capital. It aroused a certain reaction, a success of sorts, in the fact that it was defaced by a canon. The punishment imposed was that two copies were to be produced, which suggests that Bedford had use of a further copy. It may have been the case that copies of the picture and poem were circulated around the country. This is an interesting example in that it shows both the visual and literary genre working together. Bedford obviously felt that the poem was not enough and that the picture was vital in communicating the legitimacy of Lancastrian rule to the French public. Both the Donne triptych and the Bedford picture, one for essentially personal use and the other for public consumption, are important in emphasising the role of the visual genre in influencing public opinion. The Bedford picture would be a good example of what Ellul calls integration propaganda, making people accept a change in regime.

Even in death political allegiance was represented. The liveries that had been worn in life were reproduced on effigies. There are some excellent examples to be found in All Saints Church on the Harewood estate near Leeds. On the tomb of Sir Richard Redman (d. *c.* 1426) he is wearing the collar of the alternate knots and ribbon and SSs, which was the livery of the house of Lancaster. He had been made speaker of the Commons in 1415 as he had assisted in the mobilisation of the army which sailed to France with Henry V. On a later tomb of 1461, Sir William Gascoigne is wearing the Yorkist livery of a collar of suns and roses and has a lion of March pendant. He had been with the Lancastrians in the Wars of the Roses but Edward IV pardoned him in 1461, hence the Yorkist rather than the Lancastrian collar. These collars were worn in death as they had been during the lifetime of the individual as a statement of political allegiance. The fact that some effigies had collars defaced after a change of regime suggests that the political significance was very strong.[29]

Badges crystallised many messages about allegiance and ideology. Yet vital visual political messages were communicated in ways at once simpler and far more subtle. To be appropriately attired was an integral part not only of kingship but also of society as a whole; it maintained an order that was recognised and respected. Appearance could therefore be manipulated to a political advantage in times of crisis. Bolingbroke used such a method publicly to humiliate Richard II during August 1399 when returning to London: 'Not once during this time was the king allowed to change his clothes, during all the time that he rode through these towns he was dressed in the same simple set of garments.'[30] The medieval populace expected a king to be dressed in a suitable manner and not to appear so would have had a detrimental effect upon Richard's standing. It was therefore an astute piece of propaganda by Bolingbroke. It may be assumed that during the journey Bolingbroke was well attired with an impressive guard. Richard was not dressed as a king therefore those who saw him no longer perceived his authority. The image was starkly drawn in the representation of the scene in Harleian MS. 1319, where Richard is shown as humbly dressed whereas Bolingbroke is better dressed and appears to tower over him.[31]

The importance of visual appearance is further confirmed by comments in Warkworth's chronicle during the period when the earl of Warwick was trying to put Henry VI back on the throne: 'whiche was not worschipfully arrayed as a prince, and not so clenly kepte as schuld seme suche a prince'.[32] However the important point here is that Warwick understood only too well the adverse effect that this would have on his plans to reinstate Henry. In a politically cunning propagandist move he got the bishop of Winchester to smarten up Henry: 'thei hade hym oute, and newe arayed hym'.[33] As Edward IV was physically an impressive and well-dressed figure it was imperative that Henry at least tried to compete with him; he could not afford to be seen in a less than regal fashion. After the battle of Tewkesbury in 1471 Edward IV paraded Margaret of Anjou as a political statement that the Lancastrians were subdued by the triumphant Yorkists. The Crowland chronicler records: 'Queen Margaret was captured and kept in security so that she might be borne in a carriage before the king at his triumph in London, and so it was done.'[34]

Public displays that were visually imposing could act as intimidation propaganda. Henry Bolingbroke made unashamed displays of military strength. At Bristol, Bolingbroke and his followers, 'with about 100,000 fighting men in all, . . . made a splendid display of themselves and their arms and weaponry in front of the town and castle.'[35] Bolingbroke continued his journey, reaching Chester where 'he remained for several days displaying himself and his military might in splendid fashion to the people of the town'.[36] This was a particularly clever piece of political propaganda as Chester was a centre of Ricardian support. The show of strength by Bolingbroke must have had a psychologically damaging effect on Richard's supporters. How do these displays in Bristol and Chester differ from normal military movements? The fact that the event merited such a comment from the chronicler is significant. It suggests that such behaviour had overtones of a political nature and it also sounds, from the language used, like a deliberate 'staging', a show of power and intent. This was not simply a practical movement of armed men; it carried an underlying message to those who witnessed the event, and the suggested length of the display further suggests that the army wanted as many people as possible to see them.

The use of a visual demonstration to quell a rumour was apparently very necessary. Mere words were not sufficient, it had to be witnessed. Henry V's absorption with the French wars meant that any propaganda was directed to that end. Integration propaganda was in many ways as essential in a climate of war as agitation propaganda. Impressing your enemy with your apparent might before a battle may have led to an advantageous settlement before any action took place or suitably demoralised the enemy as seen by Bolingbroke's displays. Waurin provides us with a picture of the embassy that was sent to France in 1413 to negotiate the marriage of Lady Catherine. '[T]he English appeared everywhere with such display as showed they belonged to a very powerful prince, for they were so richly dressed, and adorned with cloth of gold and silk.'[37]

Although Henry V was portrayed as the epitome of chivalry he was capable of being less than honourable in victory. For example after the siege of Rouen he used explicit visual symbols to insult his conquered enemies: 'the king had a page behind him on a very handsome horse, carrying a lance to which near the blade he had tied a fox's tail after the manner of a pennon, on which many wise people made remarks'.[38] The French chronicler was aware of the inference of the fox's tail, a symbol as familiar across the Channel as at home. The use of a fox's tail was a well-recognised symbol of defiance and Henry appears to be adding insult to injury. While Henry VI was being paraded around the streets of London in an attempt to gain support for his readeption in 1470, foxes' tails were attached to poles and carried by those in his entourage.[39] Once again it is likely that Warwick would have orchestrated the use of the foxes' tails in combination with the smartening up of Henry VI. It was a two-pronged attack as Henry VI was made visually to appear regal and the opportunity was also taken to insult Edward IV.

The physical displays of magnificence as seen in processions and journeys around the kingdom were also an effective propagandist method for reassuring the subjects that all was well: they were essentially integration propaganda. Crown-wearing became increasingly important as it emphasised, visually at least, the wearer's position. Henry V's conquest of France was by no means secure and had to be emphasised at every possible opportunity. The Lancastrians were adept at using entries into Paris as a chance to demonstrate their control of government and to legitimise their usurpation of the French throne.[40] They also wore the crowned helmet as a sign of conquest at these entries.[41] This served to emphasise their legitimacy to rule together with their military prowess. These processions were particularly important for both Edward IV and Richard III whose claims to the throne were weak. As C.A.J. Armstrong points out, both Edward IV and Richard III 'went crowned' at times of relative calm and not just when their position was in danger.[42] Far from being solely spent in London, Edward IV's early years were marked by a series of royal tours around the provinces. In 1461 he travelled from Canterbury to Bristol where he presided over the trial of Sir Baldwin Fulford who was executed and his head displayed in the market place at Exeter. At Christmas, 1484 Richard III wore his crown in public and again at New Year. The Crowland chronicle shows how much trouble Richard went to visually to impress and at the same time legitimise his position to the country:

> Wishing therefore to display in the North, where he had spent most of his time previously, the superior royal rank, which he had acquired for himself in this manner, as diligently as possible, he left the royal city of London and passing through Windsor, Oxford and Coventry came at length to York. There, on a day appointed for the repetition of his crowning in the metropolitan church . . . he arranged splendid and highly expensive feasts and entertainments to attract to himself the affection of many people.[43]

If the physical presence of the monarch or other individual could not be obtained, rumour, a constant problem for medieval government, might be dispelled through the display of some personal item, especially jewellery or clothing. During the battle of Barnet rumours were circulating as to who had won. When word came that Edward had won no one believed it until a rider was despatched carrying the king's gauntlet to the queen. The sight of the king's gauntlet was apparently enough to counteract rumour whereas the oral or written word was not regarded as satisfactory proof.

The body in death was even more vital. The re-interment of Richard, duke of York, and Edmund, earl of Rutland, was not without its political significance. The bodies were transferred from Pontefract to the family vault at Fotheringhay castle in a procession that lasted five days. No opportunity was missed to reiterate the legitimacy of the Yorkist reign as the hearse was 'decked with banners and standards and guarded by an angel of silver bearing a crown of gold as a reminder that by right the duke had been a king'.[44] The displaying of a body was often the only way to quash a rumour; as with the evidence of the king's gauntlet, visual confirmation was sought. But even the display of Richard II's body did not quell the rumours of his survival. Without the acceptance that the previous king was dead it was very difficult for the new monarch, particularly a usurping one, to establish himself. The public display of a body was intended as an act of integration propaganda. After the battle of Barnet the Lancastrians perpetuated the rumour that both Warwick and Montagu were still alive, but Edward IV was astute enough to ensure that their remains were publicly displayed at St Paul's:

> Kynge Edwarde commaundyd bothe the Erle of Warwikes body and the Lord Markes body to be putt in a carte . . . and there commaundede the seide ij bodyes to be layede in the chyrche of Paulis, one the pavement, that every manne myghte see them.[45]

The use of hangings and other capital sentences which maximised visual impact as a method of propaganda was extreme but nevertheless effective in quelling unrest or imposing authority.[46] After the capture of Montereau in 1420 Henry V sent prisoners from the town to another fort in order to make them surrender. The fortress refused and in a show of visual intimidation: 'they were led back to the camp, where king Henry ordered a gibbet to be erected, on which the said prisoners were hanged in sight of the people in the castle'.[47] The public display of whole corpses, heads and assorted limbs was an effective method of exerting discipline through the use of propaganda. It sought to emphasise justice and the power and authority of the king while also acting as a deterrent to possible troublemakers. The murder of Henry VI finally ended a period of uncertainty for Edward IV and, by displaying the body, the new king was literally laying the ghost of not only the old king but the Lancastrian cause to rest. Although this appears to be a particularly macabre method for dispelling rumours it was not unusual. The heads of those of significance were usually displayed in public places, such as market squares or city gates. The unfortunate earl of Wiltshire was 'brought unto Newe Castell to the kynge. And there hys hedde was smete of, and send unto London to be sette uppon London Brygge.'[48] The visual impact of a head must have been important for heads to have been moved nationally in order to be displayed. The case of Sir Baldwin Fulford is another example. Having been beheaded in Bristol his head was carried on to Exeter and then 'sate upon the castell yate'.[49] It was not just the ruling class who sought execution as a means of propaganda. In 1451 Jack Cade had Lord Saye beheaded and publicly degraded him by having his naked corpse dragged through the streets. Cade's own death was no less symbolic. He was ritually beheaded at Newgate despite the fact that he had died previously from injuries. Subsequently, his head was displayed on London Bridge, while the towns of Norwich, Salisbury, Gloucester and Blackheath were each sent a quarter to display as an ominous warning to their citizens.

The contribution of visual propaganda to fifteenth-century politics was therefore great. The impact that it had was certainly tangible and in some instances it may have changed the course of events. The advantages that it had over its literary counterpart were its flexibility and ability to communicate to a greater audience, and the increase in literacy did not seem to detract from its influence. In fact the literary genre often adopted and recorded these visual manifestations of political propaganda, as the Crowland Continuator states:

> In the year 1485 on the 22nd day of August the tusks of the boar were blunted and the red rose, the avenger of the white, shines upon us.[50]

The boar, and white and red roses had become so synonymous with Richard III, Yorkists and Lancastrians respectively that no mention of names was necessary. These visual images had become such an integrated part of medieval life that they were recorded thus by the literary genre.

Notes

1   Erwin Panofsky, *Meaning in the Visual Arts* (first published 1955; Harmondsworth, Penguin, 1993), p. 35.

2   Paul Binski, *Painters* (London, British Museum Press, 1991), p. 35.

3   Francis Haskell, *History and its Images: Art and the Interpretation of the Past* (New Haven and London, Yale University Press, 1993), p. 5.

4   Sydney Anglo, *Images of Tudor Kingship* (London, Seaby, 1992).

5   M.V. Clarke, 'The Wilton Diptych', in L.S. Sutherland and M. McKisack (eds), *Fourteenth Century Studies by M.V. Clarke* (Oxford, Clarendon Press, 1937), pp. 272–92, esp. p. 272; reprinted from *Burlington Magazine* (June 1931).

6   Michael Michael, 'The Little Land of England is Preferred before the Great Kingdom of France: The Quartering of the Royal Arms by Edward III', in David Buckton and T.A. Heslop (eds),

Studies in Medieval Art and Architecture, presented to Peter Lasko (Stroud, Sutton, for the Trustees of the British Museum, 1994), pp. 113–26, esp. p. 113.

7   Jacques Ellul, *Propaganda: The Formation of Men's Attitudes* (New York, Vintage Books, 1973).

8   C. Richmond, 'Propaganda in the Wars of the Roses', *History Today*, 42 (1992), 12–18.

9   And there has been a more thorough coverage of literary forms: V.J. Scattergood, *Politics and Poetry in the Fifteenth Century* (London, Blandford Press, 1971); C.L. Kingsford, *English Historical Literature in the Fifteenth Century* (Oxford, Clarendon Press, 1913); Antonia Gransden, *Historical Writing in England* (2 vols, London, Routledge and Kegan Paul, 1974–82) vol. 2, c. *1307 to the Early Sixteenth Century*.

10   Evelyn Welch, *Art and Society in Italy 1350–1500* (Oxford University Press, 1997), p. 215.

11   John F. Cherry, *Medieval Decorative Art* (London, British Museum Press, 1991), p. 32.

12   David Starkey, 'Ightham Mote: Politics and Architecture in Early Tudor England', *Archaeologia*, cvii (1982), 153–63, esp. p. 154.

13   J. Warkworth, *A Chronicle of the First Thirteen Years of the Reign of King Edward the Fourth*, ed. James Orchard Halliwell (Camden Society, first series, x, 1839), p. 16.

14   Starkey, 'Ightham Mote', p. 154.

15   *Oeuvres de Froissart*, ed. Kervyn de Lettenhove and A. Scheler (25 vols in 26, Brussels, 1867–77; reprinted Osnabrück, Biblio Verlag, 1967), vol. V, pp. 416–19; E.A. Danbury, 'English and French Artistic Propaganda during the Period of the Hundred Years War: Some Evidence from Royal Charters', in C. Allmand (ed.), *Power, Culture and Religion in France* c. *1350*–c. *1550* (Woodbridge, Suffolk, Boydell, 1989), pp. 75–97, esp. p. 95.

16   'The Chronicle of Dieulacres Abbey, 1381–1403', in M.V. Clarke and V.H. Galbraith, 'The Deposition of Richard II', *Bulletin of the John Rylands Library*, 14 (1930), 125–81, at pp. 164–81 – quotation from p. 173; reprinted in Chris Given-Wilson (ed.), *Chronicles of the Revolution 1397–1400: The Reign of Richard II* (Manchester University Press, 1993), p. 155.

17   J.B. Post, 'Courts, Councils and Arbitrators in the Ladbrook Manor Dispute, 1382–1400', in R.F. Hunnisett and J.B. Post (eds), *Medieval Legal Records: Edited in Memory of C.A.F. Meeking* (London, HMSO, 1978), pp. 323–4; reprinted in Given-Wilson, *Chronicles*, p. 136.

18   *Select Cases in the Court of King's Bench under Richard II, Henry IV and Henry V* (Selden Society, 88, 1971), vol. VII, p. 154.

19   J.S. Davies (ed.), *An English Chronicle from 1377 to 1461* (Camden Society, first series, lxiv, 1855), p. 2.

20   *English Chronicle*, p. 29.

21   C. Allmand, *Henry V* (London, Methuen, 1992), p. 245.

22   'Bale's Chronicle', in Ralph Flenley (ed.), *Six Town Chronicles of England* (Oxford, Clarendon Press, 1911), p. 136.

23   *Six Town Chronicles*, p. 136.

24   Andrew R. Scoble (ed.), *The Memoirs of Philip de Commines Lord of Argenton* (2 vols, London, Henry G. Bohn, 1855), vol. I, p. 192.

25   *Memoirs of Philip de Commines*, vol. I, pp. 196–7.

26   Rosemary Horrox and P.W. Hammond (eds), *British Library Harleian Manuscript 433* (4 vols, Gloucester, Alan Sutton for the Richard III Society, 1979–83), vol. 2, p. 42 (f. 126): 'iiij Standerdes of sarcenet with bores / xiij Ml Quynysans of fustyane with bores'; G.L. Harriss, 'The King and his

Subjects', in R. Horrox (ed.), *Fifteenth-Century Attitudes: Perceptions of Society in Late Medieval England* (Cambridge University Press, 1994), pp. 13–28, at p. 21.

27   Chris Given-Wilson (ed.), *The Chronicle of Adam Usk, 1377–1421* (Oxford, Clarendon Press, 1997), pp. 82–5.

28   Shrewsbury manuscript: British Library, MS. Royal 15 E. vi, f. 3.

29   Pauline E. Routh, *Medieval Effigial Alabaster Tombs in Yorkshire* (Ipswich, Boydell, 1976).

30   George B. Stow (ed.), *Historia Vitae et Regni Ricardi Secundi* (Philadelphia, University of Pennsylvania Press, 1977), p. 156; for a translation see Given-Wilson, *Chronicles*, p. 130.

31   *Historia Vitae et Regni Ricardi Secundi*, p. 156; for a translation see Given-Wilson, *Chronicles*, p. 130 and plates.

32   Warkworth, *Chronicle*, p. 11; cf. A.H. Thomas and I.D. Thornley (eds), *The Great Chronicle of London* (London, 1938; reprinted Gloucester, Alan Sutton, 1983), p. 215; and below, pp. 41, 52 (n. 3).

33   Warkworth, *Chronicle*, p. 11.

34   Nicholas Pronay and John Cox (eds), *The Crowland Chronicle Continuations: 1459–1486* (Alan Sutton for Richard III & Yorkist History Trust, London, 1986), p. 127.

35   *Historia Vitae et Regni Ricardi Secundi*, pp. 151–60; translated in Given-Wilson, *Chronicles*, p. 128.

36   Given-Wilson, *Chronicles*, p. 129.

37   John de Waurin, *A Collection of the Chronicles and Ancient Histories of Great Britain, now called England*, trans. W. Hardy and Edward L.C.P. Hardy (Rolls Series, 40; 3 vols; London, Longman, Green, Longman, Roberts, and Green, 1864–91), vol. II, p. 171.

38   Waurin, *Collection*, vol. II, p. 254.

39   J.R. Lander, *The Wars of the Roses* (Stroud, Alan Sutton, 1992), p. 135.

40   Lawrence M. Bryant, 'The Medieval Entry Ceremony at Paris', in J.M. Bak (ed.), *Coronations: Medieval and Early Modern Monarchic Ritual* (Berkeley, CA, and Oxford, University of California Press, 1990), pp. 88–118, esp. p. 102.

41   Bryant, 'Medieval Entry Ceremony', p. 105.

42   C.A.J. Armstrong, 'The Inauguration Ceremonies of the Yorkist Kings and their Title to the Throne', *TRHS*, 4th series, XXX (1948), 51–73, at pp. 70–2; reprinted in his *England, France and Burgundy in the Fifteenth Century* (London, Hambledon, 1983), pp. 73–95.

43   *Crowland*, p. 161.

44   Cora L. Scofield, *The Life and Reign of Edward the Fourth, King of England and France and Lord of Ireland* (2 vols, 1923; new impression, London, Frank Cass, 1967), p. 167.

45   Warkworth, *Chronicle*, p. 17.

46   Michel Foucault, *Discipline and Punish: The Birth of the Prison*, tr. Alan Sheridan (London, Allen Lane, 1977).

47   Waurin, *Collection*, vol. II, p. 306.

48   'William Gregory's Chronicle of London', in *The Historical Collections of a Citizen of London in the Fifteenth Century*, ed. J. Gairdner (Camden Society, new series, xvii, 1876), pp. 55–239, esp. pp. 217–18.

49   'A Short English Chronicle', in *Three Fifteenth-Century Chronicles*, ed. James Gairdner (Camden Society, new series, xxviii, 1880), pp. 1–80, esp. p. 77.

50   *Crowland*, pp. 184–5.

3

PROPAGANDA, POLITICAL COMMUNICATION AND THE PROBLEM OF ENGLISH RESPONSES TO THE INTRODUCTION OF PRINTING[1]

Tim Thornton

This paper is intended as a contribution to the history of political communication in the half century after the introduction of printing to England. It has two main objectives. First, it will assess the current state of the historiography in this area, with its focus on the variety of the means and purposes of communication in the late fifteenth and early sixteenth centuries, and the interaction between crises of dynasty and religious policy, in conjunction with social and economic difficulties, and the stimulation of innovation, especially in the use of the printing press. Second, it will place English governmental developments in a wider context and demonstrate that the historiography has failed to tackle the most problematic element of all in the developments of this period: the relative reluctance of the government to take advantage of the opportunities on offer.

Nonetheless, it is important to point out that the regimes of English kings, from Henry VI to Henry VIII, took advantage of a wide variety of media in order to communicate messages to their people. These might be sub-divided as visual, oral, manuscript and print. At the heart of royal government was the person of the king, and the actions of the monarch were a powerful means to display and communicate messages to the audience. In any environment, the splendour of his dress, whether it be civilian or military, communicated a message about his magnificence, wealth and power.[2] Such appearance was eagerly noted and reported by observers: the diplomatic visitors of the period invariably began their summaries of English affairs with a physical description of the king, and English ambassadors to foreign courts reciprocated.[3] The royal person might also be presented in various contexts, whether at court or beyond. Hence the layout of the royal palaces, in particular the presence chamber, in which the placing and splendour of the throne provided a setting for the king's person when he met ambassadors and supplicants, or dined in public.[4] Hence too the entertainments in which the king participated, more or less directly;[5] and beyond the palace, the formal entries designed for the king when he travelled his kingdom;[6] the crown wearings revived by the Yorkists;[7] the jousts,[8] the events of the religious calendar, especially the feasts closely associated with the royal family such as that of the Garter and St George under Henry VII and his son.[9] Royal entries have been particularly closely studied; Anglo has described how the Tudors developed a style of composite displays in the Burgundian manner, culminating in probably the most complex, the reception of Catherine of Aragon.[10] Events in the royal life cycle also played an important role, for example funerals.[11] Every royal action and gesture could be highly symbolic.[12] Within this category it is also important to remember that governmental propaganda was also conveyed by the actions and persons of members of the royal family, especially the queen, and by those of the crown's chief ministers: Cavendish's description of Wolsey's procession to court is memorable.[13]

This category shades seamlessly into that of oral propaganda. On few occasions was the visual impact of the royal presence not supported by sound of some kind, and as often as not by speech. Music played an important role at the Field of Cloth of Gold, for example.[14] Meanwhile, the king consistently maintained a large group of trumpeters at court.[15] More complex harmonies and messages were communicated through the voices of the members of the chapel royal and in the words sung by courtiers.[16] Royal[17] and ministerial speeches[18] were crucial to the explanation of royal policy. Speeches were integrated into more visual forms, such as entries and jousts, highlighting the specific relevance of general visual themes.[19] Preaching also needs to be considered here, from the sermons at St Paul's Cross, which were under the control of the bishop of London and therefore more or less closely the government, to sermons preached at royal command elsewhere.[20] Oral forms of persuasion allowed messages to be communicated at some distance from the person of the king or his ministers, for example by passing words with credence, such as rings.[21]

This leads us to the manner in which royal messages might be communicated through objects, such as coins and medals;[22] portraits, including those on charters;[23] seals;[24] buildings;[25] tombs, with the projects for the tombs of Henry VII and Henry VIII being innovative and carrying many messages; and indeed anything that might carry a royal badge.[26]

From commands passed by messengers carrying credence there is only a short leap to persuasion by means of written documents. The writ is one of the startling things about Anglo-Saxon England, allowing the king's command to pass throughout the kingdom. The development of a unified writ culture has been given great prominence by writers in the emergence of a unified kingdom.[27] Yet a writ in itself cannot really be called propaganda: it is an order, and as such cannot really be described as persuasion. What is more important is the development of proclamation, for this took the order of the writ and added to it a text which was specifically designed to be interpreted orally to a group of listeners. The most important development in our period here is the consistent introduction of English texts to proclamations, a change which took place in the reign of Edward IV. This gave the government much closer control over the actual words spoken to the assembled populace.[28] Once this transition had been made, the number of proclamations issued grew rapidly, from approximately one every four months in the reign of Henry VII to around one every month in the period 1539–53.[29] Other forms of manuscript were designed for reading by their audience, as well as and combined with reading out loud and listening: bills, to be passed from hand to hand, or to be posted, became a common feature of the later fifteenth-century political scene. Longer tracts were designed for more leisurely perusal.[30]

Then, of course, there was printing. Not long after Caxton began to work in Westminster, the government used the press to demonstrate the duplicity of the French in their treaty with the Burgundians of 1483, printing it alongside the Anglo-French treaty of 1475.[31] The statutes of each parliamentary session were printed from 1484, at first fitfully and as a commercial printing operation, then from 1504 by the king's printer. From 1515 this royal printing became regular, and with individual statutes of wide relevance being reproduced in large numbers from 1510, the activity of king-in-parliament was being projected to the population at large.[32] The achievement of compliance and active support for the laws so enacted was now a clear objective, for the preambles of the acts grew in length and persuasive vigour.[33] Printing was also deployed in reproducing proclamations.[34]

The purposes of all this persuasive action and material can be divided into integration and agitation, although this actually represents a very broad and complex spectrum.[35] Propaganda might motivate someone, in a military scenario, at its most extreme, to rise and kill others; it might persuade to eager acceptance of orders and policy of government, most powerfully fiscal demands and religious instructions; or it might win peaceful compliance or acquiescence, and dissuasion from rebellion or disaffection.[36]

What focuses most attention on political communication during this period is that it was one of dynastic discontinuity and religious upheaval. Therefore all regimes had great incentives to apply the various propaganda methods to achieve their purposes. Hence Edward IV's use of proclamations;[37] the early Tudors' systematic use of badges;[38] the printing of the papal bull threatening dire sanctions against those who questioned either the legitimacy or marriage of Henry VII;[39] the growing use of printing for proclamations;[40] and the alleged masterplanning in Cromwell's control of the press as culmination of all this.[41] Roy Strong's hugely influential work on Elizabeth I suggested that a deliberately organised cult of the queen was promoted, especially through the production of royal portraits which idealised her image.[42] It was now possible for the king's government to seek 'not only to exhort but also to inform his loving subjects of the truth'.[43] The debate has tended to emphasise this combination of means and circumstances revolutionising political communication. Elton took this to perhaps its apogee. '[W]hen the new order came under attack, Cromwell employed his special staff to blast the opposition (on paper) off the face of the earth. Throughout the press was used, intensively, carefully and purposefully, to back up political action.' For him, this was the 'first such campaign ever mounted by any government in any state of Europe'.[44]

Yet there are serious problems. Of course the English governments of the period adopted new means of communication; yet they did not do so with the eagerness or system which was seen elsewhere. Printing was taken up for political purposes in Germany very rapidly: the church began printing indulgences in 1454, and in 1462 when two rivals competed for the bishopric of Mainz, print was used by the opposing parties to promote their claims.[45] In the Holy Roman Empire, the *Landfrieden* or laws for public peace made between the Emperor and the princes were printed, but not so frequently as the accompanying bans on disturbing the peace, of which as many as eighteen were printed in the twenty-two years to 1500.[46] The same period saw huge numbers of indulgences to raise money to defend against the Ottoman threat, and these were often committed to print. This reached peaks in the 1450s after the fall of Constantinople and in the 1480s at the time of the siege of Rhodes.[47] A more domestic threat in Württemberg in 1514, a peasant movement, was the occasion for the printing not just of the *Tübinger Vertrag*, the agreement reached by the duke, but of the *Nebenabschied*, the proclamation to accompany it and to coerce acceptance. A further proclamation shortly afterwards, explaining the defeat of the peasants and threatening sanctions against anyone continuing in their cause, was accompanied by printed letters carefully targeted at their chosen audience: bishops and archbishops, counts and freemen, free cities, and bailiffs.[48] Even in England, the church demonstrated a far more creative use of printing to achieve its ends. The most famous example of church printing is the guild of the Blessed Virgin at Boston, which capitalised on the exceptional benefits given to it by the papacy through the printing of indulgences, at such a volume that even the year came to be printed, it being assumed that at least one edition a year would be needed.[49] A perusal of the *Short-Title Catalogue* for Indulgences shows that religious institutions across the length of the country, and from the smallest order to the greatest, were participating.

It might be argued that this phenomenon was specific to printing, and that England's relatively late acquisition of printing technology could explain why it was not taken up so enthusiastically as it was elsewhere. As has already been shown, however, the church took up the new medium enthusiastically; yet the church had an even weaker grip on the medium in England than it did elsewhere and, with early experiments in printing at St Albans, Tavistock and elsewhere coming to nothing, it seems unlikely that this is the prime reason.[50] Indeed, the failure to take full advantage of printing seems to be echoed in the government's attitude to other means of promotion and persuasion. There are remarkably few royal entries in the early sixteenth century; the persuasive powers of the royal person were not widely displayed after the early years of Henry VII's reign, and Henry VIII travelled little outside the south-east.[51] This was even more the case in the reigns of Edward VI and Mary. Not only were there few such splendid royal appearances, but these were not promulgated in pictorial or printed form. In France, by contrast, the period from the late fifteenth century saw not only frequent royal entries but also manuscript and printed descriptions and portrayals of them.[52] Similar arguments have recently been advanced for Tudor royal portraiture and court ceremonial.[53] One sign of the failure of the Tudor monarchy to take up the challenges of the period with a full-blown propaganda campaign is the abortive proposals put forward for such an effort by Clement Urmeston and Richard Morrison. Urmeston's scheme encompassed the use of seals, which were to be affixed to declarations of obedience through a system of hierarchies from the crown, through the shires, to individual householders.[54] Morrison proposed an annual triumph with bonfires and processions to celebrate the deliverance of the realm from the papacy, along with a scheme of plays.[55]

It is especially important to explore this issue with regard to printing. The compilation of printed broadsides, the *Einblattdruke*, listed 1,574 broadsides produced in the fifteenth century, of which only 39, or 2.5 per cent, came from England.[56] It has been argued that a major impetus behind the development of printing in England was royal or aristocratic sponsorship; Colin Clair, for example in his *History of Printing in Britain*, noted the reference in Caxton's *Golden Legend* ([1483]; STC 24873) to the earl of Arundel's promise to take 'a reasonable quantyte' of the work and give him a yearly fee, and the offer of Sir Hugh Brice, alderman of London, to defray the cost of the *Mirrour of the World* ([1481]; STC 24762).[57] The usual corollary of this is that royal interests sought to use printing for propaganda purposes. Hence studies of Caxton have focused on his relationship with Margaret of Burgundy, and through her with George, duke of Clarence, as the means by which he was brought to settle again in England. Once established at Westminster, the patronage of Anthony Earl Rivers has been adduced behind an ever growing list of publications, indirectly at least drawing on his responsibilities for the prince of Wales and his interests. The emergence of William Faques as 'king's printer' in 1504,[58] later succeeded by Pynson, and the parallel description of Wynkyn de Worde as printer to the queen mother, Margaret Beaufort, has been given great significance;[59] and the period is seen to culminate in Thomas Cromwell's use of the press, both directly and through his followers such as William Marshall[60] and Richard Morrison.[61] As has recently been pointed out, however, the actual evidence for specific financial support for these printers by their supposed patrons, as currently established, is remarkably thin.[62]

If the novelty of printing does not seem to be the answer to this problem, and it in fact appears to be more widely experienced in other media of propaganda, we must find broader explanations. Sydney Anglo has recently emphasised reception, pointing out that most earlier work has failed to ask the key question of whether the complex symbolic and didactic functions of ceremony and printing were understood in anything like the way modern writers have supposed. Anglo makes valid points about the information we do have for reception, for example of the celebrations surrounding the reception of Catherine of Aragon in 1501, when observers failed to explain to their correspondents any of the complex imagery surrounding Arthur which was later interpreted in this event.[63] Anglo's reaction is therefore to emphasise the one form of Tudor propaganda which he believes to have been clearly comprehensible to all viewers: the royal badge. To an extent, his argument is undoubtedly valid: both he and David Starkey have pointed out the remarkable degree to which Tudor badges, the dual rose, the portcullis, and so on, were spread across the kingdom, with Starkey in particular associating their appearance with the presence of members of the royal household. As part of Starkey's theory of representation through intimacy, the badged courtier covered everything he touched with royal badges, so marking out the intensifying influence of the royal court.

There are two problems with this argument. The first takes us back to the comparative perspective adopted above. There are few signs that English audiences were less well educated in the languages of propaganda than their European neighbours. The means to understand were surely no less present than in France or Germany – if anything, the social structure of England meant there were more men with claims to gentility who might be able to read a coat of arms or a heraldic badge than in many other places. Levels of literacy, especially in the south and east of the country, were not catastrophically lower than in other western European countries.[64] The second problem is that Anglo underestimates the complexity of the material that he admits was projected and received. The badges of which he made so much were less simple in their construction and meaning than he implies, and their use was inevitably more complex still. The dual rose badge was not something created by royal agents and clearly understood by all, but an innovation of the authorities in York in 1486.[65] It first appeared in the pageants to welcome Henry VII to the city, pageants notable for the way they rewrote the recent past, making the city a loyal follower of the Tudor cause from the outset. Such a badge therefore represented a political statement about the nature of Henry VII's kingship – one that he was only too happy to go along with, but a controversial statement nonetheless. Their use was if anything more difficult still. We must assume that the population at large understood the message being conveyed when in 1539 three men were hanged in the prince of Wales's livery for the murder of Roger Cholmondeley.[66] A crude reading of this action would make this a blow against a member of the royal family: in reality it was a comment on the issue of the system of badges and connections which might be misused. Both problems suggest that the alleged backwardness of the English political nation is not a useful resort.

Further possible answers have been suggested by John King. One of his major theses is that the nature of the religion of the English Reformation rapidly undermined the use of many iconographic means of persuasion; similar arguments have been developed for the field of political drama by Greg Walker.[67] Once again, there is considerable evidence to support the argument. Its usefulness for our purposes, however, is more questionable. The failure of the English monarchy to participate as fully in propagandistic efforts as its western European neighbours predated the Reformation, and certainly predated the period in the 1540s when this form of Protestantism first became pre-eminent in England. A second argument put forward by King relates to the persons of the English monarchs themselves. The fact that in the 1540s England was ruled by an invalid, succeeded by an ailing minor, and that in the following decade he in turn was succeeded by two women, the first of whom occupied an ambivalent position as the wife of a prince who was rarely in the country, meant that the propaganda efforts of the royal state were bound to be limited in their ambition.[68] Once again, however, issues of chronology intrude, for in Henry VIII the English monarchy had for at least thirty years the most marketable image of princely magnificence on the European stage; and yet it did not choose to promote it strongly.

Religion does appear to play a role in the answer to this question, if not in the form adopted by King and Walker. The particular process by which Protestantism came to be accepted in England helped to preclude the development of a vigorous culture of propaganda. Until the 1540s, the admission of Protestant ideas was never more than cautious. Wolsey's resistance is well chronicled; so too is the tension between Thomas Cromwell and Henry VIII over the former's limited moves towards reform. The keynote of the religious developments of this period was royal control, whether of the defence of Catholicism, or of moves towards Protestantism. Royal religion meant a religion of instruction and proscription; there was little need to cooperate with a semi-independent church establishment in counteracting opposing tendencies, as there was for example in parts of Germany.[69] Medieval preaching guides were replaced by a single book of royally approved homilies; guides to the interpretation of the scriptures made way for Erasmus's *Paraphrases of the Gospels and Acts*, selected by the crown; and books of private devotion made way for printed primers at the king's command.[70]

These developments also owed something to the problematic relationship between the new religion and the historiography of the period: history, potentially a vital means to articulate royal aspirations, could not be used as propaganda as effectively as it might have been. The period saw some promising beginnings, in the appointment by Henry VII of a royal historian, Bernard Andre, and the commissioning of Polydore Vergil to write a history of England.[71] Vergil's work, however, was problematic. It promoted the Tudor dynasty, as might be expected given its commissioning by Henry VII; yet Vergil's challenge to the traditional account of Brutus and the British History, upon which many of the imperial claims to religious and political self-determination were made, meant his work was unwelcome at court. His *Anglica Historia* and other works, such as his edition of *Gildas*, had to be produced abroad.[72]

The nature of English political culture is also an important factor. At one level the failure to develop strong propaganda methods is a sign of its strength. Those who wish to see in England perhaps the most centralised political system in Europe may draw comfort from the fact that the royal government did not need to exert massive efforts in propaganda to hold it together and articulate it. Bonds between ruler and ruled were strong enough to ensure that even in the worst days of religious division and social crisis, fundamental breakdown was never close.[73] In this sense, the opposite case is provided by Germany, where relatively weak political bonds seem to have stimulated a vigorous propaganda culture throughout the fifteenth and sixteenth centuries. In some ways, England was still the face-to-face political culture described by Colin Richmond – one where information flowed because of personal experience and contact.[74] On the other hand, the articulation of English political society, though strong, was constructed around far more flexible and open ties than would be implied by this argument. English political society was remarkably decentralised, its political culture remarkably open. If the royal government was not an active propagandist during this period, that does not mean that other groups in society were not. Religious corporations, noblemen, towns, and others all vigorously propagated their views.[75]

It may be, in fact, that we should abandon assumptions that royal policy towards propaganda was the prime determinant of the shape of political debate in the early sixteenth century. The crown's attitude to propaganda was affected by contact with this vigorous political culture. There are signs that early in the sixteenth century, government began to use the press more actively to promote itself. The best example of this is the printing of the celebrations for the engagement between the princess Mary and Charles, the heir to the Spanish kingdoms and to the Holy Roman Empire.[76] There can be no doubt that the beginning of Henry VIII's reign saw a sudden enthusiasm for the use of the printing press, especially for the reproduction of proclamations. Under Henry VII, aside from the proclamation of the Bull for Henry's marriage and legitimacy as king, only one proclamation had been printed, that on silver coin of 1504.[77] A remarkably well-coordinated campaign accompanied Henry VIII's wars against the French and Scots between 1512 and 1513, ranging from the printing of the taxation statute, with its elaborate preamble, through the proclamation that accompanied it, to the Latin tract which set out the government's arguments, the two versions of the English poem *The Gardyners Passetaunce* which popularised them, the leading clerical poet Alexander Barclay's attack on French policy towards the church, and the glorification of victory represented by the printed

account of the battle of Flodden and attacks on James IV, including Skelton's.[78] It
has even been argued that the order to Pynson to print Lydgate's *Sege of Troye*
(STC 5579) in 1513 at the time of Henry VIII's first campaign against the French
was an attempt to generate a more militant milieu in the country.[79] This entry of
the crown into the field of printed propaganda seems to have stimulated a
remarkable response from others in the political nation. In these decades we find
everyone from the duke of Buckingham to tiny monasteries using the press to
promote their interests. Buckingham's sponsorship of the publication of *Helyas,
Knight of the Swanne* (1512; STC 7571) may have been part of his campaign to
secure the constableship, and the *Lytell Cronycle* of *c*. 1520 further promoted
Buckingham's chivalric credentials, especially in the light of the contemporary
calls for the renewal of the crusade against the Turk.[80]

There followed a period in which the crown withdrew dramatically from the
printing of political propaganda. This is particularly clear in the ministry of
Wolsey. In so many spheres a remarkable innovator, Wolsey's chancellorship saw
an almost complete withdrawal from the print propaganda market. Remarkably
few statutes were printed in the dozen years beginning with the parliamentary
sessions of 1515. Pynson produced the sessional prints of the statutes of the
parliaments of that year, and a separate printing of the act for the king's revenue, 7
Henry VIII, c. 7.[81] Another edition of the statutes of the parliament of 7 Henry
VIII appeared in about 1520.[82] There was then nothing until the parliament of
1523, which produced a sessional edition of statutes, but no specific parliamentary
acts in print.[83] The same was true of printing of proclamations. Five were printed
in the years 1514–17, but only two between then and 1526.[84] Even in the latter
year and in 1527 only one edition per year survives.[85] The nine years from 1509
to 1517 produced fourteen editions of proclamations, the nine years from 1518 to
1526 just three.[86] Another possible indication of the same phenomenon is the
reticence with which the royal records refer to Pynson, in spite of his frequent use
of the title of royal printer, and the justification for this provided by his royal
annuity. Pynson appears in the king's book of payments on ten occasions in the
period 1511 to 1517. In the subsequent book of payments he appears just once.[87]
Among these eleven occasions, he was described as king's printer on just three.
The absence of work to support the key transition to war against France after a
period of intense peace negotiations, in 1521, and the enormous efforts to
mobilise to take advantage of the French king's capture in 1525, is very striking.[88]
The main possible exception to this picture is provided by the printing of Lord
Berners' translation of Froissart's Chronicles. Berners claimed he wrote at 'the
highe comaundement of my moost redouted soverayne lorde kynge Henry the
viii.'; his philosophy of history emphasised the lessons to be learned from the past,
but he also saw: 'What pleasure shall it be to the noble gentylmen of Englande to
se, beholde, and rede the highe enterprises, famous actes, and glorious dedes done
and atchyved by their valyant aunceytours?'[89] Given that Berners was sent as

captain of Calais at the end of 1520, at a time when Henry VIII's mind was turning to war with France, there can be little doubt that the translation and the printing of the work took place against the background of a renewed effort to revive the glories of the Hundred Years War.[90] The first volume of the work was published in 1523, the year of Suffolk's march on Paris; the second appeared in 1525, perhaps after Francis I's capture at Pavia, which restored Henry's enthusiasm for French conquest, if only temporarily. Yet, as N.F. Blake has pointed out, the preface to the first volume emphasises not just Henry's commission but also Berners' own personal choice of the subject, and the preface to the second volume is fuller in its praise of the king than the first, suggesting the first volume may have been more a speculative request for patronage than a directly commissioned government propaganda piece.[91] If the argument just advanced, that the crown and its ministers were uneasy about the level of print propaganda in circulation in the early 1510s, is an explanation of why they chose to draw back thereafter, it might also be suggested that the assault on Wolsey launched by John Skelton, especially in the poem *Why Come Ye Nat to Court?*, which featured criticism of the miltary debacles of 1522 on the Scottish border, and in the play *Magnyfycence*, might have contributed to Wolsey's apparent personal unwillingness to use print propaganda for the king in the early 1520s.[92] This was of course precisely the period when royal use of the printing press to aid the attack on Luther was being superseded by an ever more restrictive attitude to works on religion in print.[93] The impressive propaganda efforts of the period from *c.* 1530 to 1538, when the break with Rome and the major actions of the Henrician Reformation were occurring, should not be seen as part of a trend, but as an isolated and unusual event produced by the exceptional stresses of the period.[94]

The kind of explosion of involvement in printing which occurred in the 1510s was not ultimately in the crown's interests – ironically, it did not have the economic power to compete effectively. It is important to recognise that printing was closely linked to existing patterns of trade, as witness the success of commercial centres and the relative failure of university towns to produce successful printing operations.[95] On the other hand, a strictly commercial interpretation of the marketing of the early printed book will not entirely suffice. Edwards and Meale have recently persuasively argued that although straightforward commercial selling of books was important in some circumstances, especially the large numbers of basic religious and educational books, in other areas different models might need to be used. On the other hand, direct subsidy or even block buying of books is very hard to demonstrate. Pynson, for example, seems to have served individuals, groups or institutions where he could be guaranteed a market for the books he produced, from the extreme example of the bulk annual printing for the Boston guild to the production of material for clerical coteries such as that associated with Syon Charterhouse.[96] The surviving contracts between Pynson and Horman for his *Vulgaria*, and especially that with Palsgrave for his *Lesclaircissement*, suggest the complexity of the arrangements which might exist even for apparently market-oriented books, in the latter case providing for a certain number of copies for the author and restricting the numbers which could be openly sold.[97] An interpretation of royal government as a similar kind of loose coterie which might provide a more or less guaranteed forum for the sale of books would be a logical and useful extrapolation of their argument – this would encompass the making of books such as the ordinances for war, where an almost guaranteed sale if not direct royal payment could be ensured, to works which less directly promoted royal policy. Thomas Berthelet's bill to the government for work done between 1541 and 1543 suggests this is the case: the printing work for which he expected payment direct from the crown was limited to editions of the statutes, collectively or individually, or of proclamations.[98] Hence resources could be drawn on more widely, although the distribution and focus of the message might be diluted.[99] Royal government therefore took the decision to operate primarily to influence what was produced elsewhere, and to concentrate on the control and direction of religion, through compulsion. This acceptance of diversity was apparent, paradoxically, in the government's willingness to buck the market and to set up regional printing centres. The dominant influence in printing for the English market continued to be foreign printers.[100] Within England, London was dominant in trade and therefore inevitably in book production. This was clear in the desperate (and vain) attempts made by printers in St Albans and Oxford to find a market by moving from Latin religious and academic texts to more popular and saleable material.[101] Government efforts to control the press inevitably eventually had centralising effects, especially in the charter to the Stationers' Company of 1557. Yet in the seventy years before the grant, on balance, the crown's efforts were in favour of regional diversity in the industry. For example, under Edward VI there were attempts to set up John Oswen in Worcester for Wales and the west, with a privilege granted on 6 January 1549;[102] and Powell was sent to Ireland to print for the crown there.[103] This acceptance of diversity also meant *de facto* permissions of different uses,[104] and subseqently for translations of the Book of Common Prayer.[105] The relationship of the English crown and printed propaganda was neither a sign of the innovative publicist genius of its ministers, nor of the simple efficacy of its government, but of its acceptance of its relative weakness and the diversity of the polity over which it ruled.

Notes

1   In this chapter, all early printed items are referred to by their number in A.W. Pollard and G.R. Redgrave, *A Short-Title Catalogue of Books Printed in England, Scotland and Ireland and of English Books Printed Abroad 1475–1640*, revised by W.A. Jackson, F.S. Ferguson, Katherine F. Pantzer and Philip M. Rider (3 vols, London, Bibliographic Society, 1976–91) (henceforth *STC*); proclamations are referred to by their number in Paul L. Hughes and James F. Larkin (eds), *Tudor Royal Proclamations* (3 vols, New Haven and London, Yale University Press, 1964–9), vol. I, *The Early Tudors, 1485–1553* (henceforth *TRP*).

2   Ernst Hartwig Kantorowicz, *The King's Two Bodies: A Study in Mediaeval Political Theology* (Princeton University Press, 1957). For magnificence as an indication of power, Anglo, *Images of Tudor Kingship*, pp. 6–10.

3   Numerous examples could be cited, for example from Rawdon Brown *et al.* (eds), *Calendar of State Papers and Manuscripts Relating to English Affairs, Existing in the Archives and Collections of Venice, and in Other Libraries in Northern Italy* (37 vols, continuing, London, Longman, Green, Longman, Roberts & Green; HMSO, 1864–1947); a particularly extreme example, not included there, is the description of Edward VI as 'a king . . . beautiful as an angel', by a valet to ambassador Domenico Bollani: C.S. Cairns, 'An Unknown Venetian Description of King Edward VI', *Bulletin of the Institute of Historical Research* (henceforth *BIHR*), XLII (1969), 110–15. For English reactions to foreign princes, see e.g. *Letters and Papers, Foreign and Domestic, of the Reign of Henry VIII, 1509–47*, ed. Brewer, Gairdner and Brodie (21 vols, 1862–1910), *Addenda*, vol. i (1929–32) (henceforth *LP*), vol. iii. nos 1078, 2136; George Cavendish, *The Life and Death of Cardinal Wolsey*, ed. Richard S. Sylvester (Early English Text Society, original series, 243, 1959 for 1957), pp. 21–2, 44–5. In 1471, the *Great Chronicle of London* emphasised the hopelessness of Henry VI's cause in a long description of his pitiful appearance as he was led through the streets of London in an attempt to rally support: A.H. Thomas and I.D. Thornley (eds), *The Great Chronicle of London* (London, 1938; reprinted Gloucester, Alan Sutton, 1983), p. 215.

4   Simon Thurley, *The Royal Palaces of Tudor England: Architecture and Court Life, 1460–1547* (New Haven, Yale University Press, 1993); David Starkey *et al.* (eds), *The English Court from the Wars of the Roses to the Civil War* (London and New York, Longman, 1987), esp. David Starkey, 'Intimacy and Innovation: The Rise of the Privy Chamber, 1485–1547', pp. 71–118; Alison Sim, *Food and Feast in Tudor England* (Stroud, Sutton, 1997), esp. chs 8–10.

5   Joycelyne Gledhill Russell, *The Field of Cloth of Gold* (London, Routledge and Kegan Paul, 1969); Greg Walker, *Plays of Persuasion: Drama and Politics at the Court of Henry VIII* (Cambridge University Press, 1991), esp. pp. 133–6; W.R. Streitberger, *Court Revels 1485–1559* (University of Toronto Press, 1994).

6   Cf. n. 10 below.

7   C.A.J. Armstrong, 'The Inauguration Ceremonies of the Yorkist Kings and their Title to the Throne', *TRHS*, 4th series, XXX (1948), 51–73; reprinted in his *England, France and Burgundy in the Fifteenth Century* (London, Hambledon, 1983), pp. 73–95; Pamela Tudor-Craig, 'Richard III's Triumphant Entry into York', in Rosemary Horrox (ed.), *Richard III and the North* (Hull, University of Hull, Centre for Regional and Local History, Studies in Regional and Local History, 6, 1986), pp. 108–16.

8   Alan Young, *Tudor and Jacobean Tournaments* (London, George Philip and Son, 1987); Steven Gunn, 'Chivalry and the Politics of the Early Tudor Court', in Sydney Anglo (ed.), *Chivalry in the Renaissance* (Woodbridge, Boydell, 1990), pp. 107–28, esp. pp. 111, 122.

9   Gunn, 'Chivalry and the Politics of the Early Tudor Court', pp. 109–16.

10   Sydney Anglo, *Spectacle, Pageantry and Early Tudor Policy* (Oxford, Clarendon Press, 1969), pp. 56–97; Gordon Kipling, *The Triumph of Honour: Burgundian Origins of the Elizabethan Renaissance* (The Hague, Leiden University Press, 1977); *The Receyt of the Ladie Kateryne*, ed. Gordon Kipling (Early English Text Society, original series, 296, 1990), provides a MS account. Gordon Kipling, *Enter the King: Theatre, Liturgy, and Ritual in Medieval Civic Triumph* (Oxford, Clarendon Press, 1998) places the

emphasis on the ritual and dramatic elements of such entries, which he contrasts with the dissemination of propaganda, although the contrast is not so stark as he implies.

11   Nigel Llewellyn, 'The Royal Body: Monuments to the Dead, for the Living', in Lucy Gent and Nigel Llewellyn (eds), *Renaissance Bodies: The Human Figure in English Culture*, c. *1540–1660* (London, Reaktion, 1990), pp. 218–40, notes pp. 275–82.

12   The history of gesture is not well developed in England, but for an exploration of the period of the Hundred Years War, see Nicolas Offenstadt, 'The Rituals of Peace during the Civil War in France, 1409–1435', in Tim Thornton (ed.), *Proceedings of the 1997 Huddersfield Conference* (Stroud, Sutton, forthcoming). If this appears to cast the net too widely, there were times when the king was not projecting a message, but it is significant that they were few and far between. It could be suggested that some of the hunting expeditions of Henry VIII, when he moved rapidly, with few attendants and with no ceremony, come into this category, although Henry's tendency to deal with business during these periods meant that even the image of the vigorous chivalrous princely hunter was a deliberately deployed one. Perhaps we have to resort to episodes such as Henry's flight from London during the outbreak of sweating sickness in the city to find a time when the king's person was not deliberately communicating a message for the regime.

13   Cavendish, *Life and Death of Cardinal Wolsey*, pp. 22–4.

14   Russell, *Field of Cloth of Gold*, pp. 160–3, 171–5.

15   For example in January 1519, payments were made to trumpeters for the New Year celebrations, and they headed the list of monthly wage payments: *LP*, iii (2), p. 1533.

16   John Stevens, *Music and Poetry in the Early Tudor Court* (1961; reprinted with corrections, Cambridge University Press, 1979); Roger Bowers, 'The Cultivation and Promotion of Music in the Household and Orbit of Thomas Wolsey', in S.J. Gunn and P.G. Lindley (eds), *Cardinal Wolsey: Church, State and Art* (Cambridge University Press, 1991), pp. 178–218.

17   Henry VIII has not been so well served as Elizabeth in this sphere of study. For the latter, see e.g. Carole Levin, *The Heart and Stomach of a King: Elizabeth I and the Politics of Sex and Power* (Philadelphia, University of Pennsylvania Press, 1994). One of the most important events of the last years of Henry VIII's reign was, however, a speech by the king, in Parliament in December 1545: Edward Halle, *Chronicle: Containing the History of England During the Reign of Henry the Fourth, and the Succeeding Monarchs to the End of the Reign of Henry the Eighth* (London, Johnson, 1809), pp. 864–6.

18   Speech of Chief Justice Huse early in Henry VII's reign: S.B. Chrimes, *Henry VII* (1972; second edn, London, Eyre Methuen, 1977), pp. 64, 184. Wolsey's speeches, 2 May 1516, May 1517, 27 October 1519: Peter Gwyn, *The King's Cardinal: The Rise and Fall of Thomas Wolsey* (London, Barrie and Jenkins, 1990), p. 116; J.A. Guy, *The Cardinal's Court: The Impact of Thomas Wolsey in Star Chamber* (Hassocks, Sussex, Harvester, 1977), pp. 30–2. For a speech to 'all the noble men, Iuges, and Iustices of the peace of euery shire' in Star Chamber on foreign policy, see Cavendish, *Life and Death of Cardinal Wolsey*, pp. 64–5.

19   For example, the reception of Catherine of Aragon in 1501, cf. n. 10 above.

20   Alan J. Fletcher, *Preaching, Politics and Poetry in Late Medieval England* (Dublin, Medieval Studies, 1998); Millar MacLure, *The Paul's Cross Sermons: 1534–1642* (University of Toronto Press, 1958); Millar MacLure, *Register of Sermons Preached at Paul's Cross 1534–1642*, revised by Jackson Campbell Boswell and Peter Pauls (Ottawa, Dovehouse edns, 1989); G.R. Elton, *Policy and Police: The Enforcement*

of the Reformation in the Age of Thomas Cromwell (Cambridge University Press, 1972; paperback edn, 1985), pp. 211–16; Peter E. McCullough, *Sermons at Court: Politics and Religion in Elizabethan and Jacobean Preaching* (Cambridge University Press, 1998).

21   NB the great power of the credence provided by the king's ring in the story told by Cavendish of the meeting between Wolsey and Henry Norris, chief gentleman of the privy chamber, in October 1529: Cavendish, *Life and Death of Cardinal Wolsey*, pp. 101–2; David Starkey, 'Representation Through Intimacy: A Study in the Symbolism of Monarchy and Court Office in Early Modern England', in I. Lewis (ed.), *Symbols and Sentiments: Cross Cultural Studies in Symbolism* (London, Academic Press, 1977), pp. 187–224.

22   C.E. Challis, *The Tudor Coinage* (Manchester University Press, 1978); P. Grierson, 'The Origins of the English Sovereign and the Symbolism of the Closed Crown', *British Numismatic Journal*, XXXIII (1964), 118–34.

23   Simon Thurley and C. Lloyd, *Henry VIII: Images of a Tudor King* (Oxford, Historic Royal Palaces Agency, 1990); Roy Strong, *Holbein and Henry VIII* (London, Routledge and Kegan Paul, 1967); John N. King, *Tudor Royal Iconography* (Princeton University Press, 1989); E.A. Danbury, 'English and French Artistic Propaganda during the Period of the Hundred Years War: Some Evidence from Royal Charters', in C. Allmand (ed.), *Power, Culture and Religion in France, c. 1350–c. 1550* (Woodbridge, Boydell, 1989), pp. 75–97; E.A. Danbury, 'The Decoration and Illumination of Royal Charters in England, 1250–1509: An Introduction', in M.C.E. Jones and M.G.A. Vale (eds), *England and Her Neighbours, 1066–1453: Essays in Honour of Pierre Chaplais* (London, Hambledon, 1989), pp. 157–79.

24   B. Bedos–Rezak, 'Ideologie royal, ambitions princières et rivalités politiques d'après le témoinage des sceaux (France, 1380–1461)', in *La 'France anglaise' au Moyen Age*, Congrès national des sociétés savantes: III colloque des historiens médiévalistes français et britannique (Paris, CTHS, 1988), pp. 483–511.

25   David Starkey, 'Ightham Mote', *Archaeologia*, 107 (1982), 153–63.

26   This is a particular emphasis of Anglo, *Images of Tudor Kingship*; and of David Starkey: 'Representation Through Intimacy', pp. 187–224; 'The Age of the Household: Politics, Society and the Arts, *c*.1350–*c*.1550', in Stephen Medcalf (ed.), *The Later Middle Ages* (London, Methuen, 1981); *The Reign of Henry VIII: Personalities and Politics* (London, George Philip, 1985).

27   John Morrill, 'The British Problem, *c*. 1534–1707', in Brendan Bradshaw and John Morrill (eds), *The British Problem, c. 1534–1707: State Formation in the Atlantic Archipelago* (Basingstoke and London, Macmillan, 1996), pp. 1–38, esp. p. 6, relying on Anglo, *Images of Tudor Kingship*, chs 2 and 5.

28   Hughes and Larkin, *Tudor Royal Proclamations*, vol. I, p. xxiii; Alison Allan, 'Royal Propaganda and the Proclamations of Edward IV', *BIHR*, 59 (1986), 146–54, esp. pp. 151–4; Charles Ross, 'Rumour, Propaganda and Public Opinion during the Wars of the Roses', in Ralph A. Griffiths (ed.), *Patronage, the Crown and the Provinces in Later Medieval England* (Gloucester, Alan Sutton, 1981), pp. 15–32.

29   Excepting the unusual period of Somerset's protectorate, when the average is 2.41 per month. Calculations: R.W. Heinze, *The Proclamations of the Tudor Kings* (Cambridge University Press, 1976), p. 5.

30   Such as those attacking the duke of York in the crisis around 1459–61: P.E. Gill, 'Politics and Propaganda in Fifteenth–Century England: The Polemical Writings of Sir John Fortescue', *Speculum*, xlvi (1971), 333–47.

31   [William de Machlinia, 1483], *STC* 9176; Gunn, *Early Tudor Government*, pp. 190–1.

32   G.R. Elton, 'The Sessional Printing of Statutes, 1484–1547', *Studies in Tudor and Stuart Politics and Government* (4 vols, Cambridge University Press, 1974–92), vol. III, pp. 92–109 (reprinted with corrections from E.W. Ives, R.J. Knecht, and J.J. Scarisbrick (eds), *Wealth and Power in Tudor England: Essays Presented to S.T. Bindoff* (London, Athlone Press, 1978)); Katharine F. Pantzer, 'Printing the English Statutes, 1484–1640', in Kenneth E. Carpenter (ed.), *Books and Society in History: Papers of the Association of College and Research Libraries Rare Book and Manuscripts Preconference, 24–28 June 1980, Boston, Massachusetts* (New York and London, R.R. Bowker, 1983), pp. 69–114; Elton, *Policy and Police*, p. 134.

33   Gunn, *Early Tudor Government*, pp. 188, 191.

34   Heinze, *Proclamations of the Tudor Kings*, pp. 5, 20–9, 68.

35   Elton attempted to draw a contrast between 'active' propaganda, designed to win support for the innovations of the 1530s in England, and 'passive' propaganda, to defend them against reaction: *Policy and Police*, p. 199.

36   The latter can be most clearly seen in the series of works aimed at the Pilgrims in 1536–7: Elton, *Policy and Police*, pp. 199–205.

37   Alison Allan, 'Royal Propaganda and the Proclamations of Edward IV', *BIHR*, 59 (1986), 146–54; Ross, 'Rumour, Propaganda and Public Opinion', pp. 25–9.

38   See above, n. 27.

39   C.S.L. Davies, 'Bishop John Morton, the Holy See, and the Accession of Henry VII', *EHR*, CII (1987), 2–30, esp. p. 15.

40   Heinze, *Proclamations of the Tudor Kings*.

41   Elton, *Policy and Police*. Elton's work built upon that by Franklin Le Van Baumer, *The Early Tudor Theory of Kingship* (1940; reprinted New York, Russell and Russell, 1966), esp. Appendix A; and W. Gordon Zeeveld, *Foundations of Tudor Policy* (Cambridge, MA, Harvard University Press, 1948).

42   Roy Strong, *Portraits of Queen Elizabeth I* (Oxford, Clarendon Press, 1963); *The Cult of Elizabeth: Elizabethan Portraiture and Pageantry* (London, Thames and Hudson, 1977); *Art and Power: Renaissance Festivals 1450–1650* (Woodbridge, Suffolk, Boydell, 1984). There was a scheme to systematically produce portraits, but it is not known whether it came to anything: Hughes and Larkin (eds), *Tudor Royal Proclamations*, vol. II, 1553–87 (1969), no. 516, cited in Anglo, *Images of Tudor Kingship*, pp. 116–17.

43   *Articles deuisid by the holle consent of the kynges counsayle* (*STC* 9177; London, Thomas Berthelet, 1533), reprinted Nicholas Pocock (ed.), *Records of the Reformation: The Divorce 1527–1533* (2 vols, London, 1870), vol. II, pp. 523–31. Elton seized on the phrase as 'obligingly' setting forth the objectives of the council and of Thomas Cromwell: *Policy and Police*, p. 180.

44   Elton, *Policy and Police*, p. 206.

45   Rudolf Hirsch, *Printing, Selling and Reading 1450–1550* (Wiesbaden, Otto Harrassowitz, 1967), p. 99.

46   Ibid., pp. 101–2. Cf. the printing of *Münzordnungen*, mint regulations to deal with the confusion arising from numerous different currencies and to combat inflation: p. 102.

47   Ibid., p. 100: 13 in the 1450s, and 185 in the 1480s; NB the total fell as low as 2 in the 1470s and 37 in the 1490s, so the nature of the threat was clearly important.

48   Rudolf Hirsch, 'The Duke Addresses his Subjects: A Study in Propaganda, 1514', *Library Quarterly*, XXII (1952), 208–13, reprinted in idem, *The Printed Word and its Distribution (Primarily in the 15th–16th Centuries)* (London, Variorum Reprints, 1978), XI.

49   *STC* 14077c.27–.34; Dennis E. Rhodes, 'Some Documents Printed by Pynson for St Botolph's, Boston, Lincs.', *The Library*, 5th series, 15 (1960), 53–7, reprinted in Rhodes, *Studies in Early European Printing and Book-Collecting* (London, Pindar, 1983), pp. 14–18; Arthur J. Slavin, 'The Gutenberg Galaxy and the Tudor Revolution', in Gerald P. Tyson and Sylvia S. Wagonheim (eds), *Print and Culture in the Renaissance: Essays on the Advent of Printing in Europe* (Newark, University of Delaware Press, London and Toronto, Associated Universities Press, 1986), pp. 90–109; A.J. Slavin, 'The Tudor Revolution and the Devil's Art: Bishop Bonner's Printed Forms', in D.J. Guth and J.W. McKenna (eds), *Tudor Rule and Revolution* (Cambridge University Press, 1982), pp. 3–23.

50   E. Gordon Duff, *The English Provincial Printers, Stationers and Bookbinders to 1557* (Cambridge University Press, 1912), pp. 34–42, 101–4 (St Albans); 98–9 (Tavistock); 99 (Abingdon).

51   Anglo, *Images of Tudor Kingship*, pp. 106–12.

52   A point made by Anglo, *Images of Tudor Kingship*, pp. 120–3.

53   Greg Walker, *Persuasive Fictions: Faction Faith and Political Culture in the Reign of Henry VIII* (Aldershot, Scolar, 1996), esp. chs 3–4; Jennifer Loach, 'The Function of Ceremonial in the Reign of Henry VIII', *Past and Present*, 144 (1994), 43–68.

54   Anglo, *Images of Tudor Kingship*, pp. 24–8; Anglo, *Spectacle*, p. 265.

55   Anglo, *Spectacle*, p. 266; Anglo, 'An Early Tudor Programme for Plays and Other Demonstrations against the Pope', *Journal of the Warburg and Courtauld Institutes*, XX (1957), 176–9. G.R. Elton, 'Reform by Statute: Thomas Starkey's *Dialogue* and Thomas Cromwell's Policy', *Proceedings of the British Academy*, LIV (1968), 165–88, at pp. 177–8.

56   It should be noted that this actually exceeded the number from Spain (26, 1.7 per cent) and France (9, 0.6 per cent): discussed in Hirsch, *Printing, Selling and Reading*, p. 103.

57   *Caxton's Own Prose*, ed. N.F. Blake (London, Deutsch, 1973), pp. 90, 115; H.S. Bennett, *English Books and Readers 1475 to 1557* (1952; 2nd edn, Cambridge University Press, 1969), p. 17; Colin Clair, *A History of Printing in Britain* (London, Cassell, 1965), pp. 6–7.

58   The title appears on the Statutes for 19 Henry VII, 1504 (*STC* 9357): Clair, *History of Printing*, p. 42. No more than eight books by him are known.

59   For de Worde and Margaret Beaufort, Clair, *History of Printing*, p. 7.

60   Dennis E. Rhodes, 'William Marshall and his Books 1533–1537', *Papers of the Bibliographical Society of America*, 58 (1964), 219–31, reprinted in Rhodes, *Studies in Early European Printing and Book-Collecting* (London, Pindar, 1983), pp. 24–36.

61   D.S. Berkowitz (ed.), *Humanist Scholarship and Public Order: Two Tracts Against the Pilgrimage of Grace by Sir Richard Morrison* (Washington, DC, Folger Shakespeare Library; London, Associated University Presses, 1984).

62   A.S.G. Edwards and Carol M. Meale, 'The Marketing of Printed Books in Late Medieval England', *The Library*, 6th series, 15 (1993), 94–124.

63   Anglo, *Images of Tudor Kingship*, p. 109. He does choose here what he himself admits is the most complex piece of ceremonial of this type.

64   François Furet and Jacques Ozouf, *Lire et écrire: l'alphabétisation des français de Calvin à Jules Ferry* (2 vols, Paris, Les éditions de minuit, 1977), vol. 1, ch. 1, and vol. 2, *passim* (the first volume published in English as *Reading and Writing: Literacy in France from Calvin to Jules Ferry* (Cambridge University Press, 1982)): in 1686–90 more than 70 per cent of men and more than 90 per cent of women were unable

to sign their names, although this figure varies considerably by region. Once material becomes available which allows us to examine it properly, it seems English political society even at its lowest levels could be remarkably sophisticated in its thinking: Adam Fox, 'Rumour, News and Popular Political Opinion in Elizabethan and Early Stuart England', *Historical Journal*, XL (1997), 597–620.

65   Anglo, *Spectacle*, pp. 22–8; Angelo Raine (ed.), *York Civic Records* (Yorkshire Archaeological Society, Records Series, XCVII–, 1939 for 1938), vol. I, pp. 155–9. King David is made to tell Henry that the city has been 'true and bolde to your Bloode'. More generally on the rose badge, Anglo, *Images of Tudor Kingship*, pp. 73–97.

66   PRO, KB 9/541/85–87; KB 27/1112, Rex, r.9–9a; Raphael Holinshed, *Chronicles of England, Scotland and Ireland* (6 vols, London, Johnson, 1807–8), vol. III, p. 807; Charles Wriothesley, *A Chronicle of England during the Reigns of the Tudors, from AD 1485 to 1559*, ed. William Douglas Hamilton, I (Camden Society, XI, 1875), p. 93; Elton, *Policy and Police*, pp. 289–90.

67   John N. King, *English Reformation Literature: The Tudor Origins of the Protestant Tradition* (Princeton University Press, 1982); Walker, *Plays of Persuasion*; Alistair Fox, *Politics and Literature in the Reigns of Henry VII and Henry VIII* (Oxford, Basil Blackwell, 1989); Anglo, *Spectacle*, p. 271.

68   Anglo, *Spectacle*, chs 8–9: an 'age of gloom'.

69   NB the comments, critical of Eisenstein's views on the fragmentational effects of printing, in John N. Wall, jnr, 'The Reformation in England and the Typographical Revolution: "By this Printing . . . the Doctrine of the Gospel Soundeth to all Nations"', in Tyson and Wagonheim (eds), *Print and Culture in the Renaissance*, pp. 208–21.

70   Wall, jnr, 'The Reformation in England and the Typographical Revolution', pp. 211–12.

71   Cf. the historical work of the late 1520s: Graham Nicholson, 'The Act of Appeals and the English Reformation', in Claire Cross, David Loades, and J.J. Scarisbrick (eds), *Law and Government under the Tudors: Essays presented to Sir Geoffrey Elton on his Retirement* (Cambridge University Press, 1988), pp. 19–30.

72   Although the preface to the *Gildas* is dated 6 April 1525, London, and the dedication is to Cuthbert Tunstall, bishop of London, it is likely that it was printed in Antwerp between 1525 and 1530: Dennis E. Rhodes, 'The First Edition of Gildas', *The Library*, 6th series, 1 (1979), 355–60, reprinted in Rhodes, *Studies in Early European Printing and Book–Collecting*, pp. 111–18; *The Anglica Historia of Polydore Vergil AD 1485–1537*, ed. Dennis Hay (Camden Society, LXXIV, 1950), pp. xiii, xv–xvi (Hay's explanation is that Vergil was waiting for the 'divorce' crisis to end).

73   In some ways this is the argument advanced by Gunn, *Early Tudor Government*, pp. 201–2, who sees flaws in the propaganda effort, such as they were, rendered relatively insignificant by the effects of 'the real achievements of early Tudor Government'.

74   Colin Richmond, 'Hand and Mouth: Information Gathering and Use in England in the Later Middle Ages', *Journal of Historical Sociology*, 1 (1988), 233–52.

75   An excellent example from the end of the sixteenth century is provided by Paul E.J. Hammer, 'Myth-making: Politics, Propaganda and the Capture of Cádiz in 1596', *Historical Journal*, XL (1997), 621–42; Rosalind Davies, 'News from the Fleet: Characterizing the Elizabethan Army in the Narratives of the Action at Cádiz, 1596', in Bertrand Taithe and Tim Thornton (eds), *War: Identities in Conflicts 1300–2000* (Stroud, Sutton, 1998), pp. 21–36.

76   '"The Spousells" of Princess Mary', ed. J. Gairdner, in *Camden Miscellany*, IX (Camden Society, new series, 53, 1895); Dennis E. Rhodes, 'Four Important End-Papers in Hereford Cathedral

Library', *The Library*, 6th series, 4 (1982), 410–15, reprinted in Rhodes, *Studies in Early European Printing and Book-Collecting* (London, Pindar, 1983), pp. 49–54, esp. 50–2.

77   *TRP* 54; *STC* 7760.4, .6, 7761 – it received one edition from W. Faques and two from W. de Worde.

78   *The Gardyners Passetaunce*, ed. Franklin B. Williams, Jr (London, Roxburghe Club, 1985); *Tudor Royal Proclamations*, vol. I, p. 65; John Skelton, *A ballade of the scottysshe kynge* (R. Faques, 1513; *STC* 22593) (*The Complete English Poems*, ed. John Scattergood (Harmondsworth, Penguin, 1985), pp. 113–21, 420–4); *Hereafter ensue the trewe encountre or batayle lately don betwene Englande and Scotlande. In whiche batayle the Scottshe kynge was slayne* (London, Richard Faques, [1513?]; *STC* 11088.5), reprinted in D. Laing (ed.), 'A Contemporary Account of the Battle of Flodden, 9th September 1513', *Proceedings of the Society of Antiquaries of Scotland*, 7 (1870), 141–52, at pp. 143–52. This concentration of governmental printed propaganda was identified by Gunn, *Early Tudor Government*, p. 191. It is interesting that the king's personal victories on the continent of Europe, especially the battle of the Spurs and the taking of Tournai, were less prominent in the print production of 1513–14 – a sign that the king was not directly in charge of the campaign, and perhaps that connections of Surrey or Catherine were? NB, for example, the high praise heaped upon Surrey and Edmund Howard, 'a coragious and an hardy yong lusty gentilman': 'Contemporary Account of the Battle of Flodden', pp. 147–8.

79   Julia Boffey and Carol M. Meale, 'Selecting the Text: Rawlinson C.86 and some other Books for London Readers', in Felicity Riddy (ed.), *Regionalism in Late-Mediaeval Manuscripts and Texts* (Cambridge, D.S. Brewer, 1991), pp. 143–69, esp. 162–3.

80   Carole Rawcliffe, *The Staffords, Earls of Stafford and Dukes of Buckingham, 1394–1521* (Cambridge University Press, 1978), pp. 1, 35–44, 96, 99–100, 182–6, 189–90; Barbara J. Harris, *Edward Stafford, 3rd Duke of Buckingham, 1478–1521* (Stanford University Press, 1986), pp. 170–1, and chs 7 and 8 for Stafford's relationship with the crown; *Chevalier au Cygne, The History of Helyas, Knight of the Swan*, tr. Robert Copland from the French version, Paris 1504, 1512 (New York, 1901); Glenn Burger, *A Lytell Cronycle: Richard Pynson's Translation (c. 1520) of 'La Fleur des Histoires de la Terre d'Orient' (c. 1307)* (University of Toronto Press, 1988), pp. xxxix–xlvii; Christopher Tyerman, *England and the Crusades, 1095–1588* (Chicago and London, Chicago University Press, 1988).

81   *STC* 9362.4, .6, .8.

82   *STC* 9362.7.

83   *STC* 9362.9; further editions appeared in 1525?, 1533?, 1543?, 1551?, 1563?, and 1575?: *STC* 9362.10, .11; 9363, 9363.2, .3, .4.

84   1514: liveries and retainers, *TRP* 77, *STC* 7765; 1515: subsidy commissioners, defining information to be given, *STC* 7766; 1515: subsidy commissioners, blank form, *STC* 7767; 1517: limiting dishes according to rank, *TRP* 81, *STC* 7768. 1520: brief for collection for T. Andrew, who has incurred losses due to fire, *STC* 7769.2; *c.* 1522: against retainers, *STC* 7769.4.

85   1526: values of coins, *TRP* 111, 112, *STC* 7769.6; 1527: against the engrossing of grain, and regarding vagabonds, *TRP* 118, STC 7769.8.

86   Overall totals are calculated from *STC*, Vol. I, pp. 356–61. According to *TRP*, annual totals of proclamations during this period are: 1509, 3; 1510, 0; 1511, 2; 1512, 5; 1513, 6; 1514, 4; 1515, 1; 1516, 0; 1517, 2; 1518, 1; 1519, 1; 1520, 0; 1521, 2; 1522, 10; 1523, 2; 1524, 4; 1525, 5; 1526, 8; 1527, 4; 1528, 3. If anything, therefore, the 1520s saw a slightly increased use of proclamations.

87   He appeared as printer once, and in the remaining cases without description: PRO, E 36/215, ff. 55, 64v., 97v., 116, 130, 139v., 160, 183, 208v., 258 (*LP.* ii, pp. 1450, 1451, 1457, 1459, 1461, 1463, 1465, 1467, 1469, 1475). PRO, E 36/216, f. 120 (*LP*, iii, p. 1544). In the Treasurer of the Chamber's accounts, E 101/420/11, ff. 22, 36 (LP. v, pp. 309, 311), he again appears without description.

88   Gunn, *Early Tudor Government*, pp. 191–2, noted this lull, but did not draw any conclusions or allow it to undermine his view of an ever-increasing royal deployment of print propaganda in the promotion of its imperial power.

89   *The Chronicle of Froissart, translated out of French by Sir John Bourchier Lord Berners annis 1523–25* (6 vols, London, David Nutt, 1901–3), vol. 1 (1901), pp. 3–7. A modernised version is available in Gillian and William Anderson (eds), *The Chronicles of Jean Froissart in Lord Berners' Translation* (London and Fontwell, Centaur Press, 1963), pp. xv–xvii. N.F. Blake, 'Lord Berners: A Survey', *Medievalia et Humanistica*, new series, 2 (1971), 119–32, esp. pp. 120–1.

90   P.J. Gwyn, 'Wolsey's Foreign Policy: The Conferences at Calais and Bruges Reconsidered', *Historical Journal*, 23 (1980), 755–72.

91   Both by Richard Pynson, London, 1523, 1525; *STC* 11396–7. Cf. S.L. Lee (ed.), *The Boke of Duke Huon of Burdeux Done into English by Sir John Bourchier, Lord Berners* (The English Charlemagne Romances, 7, 8, 9, 12; *Early English Text Society*, extra series, 40, 41, 43, 50, 1882–84, 1887). Other editions possibly connected with the French war are Barclay's *Jugurtha* and the *de gesta romanorum*: Fox, *Politics and Literature*, pp. 37–55, esp. 54–5 for the patronage of the second duke of Norfolk for Barclay and his *Jugurtha*; Sidney J.H. Herrtage (ed.), *The Early English Versions of the Gesta Romanorum* (Early English Text Society, extra series, 38, 1879), pp. xxi–xxii for de Worde's edition. On the whole, however, the patronage of the nobility followed remarkably peaceful themes: Hastings promoted Berners' *Marcus Aurelius* (*STC* 12,436); and an edition of Bernardinus was dedicated to Charles, duke of Somerset (*STC* 1967).

92   Walker, *Persuasive Fictions*, ch. 2; Walker, *Plays of Persuasion*, ch. 2; Greg Walker, *John Skelton and the Politics of the 1520s* (Cambridge University Press, 1988).

93   Richard Rex, 'The English Campaign against Luther in the 1520s', *TRHS*, 5th series, XXXIX (1989), 85–106; Frederick Seaton Siebert, *Freedom of the Press in England 1476–1776: The Rise and Decline of Government Control* (Urbana, University of Illinois Press, 1965), pp. 42–6; D.M. Loades, 'The Theory and Practice of Censorship in Sixteenth-Century England', *TRHS*, 5th series, XXIV (1974), 141–57.

94   Elton, *Policy and Police*, pp. 171–210; Steven W. Haas, 'Henry VIII's *Glasse of Truthe*', *History*, 64 (1979), 353–62; Edward Surtz and Virginia Murphy (eds), *The Divorce Tracts of Henry VIII* (Angers, Moreana, 1988); D.S. Berkowitz (ed.), *Humanist Scholarship and Public Order*. NB Elton's admission, *Policy and Police*, p. 174, that the 'whole campaign started very quietly, but more especially it started rather late'. In this light, the relative unwillingness of the Marian regime to engage in pamphlet wars is less surprising than it might otherwise seem: Jennifer Loach, 'Pamphlets and Politics, 1553–8', *BIHR*, XLVIII (1975), 31–44.

95   A Europe-wide phenomenon: Hirsch, *Printing, Selling and Reading*, p. 112.

96   Another example they use is the production of Henry Bradshaw's saints' lives for Chester Abbey; for my interpretation of this in the context of the struggles of the abbey see Tim Thornton, 'Cardinal Wolsey and the Abbot of Chester', *History Today*, 45 (8) (August 1995), 12–17.

97   PRO, SP 1/18, f. 211; /29, /30, p. 32 (*LP*, vol. III, nos 337, 3680; vol. IV, no. 39); F.J. Furnivall, 'Pynson's Contracts with Horman for his *Vulgaria*, and Palsgrave for his *Lesclaircissement*, with Pynson's Letter of Denization', *Philological Society Transactions* (1867), 362–74.

98   W.H. Black and F.H. Davies, 'Thomas Berthelet's Bill, as King's Printer, for Books Sold and Bound, and for Statutes and Proclamations Furnished to the Government in 1541–43', *Journal of the British Archaeological Association*, VII (1853), 44–52.

99   Propaganda still was attributed to the crown, but this was more usually an attempt to influence royal policy rather than promote it. It might even be that what many have seen as propaganda for the crown was no more than an attempt to subscribe to crown culture and therefore acquire something of the power that this might bestow. As Anglo has pointed out, the 'Procession' portrait of Elizabeth I, with its representation of Edward Somerset, earl of Worcester, Master of the Horse, was primarily intended to further his glorification through the medium of service to the queen: Anglo, *Images of Tudor Kingship*, pp. 112–16.

100   Even a London printer like de Worde would go abroad for the printing of missals: George D. Painter, Dennis E. Rhodes, and Howard M. Nixon, 'Two Missals Printed for Wynkyn de Worde', *British Library Journal*, 2 (1976), 159–71; cf. Frederick C. Avis, 'England's Use of Antwerp Printers 1500–1540', *Gutenberg-Jahrbuch* (1973), 234–40.

101   Norman F. Blake, 'The Spread of Printing in English during the Fifteenth Century', *Gutenberg-Jahrbuch* (1987), 26–36.

102   Duff, *English Provincial Printers*, pp. 111–16; Clair, *History of Printing*, p. 117; *Calendar of Patent Rolls*, Edward VI (6 vols, London, HMSO, 1924–9), I, p. 269; he probably also had a shop in Shrewsbury.

103   Clair, *History of Printing*, pp. 126–7. He received £20 from the king, recorded 18 July 1550: John Roche Dasent (ed.), *Acts of the Privy Council of England*, new series (continuing, London, HMSO, 1890—), vol. III, *AD 1550–1552* (1891), p. 84. Cf. also the Tavistock press: Boethius, *De consolatione philosophiae*, translated by John Walton as *The boke of comfort* (*STC* 3200), was printed by the monk Thomas Rychard in 1525; more official was the 1534 *Charter perteynynge to all the tynners wythyn the countey of Deuonshyre* (*STC* 6795.6), a 26–leaf production linked to the Boethius by a woodcut of God the Father common to both. Duff, *English Provincial Printers*, pp. 98–9; Clair, *History of Printing*, p. 116. The exception is the second manifestation of the St Albans press, which resulted in the persecution of the printer John Herford for printing conservative religious works in the 1530s. He reappeared, however, in London in 1544 to print Leland's *Assertio inclytissimi Arthurii regis Britanniae* (*STC* 15440), and the following year his *Cygnea Cantio*. Clair, *History of Printing*, p. 119.

104   Wall, jnr, 'The Reformation in England and the Typographical Revolution', p. 22, notes that printing in such a few centres must have made obvious the contrasts between the various rites.

105   For example Thomas Gaultier, King's Printer in French for the Channel Islands 1553: Bettye Chambers, 'The First French New Testament Printed in England?', in *Bibliothèque d'Humanisme et Renaissance*, 39 (1977), 143–8; Chambers, 'Thomas Gaultier Strikes Again . . . and Again?' in ibid., 41 (1979), 353–8; the French Book of Common Prayer is *STC* 16430 (1553).

4

THEMES OF POWER AND IDENTITY IN THE COURT FESTIVALS OF DUCAL LORRAINE, 1563–1624

Kate Currey

This chapter will examine the complex relationship between propaganda, political rhetoric and identity as revealed in the court festivals of ducal Lorraine between 1563 and 1624. The festivals of the Nanceian court are a fruitful source for the examination of what Peter Burke has termed the 'public image' of its ruling dynasty.[1] The term 'public image' would, however, benefit from definition on two levels, especially regarding the propaganda impact of court festivals. First, there is the 'public image' of the dynasty as it appeared to its creators or intimates (within the context of the court of Nancy, for example). Second, there is the question of how this 'public image' was received by an audience outside the confines of the court.

The court of Nancy witnessed an active festival culture, where a variety of festival forms reiterated the continuity of the house of Lorraine. These forms included baptisms, pastorals, entries, theatre, ballets, combats, weddings and funerals. Here I will concentrate the greater part of my discussion upon those forms which appear to have been consciously adopted and deployed as vehicles for the dynastic continuity of the dukes of Lorraine, namely, pastoral, entries and funerals. The theme of ducal power and its consolidation first began to emerge in festivals held during the reign of duc Charles III (1563–1608) and at the crucial juncture between its end and the beginning of that of his son and heir Henri II (1608–24). Charles III was the first ruler of Lorraine consistent in his deployment of court festival as a propaganda vehicle to promote the identity of his dynasty. One of the factors which would seem to have led Charles III to employ festivals for such self-promotion was the formative phase of his adolescence spent at the French Valois court 'dans un climat favorable à l'absolutisme'.[2] Direct evidence of Charles III's intentions for festival is absent. Yet, as Rothrock, Giesey and Choné argue, a degree of propagandistic intention can be inferred and 'we must assume the interchange of ideas' between French royal festival custom and that of the duchy.[3] The 'fabrication' of an identity (to use another Burkeian phrase) for ducal Lorraine was the political intention and end product of its festival propaganda. This is where it is important to 'read' the symbolic content of relevant festivals, for the deployment of symbolism played an active role in creating a distinct identity for the duchy. To those who formulated such symbolism, the question of Lorraine's identity existed specifically in relation to its function as an independent political entity. The court festivals of Lorraine provide a medium in which the coexistent themes of power and identity find their resolution.

This preoccupation with and use of festival to formulate an identity for the sovereign territory of Lorraine apparently coincides with an important phase in the development of 'national territorial sovereignty' in early-modern Europe.[4] This would particularly appear to have been the case of territories such as Lorraine (or perhaps Burgundy or Brittany) which had typically been identified as *pays de l'entre deux* since the Middle Ages.[5] Although the duchy of Lorraine had achieved some semblance of territorial unity by the sixteenth century, it was still a complex and fragile construction, easily under threat of incursion from its neighbours. In the second half of the sixteenth century, full ducal authority extended only to that portion of the duchy which occupied the right-hand bank of the river Meuse, the so-called *Barrois non-mouvant*. On the left-hand bank of the river, Lorraine was subject to France. The duchies of Lorraine and Bar were joined in the fifteenth century with the marriage of René d'Anjou to Isabelle de Lorraine, a union consolidated through the reign of their son, René II (1451–1508).[6] René II's victory over the Burgundian duke, Charles the Bold, at the battle of Nancy in 1477, ended the Burgundian threat.

Pierre de Blarru's *Nancéide* (1518) links René II's victory with a crucial phase in the development of the duchy's political independence. Blarru conveys this sense of threat to Lorraine through the covetous way in which Charles the Bold describes it: 'Charles de Bourgogne, portant sur les terres lorraines un regard captateur, ne cacha pas son désir et dit: "Chère petite province, tu charmes ma grandeur. Aucune plus ne me tient plus à coeur." '[7] Elsewhere Blarru comments that Charles is 'in love' with Lorraine. This amorous language and attribution of a feminine identity to the duchy is doubly interesting.[8] First, it anticipates Lorraine's personification as the nymph Lorine in Nicolas Romain's *La Salmée* (1602). As such it represents a formative stage in the development of the duchy's symbolic identity. Second, it alludes to territorial expansion by early-modern rulers in terms of sexual conquest, thus subverting dynastic marriage as the only 'acceptable' form through which territorial aggrandisement could be achieved.

Blarru's *Nancéide* is not the only text which examines the theme of threats to the duchy's political and territorial integrity by outside agencies. Equally important is Laurent Pillard's *La Rusticiade* (1548) which recounts duc Antoine de Lorraine and Claude de Guise's two-phase victory in 1525 over the German Protestant peasant army: *les Rustauds*.[9] The army crossed the border of southern Germany into Alsace and Lorraine. It was beaten back, first at Saverne and then at the entrance to the Val de Sainte-Marie. Antoine's victory had important political consequences for Lorraine. Not only did this victory check the progress of the

Reformation in the duchy, but it also placed the duke firmly on the side of its Catholic adversaries.[10] The victory was marked by a triumphal entry into Nancy by duc Antoine. Here, a ceremony traditionally associated with the affirmation of rule was deployed to reinforce the position of the ruling dynasty. This would seem to have been a formative moment in the creation of the typology which came to be associated with the rulers of the House of Lorraine, that of the *soldat de dieu*.[11]

Blarru's *Nancéide* has been described as Lorraine's first 'national' poem, *La Rusticiade* being the second.[12] It seems that both authors were creating a type of meta-historical narrative for the duchy of Lorraine based on the retrospective assimilation of such key events into a teleological structure. Indeed, this process can be observed in the dynastic historiography fostered by contemporary rulers. Ducal Burgundy presented a case where, with its diverse territories acquired over a relatively long timescale, it was difficult to integrate such separate histories into a coherent political and narrative structure.[13] In ducal Lorraine, however, the narrative's outcome was straightforward: the duchy's territorial and political cohesion and the growth of an identity underscored by the theme of Catholicism.

Duc Antoine's reign (1508–44) assured the political and territorial consolidation of the duchy. However, after France occupied the bishoprics of Metz, Toul and Verdun in 1552, the duchy's western borders faced the threat of further French incursion. Lorraine was vulnerable after the death of duc François in 1545 and during the co-regency of his widow, Christine de Denmark, and her brother-in-law, Nicolas de Vaudémont. Nicolas de Vaudémont was suspicious of Christine's pro-Empire policies and had himself made the duchy's sole regent in 1552 and the ducal heir, Charles III, taken to live at the French court. His marriage in 1559 to Claude de France, daughter of Henri II and Catherine de Medici, on the surface at least, cemented the union of France and Lorraine. Tensions still remained between France and Lorraine, centred upon Charles III's desire to secure accession to the French throne for his heir, Henri, marquis du Pont.[14] Certainly the state of many early-modern dynasties, Lorraine included, was insecure. In Lorraine, the staging of festivals confirming dynastic continuity reached its height in the early seventeenth century, just when the duchy faced several serious political threats. One was the death of Charles III after more than a half-century of rule. Another was the fact that his heir, Henri, marquis du Pont's marriage to Catherine de Bourbon (who died in 1604) was sterile. This necessitated his urgent remarriage to Margherita Gonzaga, a younger and more fertile choice of bride, in 1606. Yet another threat was the attempted assassination of Henri II in 1609.

This brings us back to the purpose and definition of propaganda itself, which can then be discussed in more explicit relation to festival literature. We know, for example, that the term did not exist until 1622, when it appeared in the title of a papal bull promulgated by Pope Gregory XV, for the *Sacra Congregatio de Propaganda Fide*. In this context, the term propaganda simply meant 'extension, increase or enlargement'. It was not actively deployed until the eighteenth century, when modes of persuasion employed by the supporters of the French Revolution were described as resembling Christian techniques of conversion.[15]

Helen Watanabe O'Kelly has argued that: 'The festival book was a propaganda weapon.'[16] While O'Kelly imputes an adversarial role to festival literature, it is interesting to compare her views with those of other scholars. Ellul has assigned a complex range of bipolar functions to propaganda, contrasting, for example, its political and sociological or its agitative or integrative aspects.[17] Bob Scribner followed Ellul's structure in identifying two kinds of early-modern propaganda. One was a 'weaker form' concerned with the sort of dynastic image-building in which early-modern rulers and their publicists were engaged, and which festival literature was commonly seen to represent.[18] The second form of propaganda was 'adversarial' in function, and aimed at undermining established modes or perceptions through opposing or countering them.[19] In the case of festival literature, however, Ellul's definition does not hold. It would seem natural to assign festival literature to the combative rather than the integrative category. This fits the pattern of European courts engaging in dynastic one-upmanship through their deployment of culture as O'Kelly asserts. Yet, as Scribner, following Ellul's integrative model, argued, another function of propaganda was to 'create solidarity', which to early-modern rulers presumably meant reinforcing their political position.[20]

Ellul's view of propaganda does not, however, allow for the coexistence of these two forms, the combative and integrative. He argues that the latter form only came into existence in the twentieth century, as a tool to aid social cohesion among the comfortably off and well informed.[21] Yet, a need existed for both forms during the early-modern period, and festival literature combined both functions. Festival literature was combative in that it issued a challenge to its audience by asserting the cultural supremacy of the court and event in question. It was intended to create a lasting impression of the event's magnificence, for, in Burke's words, 'magnificence had a political function'.[22] Festival literature also had an integrative purpose. Like its cousin, court historiography, festival literature was 'the instrument of that process whereby the political centre consciously fostered the coalescence of a wider political community around itself'.[23] In other words, festivals and their literature were becoming an important propaganda tool for early-modern state builders.

Mark Greengrass has argued that 'The peculiar feature (though it may not be unique in world history) of Europe's political past is the unusual perception that states should be viewed as primarily territorial, rather than legal, religious, cultural or dynastic entities.'[24] Yet this amorphous territorial structure was to acquire an identity both through its conception in cultural forms and its assignment of a symbolic role through festival. Every early-modern state needed a powerbase, a visible expression of its actuality. Just as the court gradually became the fixed powerbase of European rulers, so the territorial and cultural boundaries of these political entities became more defined and more closely attached to a self-seeking dynastic identity which took the form of a genealogical obsession intent on proving descent from a range of real and quasi-mythological figures as diverse as Aeneas and Charlemagne.[25]

This ties in to the progression of modes of propaganda utilised by the kings of France, described by Klaits, prior to its apogee under Louis XIV.[26] The fifteenth-century transition from oral to printed modes of propaganda ran parallel with the decreasing reliance of the French monarchy on its estates to support itself.[27] As the estates became an increasing obstacle to centralised royal control, the kings of France resorted to printed propaganda in an attempt to reaffirm royal supremacy. Ultimately, as occurred under Louis XIV, this led to the centralised control of print culture and the attempted subversion of any opposition.[28]

Obviously, early-modern rulers had considerable impact upon the switch from oral to printed propaganda. Festival literature *per se* belongs to this transition. Examples of festival books are known to exist in the last quarter of the fifteenth century, with the genre gaining full recognition by the 1520s.[29] Emperor Maximilian I is seen as the archetypal proponent of the festival book for propaganda purposes. He commissioned an important series of illustrated books (the *Theuerdank*, *Weisskunig* and *Freydal*), featuring himself as a chivalric hero. Even more important in terms of festival literature were the classically inspired *Triumphal Arch* (1517) and *Triumphal Procession* (1517) which were to prove influential for the themes and decor of early-modern entries.[30]

To understand what made festival literature such a valuable medium for the deployment of propaganda messages, it is necessary to consider the role and propaganda function of early-modern court festival itself. Recent researches into early-modern European courts have placed increasing emphasis on their importance as both political and cultural centres.[31] Scholars increasingly regard festival as not just social diversion but as a vital ingredient of power-politics.[32] Those associated with early-modern court society recognised the explicit relationship between court festival and the expression of power. As Louis XIV's secretary commented to the Dauphin, 'festivals please one's subjects and give foreigners an extremely useful impression of magnificence, power, wealth and grandeur'.[33] Here the emphasis was on making an impression on both a national and international level. It provides some indication that potential audience response was considered by those festival organisers.

The reception of festivals and festival literature by their audience is a difficult topic. However impressive the event, it was ephemeral. Even if it impressed its audience, it could only serve as an exemplar if it was recorded permanently in festival literature. This literature had many benefits. It could provide a direct record of events, 'reportage' and, with the inclusion of illustrations, could aim to recreate the total festival experience, in a form of 're-enactment'.[34]

Festivals offered a total sensory package. The role of spectator had an especial significance in early-modern culture. Crowd scenes in Jacques Callot's engravings often depict audiences watching a spectacle. Some individuals look through telescopes or stare out at the viewer.[35] Callot thereby signals to his audience that his vision of events is personal. Defining limits should be set on the 'veracity' of festival literature. As a propaganda form it was designed to manipulate its audience, just as the original event had been. It is possible to see how devices (such as those used by Callot) were inserted into the text to manipulate the mind of the reader.

What complicates the question of the reception of festivals and their literature are the two different levels of engagement demanded of their audiences on the one hand and their readers on the other. It should be recalled that the term 'audience' refers to the original method through which most individuals encountered texts, by hearing them read aloud. There were thus two very different forms of cultural reception. Festivals themselves were a largely visual experience, but with textual elements. On the other hand, festival literature made much greater use of text, with images deployed in its support. As visual spectacle, festivals were more broadly comprehensible to an audience with a large non-literate component. Festival literature, however, was probably aimed more at a literate, educated readership.

Then, of course, there is the difficulty of gauging both the intention of the propagandist and the reaction of those on the receiving end. Ellul has identified several limitations to this process. One is the 'diversity of objectives' relating to propaganda itself.[36] Another is that responses to propaganda varied according to the different levels of cultural preconditioning among social groups. Therefore the propaganda impact of those festivals whose audiences came from a broad range of social groups was somewhat problematic. Ellul argues that the most effective propaganda was aimed at a specific audience, by propagandists who knew their intellectual 'terrain'.[37] Therefore, festival literature, a genre created by the elite for the elite, had a much greater chance of conveying its message (or at least reinforcing one) than a simple festival.

In both these cases, actual evidence regarding the reception of both events and texts is almost non-existent. The sparse nature of this evidence is best illustrated by the following examples. Among Charles III's funeral literature survives a text entitled the *Derniers et mémorables propos* (1608). Its author, Durmont, perhaps a literate court functionary, describes himself as a soldier of the Nanceian guard, writing an eyewitness account of the events surrounding Charles III's death for those with no *goust à la poësie*.[38] Sometimes festivals are mentioned in private correspondence between family members at different courts. A letter survives from duke Wilhelm of Bavaria to Dorothy of Brunswick thanking her for news of the investitural entry made by Henri II of Lorraine in 1610.[39] It is obvious that Dorothy witnessed the event, but Wilhelm's response evinces nothing by way of qualitative comment. Similar conditions apply when attempting to gauge responses to texts. Graeme Small characterises the problems posed by the chronicles of the Burgundian courtier Georges Chastelain: 'Rhetoricians and courtiers thought highly of Chastelain's work, but they never say why.'[40] Nonetheless, he goes on to say that in the case of texts, 'reader reception might be classified as imitative and interpretative'.[41] In other words, festival texts could spawn imitations, through which a chain of influence or reception can be traced. This is probably our only valid route in the case of Lorraine's festival literature.

Charles III's funeral literature provides some interesting clues regarding the notion of textual influence and imitation. Two key texts recount Charles III's obsequies in 1608. Both were produced by Claude de La Ruelle, a court employee and organiser of the event. One account is purely textual while the other consists of detailed engravings.[42] La Ruelle launched a lawsuit against another man he accused of trying to subvert his monopoly over accounts of the 1608 funeral.[43] It seems that La Ruelle placed political value upon his association with the event and its publications. Identified as the first illustrated festival account generated at the court of Lorraine, La Ruelle's *Dix grand tables* possesses especial significance as a role model for later texts, such as Lorraine's ambitious *Combat à la Barrière* (1627).

Catholicism was one of the key intellectual foundations of ducal Lorraine's court propaganda. The relationship between the duchy's battle with the *Rustauds* in the 1520s and the corresponding conceptualisation of the duke as a Christian warrior has already been discussed. Such ideas became embedded in the psyche and outlook of Charles III. Maybe the martial conceptualisation of Catholicism owed something to the fact that it was a vital ingredient of the ruler's political identification with his territory. When this was threatened, as in the case of the *Rustauds*, it provided an intellectual justification for the ruler to engage in active self-defence. Otherwise, the typology of the Christian warrior would seem a little contradictory, but it was an idea at the heart of the early-modern concept of rulership and frequently occurred in festival.

A comparative example of the idea of martial Catholicism at work in shaping propaganda is to be found in ducal Bavaria, with which Lorraine was to become dynastically linked in the latter half of the sixteenth century.[44] This union reflected the duchies' shared espousal of counter-Reformation Catholicism.[45] Soergel has recounted how the dukes of Bavaria deployed Corpus Christi processions (well known as having 'important power functions for the early-modern state') to relay their adversarial stance against Protestantism.[46]

Like their ducal counterparts in Bavaria, the dukes of Lorraine were avid 'Catholic propagandists' who utilised their religious affiliation in the service of their state.[47] Charles III's foundation (1574) and continued patronage of the Jesuit university of Pont-à-Mousson would appear to suggest this.[48] One function of the university was to instil in the duchy's nobility (whom it educated) a strong sense of loyalty to the Catholic faith. The Jesuits used drama as pedagogic tool. As Burke comments, 'Given the stress on rhetoric in the education of elites at this time, they were probably more conscious of techniques of persuasion than most of us are today.'[49] Therefore, those pupils who participated in Jesuit drama at Pont-à-Mousson could well have inadvertently relayed just such a message of Catholic supremacy.

One play from Pont-à-Mousson's dramatic repertoire deserves mention here for its use of pro-Catholic propaganda and its contribution to the formation of the duchy's political identity. This is Fronton du Duc's *Histoire tragique de la Pucelle de Domrémy, aultrement d'Orléans* (1581).[50] Written for a visit by King Henri III and Louise de Lorraine to the university, the play was postponed due to an outbreak of plague. It was eventually performed in front of Charles III and the ducal court, who were visiting the town. Fronton du Duc taught at the university and was to pursue an active career as an anti-Protestant polemicist, engaging in a war of words with the French Protestant theologian Duplessis Mornay.[51] Given the co-operation between the court and the university, one of the interesting aspects of this play in terms of propaganda is the way it combines the educational rationale of the Jesuits with active support for ducal pro-Catholic policy.

In Fronton du Duc's rendition of Joan of Arc's career and martyrdom she symbolised two themes of interest and importance to ducal Lorraine. One was the duchy's espousal of counter-Reformation Catholicism as represented by Joan's acceptance of her divinely inspired mission. This could be read as a parallel to the duties of a Catholic ruler. Another theme is the identification of Joan with the territory of Lorraine and its Catholicism. This is made explicit when she correctly identifies the disguised Dauphin. A witness comments:

> Je croy que s'il est vray qu'elle de Lorraine
> Elle a veu vostre face aussi tost que la mienne.[52]

Joan's choice as heroine reflects her increasing importance and gradual rehabilitation in both Lorraine and France in the sixteenth century.[53] In a fashion typical of polemicists, she was appropriated and used by this Jesuit dramatist who regarded her as an embodiment of those precise qualities he wished to convey.

The festival forms which had a specific propaganda role during the successive reigns of Charles III and Henri II were pastoral, entries and funeral. Pastoral was a festival form intimately connected with the nature and power of rule and, as such, displays what Monga has styled 'engagement politique'.[54] It concealed the identity of rulers and their territories as idealised fictional realms inhabited by troupes of noble shepherds, evoking the golden age of classical mythology.[55] There is also a Christian element to the pastoral genre conveyed through the identification of Christ as the Good Shepherd, frequently deployed as a role model for early-modern rulers.[56]

Nicolas Romain's pastoral *La Salmée* (1602) was written to celebrate the birth of an heir to Charles III's youngest son, François, comte de Vaudémont, and Christine de Salm.[57] At this point the ducal heir, Henri, had not succeeded in producing issue from his marriage to Catherine de Bourbon. It is possible to see this work as an explicit piece of dynastic assertiveness by François de Vaudémont against his elder brother. This would have been particularly resonant if one is to consider that the birth of Henri II (1564) had itself been fêted in a pastoral which was a role model for *La Salmée*, Remy Belleau's *La Bergerie*.[58]

The nature of Lorraine's identity is made explicit in an introductory sonnet which compares Nicolas Romain with the writers of the French *Pléiade*, Belleau included:

> Si tu estois de France, et de France ton art,
> Je ne m'etonnerois: Mais que Loir'en Moselle,
> Que Romain en Ronsard, en Belleau et Baif,
> Qu'un Lorrain tout à coup en un François naif
> Soit metamorphosé, c'est chose trop nouvelle.[59]

Just as Fronton du Duc identified Joan of Arc with the virtues of her native Lorraine, so this sonnet argues that the duchy has produced writers of equal stature to those of the French *Pléiade*, but with an extra 'local' ingredient. Where could the confidence to make such a claim have come from? The answer lies in Nicolas Romain's career. Romain was one of the first generations of Lorrainers to be educated at the university of Pont-à-Mousson, where he was a doctor of law and also secretary to François de Vaudémont. Connected to the spheres of both university and court, Romain's writing (always dedicated to his employer) furnished his self-advancement. In the case of *La Salmée*, Romain used his knowledge of the court's internal affairs to advance the case of his master over that of his brother. Yet in creating propaganda to reinforce François de Vaudémont's status, Romain was subverting the position of its rightful heir during a vulnerable period in the duchy's history. *La Salmée* stands as an interesting example of propaganda aimed at the court's inner circle.

Entries were a form frequently used to assert the power of early-modern rulers in both a secular and a religious context. In particular, the investitural entries held at Nancy in 1559 and 1610 represented the undisputed control of the rulers of Lorraine over their territory. Charles III played a key role in using the entry as a form to convey his authority over the duchy. Charles III attained his majority in 1559. His accession to the ducal throne would traditionally have been marked by an entry to Nancy, but Charles III altered this pattern of events.[60] While Charles undertook his entry to Bar-le-Duc (in the *Barrois non-mouvant*) in 1559, he postponed his entry to Nancy until 1562. It appears that this was because he resented the limits which the entry's traditional form of words placed upon his ducal authority and, consequently, upon his dynastic ambitions.[61] It is interesting that, even early in his reign, Charles III was a ruler determined not to be constrained by ritual forms. Eventually, however, he had to concede, and made his solemn entry to Nancy, swearing the oath of sovereignty and loyalty to his subjects in the ducal church of St Georges adjacent to the palace.

If Charles III could not alter the form of entry ceremonies within Nancy, elsewhere his manipulation of traditional ceremonies was more successful as in the case of his entry to Remiremont in 1579, which occurred in the context of rivalry between the duchy and the abbey of Remiremont. Since 1551, the abbey had enjoyed semi-independence under the protection of Emperor Ferdinand I. In 1566, the Empire sought to consolidate its authority over the town by displaying the Imperial arms over the town gates. Charles III responded to this perceived challenge to his sovereignty by sending his representatives to remove the placards and quell any resistance.[62] His entry to Remiremont in August 1579 was very similar to the traditional form of ducal entries to Lorraine, but differed in one essential. Instead of styling himself Remiremont's guardian, as he had with Lorraine, he called himself its sovereign, thus giving him unrestricted control over the town and the abbey.[63]

By the first decade of the seventeenth century the pattern of ducal entries to Nancy had altered. It appears that the court and the Nanceian town council (through the agency of such individuals as Nicolas Remy) collaborated on a series of entries staged for Margherita Gonzaga's marriage to Charles III's heir, Henri, in 1606 and for his investitural entry in May 1610. More emphasis was placed upon Nanceian entries as a propaganda tool; they utilised the public space of the ducal capital, deployed carefully planned routes and symbolic decor to lavish effect, very much according to the pattern of entry-ceremonies elsewhere in Europe.[64] Margherita Gonzaga's wedding entry to Nancy on 17 June 1606 was part of a whole series of celebrations staged by the Nanceian court and municipality. Margherita was fêted with an entry precisely because of the political hopes invested in her, that her union with Henri II would produce an heir for the duchy. A contemporary work, Jean de Rosières's *Notables observations sur le mariage de Monseigneur Henry*, expressed the hope that a prince of Lorraine would be born, who could lead Lorraine and other Catholic powers in crusade against the Turks.[65] Margherita's entry was the first held for a Lorraine princess since that for Renée de Bourbon, wife of Antoine de Lorraine, in April 1516.[66] No such entry was held to celebrate the arrival of Henri's first wife, Catherine de Bourbon, at Nancy in 1599. Margherita's entry conveyed a significant propaganda message: that of the continuity of the ducal dynasty through her childbearing potential.

This entry was an important public event involving the court and the municipality of Nancy. Nanceian magistrate Nicolas Remy devised the entry's theme and wrote the Latin account.[67] That Remy's account was in Latin suggests that he was attempting to capture the attention of a more educated audience. The text contains many classical allusions; for example, Remy styled Margherita as the goddess Venus and punned on her name (meaning 'pearl' in Latin).[68] The route of the entry indicated that cordial relations existed between the Nancean court and municipality. Indeed, the latter wished to emphasise the symbolic union of both institutions. Thus the pageant passed through the new town of Nancy (which was still under construction). The ceremonial climax of the entry was when Margherita passed through the gates of the new town and received its keys. Symbolically linked through the festival route, the court and municipality of Nancy were thus seen as a cooperative body with a mutual interest in the ducal capital as a tool of political and civic prestige.

Two entries were staged for Henri II in 1610. The first, on 20 April, was an investiture ceremony like that finally held for his father in 1562. The second entry was originally planned for 13 September 1609, but was postponed after an incident in which Clément, a furrier from the *comté* of Vaudémont and former employee of Charles III, tried to stab Henri II.[69] The would-be assassin's death became a public spectacle. He was broken on the wheel on a site in the new town of Nancy and then beheaded. Next his head was nailed to a stake in the full presence of Henri II and his court. His body was quartered and each section displayed on one of Nancy's four main thoroughfares. Clément's punishment was exemplary in intent and served as propaganda designed to reinforce ducal supremacy.

Henri II's investiture entry took place on 20 April, on a pattern similar to those of his father and predecessors. It is recorded in a set of engravings entitled *L'ordre tenu au marcher, parmy la ville de Nancy, capitale de Lorraine* (1611) which depict the various sections of Nancean society which took part. Besides attempting to reproduce the cumulative effect of this procession, the work also conveys an important propaganda message – that the entire duchy of Lorraine was united in support for its new ruler.

The festive mood induced by the April entry led the Nancean town council to organise a second entry for 12 May. This event is described in Nicolas Remy's Latin pamphlet, *Quae primum solennius*.[70] Its theme centred upon Henri II's qualities as a ruler. Figures of Janus, Pax and Bellona on a triumphal arch outside the Nancean hôtel de ville underlined the propaganda message of the event. Janus represented Henri II's dual qualities as both a ruler and a warrior, while Pax and Bellona symbolised reconciliation between peace and war. Each figure addressed the ruler; Pax encouraged him to be pious, while Bellona encouraged him to follow the martial example of his ancestors. Through its symbolism, Remy's account encapsulates the typical presentation of early-modern rulers as warriors, peacemakers and just governors.

Charles III frequently deployed entries in the closing years of his reign and the practice continued in the opening years of Henri II's. The early seventeenth century was a pivotal phase for the dynasty, one, indeed, that was 'potentially disruptive' for its continuity.[71] Therefore, the entries of 1606 and 1610 have a common message of continuity and reassurance, which, as Remy and his associates would have recognised, were of vital importance in maintaining confidence in the face of such threats. Similarly, the propaganda message conveyed by Charles III's 1608 funeral ceremonies was imbued with a sense of local identity and continuity for the duchy. Many of the symbolic trappings and decor, such as the *chapelles ardentes* in the ducal churches of St Georges and St François, deployed local symbols such as the cross of Lorraine in their decoration. Charles III's own descent was alluded to by the banners depicting his lineage carried in the funeral procession.

Claude de la Ruelle's accounts of Charles III's 1608 funeral both provide a comprehensive reconstruction of the event. His prose *Discours* (1609) probably served as an interim measure until the lavish and detailed prints of the *Pompe funèbre* (1611) could be published. As Rothrock observed of the *Pompe funèbre*, 'we ought to make no mistake about the book's propagandistic purpose, inasmuch as it recorded the sixty-three-year reign of Charles III and the change within Lorraine during his rule from feudal duchy to dynastic nation-state bound up in the dynastic politics of Europe'.[72] This work conveyed the themes of both Charles III's ducal power and its impact upon the identity of his duchy to an internal audience and Europe's courts.

This articulation of the complex relationship between festival, festival literature and the expression of ducal power is somewhat pared down and simplistic. Nonetheless, clear trends emerge. The process of the duchy of Lorraine's territorial and dynastic consolidation was reasonably well advanced by the time Charles III acceded to the ducal throne. Certain key ingredients of its propaganda were already in place, including the martial aspect of ducal rule (underlined by the victory of the battle of Nancy in 1477) and its close alliance with Catholicism, exemplified by the victory over the *Rustauds* in 1525. The existence of such works as the *Nancéide*, the *Rusticiade* and the *Histoire tragique* serve to confirm that literature could be harnessed to express messages asserting ducal authority. From here, the step to festivals and festival literature was but a short one.

The active growth of festival as a form expressive of a propaganda message and conveying the identity of the duchy owes its inception to the reign of Charles III. His experience of French festival form and his efficiency and energy as a ruler led him and his publicists to harness festival for their own ends. This trend had a brief continuity during the reign of Henri II, but would appear to have owed more to the vigour of court publicists than to Henri himself. There was continuity in personnel between the reigns of father and son. Here, one of the most influential factors was the existence of the Jesuit university of Pont-à-Mousson. It institutionalised the thinking of the first generation of university-educated court personnel known to Lorraine. Hitherto, it had often had to deploy outside talent to create festivals expressive of its self-image, such as was the case with the French *héraut d'armes* Emond du Boullay, who was involved in the staging of funerals during the later sixteenth century. Charles III's reign instilled the confidence to utilise festivals as propaganda. His court furnished the artistic talent to realise it. The university of Pont-à-Mousson supplied the court and municipal administrators who organised and recorded festivals and conceptualised Lorraine's identity in symbolic terms.

As a relatively late political creation, which did not achieve full political unity until the fifteenth century, the court of Lorraine, unlike its longer established European colleagues, had much less opportunity to evolve a festival tradition over several hundred years. Instead, like the Florentine Medici, Charles III channelled a significant proportion of his energies into both maintaining the duchy's independence and the deployment of festival as propaganda which would allow Lorraine to compete on equal terms with other European princely courts.

Elliott has characterised Europe's smaller and less established courts, such as Lorraine, as cultural innovators, centres of new ideas and trends which forced their larger neighbours to compete with them.[73] This chapter argues instead that the court of Lorraine was important as a cultural receptor and adaptor rather than as an innovator. Only in the creation of its symbolic identity did the festivals of Lorraine break new ground – alongside the traditional iconographical or allegorical forms culled from scripture or Cesare Ripa, figures like Joan of Arc proudly affirm the political independence and Catholicism of Charles III's Lorraine.

Notes

1   P. Burke, *The Fabrication of Louis XIV* (Cambridge University Press, 1992), p. 1.

2   P. Choné, *Emblèmes et pensée symbolique en Lorraine (1525–1633)* (Paris, Klincksieck, 1991), p. 132, n. 12.

3   O.R. Rothrock, 'Jacques Callot and Court Theatre (1608–1619): Studies in Court Theatre and its Printed Propaganda in the Background of Callot's Artistic Individuality' (unpublished Ph.D. dissertation, Princeton University, 1987), p. 28.

4   P. Sahlins, *Boundaries: The Making of France and Spain in the Pyrenees* (Berkeley, University of California Press, 1989), p. 7.

5   A typical instance of the usage of this term is to be found in a work entitled *Les Pays de l' "entre-deux" au moyen age: Questions d'histoire des territoires d'Empire entre Meuse, Rhône et Rhin*, Actes du 113e congrès national des sociétés savantes, Strasbourg, 1988 (Paris, Comité des Travaux Historiques et Scientifiques, 1990).

6   René II: duc de Lorraine (1473–1508) and duc de Bar (1480–1508).

7   P. de Blarru, *La Nancéide, pages choisies par J. Barbier . . .; trad. sur le texte de 1518 imprimé par Pierre Jacobi à St-Nicolas-de-Port*, ed. R. Cuénot (Nancy, Berger-Levrault, 1978), p. 15.

8   Blarru, *Nancéide*, p. 17.

9   The original edition is Laurent Pillard, *Rusticiados libris sex* . . . (Metz, Jean Palier, 1548). I refer here to Laurent Pillard, *La Rusticiade ou la Guerre des Paysans en Lorrain*, tr. F.R. Dupeux (Nancy, Berger-Levrault, 1875).

10   R. Taveneaux, 'L'esprit de croisade en Lorraine aux XVIe et XVIIe siècles', in *L'Europe, l'Alsace et la France. Problèmes intérieures et relations internationales à l'époque moderne. Études réunies en l'honneur du Doyen Georges Linet pour son 70e anniversaire* (Strasbourg, Editions d'Alsace, 1986), pp. 256, 257–63.

11   Taveneaux, 'L'esprit de croisade', p. 256.

12   Pillard, *La Rusticiade*, p.10.

13   Graeme Small, *George Chastelain and the Shaping of Valois Burgundy: Political and Historical Culture at Court in the Fifteenth Century* (Woodbridge and Rochester (New York), Royal Historical Society/Boydell Press, 1997), pp. 104–5.

14   Charles III's motivations are analysed in L. Davillé, *Les prétentions de Charles III, duc de Lorraine, à la couronne de France* (Paris, Félix Alcan, 1909).

15   Burke, *Fabrication*, p. 4.

16   Helen Watanabe O'Kelly, 'Festival Books in Europe from the Renaissance to Rococo', *The Seventeenth Century*, 2 (1988), 181–201, esp p. 192.

17   Jacques Ellul, *Propaganda: The Formation of Men's Attitudes* (New York, Vintage, 1973), p. 70.

18   Robert Scribner, *For the Sake of Simple Folk: Popular Propaganda for the German Reformation* (Cambridge University Press, 1981), p. xxii.

19   Scribner, *For the Sake of Simple Folk*, p. xxii.

20   Scribner, *For the Sake of Simple Folk*, p. xxii.

21   Ellul, *Propaganda*, p. 70.

22   Burke, *Fabrication*, p. 5.

23   J.G.A. Pocock, 'The Limits and Divisions of British History', *American Historical Review*, 87, (1982), 311–36, p. 321, cited in Small, *George Chastelain*, p. 102.

24   Mark Greengrass (ed.), *Conquest and Coalescence: The Shaping of the State in Early Modern Europe* (London, Edward Arnold, 1991), p. 1.

25   On the descent of the French kings from Charlemagne, see Frances Yates, *Astraea: The Imperial Theme in the Sixteenth Century* (London, Ark, 1985), p. 122.

26   Joseph Klaits, *Printed Propaganda Under Louis XIV: Absolute Monarchy and Public Opinion* (Princeton University Press, 1976), pp. 5–6.

27   Klaits, *Printed Propaganda*, p. 5.

28   Klaits, *Printed Propaganda*, p. 7.

29   O'Kelly, 'Festival Books', pp. 182–3.

30   O'Kelly, 'Festival Books', pp. 182–3.

31   Such as R.G. Asch and A.M. Birke (eds), *Princes, Patronage and the Nobility: The Court at the Beginning of the Modern Age (1450–1650)* (London, German Historical Institute, 1991).

32   A typical instance of the former viewpoint was expressed by Hippolyte Roy, who regarded festival as diversion which punctuated 'la somnolence des mornes lendemains' of life at the court of Nancy: H. Roy, 'La vie à la cour de Lorraine sous le Duc Henri II', *Mémoires de la Société d'Archéologie Lorraine et du Musée Historique de Lorraine* (1913), pp. 53–206, esp. p. 72. For the latter viewpoint, Asch

and Birke argue that the devaluing of the political function of courts similarly demotes the political function of festival: Asch and Birke, *Princes*, p. 12.

33 Cited by Burke, *Fabrication*, p. 5.

34 O'Kelly, 'Festival Books', p. 192.

35 Rothrock, 'Jacques Callot', pp. 120–1.

36 Ellul, *Propaganda*, p. 266.

37 Ellul, *Propaganda*, p. 30.

38 Durmont, *Derniers et mémorables propos tenus* (Nancy, Blaise André, 1608), unpaginated.

39 Bibliothèque Nationale, Paris, *Collection de Lorraine*, t.493, ff. 73–4.

40 Small, *George Chastelain*, p. 219.

41 Small, *George Chastelain*, p. 219.

42 Claude de la Ruelle, *Discours des cérémonies* (Nancy/Clairlieu, Jean Savine, 1609) and *Pompe funèbre* (Nancy, Herman de Loye, 1611).

43 Rothrock, 'Jacques Callot', p. 134.

44 Charles III's sister, Renée, married Wilhelm of Bavaria in 1568, while his daughter Elisabeth married her first cousin Maximilian of Bavaria in 1595.

45 While here I am considering Catholicism as an ingredient of propaganda, it is important to remember that Protestant courts used their religious allegiance in a similar fashion. See Helen Watanabe O'Kelly, 'The Iconography of German Protestant Tournaments in the Years before the Thirty Years War', *Image et spectacle*, Actes du XXXIIe Colloque International d'Études Humanistes du Centre d'Études Supérieures de la Renaissance (Amsterdam, Rodopi, 1993), pp. 47–64.

46 Philip M. Soergel, *Wondrous in His Saints: Counter-Reformation Propaganda in Bavaria* (Berkeley and Los Angeles, University of California Press, 1993), p. 89. See also Miri Rubin, *Corpus Christi: The Eucharist in Late-Medieval Culture* (Cambridge University Press, 1991).

47 Soergel, *Wondrous in His Saints*, p. 5.

48 On the foundation of Pont-à-Mousson, see M. Pernot, 'Le Cardinal de Lorraine et la fondation de l'Université de Pont-à-Mousson', *L'Université de Pont-à-Mousson et les problèmes de son temps* (Nancy, Presses Universitaires de Nancy, 1972).

49 Burke, *Fabrication*, p. 4.

50 Father Fronton du Duc, *L'histoire tragique de la Pucelle de Dom-Remy, aultrement d'Orléans* (Nancy, Vve. de Jean Janson, 1581).

51 For more on Fronton du Duc's career, Charles Mazouer, 'Le Père Fronton du Duc et son Histoire Tragique de la Pucelle d'Orléans', *Les Jésuites parmi les hommes, aux XVIe et XVIIe siècles* (Clermont Ferrand, 1985), pp. 417–29.

52 Fronton du Duc, *Histoire*, p. 6.

53 On Joan's sixteenth-century rehabilitation, see Marina Warner, *Joan of Arc: The Image of Female Heroism* (London, Weidenfeld and Nicolson, 1981), ch. 9, 'The Vindication', pp. 189–200.

54 Luigi Monga, *Le genre pastoral au XVIe siècle: Sannazar et Belleau* (Paris, Éditions Universitaires, 1974), p. 63.

55 For more on the theme of the golden age in pastoral, see Erwin Panofsky, '*Et in Arcadia Ego*: Poussin and the Elegiac Tradition', *Meaning and the Visual Arts* (Harmondsworth, Peregrine, 1970), pp. 340–67.

56   For example, in Lorraine where Charles III was often styled as the Good Shepherd, see Choné, *Emblèmes*, pp. 657–8.

57   Nicolas Romain, *La Salmée, pastorelle comique ou fable bocagère* (Pont-à-Mousson, Melchior Bernard, 1602).

58   Rémy Belleau, *La Bergerie* (Paris, 1565).

59   Romain, *La Salmée*, p. 15.

60   René II (1473), Antoine (1508) and François I (1545) were the precedents.

61   Choné, *Emblèmes*, p. 132.

62   For an account of this event, see Bernard Puton, *Entrées et serments des ducs de Lorraine à Remiremont* (Bulletin de la Société Philomathique Vosgienne, Saint-Dié, 1888–9).

63   Puton, *Entrées et serments*, pp. 50–1.

64   For a general account of entries to Nancy and their decor in the later seventeenth and early eighteenth centuries, see Chantal Humbert, 'Décorations éphémères et thème dynastique à la cour de Lorraine 1650–1736', *Le Pays Lorrain* (1980), pp. 125–58.

65   Jean de Rosières, *Notables observations sur le mariage de Monseigneur Henry* (Pont-à-Mousson, Melchior Bernard, 1606), introduction, text not paginated.

66   Choné, *Emblèmes*, p. 763

67   Nicolas Remy, *Quae sunt . . .* (Nancy, Jean Savine, 1606).

68   Remy, *Quae sunt . . .* , p. 8.

69   Balthasar Guillermé, 'Mémoires de Balthasar Guillermé', *Journal de la Société d'Archéologie Lorraine* (1869–70), 67–83.

70   Nicolas Remy, *Quae primum solennius* (Nancy, Melchior Bernard, 1610).

71   Nigel Llewellyn, *The Art of Death: Visual Culture in the English Death Rituals, 1500–c.1800* (London, Victoria and Albert Museum/Reaktion, 1991), p. 28.

72   Rothrock, 'Jacques Callot', p. 152.

73   John Elliott, 'The Court of the Spanish Habsburgs: A Peculiar Institution?', *Spain and its World 1500–1700* (New Haven, Yale University Press, 1989), pp. 142–61, esp. p. 146.

Part Two

THE AGE OF REVOLUTIONS: FROM DYNASTIES TO IDEOLOGIES

This second section covers a wide chronological spread. The chapters suggest transformations in the meaning of propaganda. Steve Murdoch in his chapter discusses the propaganda deployed in northern Europe by Charles II and his Royalist party and by their opponents. This propaganda defined the remit of English Free State diplomacy, at a key point in the transition from purely dynastic associations to a world of broader geopolitical alliances. László Kontler's paper describes another key moment in the development of a definition of propaganda. By looking at the work of Burke and his German followers, his chapter demonstrates how the French Revolution shifted the meaning of the term propaganda from its original religious sense to an ideological one. The French Revolution is here crucial to this ideology. Michael Rowe, discussing identity formation in the German Rhineland, argues that ideologically based propaganda of this kind failed to address the assumptions of its intended audience and shows that the French empire could better manage its propaganda by adopting recognisable models borrowed from the church and earlier regimes. The emphasis of all this propaganda was on continuity and stability rather than ideological upheaval. This chapter and the following one dwell heavily on issues of reception. Geoff Watkins' paper especially considers the role of commercially produced nostalgic material which could then be harnessed retrospectively for a propagandistic cause. Watkins challenges the received assumption that the Napoleonic legend was produced for political ends. The second empire may well have benefited from the memory of first empire propaganda, but it cannot be said to have been the product of what was in the main a commercial enterprise.

5

THE SEARCH FOR NORTHERN ALLIES: STUART AND CROMWELLIAN PROPAGANDISTS AND PROTAGONISTS IN SCANDINAVIA, 1649–60

Steve Murdoch

The period which followed the execution of Charles I proved a fertile time for the production and dissemination of propaganda.[1] Though not called propaganda at the time – it would take another 150 years for the word to come into vogue in its modern meaning – all sides sought to appraise every section of society with their beliefs and objectives. The Scottish and English Parliaments directed their own campaigns while the Royalists were directed from the Stuart court. Later, Oliver Cromwell took a direct interest in the dissemination of information. Partisans of all persuasions contributed individually to the organised campaigns by attacking publicly the error, hypocrisy or failings in the opposition's rhetoric. In addition there were occasional spontaneous outbursts of material from continental supporters of a particular concept, such as the sanctity of monarchy or the virtues of republicanism, rather than supporters of the protagonists in Britain *per se*.

Propaganda pamphleteering and printing had however been perfected to a fine art by the late 1640s.[2] The campaign of the English Parliament had been significantly enhanced by an ordinance of September 1647 which, with amendments, governed printing in England until 1660.[3] Throughout the period of the English Free State, Royalist printers were frequently arrested – eighteen in 1653 alone – while other printing houses were commandeered to produce Cromwellian propaganda.[4] This ensured, to begin with at least, that England's Parliament controlled the greater part of the information war and drove Royalist printing underground or on to the continent. Within the mainland of Europe the Royalists scored several successes of their own. Richard Bradshaw noted that the state of Hamburg would 'not suffer anything printed in favour of the Parliament, without such a curtailing as renders it to their disadvantage'.[5] In Brussels and Antwerp too the press became a vehicle for Royalist propaganda.[6] Perhaps their greatest success occurred when the German electors declared 'a severe edict against all the rebells bookes that shall be turned into latine or dutch and there vented in Germany'.[7]

The Royalists had a significant advantage in the quest for allies at foreign courts in that they had retained open lines of communications through the network of permanent agents and the sending of frequent embassies to them.[8] Such Royalist influence did not stop English Free State propaganda being read abroad. Since the mid-1640s, the English Parliament had successfully built a diplomatic corps which had attained a high degree of credibility, notably in the succesful agreement of a trade alliance with Denmark-Norway in 1645.[9] Swedish records prove that English Parliamentary concerns were also discussed in the Swedish Riksråd (Royal Council). On 5 July 1649 a debate arose over an English newspaper from 18 June which discussed a Parliamentary victory over the Levellers.[10] Apart from showing that these issues were deemed important enough to be raised in Swedish governmental debates, this incident also tells us that it took up to two weeks for information to filter into Scandinavia. This time lag made little difference to the way propaganda was received in Scandinavia since information took the same time to travel regardless of who produced it.

The propaganda war became particularly acute in Scandinavia for several reasons. The execution of Charles I was seen in Copenhagen as the murder of a member of the Danish royal family, a first cousin of Frederik III. This was important since Denmark-Norway had the power economically to destroy the English Free State by closing the Baltic Sound, thereby ruining English trade. Sweden, on the other hand, had only recently concluded the treaty at Westphalia with the Holy Roman Empire in 1648. With her powerful army still in arms, Sweden had the capability to threaten the English Free State militarily if Royalists could bring her into their camp.

The fundamental message of the Stuarts had actually changed little since the mid-1640s. This centred around the issues of dynastic continuity, stability and legitimacy.[11] Even while he was alive Charles I had warned his neighbours that the success of his enemies would carry serious implications for all the monarchies of Christendom.[12] The harsh realities of economics had, however, even edged Charles I's closet ally, Denmark-Norway, into an economic treaty with the English Parliament in 1645.[13] Elsewhere Sweden remained hostile to the Stuarts, and Russia, Danzig, Hamburg and Poland all enjoyed the benefits of a healthy trading relationship with both Scotland and England. Yet the act of regicide by the English Parliament seriously altered the situation.

Only days before Charles I's execution the Scandinavian monarchs had been softened up by the emotive letters of the prince of Wales begging them to intercede to save his father and, indeed, the monarchy itself.[14] The potentates had also been subjected to an effective hearts and minds campaign pressed home by Montrosian Cavaliers, exiled from Scotland since 1646. After the execution of Charles I, Danish relations with the English Parliament immediately faltered. In the United Provinces shock was felt among the Orange faction and the hard-line Republican opposition alike.[15] The English Parliamentary envoy described the

City of Hamburg as England's most cordial enemies.[16] In Russia the English merchants of the Muscovy Company had their charter cancelled.[17] The Poles introduced a new tax on all traders making them pay one-tenth of all their goods to the new Stuart king, Charles II.[18] In short, Royalist propagandists in northern Europe found themselves pushing against several open doors in their quest for allies. So successfully had the Royalists sold their message that in the Riksråd itself Queen Christina could be heard reciting the Stuart mantra 'that it was of concern to all potentates to see Charles II reinstalled in his kingdoms'.[19] Indeed the Swedish State Councillor, General Magnus de la Gardie, advocated sending the Swedish army into England to avenge Charles' death, as did several other European leaders.[20]

Having seized the initiative, Royalist propagandists deployed their propaganda through literature, news-sheets and hundreds of itinerant agents. They added to the propaganda of their eulogies for Charles I by printing funeral verses on black-edged paper and sending royal letters in purple and black envelopes to emphasise their state of mourning.[21] Another form of propaganda came in the exploitation of the potent 'severed head' image of Charles I. This macabre symbol found its way on to the Royalist standard of the marquis of Montrose. Drawings of the banner were thought provocative enough to be displayed and discussed in the Swedish Riksråd in 1650.[22] The force of such imagery was not lost on the crowned heads of Europe and doubtless many of them contemplated their own positions as they mused over the spectacle of a decapitated king.

The masterstroke of the Royalist propagandists proved to be in attributing their writings to powerful leaders, both living and dead. One declaration, attributed to Tsar Alexea of Russia, appeared on the European stage very soon after Charles' execution.[23] The author, almost certainly an English Royalist, availed himself of the opportunity to give an 'outspoken "royal" retrospect of events and questions of the Civil war, richly interwoven with bitter reflections and elaborate comparisons of an historical, biblical and mythological kind'.[24] The real potency of the document, however, lay in the fact that it conveyed exactly the sort of perspective that the tsar was known to have relating to the regicides. Certainly anyone familiar with the tsar's treatment of the Muscovy Company would have found enough familiar sentiment in the document to convince them that it was genuine. It was therefore more or less irrelevant whether the tsar had in fact written the document as most people would believe that he had.

Only days after the execution of Charles I, *Eikon Basilike*, a work attributed to Charles, had been widely distributed in the British Isles and abroad.[25] Despite attempts at suppression of the book by Parliamentary authorities, it reached sixty editions in its first year, including versions in French, Latin, Dutch, German and Danish.[26] The propaganda effect of this work was devastating. Charles Stuart the Martyr became a Royalist icon in the courts of Europe, prompting numerous paintings, prints and eulogies, all feeding more grist to the Royalist propaganda mill.[27] The rulers of the English Free State were on the defensive in the battle for hearts and minds, and they knew it. To try to counter the damage being done by *Eikon Basilike*, the English Council employed skilled propagandists. Several challenges to the growing personality cult of Charles Stuart followed *Eikon Basilike*, though with little effect.[28] The task of definitively answering *Eikon Basilike* therefore fell to John Milton. Milton himself did not relish the job as he knew that the audience would be more receptive to *Eikon Basilike*'s sentimentality. At best he believed he might be able to convert a few discerning readers.[29] His answer, *Eikonoklastes*, was published in mid-October 1649. Copies reached Scandinavia but, as Milton had predicted, it did little to reverse the impression left by the 'king's book' at home or abroad.[30]

After 1649, in order to try to justify the English Free State, ambassadors were sent to the continent. Perhaps unsurprisingly, their reception was seldom friendly and many were inhibited from delivering their message. The Royalists often managed to make a mockery of Parliamentary diplomacy. In Gothenburg, Bulstrode Whitelocke had to conduct his business with the Swedish governor through a Scottish Royalist interpreter, Colonel Daniel Sinclair.[31] Similarly, in Moscow, William Prideaux blamed the failure of his embassy on the deliberate mistranslations of his Royalist interpreter, John Hebdon.[32] Royalist obstruction to the Republican message often travelled a more sinister path, however. The evening Dr Isaak Dorislaus arrived in The Hague he was assassinated by Colonel Walter Whiteford, a Scottish Catholic.[33] The following year Antony Ascham and his secretary were murdered in Madrid by English Royalists.[34] Ascham's death both removed a major propagandist of republicanism and provided the Free State with a minor propaganda opportunity.[35] When news of the assassination reached Hamburg the nationality of Ascham's assassins had been altered. Richard Bradshaw noted the assassination 'to be done by the Irish villains'.[36] Perhaps to admit that the deed had been perpetrated by Englishmen would have been to admit that England was not as unified behind Cromwell as he wished to portray. The news of an Irish atrocity against an English diplomat, however, could at least help justify Cromwell's policies in Ireland.

The actions of Royalist assassins had a significant effect on Republican envoys. Walter Strickland in The Hague, Richard Bradshaw in Hamburg and Bulstrode Whitelocke in Sweden all expressed fears about assassination.[37] Indeed, a Scottish assassin had actually infiltrated Whitelocke's retinue, and it was only by his own vigilance that Whitelocke avoided death.[38] In Hamburg Colonel John Cochrane had English Republicans beaten up in the street.[39] Bulstrode Whitelocke recorded numerous assaults on his associates, and once his residence was attacked by a drunken mob of Dutch, Danes and Swedes, who shouted 'Ye English dogges, ye King killers'.[40] These men, pronouncing judgement in English, are themselves evidence that the Royalist message had got through to every level of Scandinavian society.

Among the ruling elites in Europe there were many who felt that the hostile actions against regicides and their supporters had some justification. One would-be assassin, Halterman, captured in Hamburg, was not only released but granted costs by the Hamburg court, who made the English company pay his charges and give him 100 Rixdaler for wrongful arrest.[41] Five out of six of Ascham's assassins were allowed to escape. One Spanish nobleman said of them, 'I envy those gentlemen for having done so noble an action', and even the Spanish king declared an interest in having 'such resolute subjects'.[42] The continent of Europe remained fertile ground for Royalist vigilantes, and assassinations raised morale among the Royalist party. More importantly, the killings removed the main instruments of Parliamentary propaganda – the diplomats themselves.

With Cromwellian diplomats under siege on the continent, Charles II ordered his own ambassadors into Europe. Lord Culpepper travelled as ambassador extraordinary to Moscow to announce the regicide committed by 'those monsters of mankind'.[43] While John Cochrane toured Poland, Courland and Danzig as an ambassador, Charles ordered the marquis of Montrose to visit Frederik III of Denmark-Norway as an additional envoy.[44] Having already received money from the Danish exchequer, Montrose spent October and November recruiting soldiers in Denmark, assuring Frederik III that his support was invaluable.[45] Even anti-Royalists noted and envied the influence of Montrose in Scandinavia.[46] As William Parker put it, 'the Cavalier party was distressingly influential on the Continent'.[47] From Copenhagen and Gothenburg, Montrose produced his famous *Declaration* against the Scottish estates which incited the Scottish people to join him in his Royal expedition to liberate them.[48] To support Montrose Charles II sent the two Scottish generals, James King and Patrick Ruthven, to Queen Christina in Sweden.[49] Controversially, Queen Christina agreed to release arms and ammunition for Stuart service. Eventually the Swedish government also sold James King the frigate *Harderinne*.[50] Yet by the time Montrose sailed for Scotland, Charles II had effectively completed his negotiations with the Scottish estates.

In February 1650, Robert Meade arrived in Sweden to accept Christina's offer of mediation between Charles and the Scottish estates and no doubt brought a copy of the Scottish estates' response to the Montrosian *Declaration*.[51] The Scottish commissioners at Breda negotiated very strict conditions which the marquis of Argyll thought, or perhaps even hoped, the king would not accept.[52] Charles had to take the Covenant and banish 'any councillors prejudicial to Presbyterianism and opposed to both the National Covenant and Solemn League and Covenant'.[53] The Scots also insisted that the king had to repudiate treaties with the duke of Ormonde and the Irish Catholics, although Charles managed momentarily to sidestep this issue.[54] Despite these harsh conditions Charles really had little option but to accept the Scottish terms. If he did not establish himself in one of his kingdoms, no foreign state would treat him seriously. Charles therefore effectively sacrificed Montrose's army and his reserves were left stranded in various Baltic ports. When Montrose met the Covenanting forces in Scotland he had little chance of success.[55] In total more than half of the Royalist force, about 600, were killed and about 400 captured.[56] Montrose was transported to Edinburgh where he was tried and executed. The estates had won their king from their worst enemy and, as a bonus, the most successful protagonist for extreme Royalism was removed with one stroke of the axe.

The political impact of Montrose's defeat went far beyond the loss of some Cavalier officers and a few hundred Danish and German mercenaries. True, Charles had secured the first of his three kingdoms – but his duplicity also grated with the majority of his northern supporters. From Hamburg, Richard Bradshaw observed that, 'the smart handling of Montrose hath turned the edge of the fury of this people from the English now to the Scots'.[57] The Danish king could surely not have been happy at the callous sacrifice of his subjects. Heavyweight Danish support from Hannibal Sehested and Korfits Ulfeldt, both close relatives of the Danish king, had also been lost. Neither were Montrose's financiers, John Maclean in Sweden and Ivor Krabbe in Denmark-Norway, likely to become involved in any future Stuart scheme. The remaining Montrosians could not forgive the sacrifice of their friends. John Cochrane abandoned the Stuart cause, absconding with all the funds he had raised in the Baltic and one of the duke of Courland's ships. John Henderson took his revenge on Charles by turning informant for the Cromwellian government.[58] General King, among others, also gave up the cause and died in exile in Sweden.

When Charles II arrived in his kingdom of Scotland in 1650 the peace between Scotland and England grew increasingly fragile. The Stuart king's presence, albeit within Scotland, would inevitably act as a destabilising element within England. Despite the abolition of monarchy in England, some people still argued that the prince of Wales had legally succeeded his father under English constitutional law. On this point the Royalist propagandists had a strong case to argue given that Charles II had been proclaimed king of Great Britain and Ireland in Edinburgh, his status being confirmed in proclamations by English and Irish Royalists.[59] Obviously the Cromwellian faction did not, and could not, accept these proclamations. Their solution to the growing strength of the Stuart party was to invade Scotland and attempt to capture or kill the young king in what Derek Hirst has described as 'a pre-emptive strike against the Scottish kingdom'.[60] Invading Scotland, however, was an act which many people in England, including General Fairfax, the chosen leader for the campaign, felt tested the bounds of legality.[61] Nonetheless, Free State propagandists sought to discredit Charles II's position by destroying the legitimacy of his father's, and even his grandfather's, succession in England. The Free State pamphleteer, J. L. Philalethes, wrote that:

forty yeares were the English under the government of two Scottish kings, even just as many yeares as the Children of Israel did wander in the Wildernesse before they came in to rest, God hath now delivered us from that servitude, and wee are very neere entring into the Land of Canaan, viz. liberty . . . wee having cast off their king, it is their designe to settle hime upon us againe, by force, they proclaimed him king of Great Brittaine, etc. But wee have more reason to breake this succession, made up of tyranny, cruelty and oppression . . . our late Tyrant king CHARLES . . . by vertue whereof his father K. James, by the unhappy policie of some Courtiers, did obtaine the crowne, who was then attended with a heavy curse, and terrible plague, into *England*, if it were no more but the weake and unjust title of the usurping pretenders, the English Nation have sufficient cause to cast off this accursed Monarchie.[62]

Having effectively rewritten the circumstances of the succession of 1603, the propagandists now associated the new king with his father's country of birth. Englishmen of the conviction of Richard Bradshaw referred to Charles Stuart and his party as the 'Pretender and his blue caps', illegitimising the king and linking all Royalists with the Scots in a sentence.[63] The vilification of the Scots by Cromwell even led many Stuart sympathisers abroad to equate all English men with the Free State government, perversely working in favour of Cromwell's intention to portray a unified image of England. The Dutchman, Crispin Van De Pas, produced a print depicting Cromwell's demise being carried out by the Dutch, Scots and Irish, ignoring the vast numbers of English Royalists and disaffected 'others'.[64]

The army which Cromwell faced in Scotland represented only a fraction of the fighting capability of the country. The pulpit propaganda espoused by the Scottish clergy clearly worked against the Scottish military interest. Believing their position to be supported by God, the leadership of the Scottish estates spent weeks purging the army of all suspected Cavaliers and Royalists as well as the 'ungodly'.[65] By doing so the Scottish estates whittled down the numbers in the army by as much as twenty thousand men and deprived it of many of Scotland's most experienced soldiers. The Covenanting army gave up its secure position near Edinburgh only to be defeated by Cromwell outside Dunbar. Richard Bradshaw particularly relished the task of spreading the news of Cromwell's victory through 'the most considerable parts of Germany, Sweden, Poland, &'.[66] Dunbar presented Parliamentary propagandists with a golden opportunity to ascribe their victory to 'divine providence'.[67] They could also press the message that the (unified) English nation had defeated the (Royalist) Scottish nation rather than simply the Covenanted faction within it. This version of events, a superb exercise in English nation building, ignored the fact that there were as many Scottish soldiers denied access to the army as were fighting in it, or that the king himself expressed great delight at the news of the Covenanters' defeat. The earl of Clarendon recorded that Dunbar was the first good fortune for Charles II since it meant that he would not be the prisoner of the Covenanters for much longer.[68] To compound the confusion of the situation, there were probably more Englishmen hoping that the Covenanters would beat Cromwell than Scotsmen fighting him – but again admitting that would be to admit a fracture in the English nation.

On 1 January 1651 Charles Stuart underwent his coronation ceremony at Scone.[69] A bizarre episode preceded the service when Charles had to denounce his father's crimes and his mother's papist idolatry. After this Charles II swore, as the king of Great Britain and Ireland, to introduce the Covenant into all his kingdoms.[70] The preamble to the coronation was immediately picked up by the satirists. In *Old Sayings and Predictions Verified* the image of King Charles II with his nose being held to the grindstone by the Scots clearly demonstrated one Republican interpretation of the coronation.[71] The Royalist view, publicly at least, was somewhat different. A Royalist print appeared which showed the crowning of Charles II by Argyll. In the foreground an image of the king was shown being dressed for war by 'Ireland' while 'Scotland' handed him a pistol labelled 'revenge'.[72] The message was obvious. The newly crowned Charles now sought to build a truly Royalist army in Scotland (from all his kingdoms) to tackle Cromwell.[73] Unfortunately for Charles, and despite the attempted 'patriotic accommodation',[74] Scotland found itself to be 'a victim of military and financial, if not ideological, exhaustion'.[75] His Irish supporters were kept occupied and significant English Royalist support failed to materialise. The king's Scottish army of accommodation was soundly defeated at Worcester through the superior numbers of Cromwell's forces.[76] With no army left in Scotland, and no faction now strong enough to form one, Cromwell concluded a 'conquest and incorporative union with [England's] northern Protestant neighbour'.[77] The Scots vigorously challenged the legitimacy of their incorporation into the English Commonwealth, arguing that it had no basis in constitutional law. They now turned the metaphor of 'the pretender' against Cromwell's 'pretended Parliament'.[78]

Perversely, Dunbar and Worcester also granted the Scottish Covenanter and Royalist factions a propaganda opportunity. They vigorously argued that God often gave success to his enemies to make their subsequent fall the greater and more instructive, and this was an argument which many Cromwellians reluctantly accepted had biblical vindication.[79] To add to the abundance of biblical metaphors the Scottish Royalists argued that, as the Israelites had been cast into the wilderness, so now the Royalist leadership went into exile.[80]

Charles II accounted for his escape from Worcester by attributing it to a 'firme argument of God's mercy and future protection of us'.[81] God's mercy in sparing him was all well and good, but unless Charles could rebuild his credibility with the decision-making states his cause was ruined. Armed with a newfound belief in providence, Charles hoped to regain the support of the royal houses of Denmark-Norway and Sweden, lost to the Stuarts after the Montrosian debacle. He sought to dissuade the Scandinavians from harbouring agents of the Commonwealth or legitimising that regime by official recognition.[82] In a clever attempt at bolstering his claims of sovereignty, Charles constantly referred to the Free State government as 'Our rebels'. Charles also filled his letters with extremely emotive language. He appealed to Frederik III to unite with him to aid his subjects 'the greatest number of whom groan under the intolerable yoke of the traitors and are oppressed by tyranny'.[83] With Danish help Charles argued he could wipe out this 'progeny of parricides'.[84] But the complexities of northern diplomacy were to impede Stuart designs to stop recognition for the new Commonwealth of England, Scotland and Ireland.

Since the sacrifice of Montrose in 1650, the Royalist cause had remained buoyant in Scandinavia largely due to the work of Salmasius, a courtier of Queen Christina's. His book *Defensio Regia*, published in 1649, 'damned the English Free State as a stain on the story of humanity'.[85] This book, like *Eikon Basilike*, significantly troubled the Free State leadership who had it banned and tried to prevent its importation. Once more John Milton was called upon to respond to 'the mischief being done in European capitals by that publication'.[86] Milton's response came in the shape of his *Defence of the English People*. Published in February 1651, *Defence* appeared in many European cities, though in some like Paris and Toulouse it was burned by the public executioner.[87] The first copies of *Defence* arrived in Stockholm by April and immediately caught the attention of Queen Christina, who commented openly on the author's genius and style. Indeed Milton's argument appeared so strong that Salmasius was thereafter shunned at court. Rumours also flourished that the queen had forbidden him to undertake a response to Milton from Sweden. Reports of Salmasius having to leave the Swedish court were printed in *Mercurius Politicus* and by Royalist sympathisers gifting another propaganda coup to the Republicans.[88] Milton, however, was sought out in London by foreign ambassadors and diplomats and he became internationally recognised as the defender of the English Free State.[89] For the first time since 1649, the Republicans were no longer playing catch-up in the propaganda war.

After the death of Charles Stuart's relative, William of Orange, the new Dutch leadership contemplated the economic possibilities of the Commonwealth and recognised the English Free State.[90] With the usual entourage of Scottish Cavaliers remaining remarkably silent, the Swedish Chancellor, Axel Oxenstierna, argued that the Swedes too should establish links with the English Parliament, and Harold Appelbom travelled to England to establish a treaty dealing with free trade.[91] In late 1651, with little immediate prospect of a restored Stuart regime, Frederik III of Denmark-Norway also decided to send an embassy to secure better relations with the English Free State.[92]

Despite all efforts, by October 1651 the fledgling relationship between the Dutch Republic and England was faltering and war appeared imminent.[93] Denmark-Norway had had an ongoing military alliance with the Dutch. Charles II saw an advantage in this situation. He strongly urged Frederik III to support the United Provinces against the English 'rebels'.[94] Charles pressed the notion of a three-way alliance of Denmark-Norway, the United Provinces and the exiled Royalists, and offered his fleet under Prince Rupert as his commitment to the war.[95] However, in June 1653, after a series of bitter naval exchanges, the Dutch sent envoys to England to settle a peace with the Commonwealth, which was secured by April 1654. These talks also led to the May 1654 Act of Exclusion which guaranteed the expulsion of Stuart Royalists from the United Provinces.[96] The military strength of the English Free State was proving to have more weight in northern politics than Stuart propaganda could counter. With the Dutch out of the war, Frederik III reluctantly signed a treaty with Cromwell on 15 September 1654.[97] Denmark-Norway, a country bound to the Stuarts through blood ties, had now effectively declared for the enemy. Peace between the Protectorate and the United Provinces and also with Denmark-Norway was indicative of the growing strength of Cromwell's foreign policy.[98] The English Parliament now wanted to complete their success and secure a trade agreement with Queen Christina of Sweden. At the beginning of January 1654, Christina wrote to Charles II rejecting his requests for support, making sure that Whitelocke saw a copy of her letter. She achieved a trade agreement with England in March 1654 just before her abdication.[99] For Stuart Royalists 1654 marked their darkest period since 1649. The vacillation of the northern potentates which had been in evidence since late 1650 had transformed into a public declaration for the English Protectorate. Sweden in particular had become absolutely hostile.[100]

The obvious strength of England at home and abroad turned the thoughts of many Englishmen to rewarding their leader by having him crowned king. When James Waynwright suggested that the crowning of Cromwell was something 'which all men desire generally' he was clearly toeing the party line.[101] The prospect of Cromwell becoming king caused abject horror among the Royalists and even genuine Republicans. Such a move would seriously retard the cause of the house of Stuart. Sir Edward Nicholas summed up the Royalist perspective when he wrote: 'I assure you I do with you apprehend nothing more prejudicial or pernicious to his majesty's interest than that Cromwell should by any title take on himself (as is evident in his design) the sovereign power in England.' A major reason behind this fear would be the recognition Cromwell might receive from foreign potentates who, as Nicholas observed, were 'not yet sensible how much they are concerned in this prodigious userpation in England'.[102]

Though Cromwell declined the title of king he gained essentially the same status when the Parliament voted him 'Royal Protector'. Queen Christina reacted favourably to the news of Cromwell's elevation largely due to the strong influence of Bulstrode Whitelocke at her court.[103] Royalist propagandists could only respond by lampooning Cromwell and the quasi-republicanism of England in satires and prints of mock coronations.[104] Yet, regardless of Royalist attempts to discredit him, Cromwell's power continued to grow. Indeed a particularly strong relationship developed between Cromwell and the new Swedish monarch, Charles X. Between them they strove to dominate the Baltic trade especially at the expense of Denmark-Norway and the Dutch.[105] Compared with the emotive ramblings of Charles II, Cromwell's letters were direct and largely devoid of propaganda.[106] Rather, Cromwell tended to rely on his military and economic strength as the guarantor of his intentions and objectives.

After the death of Oliver Cromwell in 1658, Scandinavia reverted once more to a situation of vacillation in relation to the contesting British factions. Frederik III certainly congratulated Richard Cromwell on his succession, as did Charles X.[107] But the political stability of the Protectorate proved fragile. Richard Cromwell was soon displaced and turmoil loomed again in the Commonwealth. The English Parliament wrote to Charles X to announce that God had restored them to 'our Pristine Authority'.[108] However, even relations between the English authorities and Sweden deteriorated after Charles X resumed his hostilities against Denmark-Norway, flouting the English-brokered Roskilde treaty of 1658.[109] These divisions allowed Charles II to once more project his cause in northern Europe. The Royalists presented Charles Stuart as one of the few men who could govern the British Isles by constitutional and legal methods. Louis Potter has argued that there also remained a residual sentiment developed by *Eikon Basilike* which significantly contributed to the mood for a Stuart Restoration.[110] Indeed, to many contemporaries, Charles appeared to promise a fulfilment of the sound advice which his father had reputedly offered in *Eikon Basilike*. Elizabeth Skerpan has described Charles in this incarnation as a 'model of sanity and cohesion amid the chaos of contemporary politics'.[111] Charles II offered the prospect of a return to a notional idyllic Stuart past which seemed to guarantee a secure future. When Charles II arrived at Dover on 16 May 1660 he had been restored without any significant help from a foreign power but by his subjects themselves.[112] He had ensured, however, that foreign powers would not become obstacles to his restoration.

The execution of Charles I allowed the British Royalists a golden opportunity to pursue their propaganda message vigorously throughout Europe. The majority of governments were receptive to the idea that the heinous crime of regicide required punishment. In Scandinavia in particular their cause had been aided by a corps of Scottish Cavaliers who exercised considerable influence and formed part of the ruling elite in those kingdoms. The northern potentates were quick to supply money, arms, men and ships to the Stuart cause and even sent diplomats to ease the negotiations with the Scottish commissioners at Breda. In short the Stuarts had won a significant propaganda victory, winning back their old ally Denmark-Norway and finding a friend in Sweden for the first time. By sacrificing his most ardent supporters in the Montrosian debacle, however, Charles then squandered his newly won resource and allies. Perhaps more significantly he lost the important influence of the Scottish exiles in Sweden and Denmark-Norway. Despite innovative literature from the Stuart camp, the Royalists had lost the propaganda initiative. Only the tsar of Russia remained loyal to their cause.

The English Free State leadership capitalised on Charles' perceived duplicity with a sustained attack on the claims of the Royalist propagandists. Propaganda gains were bolstered by the military and economic power of the English Free State which proved irresistible to the northern powers. Only the instability of the Commonwealth in the period following Oliver Cromwell's death changed this situation. During this time the residual message of *Eikon Basilike*, coupled with the careful cultivation of the Stuart image, brought the king and his kingdoms closer together. In reviewing the influence of propagandists and their message, four clear phases can be described within the eleven-year period between the execution of Charles I and the return of Charles II to Westminster. This variously saw the northern potentates supporting Charles II (1649–51), then vacillating once more (1658–60). Interestingly then, while both sides managed to win allies in the north through their propaganda campaigns, neither side had managed to keep them. The culmination of the period saw a renewed propaganda push from the Royalists which attempted to obliterate the memory of the first eleven years of Charles' reign.[113]

Although Royalist propaganda survived the 1650s and contributed to the Restoration, it is Cromwellian propaganda that has proved the more robust. Historians have subscribed to the idea that Cromwell's victories at Dunbar and Worcester represent national conflicts between Scotland and England rather than contesting factions made up of armies stemming predominantly from each of those nations. Further, rather than talk of the 'Cromwellian Usurpation' historians discuss the 'Interregnum' as if Charles II had never been proclaimed king in England and Ireland or crowned in Scotland. To say he was not really king in England until 1660 simply because he was not crowned, in control or there in person, is by the same rationale to suggest an interregnum in Scotland between 1625 and 1633, or 1638 and 1640. It seems that despite all the Restoration rhetoric pursued by Charles II, the Free State propagandists have successfully legitimised Cromwell's niche in history.

Notes

1   G.S. Jowett and V. O'Donnel, *Propaganda and Persuasion* (Beverly Hills, Sage Publications, 1986), p. 15. They offer the following definition of propaganda: 'the purpose of propaganda is to send out an ideology to an audience with a related objective'.

2   D. Kunzle, *The Early Comic Strip: Narrative Strips and Picture Stories in the European Broadsheet from* c. *1450–1825* (Berkeley, University of California Press, 1973), p. 125.

3   L. Potter, *Secret Rites and Secret Writing: Royalist Literature 1641–1660* (Cambridge University Press, 1989), p. 4.

4   Ibid., p. 11; W.C. Abbott, *The Writings and Speeches of Oliver Cromwell* (4 vols, Cambridge MA, Harvard University Press, 1938–47), III, p. 246. Instructions to General Monk, 6 April 1654. Cromwell ordered that Monk should either utilise Scottish printing presses to his advantage or destroy them to prevent his opponents from using them. The term 'English Free State' is used to cover all regimes in England 1649–60.

5   *HMC, Sixth Report*, pp. 431–2. Bradshaw to Frost, 24 September 1650.

6   G.F. Warner (ed.), *The Nicholas Papers; Correspondence of Sir Edward Nicholas, Secretary of State,* [hereafter *Nicholas Papers*] (4 vols, London, Camden Society, 1892–1920), III, pp. 67–9. Langdale to Nicholas, 4 October 1655.

7   *Nicholas Papers*, II, pp. 39–42. Hatton to Nicholas, 2 January 1653/4.

8   G.M. Bell, *A Handlist of British Diplomatic Representatives, 1509–1688* (London, Royal Historical Society, 1990), *passim*.

9   Rigsarkivet, Denmark [hereafter Da. Ra.] TKUA, England, II 15, f.49b. Trade alliance between Christian IV and the English Parliament, April 1645.

10   *Svenska Riksrådets Protokol* [hereafter *SRP*] (18 vols, Stockholm, P.A. Nordstedt & Söner, 1878–1959), vol. 13, p. 165, 5 July 1649.

11   D. Hirst, 'The Politics of Literature in the English Republic', *The Seventeenth Century*, V (1990), 133–55, esp. p. 137; N. Smith, *Literature and Revolution in England 1640–1660* (New Haven, Yale University Press, 1994), p. 177.

12   Da. Ra. TKUA, England, A I. Charles I to Christian IV, 26 February 1645.

13   L. Laursen (ed.), *Danmark-Norges Traktater 1523–1750* (11 vols, Copenhagen, Nielsen & Lydiche, 1917), IV, pp. 402–12.

14   Da. Ra. TKUA, England, A I. Charles, Prince of Wales, to Frederik III, 23 January 1649; Riksarkivet, Sweden [hereafter Ra. Sv.] Anglica 517. Prince Charles to Queen Christina, 29 January 1649.

15   Laursen, *Danmark-Norges Traktater*, V, p. 16; Abbott, *Oliver Cromwell*, II, p. 267.

16   *HMC, Sixth Report*, p. 430. Bradshaw to Strickland, 16 July 1650.

17   PRO SP 91/3 f.77–79. 'The humble remonstrance of John Hebdon, 16 March 1660'; L. Leowenson, 'Did Russia Intervene after the Execution of Charles I?', *Bulletin of the Institute of Historical Research*, XVIII (1940–1), 13–20, esp. p. 15; G.P. Herd, 'General Patrick Gordon of Auchleuchries – A Scot in Seventeenth Century Russian Service' (unpublished Ph.D. thesis, University of Aberdeen, 1994), p. 33.

18   F.A. Patterson *et al.*, *The Works of John Milton: State Papers* (New York, Columbia University Press, 1937), XIII, pp. 44–5. English Parliament to the city of Danzig, 6 February 1650.

19   *SRP*, vol.14, pp. 51–2, 20 February 1650.

20   A. Fryxell, *Handlingar Rörande Sverges Historia* (Stockholm, L.J. Hjerta, 1836), I, p. 36. Peder Juel's report to his Council, 10 April 1649; Leowenson, 'Did Russia Intervene?', 19.

21   *SRP*, vol.15, pp. 51–2. 20 February 1650; Hirst, 'The Politics of Literature', 142.

22   S.R. Gardiner (ed.), *Letters and papers illustrating the relations between Charles II and Scotland in 1650* (Edinburgh, Scottish Historical Texts Society, 1894), p. 6; G. Wishart, *The Memoirs of James Marquis of Montrose 1639–1650*, eds A.D. Murdoch and H.F.M. Simpson [hereafter *Memoirs of Montrose*] (London, Longmans, 1893), pp. 280–1; B. Steckzén, *Svenskt och Brittiskt* (Stockholm, Almqvist & Wiksell, 1959), p. 158.

23   BL, Thomason Tract E. 623 (17), '*A Declaration of His Imperial Majestie, the most high and mighty Potentate Alexea . . .*' (1650).

24   Leowenson, 'Did Russia Intervene?', 14.

25   F.F. Madan, *A New Bibliography of the* Eikon Basilike *of King Charles the First* (London, Bernard Quaritch, 1950); W.R. Parker, *Milton: A Biography* (Oxford, Clarendon Press, 1968), pp. 360–1; E. Skerpan, *The Rhetoric of Politics in the English Revolution 1642–1660* (Columbia, University of Missouri Press, 1992), pp. 110–12; Hirst, 'Politics of Literature', p. 7.

26   Madan, *Eikon Basilike, passim*; Parker, *Milton*, pp. 360–1.

27   Skerpan, *The Rhetoric of Politics*, p. 112. For engravings and paintings, see Anon., 'Endhauptung dess Königs in Engelandt anno 1649', reprinted in F. Maclean, *A Concise History of Scotland* (London, Book Club Associates, 1970), p. 131; Scottish National Portrait Gallery, Anon., 'The execution of Charles I 1600–1649'.

28   Skerpan, *Rhetoric of Politics*, p. 113.

29   Parker, *Milton*, p. 361.

30   Parker, *Milton*, p. 361; Skerpan, *Rhetoric of Politics*, p. 113; Potter, *Secret Rites*, p. 10.

31   R. Spalding (ed.), *The Diary of Bulstrode Whitelocke 1605–1675* (Oxford, The British Academy, 1990), p. 301.

32   Herd, 'General Patrick Gordon', p. 38.

33   Edward, Earl of Clarendon, *The History of the Rebellion and Civil Wars in England together with an historical view of the affairs of Ireland* (6 vols, Oxford University Press, 1849), V, p. 127; Abbott, *Oliver Cromwell*, II, pp. 76–7. The death of Dorislaus was used in the Royalist literature of John Couch. In his play *New Market Fair*, Couch portrayed Dorislaus' ghost returning from hell to announce that it was full of Roundheads and that Charles I was in heaven. For a fuller discussion of the assassination of Free State diplomats, see Jason T. Peacey, 'Order and Disorder in Europe: Parliamentary Agents and Royalist Thugs, 1649–1650', *Historical Journal*, XL (1997), 953–76.

34   S.R. Gardiner, *History of the Commonwealth and Protectorate* (4 vols, Gloucestershire, The Windrush Press, 1988), I, pp. 308–9; Clarendon, *History of the Rebellion*, V, pp. 150–6.

35   Ascham has been described as having played a major role in the development of English Republican thought, publishing under several names. For a discussion see Smith, *Literature and Revolution*, p. 181.

36   *Nicholas Papers*, III, p. 428. Bradshaw to Frost, 25 June 1650.

37   Abbott, *Oliver Cromwell*, II, p. 167; *HMC, Sixth Report*, pp. 427–9. Bradshaw to Frost, 25 June 1650; Spalding, *Bulstrode Whitelocke*, p. 9; Parker, *Milton*, pp. 368–75.

38   Spalding, *Bulstrode Whitelocke*, pp. 292, 312 and 337.

39   J.N.M. Maclean, 'Montrose's Preparations for the Invasion of Scotland and Royalist Mission to Sweden 1649–1651', in R. Hatton and M. Anderson (eds), *Studies in Diplomatic History* (London, Longman, 1970), p. 14; Spalding, *Bulstrode Whitelocke*, p. 337.

40   Ibid., 21 February 1650.

41   *HMC, Sixth Report*, pp. 432–3. Bradshaw to Frost, 1, 8 and 15 October 1650.

42   Clarendon, *History of the Rebellion*, V, p. 157.

43   PRO, SP 22/60 f. 76 (copy). Charles II to Tsar Alexsei, 16 April 1649.

44   Da. Ra. TKUA, England, A II 16. John Cochrane to Frederick III, 28 July 1649.

45   In The Hague, Corfits Ulfeldt gave Montrose about £5,400 (24,000 Rixdaler) from the royal Danish purse and a further sum from his own resources. See Clarendon, *History of the Rebellion*, V, pp. 41–3; *Memoirs of Montrose*, pp. 244–5, 260, 508–9; Maclean, 'Montrose's Preparations', pp. 14–15.

46   Gardiner, *Charles II and Scotland*, pp. 29–31. Letter from Rollen, 6/16 March 1649/50.

47   Parker, *Milton*, p. 368.

48   BL, Thomason Tract E.1294 (3), *Declaration of His Excellency James Marques of Montrose, Earl of Kincairn, Lord Graeme, Baron of Montdev, Lieutenant Governor and Captaine Generall for His Majestie of the Kingdom of Scotland* (Gothenburg, 1649).

49   Sv. Ra. Anglica 517, Charles II to Queen Christina, 28 May 1649. BL, Thomason Tract E.549 (22), *Declaration of the Committee of Estates of the Parliament of Scotland in vindication of their proceedings from the asperations of a scandelous pamphlet published by that excommunicate traytor James Grahame* (Edinburgh, January 1650).

50   *SRP*, vol. 13, p. 43, 31 March and 2 April 1649. Christina decided that he would receive 6,000 muskets, 5,000 pikes, 3,000 bandoleers, 4,000 infantry swords, 50 drums, 1,800 pistols, 600 cavalry swords and 2,000 cavalry harnesses. The state marshal noted that 12 cannon could also be provided to General Patrick Ruthven; Steckzén, *Svenskt och Brittiskt*, pp. 155–7.

51   *SRP*, vol. 14, pp. 51–2. 20 February 1650.

52   Clarendon, *History of the Rebellion*, V, pp. 117–19. The Breda negotiations and treaty are discussed in J.R. Young, *The Scottish Parliament 1639–1661: A Political and Constitutional Analysis* (Edinburgh, John Donald, 1996), pp. 246–58.

53   Young, *Scottish Parliament*, p. 224.

54   Gardiner, *Charles II and Scotland*, pp. 140–2, the Dean of Tuam to Ormonde, 15 October 1650; R. Hutton, *The British Republic, 1649–1660* (London, Macmillan, 1990), p. 51.

55   Abbott, *Oliver Cromwell*, II, p. 254. Abbott also mentions that Montrose's forces were depleted by 1,000 men who were lost in shipwrecks.

56   *Memoirs of Montrose*, pp. 493–4. Appendix of prisoners taken at Carbisdale; David Stevenson, *Revolution and Counter Revolution in Scotland, 1644–1651* (London, Royal Historical Society, 1977), p. 162; Clarendon, *History of the Rebellion*, V, p. 127.

57   *HMC, Sixth Report*, p. 426. Bradshaw to Fleming, 18 June 1650; same to Ac'ton, 19 June 1650.

58   *HMC, Sixth Report*, pp. 421 and 427. Bradshaw to Frost, 3 September 1650; same to Ac'ton, 19 June 1650.

59   BL, Thomason Tract 669 f. 13 (79); 669 f. 13 (82); and E.544 (12). *Broadside in the form of a proclamation declaring Prince Charles to be king, February 1649* and *Charles II proclaimed king by Ormonde, February 1649*; J.R. Jones, *Charles II: Royal Politician* (London, Allen & Unwin, 1987), p. 13; J. Morrill,

'The Britishness of the English Revolution 1640–1660', in R.G. Asch (ed.), *Three Nations – A Common History? England, Scotland, Ireland and British History* c. *1600–1920* (Bochum University Press, 1993), p. 101.

60   D. Hirst, 'The English Republic and the Meaning of Britain', in B. Bradshaw and J. Morrill (eds), *The British Problem*, c. *1534–1707: State Formation in the Atlantic Archipelago* (London, Macmillan, 1996), pp. 197 and 200.

61   Thomas Fairfax held a Scottish peerage as Lord Fairfax of Cameron and this may have influenced his desire not to invade Scotland. Other people claim Fairfax simply did not want to fight fellow Presbyterians or had not 'reconciled himself to the abolition of monarchy and did not wish to destroy the last monarchical state in the British Isles'. See Hutton, *The British Republic*, p. 23; M. Wilding, *Dragon's Teeth, Literature in the English Revolution* (Oxford, Clarendon, 1987), pp. 134–42; J. Morrill, 'Three Kingdoms and One Commonwealth? The Enigma of Mid-Seventeenth Century Britain and Ireland', in A. Grant and K.J. Stinger (eds), *Uniting the Kingdom? The Making of British History* (London, Routledge, 1995), p. 186; Hirst, 'The English Republic', p. 197; Clarendon, *History of the Rebellion*, V, p. 159; Abbott, *Oliver Cromwell*, II, p. 267.

62   BL, Thomason Tract 669 f. 16 (13), J.L. Philalethes, *Old Sayings and Predictions Verified and Fulfilled, Touching the Young King of Scotland and his Gued Subjects* (London, J.L. Philalethes, 1651).

63   *HMC, Sixth Report*, pp. 427 and 430. Bradshaw to Strickland, 21 June 1650/16 July 1650 and p. 429, Bradshaw to the Council of State, 2 July 1650. Cromwell's association of Charles II as 'the King of Scots' stuck in the minds of both the Free State and some of the European heads of state. See Abbott, *Oliver Cromwell*, IV, speech to Parliament, 4 February 1657/8, pp. 731–2; *HMC, Sixth Report*, pp. 426–44, *passim*; *SRP*, vol. 18, p. 39.

64   Crispin Van De Pas, *Uytbeeldinge van de Hoogmoedige Republijk van Engelandt (*c. *1653)*, reproduced and discussed in Kunzle, *The Early Comic Strip*, p. 94; Robert Philippe, *Political Graphics: Art as a Weapon* (New York, Abbeville Press, 1982), p. 76.

65   John Nicoll, 'A Diary of Public Transactions and Other Occurrences, Chiefly in Scotland, from January 1650 to June 1667', in A. Peterkin (ed.), *Records of the Kirk of Scotland, containing the Acts and Proceedings of the General Assemblies from the Year 1638 Downwards* (Edinburgh, Church of Scotland, 1843), pp. 612–17.

66   *HMC, Sixth Report*, pp. 431–2. Bradshaw to Frost, 24 September 1650.

67   Abbott, *Oliver Cromwell*, II, p. 173 and III, pp. 53 and 587; B. Worden, 'Providence and Politics in Cromwellian England', *Past and Present*, 109 (1985), 67 and 83.

68   Clarendon, *History of the Rebellion*, V, p. 179; Jones, *Royal Politician*, p. 21; Young, *Scottish Parliament*, p. 250.

69   Clarendon, *History of the Rebellion*, V, p. 189.

70   Jones, *Royal Politician*, p. 21; Morrill, 'The Britishness of the English Revolution', p. 108.

71   Philalethes, *Old Sayings and Predictions Verified*.

72   British Museum, Huych Allaerdt, *Crowning of Charles II at Scone, 1st of January 1651*, reproduced in F. Maclean, *A Concise History of Scotland* (London, Book Club Associates, 1970), p. 131.

73   Jones, *Royal Politician*, p. 21; Morrill, 'The Britishness of the English Revolution', p. 101.

74   John Young notes that the 'Patriotic Settlement' which led to the repeal of the Act of Classes in June 1651 formed a major component of the Sixth, Seventh and Eighth sessions of the Second

Triennial Parliament beginning in November 1650, two months after the battle of Dunbar. See J.R. Young, 'The Scottish Parliament and the Covenanting Revolution: The Emergence of a Scottish Commons', in J.R. Young (ed.), *Celtic Dimensions of the British Civil Wars* (Edinburgh, John Donald, 1997), p.164; Young, *Scottish Parliament*, pp. 244–61.

75   A.I. Macinnes, 'The Scottish Constitution, 1638-1651: The Rise and Fall of Oligarchic Centralism', in J. Morrill (ed.), *The Scottish National Covenant in its British Context* (Edinburgh University Press, 1990), p. 128.

76   PRO SP 75/16 ff. 218–20. Charles II to Frederik III of Denmark-Norway and Queen Christina of Sweden, 20/30 August 1652; Clarendon, *History of the Rebellion*, V, pp. 197–209.

77   Morrill, 'The Britishness of the English Revolution', p. 108; Hirst, 'The English Republic', pp. 198–201. Morrill has argued that Charles II was not crowned as the king of the [Scottish] nation in 1651, but only a faction of it. It follows logically, therefore, that it was not the Scottish nation which was defeated at Worcester, but only a faction of it. The Royalist defeat is usually presented as an English defeat of Scotland. See Morrill, 'The Scottish National Covenant', in Morrill, *The Scottish National Covenant in its British Context*, p. 21.

78   'The Earl of Louden's Narrative of the Union of England and Scotland', in C.H. Firth (ed.), *Scotland and the Commonwealth* (Edinburgh, Scottish History Society, 1895), pp. 208–13.

79   Worden, 'Providence and Politics', pp. 82–3.

80   Iain Lom, 'Oran Cumhaidh air Cor na Rioghachd', *c.* 1651. See C.O. Baoill (ed.), *Gair nan Clarsach: The Harper's Cry, an Anthology of 17th Century Gaelic Poetry* (Edinburgh, Birlinn, 1994), pp. 130–4. The same metaphor can be found in Fear Dorcha O Mealláin's *An Díbirt Go Connachta, c.* 1652; see S.O Tuama, *An Duanaire 1600–1900: Poems of the Dispossessed* (Mountrath, The Dolmen Press, 1981), pp. 104–9; for English Royalists' claims to be the lost tribe see Potter, *Secret Rites*, pp. 33–4.

81   PRO SP 75/16 ff. 218–20, Charles II to Frederik III of Denmark-Norway and Queen Christina of Sweden, 20/30 August 1652.

82   PRO SP 75/16 ff. 218–20.

83   Da. Ra. TKUA, England, A I, Charles II to Frederik III, February 1653.

84   Da. Ra. TKUA, England, A I, Charles II to Frederik III from Paris, 8 August 1653.

85   Parker, *Milton*, p. 372.

86   Parker, *Milton*, p. 372, p. 369; Smith, *Literature and Revolution*, p. 190.

87   Parker, *Milton*, pp. 387–8.

88   *Mercurius Politicus*, no. 66, 4–11 September 1651; *Nicholas Papers*, I, pp. 317–18.

89   Parker, *Milton*, pp. 389, 395.

90   Laursen, *Danmark-Norges Traktater*, V, p. 16; G.M.D. Howatt, *Stuart and Cromwellian Foreign Policy* (London, Adam and Charles Black, 1974), p. 70.

91   *SRP*, vol. 15, pp. 97–9, 14 August 1651; and p. 101, 28 August 1651.

92   Abbott, *Oliver Cromwell*, II, pp. 489, 524; Laursen, *Danmark-Norges Traktater*, V, p. 136.

93   Abbott, *Oliver Cromwell*, II, pp. 541–71; Laursen, *Danmark-Norges Traktater*, V, pp. 16–17 and 139–142; J.A. Fridericia, *Adelsvældens Sidste Dage Danmarks Historie fra Christian IV's Død til Enevældens Indførelse 1648–1660* (Copenhagen, P.G. Philipsens Forlag, 1894), p. 210; G.D.M. Howatt, *Stuart and Cromwellian Foreign Policy* (London, A&C Black, 1974), pp. 71–2; Jones, *Royal Politician*, p. 22.

94   PRO SP 75/16 ff. 218–20, Charles II to Frederik of Denmark-Norway and Queen Christina of Sweden, 20/30 August 1652.

95   Da. Ra. TKUA, England, A I, Charles II to Frederick III, *c.* February 1653.

96   Abbott, *Oliver Cromwell*, II, p. 300; *HMC, Sixth Report*, p. 437. Waynwright to Bradshaw, 7, 21 and 28 April 1654; D. Laing (ed.), *The Letters and Journals of Robert Baillie, A.M. Principal of the University of Glasgow* (3 vols, Hamilton, London, 1844), III, p. 256; Howatt, *Stuart and Cromwellian Foreign Policy*, p. 75; Jones, *Royal Politician*, p. 26.

97   Laursen, *Danmark-Norges Traktater*, V, p. 152. Treaty between Oliver Cromwell and King Frederik III of Denmark-Norway, 15 September 1654.

98   Abbott, *Oliver Cromwell*, III, p. 267.

99   Spalding, *Bulstrode Whitelocke*, p. 321, 2 January 1654; Fryxell, *Sverges Historia*, I, p. 100, 17 March 1654.

100   Milton rewarded Queen Christina for her rejection of the Stuarts in a lengthy panegyric which formed part of his famous 'Second Defence of the People of England'. See J. Milton, *Pro populo anglicano defensio secunda* (London, 1654), *passim*.

101   *HMC, Sixth Report*, p. 437. Waynwright to Bradshaw, 4 May 1655.

102   *Nicholas Papers*, II, p. 32. Nicholas to Hyde, 8/18 December 1653.

103   G. Masson, *Queen Christina* (London, Sphere Books, 1974), p. 199.

104   Crispin Van De Pas, *Uytbeeldinge van de Hoogmoedige Republijk and Rombout van den Hoeyen, Ik wist het blinde graauw an 't Hol-ziek England (c. 1653)* are discussed in Kunzle, *The Early Comic Strip*, pp. 75 and 94; Philippe, *Political Graphics*, p. 76.

105   Patterson, *Milton State Papers, passim.*

106   Patterson, *Milton State Papers*. This was with the exception of the pan-Protestantism advocated by the Scottish cleric John Dury. Cromwell sometimes embellished his letters to the Scandinavians with some propaganda on this subject. See ibid., pp. 167–89, Cromwell to Frederik III and Cromwell to Charles X, 25 May 1655.

107   Da. Ra. TKUA, England, A I, Richard Cromwell to Frederik III, 15 November 1658.

108   Patterson, *Milton State Papers*, p. 429, Parliament to Charles X, 15 May 1659.

109   Da. Ra. TKUA, England, A II 16, Swedish and Danish acceptance of English mediation; Abbott, *Oliver Cromwell*, I, pp. 605–10; Laursen, *Danmark-Norges Traktater*, V, pp. 218–43.

110   Potter, *Secret Rites*, p. 10.

111   Skerpan, *The Rhetoric of Politics*, p. 111.

112   Howatt, *Stuart and Cromwellian Foreign Policy*, p. 95.

113   See J. Sawday, 'Re-writing a Revolution: History, Symbol and Text in the Restoration', *Seventeenth Century*, VII, no. 2 (1992).

6

SUPERSTITION, ENTHUSIASM AND PROPAGANDISM: BURKE AND GENTZ ON THE NATURE OF THE FRENCH REVOLUTION[1]

László Kontler

U nlike other contributions to this volume, the present chapter will not be concerned with the exercise, reception and impact of propaganda in the sense of a concerted activity aimed at persuading people to adopt or simply recognise a particular creed, doctrine or practice. Instead, this chapter will examine through a few examples a crucial phase in the history of the notion of propaganda, which underwent remarkable changes in western political discourse before acquiring its present technical sense as a method of policy making. As in many other cases, that crucial moment is the period of the French Revolution, at the outbreak of which the earlier, predominantly religious and neutral understanding of the concept – largely through its interchangeable equivalents, 'proselytising' and 'propagation' – had already become politicised, with negative implications conferred on it as a result of its identification with a theory of papalist conspiracy against Protestantism. I shall argue that the dichotomy of superstition and enthusiasm worked out in Enlightenment sociology of religion and philosophical history was of great consequence to this latter development; and that this heuristic device was also of great service for anti-revolutionary authors like Edmund Burke and Friedrich Gentz in developing the argument that one of the reasons why the powers allied against revolutionary France ought to carry out an uncompromising fight was that abominable 'propaganda' was an integral part of the revolutionary machinery aimed at pulling down the whole edifice of European old regime civilisation.

The notion of propaganda rose in post-Tridentine Catholicism to describe the missionary activity of the church, and also gave the name to the institution devoted to that task: the *Congregatio de Propaganda Fide*. Originally titled *Sacra Congregatio Christiano Nomini Propagando*, it grew out of a commission of three cardinals set up by Pope Gregory XIII (1572–85) to answer the needs of communicating with recently discovered lands and to promote the union of Rome and Oriental Christians. As a part of the new system of papal government by congregations adopted during the counter-Reformation – a complete system of administrative departments, each assigned a special branch of the Catholic interest – it was officially established by the bull *Inscrutabili Divinae* of Gregory XV in 1622, and received its fully fledged organisational structure under Urban VIII (1623–44), who had been one of its initial members.[2] Throughout the rest of the seventeenth and for the entire eighteenth century, the derivative of the Latin term 'propagation' or its synonym 'proselytising' enjoyed preference in the European vernaculars to express the same phenomenon. The fact that the notion, though certainly not the organisation, of 'propaganda' might look harmless to other denominations is shown by similar names suggested for similarly motivated Protestant initiatives. In 1697, the Anglican minister Thomas Bray published *A General Plan of the Constitution of a Protestant Congregation or Society for Propagating Christian Knowledge*, consciously modelled after its Catholic counterpart.[3] At the same time, since the *Congregatio* was juxtaposed with other agencies of the papacy, such as the Inquisition and the Society of Jesus, 'proselytism' was occasionally seen as part of a diabolical machinery aimed at ecclesiastical tyranny where Catholicism was established, and at subversive plotting where it was a minority religion. This association of ideas was communicated to the public on different levels of Enlightenment literature. According to the article *Jésuite* of the *Encyclopédie*, the followers of Ignatius of Loyola were a sect of 'the impious and the fanatic, of corrupters and regicides . . . commanded by a foreign chief, Machiavellian by institution', who replaced true Christianity with magic and superstition, and who were proven disturbers of the public peace everywhere they appeared.[4] The Göttingen scholar Ludwig Timotheus Spittler wrote in his *Outline of the History of the Christian Church* that these 'Janissaries of the Holy See', who were simultaneously 'the defense and the terror of despots', provided that 'artificial mixture of light and darkness . . . through which alone could the Papacy save itself after the times of Luther and Calvin', the proof being that at least in Germany there was 'hardly one proselyte' to be found who was not converted by a Jesuit. In fact, '[t]he entire history of the Catholic Church from the time of the Synod of Trent to the first quarter of the present century is a Jesuitical cabal'.[5] It is noteworthy that one of the main charges levelled against Jesuit proselytising – in a striking anticipation of anti-revolutionary polemic – was its destabilising effect on the position of secular authorities: the idea that the Pope could absolve subjects from their allegiance to heretic rulers, attributed to the Jesuit neo-Thomists Francisco Suárez and Juan Mariana, looked particularly dangerous in view of the Jesuits' role in educating the young.[6]

Such sentiments were especially deeply rooted and long lasting in Britain. As late as 1829 – obviously in the heat of the debates on Catholic emancipation, and quite wrongly as regards its main assertion – it was claimed in the *Blackwell's Magazine* that '[t]he very word proselytism was scarcely known to the English language, until it was added to it a few years ago by the barbarous jargon of

Catholicism'.[7] In fact, it has been suggested that in the England of the 1530s to the 1830s 'the most consistent theme both of popular sentiment and of ideological exegesis was anti-Catholicism',[8] with the nightmarish image of an international conspiracy, whose agents were proselytising Jesuits, being a chief motive force behind it. From the attempts at Queen Elizabeth's life, through the Gunpowder Plot and the Popish Plot, to the Jacobite rebellions, the wars of the 1740s against 'Popish' powers and the Gordon Riots, the same ambiguity as described above asserted itself in the portrayal of the relationship between popery and established authority: from an agent of subverting lawful rulers, it became viewed as one of arbitrary power. The latter allegation was made initially possible by the practice of collapsing Roman Catholicism with Roman law and its idea of unitary, tyrannical sovereignty, and, by implication, divine right (in salient contradiction to the fact that divine right authors were profoundly critical of the Jesuit notions of the secular origin of the state, social contract and the consequent superiority of papal authority). In the eighteenth century, however, this argument gained reinforcement from the works of philosophical historians – Voltaire, David Hume, William Robertson and Edward Gibbon in the first place – who examined the corrupting effects of two forms of 'false religion', superstition and enthusiasm, in the history of western civilisation.[9] The dichotomy became most influential in the succinct form Hume gave to it. In terms of political consequences, superstition, whose true sources were 'weakness, fear, melancholy, together with ignorance', rendered men 'tame', 'submissive' and 'abject' and was, therefore, 'an enemy to civil liberty'. On the other hand, enthusiasm, founded on 'hope, pride, presumption, a warm imagination, together with ignorance' was a friend to liberty, notwithstanding the fact that its first outbursts were always 'furious and violent', and produced 'the most cruel disorders in human society'.[10] Through the notion of tyranny, therefore, a link was established between proselytising and superstititon: a superstitious religion – like Catholicism – would be at the same time, by definition, a proselytising religion, and the other way round.

Edmund Burke thought of the proselytising potential of Catholicism on quite different grounds: observing that Catholics made far more converts among pagan peoples than Protestants, he ascribed this phenomenon to the fact that Catholicism was a 'full' form of Christianity, while Protestantism was a 'diminished' form.[11] Not that he could with any certainty be identified as a crypto-Catholic. Recently, he has been described as 'an honest sceptic' who perceived religion as 'a set of complex social data which has to be borne in mind' to prevent it from aggravating conflicts already difficult to solve without it; though even if he was one, he did have a predilection towards Trinitarian Christianity and an early conceived, deep-seated and later (to him) all too powerfully vindicated suspicion towards the 'enthusiasm' of heterodox Dissent.[12] Still, if there was a figure on the British public scene in the eighteenth century who felt the edge of anti-Catholicism, it was Edmund Burke.[13] An Irishman from a Catholic environment whose father (presumably) had only conformed with the Church of England for the sake of pursuing a legal career a few years before Edmund's birth, and whose mother and wife (also presumably) remained Catholic throughout their lives, Burke became a target for charges of being an agent of popery as soon as his lifelong political commitment on behalf of Irish Catholics had commenced. Shortly after having written the *Tract Relative to the Laws against Popery in Ireland* (between 1761 and 1764), Burke found himself accused of being an Irish papist educated by Jesuits at St Omer (a usual venue of training Irish Catholic priests in the period) who had been sent to England as a Jesuit spy.[14] It was to remain a lasting stigma, and Burke could not be circumspect enough in his support for Catholic relief to rid himself of it (even though he tried hard, precisely in the interest of rendering efficacious help). It earned him portrayals in Jesuit garb in countless caricatures down to the period of the Revolution; it cost him his seat for Bristol after having played a discreet, but essential part in bringing about the Catholic Relief Act of 1778; and it brought him, as one of the supporters of the Act, threats to his life during the Gordon Riots of 1780.

The Gordon Riots are an important episode for the present subject. The worst anti-Catholic disturbances of the eighteenth century have recently been persuasively described as a *revolution manquée*.[15] Their origins fit the pattern of popish conspiracy against liberty: the prospect of relief in 1778 was held out, as it were, in return for recruiting Catholics from Gordon's native Scotland into the armed forces to fight the American colonists, whose cause was dear to Burke as well as Gordon, but whereas the former opted for toleration, the latter launched a campaign of the Protestant Association to unveil 'the diabolical purpose' of the bill, which was allegedly 'to arm Roman Catholics'.[16] They also fit the pattern of superstition and proselytism versus enthusiasm: Gordon's campaign employed the whole paraphernalia of anti-Catholic demonology from conspiratorial Jesuits to idolatrous relics, while Burke commented on the riots by describing those involved in it as a 'Body of Zealots' who 'on pretended principles of religion have declared war . . . on Mankind'.[17] Indeed, the period of the first Relief Act was one in which Catholics were themselves beginning to employ the Humean dichotomy to their own advantage, suggesting that the days when 'reason of state gave a sanction to the fury of enthusiasm' had come to an end, and that to continue discriminating against papists as dangerous to civil society was 'contrary to those benevolent principles in which this enlightened age glories'.[18] Burke was thinking in similar terms. He suggested that the times when superstition and 'the enthusiasm of religion threw a gloom over the politics; and political interests poisoned and perverted the spirit of religion on all sides', and when it was 'necessary, perhaps, to oppose to Popery another Popery, to get the better of it', were, or ought to be, over. Having felt charged by his Bristol electors to have advanced the cause of Roman Catholics his politeness failed him and he retorted:

'The calumny is fitter to be scrawled with the midnight chalk of incendiaries, with "No Popery," on walls and doors of devoted houses, than to be mentioned in any civilised company.'[19] At the same time, he disclaimed having played a part of any direct importance in bringing in the Relief Act of 1778 – thus rejecting the charge that he had contributed to 'provoking' the Gordon Riots and was just as extremist as the rioters themselves in the eyes of many an observer. Disregarding the slight tension between these two lines of argument, Burke's strategy was to shift familiar accents in order to impress hearers and readers: the opposite of sober, firm and civilised policy was now enthusiasm armed with the weapons formerly used by superstition. The experience of the riots helped Burke lay the foundations of his understanding of the dynamic of revolutionary ferment that he was to develop in the *Reflections on the Revolution in France*. Given the qualified assent of rational Dissent, and the active agency of some prominent Dissenters, besides the 'Church-and-King' mob in the disturbances, a combination of lower-class radicalism inspired by blind neo-Puritanic enthusiasm and the ambition of cool, calculating political men of letters seemed to be in the making.[20] Looking back from 1796, Burke thought that only the absence of the rights of man from the British political scene during the years 1780 to 1782 had prevented 'all the vices, crimes, horrors and miseries of the French Revolution'.[21]

Catholic superstition, allied to conspiratorial and proselytising devices, with Protestant enthusiasm as its mighty rival, constituted a comprehensible model of interpreting social upheaval in the eighteenth century, and Burke thus started to build a new frame of reference for describing revolution by reshaping this model well before the French Revolution.[22] As it broke out, and in the way it proceeded in France and was viewed in Britain, Burke perceived an opportunity, not merely to re-establish Whiggery on its old principles and assert his own position within it, while re-emphasising his commitment to the eighteenth-century modernity that he now saw threatened (although these are undoubtedly grand themes of the *Reflections* and his other anti-revolutionary writings), but also subtly to vindicate his own longstanding support for the adherents of a supposedly superstitious and proselytising religion, relieving Catholicism of the stigma of superstition and proselytising. This was the implication of the only conclusion that, he thought, could be drawn from the experience of the Revolution: that 'superstition' was to be preferred to proselytising enthusiasm, and that the political counterparts of these religious attitudes were not slavery and liberty but stability and anarchy, the former maintaining a civilisational standard achieved at considerable sacrifice and leading to the safe enjoyment of reasonable liberty, and the latter hazarding those achievements of modernity and leading to tyranny.[23]

In order to evoke this effect, Burke first relied on a thoroughly ironic use of the dichotomy of superstition and enthusiasm. The latter is presented in the *Reflections* as emerging in full vigour, recalling the worst memories of religious and civil strife in the preceding centuries. The respectable Unitarian preacher

Richard Price, author of the pamphlet that awakened Burke to the dangerous possibility of French revolutionary doctrines falling on fertile ground in Britain, is cast in the role of Civil War enthusiast and regicide Hugh Peter[24] – a choice which is not explained by the relations between rational Dissent and the French *philosophes* and members of the National Assembly, but by its earlier association with the rioters of Gordon, who appears quite frequently in the pages of Burke's anti-revolutionary writings.[25] Against this background, references to Gordon's conversion to Judaism in 1787 were meant to establish the link between the enthusiasm of Dissent and the fanatical Puritan millenarianism of the Fifth Monarchy Men. Their 'prophetic enthusiasm' was intended to 'vanquish all the mean superstitions of the heart', to 'undermine superstition and error'.[26] But what is, in fact, superstition? Burke's irony is at its most thorough here. 'On this scheme of things . . . [r]egicide, parricide, and sacrilege, are but fictions of superstition.'[27] What the 'barbarous philosophy' of the revolutionaries and their British fellow travellers considers superstition is in fact a firm commitment to moral beliefs passed down through centuries, not necessarily rational, but more or less universally shared and proven useful. Superstition, far from being the high road to slavery, is collapsed into another, peculiarly Burkean category: innocent, even beneficial, prejudice.[28]

Proselytism could hardly be an instrument of such a sober disposition. On the contrary, it is the inevitable corollary of religious and political enthusiasm. Having unmasked the true character of the British admirers of the French Revolution, Burke leaves no doubt about the fact that the attitudes displayed by them are identical with those that motivate their French idols, and bear supreme responsibility for the calamitous state of France.

> The literary cabal had some years ago formed something like a regular plan for the destruction of the Christian religion. This object they pursued with a degree of zeal which hitherto had been discovered only in propagators of some system of piety. They were possessed with a spirit of proselytism in the most fanatical degree; and from thence, by an easy progress, with the spirit of persecution according to their means.[29]

From here onwards, zeal, fanaticism and enthusiasm – often described as 'atheistic' – occur on a regular basis as inseparable from proselytism and propagation in the *Reflections* as well as in Burke's later anti-revolutionary writings. He also clearly recognised the significance of the printed word which, properly managed, might become a self-contained machinery for disseminating propaganda.

> What direction the French spirit of proselytism is likely to take, and in what order it is likely to prevail, it is not easy to determine. The seeds are sown almost everywhere, chiefly by newspaper circulation, infinitely more efficacious and extensive than ever they were. And they are a more important

instrument than generally is imagined. They are a part of the reading of all, they are the whole of the reading of the far greater number.[30]

Thus, the link gradually forged by the period of the High Enlightenment between superstition – Catholicism, Popery, Jesuitism – and proselytising is broken by Burke, who associates proselytism with revolutionary turbulence inspired by a mixture of religious and secular enthusiasm. It is on these grounds that he develops the famous dictum on the Revolution as one of *'doctrine and theoretick dogma'* which 'has a much greater resemblance to those changes which have been made upon religious grounds, in which a spirit of proselytism makes an essential part'.[31] The joint, and mutually reinforcing momentum of enthusiasm and proselytism – old forces only too well known to Burke, if in a new guise – is the reason for Burke's almost paranoiac apprehension of the activities of 'factious clubs' within and outside France.[32] If there is an element of the conspiracy theory in Burke, it is intertwined in a sophisticated manner with the themes of superstition, proselytism and enthusiasm.[33] The full appreciation of this combination is also essential for an assessment of Burke's other well-known statement about the nature of the revolutionary wars:

> We are at war with a system, which, by its very essence, is inimical to all other governments, and which makes peace or war, as peace and war may best contribute to their subversion. It is with an *armed doctrine*, that we are at war. It has, by its essence, a faction of opinion, and of interest, and of enthusiasm, in every country.[34]

Whereas Burke quite clearly defined the phenomenon and provided a novel analysis of it within the linguistic conventions available to contemporaries for the interpretation of socio-political conflict, he did not use the word 'propaganda' and was content with its old-fashioned equivalents 'proselytism' and 'propagation'. This is all the more puzzling since after the uprising of August 1792 a central propaganda agency, the *Bureau de l'esprit public,* was set up in Paris by Minister of the Interior Jean Marie Roland de la Platiére, followed by the issue of 'Propagandist Decrees' from the Republican government. The 'Propaganda', with a definite article and often with a capital letter, had in fact been identified as a dangerous agent of the Revolution by a correspondent of the prince of Wales as early as September 1790: 'All Kings have . . . a new race of Pretenders to contend with, the disciples of the propaganda at Paris, or as they call themselves, *Les Ambassadeurs du genre humain.'*[35] Similarly, the *Gentleman's Magazine* reported about '[t]he Propaganda, a society whose members are bound, by solemn engagements, to stir up subjects against their lawful rulers.'[36] But this is the old notion of propaganda being one particular organ within a huge machinery aiming at universal tyranny – as the Propaganda, the Inquisition and Jesuitism were facets of popish expansionism – which Burke had actually superseded.

'Proselytising', as well as 'propaganda' in the former, reductionist sense, figured quite prominently in a debate during the German High Enlightenment, which also served to some extent as a prelude to the discussion of the same phenomena in the French Revolution. Without resulting in physical violence, but with an intellectual fervour as powerful as in the most intense periods of anti-popery in Britain, influential figures of the Prussian Enlightenment launched a full-scale campaign to avert, as they conceived of it, a conspiratorial offensive of the Catholic Church against Protestantism and Enlightenment.[37] The Berlin *Aufklärer* Friedrich Nicolai set the tone in an account of his travels in Germany in 1781, alleging that there was an ever more intensive missionary activity of Catholic priests in North Germany as a result of an '*Actus de propaganda fide*, whose pursuit shall never be abandoned'.[38] During the following years, the chief organ of the Berlin Enlightenment, the *Berlinische Monatsschrift*, devoted substantial energies to the 'unmasking' of the 'project' of 'the College of Propaganda' to strengthen 'the obscurantist party' through 'proselytism', by sending out 'disguised ex-Jesuits' to convert more 'crypto-Catholics'. The editor of the journal, Johann Erich Biester, was initially mainly worried about the integrity of Protestant souls when he lamented that 'the Collegium de propaganda fide is exerting an extraordinary activity'.[39] At the same time, especially since in this period of the decline of Freemasonry most of the still active secret societies were anti-rationalist sects, in the strategy of the *Aufklärer* 'secrecy' also acquired politically subversive implications. Thus, the jurist Johann Friedrich Le Bret argued that 'the Pope and the Propaganda can always influence the constitution of Germany'; similarly, in his preface to a contribution by the same author in the *Berlinische Monatsschrift*, Biester claimed that the Peace of Westphalia would in this way be undermined, princes would be deprived of their prerogative of *placetum regium* and lose their sovereign status, and that 'the subversive evil of a secret state within the state' threatened the whole of North Germany.[40]

Most sober *Aufklärer* distanced themselves from this anti-Catholic militancy, as did Christian Garve, emphasising his unshaken belief in the power of reason: 'As long as the ever widening dissemination of the principles of sound philosophy, statecraft and natural science counter opinions not sufficiently demonstated', there was no reason to worry about suspected machinations of the *Congregatio*.[41] However, there was also another line of criticism levelled against the campaign of the *Berlinische Monatsschrift*, one which turned the charges of proselytism back on its enlightened architects, and thus contributed to the rise of the notion of a conspiracy of *philosophes* against the old regime, culminating in the French Revolution. Its author, Johann August Starck, court preacher and councillor in Darmstadt, later became one of the editors of the chief German reactionary journal, *Eudämonia* (1795–8), and wrote one of the most notorious anti-Enlightenment indictments.[42] In 1787, Starck published two weighty volumes, and in 1788 a third one, taking issue with the perpetrators of what he regarded a 'hunt for heretics' by 'a kind of Inquisition tribunal', and drawing a remarkable parallel: 'A few years ago people witnessed a quite similar scene in England, when the enthusiast Lord George Gordon rose and dreamt of terrible secret attempts of the Catholics to undermine Protestantism.'[43] No one could have predicted 'that in our enlightened times, when the old spirit of enmity between Protestants and Catholics started to subside, and the thinking and conduct of both parties became milder and more Christian towards the other, the fire once extinguished would be rekindled'; and Gordon is mentioned again as the author of this new persecuting spirit.[44] Though he expressed some surprise at the phenomenon, Starck had no doubt about the motivation fuelling this hysteria. The *Aufklärer* wanted to root out Christianity and to replace it with their pure rational religion and naturalism, an end which could not be better served than by stigmatising as missionaries of the Propaganda – as it were, heretics – those who were in fact honest defenders of the Gospel against Socinians and Deists. Biester, who used the pretext of giving an acount of Christianity at the time of the Roman Emperor Julianus to produce a 'panegyric of pure Deism', and his colleagues were themselves enthusiasts of the worst kind, and their campaign was 'disguised proselytising of another sort, though just as harmful and much more shameful than disguised proselytising on behalf of Popery'.[45] They were also dangerous demagogues, themselves displaying Jesuit attitudes and foreshadowing Jacobin ones in the peculiar implication of their argument: 'think as we do, or else we shall condemn you as a Jesuit or an instrument of Jesuitism'.[46]

After such antecedents it was only natural that Starck became one in a chorus of several German authors who later disseminated and maintained the view that the French Revolutionaries 'established their own Propaganda . . . in imitation of the Roman "*Collegii de propaganda fide*", which contributed so greatly to the spread of Christianity in the farthest corners of the Earth', the only difference being that the revolutionary replica of the *Congregatio* was committed to the propagation of atheism and subversion.[47] In fact, statements by leading radicals of the Revolution describing the role of the Jacobin Club in propagating the religion of patriotism and philanthropy as analogous to that of Rome in Christianity, were largely responsible for the apprehensions about Propaganda as a club or society intended to pull the strings of an 'infernal machinery' whose goal was 'to destroy all order . . . to mock religion and laws . . . to pull down all thrones'.[48] Reports 'about the so-called Propaganda' started to proliferate and were speculated on abundantly. In his widely read *Historische Nachrichten und politische Untersuchungen über die französische Revolution* Christoph Girtanner alleged that the organisation had been established as early as 1786 by Rochefoucauld, Condorcet and Sieyés, and was anxious to lend credibility to his account of its activity by a minute description of the operative regulations of the 'club' after the model of contemporary secret societies.[49] 'Propaganda' was a frequent topic of the documents collected in the eight volumes of *Politische Annalen* (Berlin, 1793–4),

also edited by Girtanner, as well as in the preface and notes he wrote to
Denkwürdigkeiten des Generals Dumouriez. There it is claimed that if the powers at war
against France neglect their task and the Jacobins retain the upper hand in
France, 'the Propaganda will regain its full vigour; and first the neighbouring
peoples, and later the more remote ones will be required to follow the example of
the French'. Roland and the Girondins in general are described as 'the Jesuits of
the Revolution'.[50]

The German authors I have hitherto examined were interested mainly in
diabolising the Revolution and identifying its evil character, and circumstances
allowed them simply to turn the pattern of old Enlightenment and Protestant
apprehensions about Propaganda inside out. This resulted in what might be
described as a 'pure' conspiracy theory. Unlike them, and resembling Burke,
Friedrich Gentz used the phenomenon of propagandism – significantly, not the
crude model of the 'Club of Propaganda' – as one of the analytical tools to
produce a subtler view of the whole of the dynamic of revolution. 'The German
Burke' was indeed far from being an exact replica of the master: instead of
Burke's traditionalism, which remained alien to him, Gentz described Kantian
philosophy as his spiritual nurse, and he was in general a rather critical admirer
of Burke.[51] But there are a number of points at which they are closer to each
other than at others,[52] and the analysis of the dynamic of revolution in terms of
enthusiasm and propagandism is one of them. The work in which most of
Gentz's relevant views are set forth, *On the Origin and Character of the War against the
French Revolution* (1801)[53], was a relatively late contribution to the debate on the
Revolution, urged by a motivation similar to that of Burke's *Letters on a Regicide
Peace*: to prevent making peace with revolutionary France. Whereas in the case of
Burke, pragmatic considerations were ever more powerfully mixed with passion
and moral indignation, Gentz fairly dispassionately weighed all circumstances
and argued that, despite the little success achieved by the coalition against France
at the expense of much suffering to the whole of the continent of Europe, the evil
arising from the war was still smaller than what would have resulted from not
resisting the tide of revolution, and that the failure to contain the danger
stemmed largely from an imperfect assessment of the forces let loose by the
Revolution in France. Gentz also suggested that a correction of this assessment
might hold out the prospect of putting up a more efficacious fight.

In the first section of the book, Gentz examines the question of whether the
allied powers have been waging a just war against France. Initially, his argument
relies heavily on natural and international law, in an effort to point out that
because of the sophisticated network of interconnections between the European
states and the assault of the Revolution against the very principles upon which
they are all established, the Revolution is not a mere internal affair, and therefore
the war against it is in fact a civil war within the 'European republic' or
'commonwealth of nations'.[54] In addition, despite the solemn declaration of the

National Assembly to abandon wars of conquest, it soon declared a 'new kind of international law' whose fundamental idea was that treaties made with tyrants were not binding. Together with their paranoiac fear of plots against the new order, this accounted for the 'fanatical passion' of the 'enthusiasts' of the Revolution to propagate their doctrines by arms. Gentz quotes Brissot, the head of the 'sect' of zealots: 'A nation that has conquered her liberty, needs war. The war of liberty is a sacred war ordained by Heaven', and comments that '[t]he crusade for universal liberty thus commenced. Each soldier became a Peter or a Bernard.'[55]

Gentz had already analysed in some detail the affinities between religious and political enthusiasm in one of the tracts published as appendices to his translation of Burke's *Reflections* in 1793. There was no difference in kind between them, Gentz suggested, and he regarded political fanaticism as 'a terrible malady of nations', which had for some time disappeared from the European scene, but which in recent years had returned to replace its 'twin sister, religious enthusiasm' in haunting peoples with a kind of secular idolatry and intolerance: 'it has raged more blindly, desperately and irresistibly for ribbons, flags and cockades than that antiquated weakness of the human spirit had for relics, images and amulets'. The 'Inquisition, the torches, the dungeons, the martial courts, the inhuman triumphal marches' were all taken over from religious fanaticism. It is significant that Gentz, even after his conservative turn, preserved enough of his enlightened rationalism for him to see no difference between the fanaticism of 'superstition' and 'enthusiasm'. To him, both were equally lethal to religion as well as to liberty, which are better preserved by what he calls 'the indifference of reason' (as distinguished from the 'indifference of scorn').[56]

Enthusiasm, therefore, a disposition in which the character of a Jesuit and that of a Protestant zealot are mixed, was at the bottom of the project that 'the soldier . . . ought to carry in his cartridge pouch not merely powder and bullet, but also a copy of the constitution in order to disseminate the revolution'[57] – in a word, at the bottom of 'the restless propagandism of the *Girondists*', which 'undermined the very possibility of peace'.[58] But propagandism, fuelled by enthusiasm, was not merely one of the main reasons why the war broke out at all, nor why it was a 'just' war on the part of the anti-revolutionary coalition. It had also played a major part in making the war difficult to bring to a conclusion, for it supplied France with a source of energy which was not recognised early enough, and because of the very novelty of the phenomenon it could not have been responded to early enough to defeat it. The major difference between Gentz and the German authors mentioned earlier – and also the main point of agreement between him and Burke – is that although he, too, speaks of propagandism mainly as an external exertion of French power to undermine the governments at war against it, at the same time he recognises in it an instrument of maintaining the 'invincible enthusiasm' which the Revolution had awakened in Frenchmen, at least among the soldiers sent to the front. The 'feverish enthusiasm' led the French to commit the most heinous crimes within the country, while in order to defy the alleged conspiracy of tyrannical neighbours 'war was ennobled and hallowed'. As a result, '[d]riven by enthusiastic pride, amidst all the Magic of the Revolution, under flags and trees of liberty, and heated by wild decrees and lofty orations . . . the courage of the French soldier rose to an all-consuming impetuosity.'[59] But as the Revolution fell into the Terror and the rule of the Directory, the initial enthusiasm for liberty gave way to enthusiasm for independence, and finally to enthusiasm for triumph and fame; once unleashed and fuelled, its energy could be utilised by the successors of the Gironde and the Jacobins, too.[60] And since the same enthusiasm for the principles of the Revolution had given rise to 'parties' sympathetic to them in the very bosom of their enemies, it was all the easier for the French through the 'non-fictitious Propaganda, even before they triumphed, to pave a smooth and comfortable way into the hearts of all states'.[61]

The question was to find a way to fight the revolutionary enthusiasm and propagandism, which were the main sources of French strength alongside the new military system favouring the rise of talents, the moral unscrupulousness generated by the Revolution, and the extraordinary economic resources that could be mobilised through revolutionary decrees. 'Through a happily calculated influence upon sentiments', Gentz's answer befitted the man who, on the side of Prince Metternich, was to become the *eminence grise* of a system which employed a great deal of 'influence on the sentiments', happily and less happily calculated. Among the circumstances that arose as a result of the French Revolution,

> public opinion ought not to be neglected or disdained for a single moment. Instruction and guidance must be the permanent concern of the princes. They should exert their influence upon the ideas and principles of the age in all expedient ways, through frequently repeated solemn declarations, through publications, through sermons, through the education of the people, through the support and encouragement of talents. . . . It is not sufficient to have the revolutionary principle denounced as a product of madness and lunacy in isolated proclamations and ephemeral pamphlets; one must penetrate into the very fundaments, and the evil ought to be chased back relentlessly to its first spring.[62]

The Revolution cannot be defied but by revolutionary means; this is precisely what the powers allied against it had, in Gentz's opinion, not sufficiently recognised, or they had not acted upon that recognition. To the critic of revolutionary propagandism this implied, among other things, counter-propaganda. From its long association with dark forces scheming to bring down what is lawful, civilised, orderly and free, the notion still sounded ominous, so Gentz refrained from calling it by name. Nevertheless, he concluded his analysis of the nature of the revolutionary wars by providing the guidelines for creating and operating a system of propaganda.

Notes

1   I am grateful to the OTKA (Hungarian National Fund for Scientific Research) and the Junior Faculty Research Support Scheme of the Central European University, which enabled me to do the research for this article.

2   Umberto Benigni, 'Propaganda', in *The Catholic Encyclopedia*, vol. XII (New York, Robert Appleton, 1911), pp. 456 ff. For the early history of the concept, see also Wolfgang Schieder and Christof Dipper, 'Propaganda', in Otto Brunner, Werner Conze and Reinhart Koselleck (eds), *Geschichtliche Grundbegriffe. Historisches Lexikon für politisch-sozialen Sprache in Deutschland* (7 vols, Stuttgart, Klett-Cotta, 1972–95), vol. V, pp. 69 ff.

3   However, as this foremost voluntary society within the Church of England was established in reality, our key word fell out of its name, which became Society for Promoting Christian Knowledge. On its early history, see most recently Craig Rose, 'The Origins and Ideals of the SPCK 1699–1716', in John Walsh, Colin Haydon and Stephen Taylor (eds), *The Church of England c. 1689–c. 1833: From Toleration to Tractarianism* (Cambridge University Press, 1993), pp. 172–90.

4   *Encyclopédie, ou dictionnaire raisonné des sciences, des arts et des métiers*, tome VIII, pp. 513–15 (repr. New York, Pergamon Press, 1969), vol. II, p. 409.

5   Ludwig Timotheus Spittler, *Grundriß der Geschichte der christlichen Kirche* (1782), in *Sämmtliche Werke*, ed. Karl Wächter (10 vols, Stuttgart-Tübingen, Cotta, 1827–36), vol. II, pp. 341, 397. Cf. idem., *Vorlesungen über die Geschichte des Papstthums im achtzehnten Jahrhundert*, in *Werke*, vol. IX (1836), p. 339; *Vorlesungen über die Geschichte der Mönchsorden*, in *Werke*, vol. X (1836), pp. 117, 133.

6   *Encyclopédie*, vol. II, p. 409; Ludwig Timotheus Spittler, *Ueber die Geschichte und Verfassung der Jesuiten-Orden*, in *Werke*, vol. IX (1836), pp. 77–8.

7   *Blackwell's Magazine*, XXV (1829), p. 59.

8   J.C.D. Clark, *The Language of Liberty 1660–1832: Political Discourse and Social Dynamics in the Anglo-American World* (Cambridge University Press, 1994), p. 238. In more detail, see Edward Norman, *Roman Catholicism in England from the Elizabethan Settlement to the Second Vatican Council* (Oxford University Press, 1985), chs 1–4; Colin Haydon, *Anti-Catholicism in Eighteenth-Century England, c. 1714–1780: A Political and Social Study* (Manchester University Press, 1993). For the role of anti-Catholicism in shaping British identity, see Linda Colley, *Britons: Forging the Nation, 1707–1837* (New Haven, Yale University Press, 1992), ch. 1.

9   For a concise presentation of this theme and its examination of the particular example of Robertson, see Nicholas Phillipson, 'Providence and Progress: An Introduction to the Historical Thought of William Robertson', in Stewart J. Brown (ed.), *William Robertson and the Expansion of Empire* (Cambridge University Press, 1997), pp. 55–73.

10   David Hume, 'Of Superstition and Enthusiasm', in Eugene F. Miller (ed.), *Essays Moral, Political, and Literary* (Indianapolis, Liberty Press, 1985), pp. 74, 76, 78. Hume is undoubtedly the 'English author' referred to in the article 'fanatisme' of the *Encyclopédie*, tome VI, p. 400, or vol. I,

p. 1358, where superstition is identified with the prerogative, or the subjection and degradation of the people, and fanaticism with a republican spirit and the elevation of the people, while both are regarded as *mauvais politiques*. The distinction is also echoed in the famous theory about the 'oscillation' of the religious spirit between polytheism and monotheism as expounded in Hume's *The Natural History of Religion* and as adopted in Gibbon's *The Decline and Fall of the Roman Empire*. See also M. Andreas Weber, *Hume und Gibbon, Religionssoziologie in der Aufklärung* (Mannheim, Antnon Hain, 1990); J.G.A. Pocock, 'Edward Gibbon and the World View of the Late Enlightenment', in *Virtue, Commerce, and History* (Cambridge University Press, 1985), pp. 143–57.

11   *A Note-Book of Edmund Burke*, ed. H.V.F. Somerset (Cambridge University Press, 1957), pp. 100–1.

12   For the first of these views, see Michel Fuchs, *Edmund Burke, Ireland, and the Fashioning of Self* (Oxford Voltaire Foundation, 1996), pp. 18–19; for the second, J.C.D. Clark, *English Society 1688–1832* (Cambridge University Press, 1985), p. 252; for Burke's early view on enthusiasm, *Note-Book of Edmund Burke*, pp. 64, 97.

13   Burke's Irish and Catholic background and its relevance to all stages of his career is suggestively, if somewhat speculatively, analysed in the most recent full-scale biography, Conor Cruise O'Brien, *The Great Melody: A Thematic Biography and Commented Anthology of Edmund Burke* (Chicago University Press, 1992).

14   Since this image of Burke was presented to the marquess of Rockingham by the duke of Newcastle shortly after Burke had been appointed the former's secretary in July 1765, it might have seriously harmed his career at its very beginning, but he was able to convince his patron that the allegations were unfounded. The episode is described in Francis Hardy, *Memoirs of the Earl of Charlemont* (2nd edition, 2 vols, London, 1812), vol. II, pp. 281–3. Earlier, Burke had quarrelled over the affairs of Irish Catholics, among other things, with his former employer, Chief Secretary for Ireland William Gerard Hamilton, who in notes on Burke's conduct angrily described him as 'a Jew, and a Jesuit'. *The Correspondence of Edmund Burke* (hereafter *Correspondence*), ed. Thomas W. Copeland *et al.* (10 vols, Cambridge University Press, 1958–70), vol. I. p. 190. The 'St Omer' charge was later in Parliament in 1770, as reported by Burke's kinsman William to an old friend: *Correspondence*, vol. II, pp. 126–9.

15   Iain McCalman, 'Mad Lord George and Madame La Motte: Riot and Sexuality in the Genesis of Burke's *Reflections on the Revolution in France*', *Journal of British Studies*, 36 (1996), 343–67.

16   Robert Kent Donovan, 'The Military Origins of the Catholic Relief Programme of 1778', *Historical Journal*, 28 (1985), 79–102; J. Paul de Castro, *The Gordon Riots* (London, 1926), pp. 19–20.

17   McCalman, 'Mad Lord George', pp. 350–2; Burke, *Correspondence*, vol. IV, p. 243.

18   George Hay, *Letters on Usury and Interest* (1774), cited in Mark Goldie, 'The Scottish Catholic Enlightenment', *Journal of British Studies*, 30 (1991), 36.

19   Burke, *Speech at Bristol Previous to the Election* (1780), in *The Writings and Speeches of Edmund Burke* (hereafter *WS*), general ed. Paul Langford (Oxford, 1989–), vol. III, pp. 638–40. Though there was relatively little anti-popery in Bristol, the 'affairs of Roman Catholics' occupy a substantial portion in Burke's defence of his conduct to his electors, showing the importance he ascribed to the issue. Cf. O'Brien, *Great Melody*, pp. 79 ff.

20   Burke, *Speech at Bristol*, pp. 654 ff.; *Correspondence*, vol. IV, pp. 246, 263–4.

21   Burke, *Letter to a Noble Lord* (1796), in *WS*, vol. IX, pp. 151–2.

22   Burke went the farthest in turning the experience of the Gordon Riots to drawing consequences for socio-political analysis, though he was certainly only one among many who were shocked by the inflammatory potential of Dissenting enthusiasm. The most frequently quoted testimony is that of Edward Gibbon: 'forty thousand Puritans such as there might be in the time of Cromwell have started out of their graves': *The Letters of Edward Gibbon*, ed. J.E. Norton (3 vols, London, Cassell 1956), vol. II, p. 243. But there were others, including Horace Walpole, Samuel Romilly, Frederick Reynolds, and more; see McCalman, 'Mad Lord George', pp. 352–4. For Gibbon as a parallel of Burke in more than just recalling the gloomy image of religious and civil strife awakened from the unenlightened sixteenth and seventeenth centuries, see Pocock, 'Gibbon and the Late Enlightenment', p. 155.

23   On Burke's assessment of the Revolution in terms of enthusiasm in general, see J.G.A. Pocock, 'Edmund Burke and the Redefinition of Enthusiasm: the Context as Counter-Revolution', in François Furet and Mona Ozouf (eds), *The Transformation of Political Culture 1789–1848*, The French Revolution and the Creation of Modern Political Culture, 3 (Oxford, Pergamon Press, 1989), 19–43.

24   Burke, *Reflections on the Revolution in France*, in *WS*, vol. VIII, p. 116.

25   For the most complex reference to Gordon, see *WS*, vol. VIII, p. 135. A further link between the Gordon Riots and rational Dissent was provided in Burke's mind by the fact that his political rival, the earl of Shelburne, whom he suspected of having fomented the former, was now, as the marquess of Lansdowne, also a patron of Price and like-minded figures. To the public at large, the relationship Gordon maintained even from prison with leading French reformers and revolutionaries, and the National Assembly's moves to free him, might suggest the same association. Cf. O'Brien, *The Great Melody*, pp. 236, 396; Leslie Mitchell, 'Introduction', in *WS*, vol. VIII, pp. 9 ff.; Albert Goodwin, *The Friends of Liberty: The English Democratic Movement in the Age of the French Revolution* (London, 1973), pp. 101–2; McCalman, 'Mad Lord George', pp. 361–2.

26   Burke, *Reflections*, p. 123.

27   Burke, *Reflections*, p. 128.

28   Burke's thought here again echoes that of Hume, the sceptic: prejudice, like the latter's 'opinion' or 'belief', is rationally unsubstantiated, but nevertheless a firmly held conviction. At the same time, all of this seemed less than fully convincing for a sympathetic but firm sceptic like Edward Gibbon, who wrote of Burke: 'I admire his eloquence, approve of his politics, I adore his chivalry, and I can *almost* excuse his reverence for church establishments' – which to his mind amounted to superstition [author's italics]. But Gibbon immediately added: 'I have sometimes thought of writing a dialogue, in which Lucian, Erasmus and Voltaire should mutually acknowledge the danger of exposing an *old* superstition to the contempt of the blind and fanatic multitude.' Edward Gibbon, *Memoirs of my own Life*, ed. Betty Radice (London, 1984), p. 194.

29   Burke, *Reflections*, p. 160.

30   Burke, *Thoughts on French Affairs* (1791), in *WS*, vol. VIII, pp. 347–8. For other combinations of the idea of enthusiasm and proselytism, see Burke, *Reflections*, pp. 161–2, 192, 197, 202; Burke, *Remarks on the Policy of the Allies* (1793), in *WS*, vol. VIII, p. 477.

31   Burke, *Thoughts on French Affairs*, p. 341.

32   See e.g. ibid., p. 397.

33   The centrality of the concept of conspiracy throughout Burke's career, as an organising

principle of all his pursuits, has been recently emphasised again by Louis Cullan, 'Burke, Ireland, and Revolution', *Eighteenth-Century Life*, 16 (1992), 21–42.

34   Burke, *First Letter on a Regicide Peace*, in *WS*, vol. IX, p. 199.

35   *The Correspondence of George, Prince of Wales*, ed. A. Aspinall (London, 1964), vol. II, p. 98.

36   *Gentleman's Magazine*, August 1797, p. 687.

37   The causes of the initiative, and especially of its bitterness, have not been sufficiently explored. General explanations, such as the crisis of Protestant rationalism, or the relatively weak self-confidence of the *Aufklärung*, are hardly satisfactory. For an overview, see Johannes Rogalla von Bieberstein, *Die These von der Verschwörung 1776–1945* (Bern and Frankfurt, 1976), ch. 1. Aspects of this episode relevant to the present subject are summarised in Schieder and Dipper, 'Propaganda', pp. 71–6.

38   Christian Friedrich Nicolai, *Beschreibung einer Reise durch Deutschland und die Schweiz im Jahre 1781. Nebst Bemerkungen über Belehrsamkeit, Industrie, Religion und Sitten* (Berlin and Stettin, 1783), vol. II, p. 499 n. Translations from German are the author's throughout.

39   Akatholikus Tolerans [i.e., Johann Erich Biester], 'Falsche toleranz einiger Märkischen und Pommerschen Städte in Ansehung der Einräumung der Protestantischen Kirchen zum Katholischen Gottesdienst', *Berlinische Monatsschrift*, 1784, vol. III, p. 190.

40   Johann Friedrich Le Bret, *Magazin zum Gebrauch der Staaten- und Kirchengeschichte*, vol. X (Ulm, 1788), p. 131; [Johann Erich Biester], Preface to Johann Friedrich Le Bret, 'Von den Päpstlichen Missionsanstalten und Vikariaten in protestantischen Ländern', *Berlinische Monatsschrift*, 1793, vols XXI, XXVII. Another characteristic contribution to the torrent of anti-Catholic polemic was the anonymous 'Beitrag zur Geschichte itziger geheimer Proselytenmacherei', *Berlinische Monatsschrift*, 1785, vol. V.

41   Christian Garve, 'Ueber die Besorgnisse der Protestanten in Ansehung der Verbreitung des Katholicismus', *Berlinische Monatsschrift*, 1795, vol. VI, pp. 37–8.

42   Johann August Starck, *Der Triumph der Philosophie im achtzehnten Jahrhundert* (2 vols, Germatown [Frankfurt], 1804). On Starck and the *Eudämonia*, see Frederick C. Beiser, *Enlightenment, Revolution and Romanticism: The Genesis of Modern German Political Thought 1790–1800* (Cambridge, MA, Harvard University Press, 1992), pp. 326–34.

43   Johann August Starck, *Ueber Krypto-Katholicismus, Proselytenmacherei, Jesuitismus, geheime Gesellschaften, und besonders die ihm selbst von dem Verfassern der Berliner Monatsschrift gemachte Beschuldigungen mit Actenstücken belegt* (2 vols, Frankfurt-Leipzig, J.G. Fleischer, 1787), vol. I, p. 1.

44   Starck, *Ueber Krypto-Katholicismus*, vol. I, p. 32. The parallel between Gordon and the authors of the *Berlinische Monatsschrift* is mentioned again on p. 215.

45   Starck, *Ueber Krypto-Katholicismus*, vol. I, pp. 209–10, and vol. II, pp. 314–15.

46   Starck, *Ueber Krypto-Katholicismus*, vol. I, p. 11. For parallels, see Spittler, *Ueber die Geschichte und Verfassung der Jesuiten-Orden*, pp. 84 ff. on the ultimate decision on who is a heretic and a tyrant belonging to the leaders of the order, and Burke, *Reflections*, p. 173 on the peculiar 'he who is not with us is against us' argument of the revolutionaries

47   Starck, *Triumph der Philosophie*, vol. II, p. 526.

48   Friedrich Daniel Schubart, 'Ein allgemeiner Verschwörungsplan', *Vaterlandschronik*, 1790, in *Gesammelte Schriften und Schicksale* (10 vols, repr. Hildesheim, Georg Olras Verlag, 1972), vol. VIII,

p. 250. Camille Desmoulins on the Jacobin Club–Rome analogy is cited in Albert Soboul, *Précis d'histoire de la Révolution française* (Paris, 1962), p. 135.

49   Christoph Girtanner, *Historische Nachrichten und politische Betrachtungen über die französische Revolution* (13 vols, Berlin, F. Unger, 1792–97), vol. III, pp. 470–2.

50   *Denkwürdigkeiten des Generals Dumouriez* (Berlin, Lagarde-Unger, 1794), Preface, p. xxviii; Introduction, pp. iv–lv.

51   For sceptical views of the intellectual community between Burke and Gentz, see Rod Preece, 'Edmund Burke and his European Reception', *The Eighteenth Century*, 21 (1980), 255–73, esp. pp. 264 ff; Beiser, *Enlightenment, Revolution and Romanticism*, pp. 317 ff.

52   See László Kontler, 'The Ancien Régime in Memory and Theory: Edmund Burke and his German Followers', *European Review of History*, 4 (1997), 31–43, esp. pp. 40 ff.

53   *Ueber den Ursprung und Charakter des Krieges gegen die französische Revolution*, in *Ausgewählte Schriften von Friedrich von Gentz*, ed. Wilderich Weich (5 vols, Stuttgart-Leipzig, Rieger, 1837). This is a text which has received relatively little attention from Gentz scholars, even in the excellent monograph of Günther Kronenbitter, *Wort und Macht. Friedrich Gentz als politischer Schriftsteller* (Berlin, Duncker & Humboldt, 1994).

54   Gentz, *Ueber den Ursprung und Charakter*, pp. 192–9.

55   Gentz, *Ueber den Ursprung und Charakter*, pp. 204–8, 230–3.

56   Friedrich von Gentz, *Ueber politische Freiheit und das Verhältniß derselben zur Regierung*, in *Ausgewählte Schriften*, vol. II, esp. pp. 25–9.

57   Quoted from a speech by Camille Desmoulins on 25 December 1791. Gentz, *Ueber den Ursprung und Charakter*, p. 234 n.

58   Gentz, *Ueber den Ursprung*, p. 236.

59   Gentz, *Ueber den Ursprung*, pp. 308–11.

60   Gentz, *Ueber den Ursprung*, p. 317. This is what Burke also has in mind when suggesting that 'out of the tomb of the murdered monarchy of France, has arisen a vast, tremendous, unformed spectre, in a far more terrific guise than any which ever yet have overpowered the imagination, and subdued the fortitude of man': Burke, *First Letter on the Regicide Peace*, in *WS*, vol. IX, pp. 190–1.

61   Gentz, *Ueber den Ursprung und Charakter*, pp. 341, 343. This is the single place where Gentz refers to 'Propaganda' in the restrictive sense of a particular organisation engineering plots in hostile states. He overwhelmingly uses the broader concept of 'propagandism'.

62   Gentz, *Ueber den Ursprung*, pp. 355–7.

7

Forging 'New Frenchmen': State Propaganda in the Rhineland, 1794–1814

Michael Rowe

The study of propaganda, especially of its impact on those at the receiving end, represents a challenge for the historian. The most effective propaganda is that of which people are unaware. Propaganda is not merely the dissemination of lies, in opposition to a well-defined, generally accepted, measurable 'truth'.[1] Furthermore, the cultural and especially linguistic turns in the classical disciplines, embracing also history, make the boundaries of the previously relatively well-defined concept of 'propaganda' increasingly nebulous. Language, and more broadly culture as a whole, are now recognised, more than ever before, as social institutions where conventions are not somehow politically or socially neutral.[2] Since at least the eighteenth century, the relationship between ruler and ruled, propagandist and propagandised, has been one of continuous *two-way* communication rather than static and one-way.[3] Hence the increased importance of examining not only the forms of 'representation' of authority from the perspective of their designers, but also the type of reception by a population often dismissed as essentially passive. This is where the researcher comes against the limitations determined by the sources, not least because the meaning accorded symbols is so closely bound to the narrow context in which they are displayed.

The history of the Rhineland at the turn of the eighteenth and nineteenth centuries offers much for those interested in identity, and in efforts by the state to mould identity through what might be termed propaganda. This was, after all, where and when the term 'propaganda' was first given its modern, secular, political and pejorative meaning, by French *émigrés*, who compared the missionary zeal of their revolutionary foes with the proselytising activities of the Roman curia.[4] For much of their history, the inhabitants of the Rhineland possessed foci of loyalty and reference points that were both local and supra-regional. They lived in a peripheral area located at the heart of the continent, astride the east–west fissure that delineates the boundary between French and German-speaking Europe, and along that great artery that since ancient times connected the Mediterranean to the south with the Low Countries to the north. Supra-regional loyalties to the Catholic church and *Reich* remained peculiarly

strong in the Rhineland, unchallenged as they were by the rise of the sovereign
state. A reminder of these loyalties to universal church and empire survives today
in the form of the two prebendal stools reserved in Cologne cathedral for the
emperor and the Pope. These loose, though wide, loyalties harmonised with and
mutually reinforced points of reference that were of a more parochial nature. It
should be remembered that by 1789 the 1.6 million inhabitants of the Rhineland
found themselves scattered among nearly one hundred territorial entities, some
with populations of a few hundred souls.[5] Small-town civic pride, closed patrician
elites with narrow horizons, and religiously bigoted peasants and guilds, were
among other attributes common to the region, at least if eighteenth-century
travel literature is to be believed.[6] Yet, it was these very factors that made the new
sociability and cosmopolitanism of the Enlightenment so attractive to those
seeking to escape the confinements of provincial life. This new movement freely
crossed the plethora of borders in the Rhineland, something which was quite
natural in an era before the consolidation of the modern nation state, and the
enclosure of humanity into cultural pockets. This would, of course, change after
1789. The outbreak of the French Revolution represented the triumph of
principles contrary to those that underlay the Holy Roman Empire and its
constituent parts. Legitimacy based on historic right clashed head-on with the
absolute demands made in the name of national sovereignty. The need to bridge
the gap – between the absolute demands of the nation state, and the failure of the
people to recognise the legitimacy of those claims – would pose no greater
challenge than on the banks of the Rhine.

The initial revolutionary invasion of the Rhine in 1792 was reversed the
following year, and it took a renewed effort in the autumn of 1794 before *de facto*
French rule was finally established. Even then, no official decision on the
integration of the region with France was taken. This would come only in late
1797. Prior to that point, the occupying revolutionary armies had their hands full
supplying their own needs.[7] They were more concerned with fighting the war
than forming public opinion. Political education and the imposition of cultural
uniformity did not appear on their list of priorities. Indeed, French officials on
the ground were happy to make concessions to old regime particularism if that
helped the supply of the army. It is therefore not surprising to find the Abbé
Grégoire, who had earlier denounced the German language in Alsace-Lorraine
as the language of slaves, justifying the introduction of revolutionary municipal
government to the inhabitants of Mainz by arguing that it conformed to the old
Germanic custom of the *Volk* electing its leaders![8]

The first dose of revolutionary festive culture to reach German soil did so with
the liberty-tree plantings conducted by and for the French army on the Rhine
from 1792 onwards. By that time this ancient symbol had asserted itself as an
emblem of national freedom. The liberty-tree was immediately adopted by
Rhenish supporters of the Revolution, including the 'Clubbists' who set up the

Mainz republic of 1792–3 under French protection. It is estimated that about a hundred such liberty-tree plantings were conducted in the Rhineland until they ceased with the beginning of Napoleonic rule.[9] These and similar events, especially those organised by local radicals, were highly provocative to the rest of the community, which remained overwhelmingly loyal to the old regime.[10] For despite the occasional aping of French revolutionary rhetoric to lend force to their demands for redress from their princes, ordinary Rhinelanders viewed the invasion not so much as liberation, but as a repetition of earlier French visitations, notably under Louis XIV over a century earlier.

The minority of Rhinelanders who supported revolution might preach the language of equality. In reality, they gloried in their role as members of an exclusive, enlightened elite battling amid a sea of fanaticism and stupidity. Home-grown revolutionaries, like the radical Masons besieged in ultra-Catholic Cologne and Aachen, were elitists through and through, equalling if not surpassing Napoleon in this respect. This self-perception as a besieged elite had been reinforced in the years between the French Revolution and the actual invasion, a period when the formerly tolerant and enlightened Rhenish princes reversed their previous policies and clamped down on dissent out of fear of revolution. Censorship was tightened, and reading societies closed down. The isolation of Rhenish radicals at the revolutionary ceremonies following the invasion could only reinforce this siege mentality. The festivities themselves regularly involved the provocative public burning of insignia representing the old regime – electoral caps, episcopal staffs, and so forth – and speeches attacking the former princes and electors, and the Catholic church. The focal point for most of these celebrations were national altars, erected in the main town squares, and decorated with classical symbols such as fasces and statues of Hercules to denote strength, or with offerings to such historic figures as Demosthenes, Cicero, Franklin and Rousseau.

This festive culture reached a far wider audience than merely those present through popular almanacs, pamphlets, fly-sheets and prints. On the whole, the old regime governments in exile proved extremely reluctant to sanction their own propaganda campaigns, trusting instead that their subjects would see through Republican assertions.[11] Despite this, satirical representations of celebrations around the liberty-tree became a staple of anti-revolutionary propaganda on the Rhine. Much of this material was smuggled in from across the river. It reinterpreted the symbolism of the liberty-tree, by pointing, for example, to its lack of roots – many liberty-trees were little more than poles – and underlining the fact that the liberty-cap stuck on top of these trees lacked a head, let alone a brain.[12] Pro-revolutionary prints and paintings of these, and later Republican ceremonies, showed French soldiers and Rhinelanders of all classes fraternising, and symbols of liberty surrounded by dancing women. Anti-revolutionary reproductions showed the exact opposite: symbols of liberty surrounded by troops with fixed bayonets, and the ordinary people either largely absent, or kept at a distance.[13] The liberty-tree phase of festive culture came to an end with a last wave of plantings in early 1798, an officially sponsored effort designed to demonstrate popular support for annexation to France, but which showed the exact opposite.

Plans for the long-term education of the 'new Frenchmen' of the Rhine only made any sense following the policy decision to annex the region, which was taken in late 1797. In the following January, Lambrechts, the minister of justice, who was now responsible for the region, sent a memorandum to the senior commissioner in Mainz, Rudler, outlining the government's educational policies. Ignorance, he wrote, always accompanies servitude, and enlightenment must always precede conferment of the benefits of liberty. This was especially true in the Rhineland, which had been crushed for centuries by 'fanaticism' and 'tyranny'. People would be liberated from this yoke by the spread of French. This would facilitate rapid communication between natives and Frenchmen, which in turn would result in the former being inculcated with a knowledge of both their rights and duties. The provision of French teaching in schools, the minister continued, was a necessity, though it would only bear fruit in the long term. It is interesting that public festivals were included in this document concerned with education policy. In fact, the minister seized upon festivals devoted to the 'love of republican virtues' – *fêtes patriotiques* – as being especially influential and effective in the short term in leaving strong impressions and profound memories. Within France itself, he wrote, their influence during the course of the Revolution had been 'remarkable'.[14] The minister of course ignored the fact that such festivals, even within France itself, never overcame the inherent tension between the need to create the illusion of spontaneity and the reality of careful preplanning and organisation.[15] This tension was even more extreme in the Rhineland, where it was reinforced by the inherent contradiction between the rigours of occupation and rhetoric of liberation.[16] This last contradiction was made painfully apparent in the discussion about whether to celebrate the festival of the sovereignty of the people in the Rhineland on 20 March 1798. This celebration was to have as its theme the right of French citizens to vote in elections. Rhinelanders, however, did not enjoy the rights of citizenship at this stage, so the authorities eventually decided to authorise only a modified version of this festivity in the occupied region.[17]

On 26 April 1798, several months after the policy decision to proceed with the administrative integration of the Rhineland into France, commissioner Rudler introduced to the region the fest-cycle then current in France itself, as laid down in the law of 3 Brumaire IV (25 October 1795). In his instructions to subaltern Rhenish officials, Rudler wrote: 'The French Republic, in order to remind man of his dignity, orders the annual celebration of solemn festivities throughout the breadth of its territory; these take their name from the most beautiful and useful of virtues, or from the principal events of our Revolution.' The decree itself, which dealt primarily with education – public festivities only came under section six – ordained seven national festivities: the foundation of the Republic (22 September); the festival of youth (30 March); the festival of married couples (29 April); the day of gratitude (29 May); the day of agriculture (28 June); the day of liberty (marking the fall of Robespierre, on 27–8 July); and the festival of the aged (27 August). The decree stated that all these festivals should be marked by patriotic songs, moralising speeches, fraternal banquets, and public games that were 'appropriate to each locality'. Rudler, interestingly, also stressed the need for economy, a noteworthy contrast to Napoleon's later observation that it was worse to stage a festival on the cheap than none at all.[18] French and radical native officials in the ultra-Catholic Rhineland viewed festivities as a means of substituting the exuberant displays of baroque religiosity that so dominated the cultural life of the region under the old regime. For example, the commissioner for the northern Roër department, Dorsch, a revolutionary ex-priest, wrote, in March 1798: 'Religious charlatans [priests] are only successful and triumphant for so long as they master the sensations of the people, and it will be easy to attach them firmly to the republican regime through national festivities.'[19] Dorsch repeated these observations in a letter to Lambrechts the following month in which he stated that festivals were necessary to replace suppressed religious processions and other *farces religieuses*, because 'the imagination of the people needs to be occupied' and the 'void needs to be filled'.[20] The fact that Republican festivities were increasingly held in churches requisitioned for the purpose further demonstrated their ersatz religious function.

One of the first festivals celebrated following Rudler's decree was that of married couples, on 29 April 1798. In Aachen, the day was pealed in by church bells from five o'clock onwards. At ten a festive procession including the oldest couple in the city and twenty-four virgins dressed in white was received at the town hall. The procession then moved on, accompanied by the local garrison, administration and municipality, and local radicals arm-in-arm, to the nearby altar of freedom. In Bonn, the participants in the day's events were confined to school children, local radicals, officials and the military; again, the mass of the population was absent. In Cologne, a more blatant attack on the prerogatives of the church was conducted in the form of public, festive civil marriage ceremonies.[21] Other festivities were equally provocative and divisive. A special one-off which was accorded much prominence in the Rhineland, the commemoration of the murder of French delegates at the Rastatt Congress by Austrian cavalry in April 1799, caused particular controversy in the largely pro-Habsburg region.

The same was true of the revolutionary calendar, extended to the Rhineland on 19 July 1798. This replaced the seven-day week with the ten-day week, and at a stroke abolished Sundays, all other religious holidays, and market days, introducing in their stead 'decade days', and the five (or six in a leap year) 'supplementary days' left over following the division of the year into twelve thirty-day months. Its very scope and radicalism made it virtually impossible to enforce this calendar, except among native officials employed by the administration. What could the authorities do to stop ordinary people ostentatiously sweeping the streets on Saturday evenings, or wearing their Sunday best the following day? Rudler advised Paris of the futility of trying to impose 'decade-holidays' because of the continued influence of the clergy, which needed to be broken before *mentalités* might be changed. The government subsequently gave up the attempt to impose the revolutionary calendar, so as not to further antagonise opinion following the outbreak of the War of the Second Coalition.[22] Revolutionary festivals in general in the pre-Napoleonic phase tended only to illustrate all the more dramatically the ideological gulf that separated the mass of the native population from the French administration and its local supporters. Yet even before Napoleon came to power, the French were beginning to learn that relying upon the small elite of native revolutionaries, whom the military in any case viewed as unrepresentative troublemakers, would not prove a sufficient basis on which to found their rule in the Rhineland.

Napoleon's coup of 18 Brumaire Year VIII brought to an end the political instability of the revolutionary decade. The one theme that dominated all official propaganda in the Rhineland thereafter was that of restoration: the restoration of order, of religion, of legitimate administration, of civic pride, even of universal empire.[23] Politically divisive ceremonies fell out of favour. Napoleon wanted 'only those festivals retained which belonged to periods when public opinion was unanimous'.[24] The authorities quietly removed liberty-trees from the Rhenish towns where they had created most offence.[25] Revolutionary rhetoric was toned down in all public pronouncements. Though the administrative structures that were now introduced were marked by uniformity to a greater extent than ever before, propaganda itself was targeted to local conditions, and therefore much more effective than previously. For example, in 1805 the interior minister received instructions to authorise celebrations that were in keeping with the customs of each *pays*.[26] This decentralised, targeted aspect of Napoleonic propaganda is often lost in general accounts, which either focus on the imperial personality cult as applied to the empire as a whole, or on studies which concentrate on the outer reaches of the empire, where the gap between the official, enlightened culture and that of the localities was well nigh unbridgeable. In these peripheries – along the Dalmatian coast, for example – one well understands the fears entertained by Napoleonic officials, besieged in their administrative seats, of the 'irrational' comportment of the mass of natives, whose cultural diversities they only studied, if at all, with a mixture of contempt and curiosity.[27]

The Rhineland fell into a somewhat different category, and provided rich seams of historical and local cultural material which the French might excavate for the construction of an image for the new regime. Napoleon, unlike his revolutionary predecessors, felt few inhibitions in associating himself with the essentially clerical and monarchical traditions of the old regime. Thus, when he visited the former Hohenzollern city of Cleves in 1804, he felt no compunction in publicly drinking a toast to the king of Prussia – with whom he would be at war only two years later – and consenting that the main street in the town regain its old name, *Königsstrasse* ('King's Street').[28] The enlightened prince-bishops, the threat of whose return had been banished forever, and who had provided an early target for revolutionary vitriol, could now be safely praised for their reforming zeal.[29] Napoleon also actively rehabilitated the ancient past in order to legitimise himself; and the Rhineland offered plenty of relics which he could safely draw upon, both to emphasise his respect for local, civic traditions, and to bind these with his self-portrayal as a successor of the Roman caesars and Carolingian emperors.

A new official interest was shown for the preservation of significant historical monuments. In 1804, during his visit to Trier, Napoleon himself symbolically ordered the removal of non-Roman accretions that had built up over the centuries around the famous Porta Nigra.[30] His prefects participated in setting up *sociétés d'émulation* in Rhenish cities as a means of both furthering integration between Rhinelanders and Frenchmen, and demonstrating official concern for the preservation and investigation of local history and culture. Some of these societies survived Napoleonic rule, and indeed a few are still in existence.[31] Equally symbolic, Napoleon made good some of the cultural vandalism inflicted by the revolutionaries in the 1790s, when Paris had sent in special commissions to extract trophies.[32] Napoleon subsequently restored much of this cultural material. The statue of Charlemagne, stolen by the revolutionary armies, was returned to Aachen in 1804.[33] The Magi were restored to Cologne, amidst equal popular jubilation.[34] Most spectacularly of all, in 1810 Napoleon ordered the return of the Shrine of the Holy Rock from Augsburg to Trier. In an impressive display of baroque piety, 200,000 pilgrims visited the shrine when it was put on show in September of that year.[35]

Official ceremonies, meanwhile, became less specifically French, and more Napoleonic interpretations of Roman, Carolingian and even Germanic traditions.[36] To a degree, this reflected the changing nature of the expanding empire. The centre of power, Napoleon's court, itself took on a more 'European' or 'imperial' flavour following the emperor's marriage to an Austrian princess, Marie-Louise, in 1810, much to the chagrin of the 'national' party.[37] In March the following year, Napoleon declared to the committee responsible for ecclesiastical affairs: 'The present epoch carries us back to the time of Charlemagne. All the kingdoms, principalities and duchies which formed themselves out of the debris of the empire have been rejuvenated under our laws. The church of my empire is the church of the Occident and of almost the whole of Christendom.' Napoleon also declared Rome 'the second city of the empire' following its annexation to the French empire, and stipulated that his successors should be crowned in that city within ten years of their coronation in Paris.[38]

Napoleon was a complete agnostic when it came to nationalism. Influenced more by the ideology of enlightened cosmopolitanism, he was nonetheless prepared to use nationalism where it suited him, notably in Poland. The French nation was merely a tool that allowed him to fulfil his destiny, which of course was never defined. It seems doubtful that the idea of an imperial revival, of Napoleon as 'Charlemagne II', had much of an impact on the Rhineland. His marriage to Marie-Louise was undoubtedly a propaganda triumph in the mainly Catholic region, which was traditionally pro-Habsburg. Symbols of the empire conceivably reinforced the legitimacy of the regime; at the very least, they did little harm. However, it should be remembered that old Rhenish attachments to the *Reich* were motivated less by abstract notions of universal empire and more by the protection afforded by imperial institutions, notably imperial law and the imperial courts, against the pretensions of the more powerful German princes and, latterly, revolutionary France. In short, Rhinelanders recognised in these institutions a defence against the demanding sovereign state. Napoleon's empire, on the other hand, was a continuation of the most demanding state the world had yet seen. Hence the Rhenish lack of interest in his vision of a neo-Carolingian empire. Of greater concern to them was the degree of autonomy they might preserve within the new French structures. French law itself, rather than dreams of empire, would prove more fruitful in this respect.

Napoleonic ceremonies also bore all the hallmarks Mona Ozouf ascribes to 'aristocratic' festivities, in that participants and audience were carefully segregated, enclosed and isolated.[39] The common people were carefully kept at bay by cordons of soldiers, and could do little but gape at the proceedings through a forest of bayonets. Their presence was nonetheless necessary, for it symbolised the second part of the Abbé Sieyès' dictum that 'authority comes from above, and confidence from below'.[40] The proceedings themselves impressed the first part through, among other things, the prominent position accorded all public officials on such occasions, the splendour of their uniforms, and the honour guards who escorted them. This was nothing less than the sacralisation of the state, a process that found its culmination in the introduction of the imperial catechism in 1806. The Catholic church, which knew how to put on a good show, was now always involved in official ceremonies. For propaganda, to be really effective, needs to be total, all encompassing, and leave no gaps.[41] This was clearly beyond the capabilities of the pre-twentieth-century state. The revolutionaries, with their calendar, aspired to totality but failed. All that survived were the individual revolutionary festivities, which were merely episodic, not total. They served only to illustrate the isolation of the new regime, both in time and space. Rhenish radicals might rejoice in this state of affairs. The French government, and especially Napoleon, did not. Hence the importance of enlisting the support of the church, or rather, grafting government propaganda on top of it. It – the church – would fill the gaps. In addition, a tightening of press censorship – for which a new 'division for press liberty' within the police ministry was set up – made alternative interpretations of the new official Napoleonic *Festkultur* difficult to publicise.

Involvement of the church also made ridicule by the regime's opponents less easy, unless they were prepared to run the risk of ridiculing the church at the same time. By 1805 it was even appropriate for leading French officials to have their own reserved pews in church.[42] Atheistic vestiges such as the revolutionary calendar were soon abolished (1 January 1806), and a new festive cycle instituted around a cult of personality centred on Napoleon himself. A deliberate attempt was made to graft this on to the religious cycle, thereby associating the new state religion with the baroque piety that both the French revolutionaries and enlightened Rhenish prince-bishops had failed to stamp out. Thus, the Assumption of the Virgin on 15 August was declared a national holiday, as the day of St Napoleon, an obscure figure dug up from the Middle Ages, and whose feast day was shifted to a more prominent place on the calendar. The other most important day in the new cycle was the first Sunday of December, which commemorated both Napoleon's coronation on 2 December 1804, and the battle of Austerlitz, which had conveniently been won exactly one year later.

The official thinking behind these new imperial festivities was revealed by Portalis, Napoleon's minister of ecclesiastical affairs, in his memorandum of February 1806. He wrote:

> . . . periodic, national solemnities represent imperishable monuments. Linked to the seasonal and annual cycle, they connect great earthly events to the inalterable course of the heavens: they are living representations of events of ancient times; they make them contemporary to every age, and the nation draws strength and power from these institutions; they have the advantage over dead inscriptions, as has the present over the past.

Portalis drew the logical conclusion from these observations by stating that civil ceremonies were 'nothing' – '[ils] ne sont rien' – if they were not 'attached' to religious ceremonies. Only this would connect earthly events with heaven, and provide a mysterious and subliminal character to state occasions. The 15 August, or St Napoleon day, represented for Portalis peace between church and state, as established in the Concordat. France, founded upon a new moral and Christian order, was now at peace with itself; 'a new organisation for the entire rejuvenated social order, which though re-established upon its ancient foundations has been reinvigorated by a new spirit and by new forms: in a word, it [the feast of St Napoleon] will be destined to perpetuate the memory of our domestic regeneration'. Meanwhile, the second annual public feast day, on 2 December, would mark the French victory over 'northern barbarism' at the battle of Austerlitz in 1805.[43] In addition to these two festivals, one-off celebrations, usually culminating in *Te Deums* in church, marked later Napoleonic victories, or dynastic occurrences such as the birth and later baptism of the king of Rome.

Napoleon personally took public ceremonial as a form of propaganda extremely seriously. He was determined that it should not show up political divisions within society. Instead, his regime made efforts to graft the official ideology of the state and empire on to the local, civic, religious and historical traditions that still remained the focus of loyalty for the vast majority. Still, such festivities, however manipulative and well managed, always presented a risk. They might be ridiculed, deliberately misinterpreted, or else simply present a risk to public order through the large number of people they attracted. Alternately, and equally damagingly, they might face a boycott. This last problem also occurred with the officially sanctioned press, which was so heavily censored (Napoleon once stated that if he allowed the press a completely free rein, he would be out of power within three months) and so obviously propagandised that fewer and fewer people were prepared to subscribe.[44] The solution to the threat of boycotts of festivities was to involve the church, remove repulsive political and divisive ideological elements, and to transform them instead into colourful, entertaining events. Indeed, they were advertised as such in officially approved broadsheets: '*Il y aura Spectacle, gratis*' ('there will be a spectacle, *for free*'), as the solemn installation of one Rhenish prefect was billed beforehand.[45]

The revolutionaries had been far more ambitious than Napoleon. Whereas they attempted to create something new, he simply restored. The last thing Napoleon wanted was popular mobilisation of the kind aimed at by what Jacques Ellul has termed 'agitational' propaganda. The revolutionary decade showed where that might lead. Far from wishing to break the psychological patterns of habit, belief and judgement, Napoleon aimed at reinforcing them through 'integrational' propaganda and social healing.[46] Napoleon's cynical remarks about religion as the basis of social order, and the fact that without it the poor would turn into highway robbers, are the best illustration of this, and of his Machiavellian instrumentalisation of the Catholic church to achieve this end. For religion allowed the unfortunate to rationalise their miserable position, while at the same time holding out the hope of equality in the life to come.

Apart from his more limited objectives, Napoleon was fortunate in that he could build upon the preponderance of French culture among elites in eighteenth-century Europe.[47] One might compare this with Ellul's 'sociological' propaganda, 'the penetration of an ideology by means of its sociological context', something which informed lifestyle rather than merely opinion, and which one might describe as the preparation of soil for the sowing of 'direct' propaganda.[48]

In particular, the sociability and enlightened ethos of the late eighteenth century provided tools that Napoleon subsequently employed throughout much of Europe. The Rhineland too had witnessed a proliferation of this culture, as represented by the Masonic lodges and reading clubs, in the final decades of the old regime. The vast majority of these societies dedicated themselves to the propagation of useful knowledge and combating superstition rather than in engaging in overt, radical politics. They met the craving for news – *Lesesucht* – which was on the increase from the 1770s and 1780s onwards. Rhenish Masonic societies, some of which had been affiliated to the Grand Orient in Paris *before* 1789, proved rich in potential as tools for the integration of the Rhineland into France.[49] Napoleon posed as the restorer of Masonic harmony following prior revolutionary disruption. His patronage of Masonry gave its members, especially those of *petit-bourgeois* background, a sense of being favoured children within the Napoleonic system.[50] Within their lodges they might mingle on supposedly equal terms with French prefects and other leading officials, while these in turn spread government propaganda and rumours – as set out by the minister of the interior in weekly circulars – in a seemingly relaxed atmosphere.[51] From 1805 onwards, the government ordered meetings of Masonic lodges to open and close with a triple cry, '*Vive Napoléon le Grand et son auguste famille*'.[52] French Masonic imperialism eventually extended into the German satellite states, along with French military power. Lodges in these states were subordinated to the Grand Orient in Paris, and links with rival mother lodges, notably those in Berlin, were cut.[53] France, according to the official Napoleonic world view, was the sole repository of enlightenment, and the enlightened always supported Napoleon. The enemies of France, on the other hand, were condemned as purely destructive, and denounced either as religious 'fanatics', or, more bizarrely, as revolutionary, as for example when Britain was accused of pursuing 'Jacobinism' on the high seas.[54]

Following his defeat in Russia in 1812, these 'unenlightened' forces began closing in on Napoleon. In January 1814 allied forces crossed the Rhine. Thus ended the two decades of French rule on the left bank. Prussian reformers, who dominated the provisional allied administration in the Rhineland, seized their opportunity to 'renationalise' – or 'revolutionise', according to Napoleonic propaganda – the region. In this they relied primarily upon the press, and on leading German nationalist writers, such as Ernst Moritz Arndt and Joseph Görres, whom they enlisted in support. They also recognised the potential of public festivities. Among the first to be celebrated were those commemorating the allied capture of Paris on 31 March 1814. To mark the event in Cologne, the Prussian authorities, like the French before them, paraded the old city banner in a conscious attempt to link civic traditions with their own cause.[55] Later that year, on 18 October, larger festivities throughout Germany, including the Rhineland, marked the anniversary of the destruction of Napoleonic power in Central

Europe at the battle of Leipzig. On this occasion spectacular nocturnal illuminations lit up the night sky, symbolising German unity, while church services were offered in thanksgiving for deliverance from the ogre.[56] The anti-Napoleonic flavour of state festivities continued in following years, which was hardly surprising given the fact that the legitimacy of Prussian rule on the Rhine derived from its role as defender of Germany's western marches. Shortly after Prussia's annexation of the Rhineland in April 1815, therefore, Berlin instituted its own cycle of annual national holidays, or '*vaterländische Festtage*', commemorating the battle of Leipzig (18 October), the capture of Paris (31 March) and the battle of Belle-Alliance (or Waterloo, 18 June).[57]

In conclusion, one might seek the elusive answer to the question posed in the introduction: how were official festivities received by the Rhenish population? The answer is easier to supply for the first, revolutionary, period of French rule, in the 1790s. Official reports from a variety of sources, together with the contemporary observations of private individuals, generally indicate that the official, revolutionary festivities met with near-universal popular hostility. The mass of the population was excluded from these events, which were confined to the French army and the minority of radicals. Contemporary paintings and prints of these affairs usually show the mass of the population kept well away from the central proceedings, more often than not confined to the windows of the houses overlooking the open spaces in which they were performed.[58] The new festive cycle that followed in 1798, and which included a completely new calendar, was simply not observed. In addition, liberty-trees were hacked down and Republican symbols desecrated. Ceremonies organised by the French and their supporters became the subject of ridicule in subversive pamphlets and in foreign newspaper reports smuggled in from across the Rhine. Above all, people resisted through publicly adhering to the old, Christian calendar and its holidays. They laid down their tools on Sundays, and other abolished holidays, and ostentatiously wore their best clothes; and there was little the government could do about this. Frontal attacks against accepted opinions are generally doomed to failure, for propaganda cannot be created out of nothing. Revolutionary propaganda, with its rhetoric of liberation and fraternity, stood too far removed from reality, which in the Rhineland from 1792 to 1800 consisted of military occupation by close to two hundred thousand under-supplied troops who lived off a civilian population of 1.6 million. The sight of French soldiers defecating into tabernacles and abusing statues of the Virgin Mary challenged in the most brutal and stark way possible the deeply ingrained beliefs of the vast majority of Rhinelanders. As Ellul writes: 'We can conclude from a large body of experience that the propagandist cannot go contrary to what is in an individual; he cannot create just any new psychological mechanism or obtain just any decision or action.'[59]

Napoleon's objectives were ultimately more limited than his revolutionary predecessors, as the importance of Rhenish public opinion to the new regime was diminished following the Peace of Lunéville and the stabilisation of French rule on the Rhine. Napoleon's wars would be fought elsewhere in Europe. The Rhineland entered a period of relative peace and security. Conflict between church and state ended, for the time being, with the Concordat, which was published in 1802. Thanks to this relatively secure position, Napoleon and his prefects could afford to tolerate a measure of nostalgia for the old regime in a way the besieged revolutionaries could not.[60] This relative tolerance should not be interpreted as indifference, however, for Napoleon demonstrated a keen interest in public opinion. He once stated: 'Power is based upon opinion. What is a government not supported by opinion? Nothing.'[61] The Napoleonic method of government aimed at creating institutions such as councils, chambers of commerce and electoral colleges where 'useful' opinion might express itself, though in a way that did not endanger the existing social and political order. Such institutions, of course, were reserved for the elites, the so-called 'notables' who alone had 'useful' opinions to offer. The wider public had to make do with a more passive role at festivities. The fact that the public reaction to these festivities is so hard to discern is in itself indicative of their success, at least from Napoleon's point of view. Bonapartism was, after all, largely about the depoliticisation of society, and the neutralisation of the factionalism and conflict of the 1790s. Much of this had been centred on controversial revolutionary festivities, each regime introducing a new cycle providing its own interpretation of the Revolution itself. Napoleon ended this practice, introducing in its stead his own cult with its attendant feast days. Furthermore, Napoleon, in restoring the Gregorian calendar, and in grafting many state festivities on to those of the church, removed the most effective means that opponents of his regime had to publicly display their opposition. Instead, festivities were transformed into free entertainment, devoid of ideological content. Attendance at such events provides little evidence for either support or opposition to the regime. That met the limited requirements of the new regime.

Paradoxically, Napoleonic propaganda proved most effective in the Rhineland in the long term. As people looked back with fading memories, in the decades following the end of French rule, they tended to forget such negative aspects as high taxation and conscription, and instead focused on the festive, carnivalesque features of the Napoleonic episode: on the splendid uniforms, the cannon fire, church bells and martial music that accompanied official ceremonies. Such memories were significant, in that they recalled events that provided a direct contrast to the rather dour Prussians, who had succeeded the French as masters in the Rhineland, and who explicitly contrasted the sobriety of their own festivals with the frivolity of the French. Rhinelanders who opposed Prussian rule needed a counter-culture that was both provocative, immediately recognisable and readily available. Symbols such as the *Marseillaise* and tricolour flags proved ideal. In the longer term, therefore, French propaganda made its mark.

Notes

1   Jacques Ellul, *Propaganda: The Formation of Men's Attitudes*, translated from the French by Konrad Kellen and Jean Lerner, with an introduction by Konrad Kellen (New York, Knopf, 1968), p. x.

2   Peter Burke, 'Introduction', in Peter Burke and Roy Porter (eds), *The Social History of Language* (Cambridge University Press, 1987), pp. 1–20.

3   For the eighteenth century, see Andreas Gestrich, *Absolutismus und Öffentlichkeit. Politische Kommunikation in Deutschland zu Beginn des 18. Jahrhunderts* (Göttingen, Vandenhoeck & Ruprecht, 1994). For the older paradigm see Jürgen Habermas, *The Structural Transformation of the Public Sphere: An Inquiry into a Category of Bourgeois Society*, translated by Thomas Burger (Cambridge, Polity, 1989).

4   Wolfgang Schieder and Christof Dipper, 'Propaganda', in Otto Brunner, Werner Conze and Reinhart Koselleck (eds), *Geschichtliche Grundbegriffe: historisches Lexikon zur politisch-sozialen Sprache in Deutschland* (8 vols, Stuttgart, Klett, 1972–97), vol. 5, pp. 77–82.

5   Wilhelm Fabricius, *Erläuterungen zum geschichtlichen Atlas der Rheinprovinz*, vol. 2: *Die Karte von 1789. Einteilung und Entwicklung der Territorien von 1600–1794* (Bonn, Publikationen der Gesellschaft für Rheinische Geschichtskunde, 1898); Franz Irsigler, *Herrschaftsgebiete im Jahre 1789* (Cologne, Rheinland Verlag, 1982).

6   Uwe Hentschel, 'Revolutionserlebnis und Deutschlandbild', *Zeitschrift für historische Forschung*, 20 (1993), 321–44.

7   T.C.W. Blanning, *The French Revolution in Germany: Occupation and Resistance in the Rhineland* (Oxford, Clarendon Press, 1983).

8   Justus Hashagen, *Das Rheinland und die französische Herrschaft. Beiträge zur Characteristik ihres Gegensatzes* (Bonn, P. Hanstein, 1908), p. 188. For an excellent recent account of French cultural policies in neighbouring Alsace-Lorraine, see David A. Bell, 'Nation-Building and Cultural Particularism in Eighteenth-Century France: The Case of Alsace', *Eighteenth-Century Studies*, 21 (1988), 472–90.

9   Wolfgang Hans Stein, 'Die Ikonographie der rheinischen Revolutionsfeste', *Jahrbuch für westdeutsche Landesgeschichte*, 15 (1989), 190–5.

10   Especially provocative were celebrations marking the execution of Louis XVI, held on 21 January. Joseph Hansen, *Quellen zur Geschichte des Rheinlandes im Zeitalter der französischen Revolution 1780–1801* (4 vols, Bonn, P. Hanstein, 1931–8), vol. 4, pp. 516–18.

11   Hansgeorg Molitor, *Vom Untertan zum Administré. Studien zur französischen Herrschaft und zum Verhalten der Bevölkerung im Rhein-Mosel-Raum von den Revolutionskriegen bis zum Ende der napoleonischen Zeit* (Wiesbaden, Steiner, 1980), pp. 104–7.

12   Stein, 'Ikonographie', pp. 194–202.

13   Stein, 'Ikonographie', pp. 201–12.

14   Lambrechts (minister of justice) to Rudler (government commissioner for the Rhineland), 14 Jan. 1798. Hansen, *Quellen*, vol. 4, pp. 503–5.

15   Mona Ozouf, *Festivals and the French Revolution* (Cambridge, MA, Harvard University Press, 1988), *passim*.

16   Stein, 'Ikonographie', p. 190.

17   Hansen, *Quellen*, vol. 4, pp. 619–29.

18   Hansen, *Quellen*, vol. 4, pp. 642–4. For Napoleon's comment on public festivals, see Robert B. Holtman, *Napoleonic Propaganda* (Baton Rouge, Louisiana State University Press, 1950), p. 110.

19   Hansen, *Quellen*, vol. 4, p. 619.

20   Hansen, *Quellen*, vol. 4, p. 653, n. 2.

21   Hansen, *Quellen*, vol. 4, pp. 822–5.

22   Blanning, *Revolution*, pp. 225–6.

23   Representative of a larger number of examples from the Rhineland is the public speech of the garrison commander of Aachen on the first Bastille Day following Brumaire (Archives Nationales, Paris (AN), F¹ᶜIII Roër 4, dossier 1, nos 92–3), and the speeches delivered on the occasion of the installation of Cologne's former *Bürgermeister*, Johann Jacob von Wittgenstein, as *maire* in August 1803 (Historisches Archiv der Stadt Köln (HASK), Bestand 1123, carton 22, dossier 'Französische Ehrenlegion betreffend').

24   Holtman, *Propaganda*, p. 106.

25   Hansen, *Quellen*, vol. 4, p. 1260, n. 3.

26   Holtman, *Propaganda*, p. 109.

27   Stuart Woolf, 'French Civilisation and Ethnicity in the Napoleonic Empire', *Past and Present*, 124 (1989), 96–120.

28   Hashagen, *Rheinland*, p. 109.

29   Molitor, *Untertan*, p. 177.

30   Eva Brües, *Die Rheinlande. Unter Verwendung des von Ehler W. Grashoff gesammelten Materials* (Munich, Deutsche Kunstverlag, 1968), p. 412.

31   Klaus Pabst, 'Bildungs- und Kulturpolitik der Franzosen im Rheinland zwischen 1794 und 1814', in Peter Hüttenberger and Hansgeorg Molitor (eds), *Franzosen und Deutsche am Rhein 1789–1918–1945* (Essen, Klartext, 1989), p. 195.

32   Ferdinand Boyer, 'Les Conquêtes Scientifiques de la Convention en Belgique et dans les Pays Rhénans (1794–1795)', *Revue d'histoire moderne et contemporaine*, 18 (1971), 366–7.

33   Pabst, 'Bildungs- und Kulturpolitik', p. 196.

34   HASK, FV 2058, no. 18. See also Eduard Hegel, *Das Erzbistum Köln zwischen Barock und Aufklärung vom Pfälzischen Krieg bis zum Ende der französischen Zeit 1688–1814* (Cologne, Bachem, 1979), p. 513.

35   Elisabeth Wagner, 'Revolution, Religiosität und Kirchen im Rheinland um 1800', in Peter Hüttenberger and Hansgeorg Molitor, *Französen und Deutsche am Rhein 1789–1918–1945* (Essen, Klartext, 1989), p. 284.

36   Hashagen, *Rheinland*, pp. 191–5.

37   Philip Mansel, *The Court of France 1789–1830* (Cambridge University Press, 1988), pp. 57–69.

38   Hans Kohn, *Prelude to Nation-States: The French and German Experience, 1789–1815* (Princeton, Van Nostrand, 1969), pp. 94–6, 102–5.

39   Ozouf, *Festivals*, p. 128.

40   Jean-Denis Bredin, *Sieyès. La clé de la Révolution française* (Paris, Éditions de Fallois, 1988), p. 469.

41   Ellul, *Propaganda*, pp. 9 ff, 17.

42   Karl-Georg Faber, *Andreas van Recum 1765–1828. Ein rheinischer Kosmopolit* (Bonn, Röhrscheid, 1969), p. 195.

43   A copy of Portalis' memorandum was circulated in the Roër department, for the benefit of local officials, in the official journal of the prefecture, the *Recueil des actes de la préfecture de la Roër* (Aachen, 1806), pp. 414–16.

44   Hansgeorg Molitor, 'Zensur, Propaganda und Überwachung zwischen 1780 und 1815 im mittleren Rheinland', in *Vom alten Reich zu neuer Staatlichkeit: Alzeyer Kollequium: Kontinuität und Wandel im Gefolge der Französischen Revolution am Mittelrhein* (Wiesbaden, Steiner, 1982), pp. 30–4.

45   Stadtarchiv Aachen (StAA), Bestand RA Allgemeine Akten, 552, no. 10.

46   Ellul, *Propaganda*, pp. 70–9.

47   Jean Tulard, *Le Grand Empire, 1804–1815* (Paris, A. Michel, 1982), pp. 13–16.

48   Ellul, *Propaganda*, pp. 15, 30, 62–70.

49   Winfried Dotzauer, *Freimaurergesellschaften am Rhein. Aufgeklärte Sozietäten auf dem linken Rheinufer vom Ausgang des Ancien Régime bis zum Ende der napoleonischen Herrschaft* (Wiesbaden, Steiner, 1977), p. 235.

50   Dotzauer, *Freimaurergesellschaften am Rhein*, p. 237.

51   Dotzauer, *Freimaurergesellschaften am Rhein*, pp. 199–201.

52   Holtman, *Propaganda*, p. 116.

53   Heinz Gürtler, *Deutsche Freimaurer im Dienste napoleonischer Politik: die Freimaurer im Königreich Westfalen 1807–1813* (Struckum, Verl. für Ganzheitl. Forschung u. Kultur, 1988).

54   Holtman, *Propaganda*, pp. 25–6, 30.

55   *Kölnische Zeitung* (19/04/1814).

56   *Kölnische Zeitung* (18/10/, 20/10/, 25/10/, 27/10/, 29/10/, 3/11/, 5/11/1814); *Rheinischer Merkur* (21/10/, 27/10/, 16/11/, 22/11/1814).

57   *Amtsblatt der Regierung zu Aachen* (Aachen, 1816), pp. 304–5. For the development of official festivities in the Prussian Rhineland up until the end of the First World War, see Ute Schneider, *Politische Festkultur im 19. Jahrhundert. Die Rheinprovinz von der französischen Zeit bis zum Ende des Ersten Weltkrieges* (1806–1918) (Essen, Klartext, 1995).

58   Stein, 'Ikonographie', pp. 201–12.

59   Ellul, *Propaganda*, p. 33.

60   Molitor, *Untertan*, pp. 176–7.

61   Ellul, *Propaganda*, p. 123.

8

SELLING BONAPARTISM OR SIMPLY SELLING COPIES? THE NAPOLEONIC LEGEND AND POPULAR ALMANACS

Geoff Watkins

In his studies of Napoleonic propaganda, Robert Holtman suggests that propaganda should be understood as the expression of only one side of an argument, in order to create a desired response from the target recipients and to affect their attitudes in a predetermined manner.[1] This is undoubtedly appropriate to the subject of Holtman's own analysis, the dissemination of propaganda by Napoleon I himself. From the early stages of his career as commander of the army of Italy, Bonaparte had used newspapers and *bulletins du jour* to present a highly favourable version of his achievements, and this practice was extended after he came to power to embrace a wide range of media, including the press, painting and engraving, theatre and education.[2]

It is by no means so clear, however, that this remains an appropriate definition for the way the Napoleonic legend exerted a political influence after the death of the emperor, particularly in contributing to the success of his nephew and self-proclaimed heir, Louis-Napoleon. Holtman's definition includes a sense of clear and deliberate purpose on the part of the producers of propagandistic material. This is applicable to much that was produced by Louis-Napoleon and his supporters, as we shall see, but it does not take into account large amounts of material which did not have the promotion of his political career as its motive, but which nevertheless did without doubt serve to reinforce the claims made by him.

It is commonplace among historians of propaganda to insist that the impact is greatest when existing attitudes and prejudices are exploited, in terms both of antipathies[3] and of sympathies.[4] In the case of nineteenth-century Bonapartism, it is equally a commonplace to assume that the exploitation of the attachment to Napoleon I and the empire was a major factor in the success of Louis-Napoleon Bonaparte. Indeed, almost every discussion of his election to the presidency in 1848 asserts this fact as unquestionable.[5]

Those few historians who have considered Bonapartism itself after 1815 in more detail are agreed, however, that a clear distinction must be drawn between a sentimental attachment to the name of Napoleon and a collection of political ideas (possibly constituting an ideology) grouped together under the name of

Bonapartism. It is then argued that the Napoleonic legend was not first and foremost a political instrument, and that in itself it could not mobilise support for a Bonapartist challenge to the restored monarchy.[6] Taken at face value, it would seem that these judgements leave us with a situation in which a nostalgic cult suddenly becomes a potent tool of political propaganda in a particular context. It is the purpose of this chapter to show that the relationship between the Napoleonic legend and popular Bonapartism was in fact a fluctuating and complex one and that it was driven by a variety of concerns, not all of them political in nature; evidence for this will be sought primarily from one particular form in which ideas were diffused, namely the popular almanac.

The popular almanac enjoyed considerable success in the 1840s and 1850s, despite its often seemingly outdated features, but as a format it was by no means new. For centuries, almanacs had been produced by local printers and sold by peddlers, combining practical information such as the dates of country fairs with, for example, astrological speculations.[7] The Revolution did little to change the routine entries, apart from the removal of saints' days from most almanacs during the Terror.[8] Napoleon I encouraged the creation of an *Imperial Almanac* which would combine the traditional features with entries aimed at glorifying the achievements of both himself and the French nation, for, like the revolutionaries, he sought to encourage a sense of national, rather than local, identity. At this time, however, a French national market for printed matter was in its infancy, especially as the Napoleonic regime exerted strict controls over the distribution of all kinds of material. This did not mean that editions of a fairly large size were unknown: statistics for 1810 reveal printings of up to 60,000, and nine almanacs in the Nord in 1813 totalled 128,200 (compared with 36,500 for twelve works of literature produced at the same time and place), but these remained the result of local, or at best regional, markets.[9]

During the Bourbon restoration all references in print to the former emperor were liable to harsh censorship, particularly in popular publications, but after 1830 this was no longer the case, and a sudden revival of public interest[10] coincided with the rapid expansion of the production of printed matter, most notably the popular press. In the late 1830s and 1840s the mass-produced almanac was able to develop as an intermediary form between popular newspapers and conventional book publishing, and those produced in Paris in particular began to acquire a wider circulation. Then, with the introduction of universal male suffrage in 1848 and the consequent perceived need to inform the newly significant masses, the market for popular printed material increased still further. Almanacs were produced sometimes as large broadsheets, but more often in a small format similar to that of a prayer-book or breviary. The language was generally still simple, and in the case of Napoleonic almanacs it imitated that of the storyteller, evoking the oral tradition attributed in particular to army veterans;[11] in addition, almost all were extensively illustrated, so that the producers of Napoleonic almanacs were able to link the storytelling tradition with that of the cheap engravings and prints which had proved popular both in Napoleon's own time[12] and since his death.[13]

Whereas simple nostalgia for a glorious past is the dominant mood of all these products, it is clear that Louis-Napoleon Bonaparte himself did consciously and consistently seek to exploit his uncle's reputation as a political tool, in a manner which is compatible with the definition offered by Holtman. Addressing the Strasbourg garrison during the abortive coup of 1836, he pointed to the standards he bore and shouted: 'Soldiers! look at this eagle; it is the eagle of Austerlitz, the emblem of a great nation and a great army', and he referred to himself as 'the nephew of Napoleon, who has inherited his name and, above all, his love of the French'.[14] Similarly, the proclamation he had planned to deliver had the Boulogne coup of 1840 succeeded, ends, 'The spirit of the great Napoleon speaks to you through my voice.'[15]

He also sought to exploit the publicity surrounding the Return of the Ashes by publishing his *Napoleonic Ideas* and a short pamphlet entitled *Aux Mânes de L'Empereur (To the Shade of the Emperor)*. In the latter he accused France's rulers of rejecting Napoleon's 'creed, ideas, glory and blood' by rejecting his own claims for recognition; in this pamphlet he also utilises the sentimental appeal common to Napoleonic literature, by dating the piece 'Citadel of Ham, 15 December 1840' and referring to his inability to join the celebrations due to his incarceration.[16]

In addition, he encouraged the magazine *La Revue de l'Empire*,[17] founded in 1842 by Charles-Edouard Temblaire, a journalist with transparent Bonapartist sympathies; this journal, which ran until the end of 1847 with the sub-title 'historical review in praise of the first Empire', purported to be devoted to 'all the glories of the Consulate and the Empire',[18] but in fact mixed its exaltations of the past with praise of Louis-Napoleon, including, for instance, a eulogistic review of his *Extinction of Pauperism*. Moreover, Temblaire subsequently sent former subscribers letters urging them to vote for Louis-Napoleon in the presidential election of 1848.

In the above examples the propagandistic intent of the references to Napoleon and the empire is clear. This is also the case with a number of short-lived almanacs produced in 1848 itself as an explicit part of Louis-Napoleon's campaign for the presidency. Thus, such publications as *Almanach de Louis-Napoléon, Candidat à la Présidence de la République*[19] leave the reader in no doubt as to their intention; they were distributed alongside campaigning songs with titles making explicit the link between the two Bonapartes: *The Emperor's Nephew*,[20] *The Ghost of Napoleon Addresses his Nephew*[21] and *Louis-Napoleon at the Tomb of the Great Man*.[22] The almanac itself contains biographical sketches of Napoleon and his nephew. At this stage there were very few almanacs which dealt solely with the present age, rare exceptions being *L'Almanach constitutionnel de l'Empire Français* of

1853[23] and *Le Triple Almanach Impérial* of 1853 and 1854,[24] which were both published in Lille[25] and are devoted entirely to the newly established second empire, with no reference to the past.[26] Even with the establishment of this new empire, the vogue for almanacs doing nothing more than celebrating and sentimentalising the past continued for a while. The *Almanach des Souvenirs de L'Empire, Bonapartiana*[27] of 1853, for instance, reprinted parts of the popular *Bonapartiana* of 1833, quoted long-standing admirers of Napoleon such as the lyricist Bérenger, and contained sentimental descriptions of Napoleon's life, campaigns and death; nowhere in its 180 pages, however, is there even an indirect reference to Napoleon III or the second empire.

This purely retrospective approach is typical of the great majority of the popular literature and prints produced before 1848. Although a steady stream of such products came on to the market from 1830 onwards, it was in the 1840s, in the wake of the publicity attendant upon the Return of the Ashes in December 1840, that levels of production increased rapidly. It was in this context that a new wave of explicitly Napoleonic almanacs began to appear, first and foremost, as the publishers' forewords make clear, as a commercial venture. A good example of this kind of almanac is the *Almanach Napoléonien* of 1844,[28] the general tone of which is set by its full title page: *Napoleonic Annual or French Historical Almanac, containing 366 deeds and gestures of the great man and his glorious epoch.* Each day in the calendar is accompanied by a maxim from Napoleon and an event from his career for which it is the anniversary. There is a potted history of France which culminates in the triumph of Napoleon as the man who 'succeeded in bringing order to the achievements of the Revolution' and whose victories 'taught foreigners to respect the name of France in its modern greatness'.[29] The comparisons with Alexander, Caesar and Charlemagne are a familiar feature; less usual is the direct comparison with Cromwell, unsurprisingly in a manner favourable to Napoleon: 'the former [Cromwell] was the great man of a people and a century, the latter was the great man of a world and of every century'.[30]

This adulation of Napoleon was not presented without reservation, however; the significance of introducing Cromwell lay in his representation as a great *Republican* leader. The *Almanach Napoléonien* demonstrates that admiration for Napoleon can be unrelated to support for imperial Bonapartism, or can even oppose it. Inasmuch as this almanac has an underlying political message, it is a Republican one; having indulged in sentimental melancholy at contemplation of Napoleon's final years, it goes on to claim that he 'died in exile because he betrayed the principles from which he had sprung', adding that while Caesar had killed the republic, Napoleon 'could only delay its establishment, having undermined every throne'.[31]

In 1848, it was not unusual for Louis-Napoleon to represent himself as a Republican, stressing his uncle's consolidation of the Revolution more than his military glories. He adopted precisely this approach in his presidential manifesto, and he was supported by newspapers with such titles as *L'Aigle Républicaine* (*The Republican Eagle*)[32] and *Napoléon Républicain*;[33] however, both of these were short-lived and clearly linked to the specific political context created by the February Revolution. None of the almanacs launched before 1848 provided any evidence of a link between Louis-Napoleon and the Republican cause. While such distancing from the Imperial cause as that found in the *Almanach Napoléonien de 1844* is not common, there are no known examples of almanacs before 1848 which would link their reverence for the Napoleonic past to a restoration of Napoleon's self-proclaimed heir. It is by their very existence and their generally wide distribution that they contributed to a climate which would be exploited for political ends, not by anything in their specific content or by any discernible editorial policy which might aim to create a desired response from the target recipients.[34] The explicit links in this kind of publication are to be found after Louis-Napoleon's success in the presidential election, and particularly in the period surrounding the *coup d'état* of December 1851 and the proclamation of a new empire a year later. The propaganda in this instance then reinforced the power and stature of the prince-president and future emperor, rather than contributing to his acquiring of office.

L'Aigle (*The Eagle*)[35] of 1852, for instance, a large-format product of eight pages, sub-titled *National and Napoleonic Almanac*, stresses a continuity between the two emperors. It opens and closes with line-drawings of Louis-Napoleon accompanying the results of the plebiscite on his 1851 coup, a decree restoring the eagle to flags and the Legion of Honour, and the speech he gave in response to the plebiscite. The final picture, covering almost the full page, depicts him in a pose virtually identical to that of Napoleon in his official portraits as First Consul (by Ingres and Gérard); where Napoleon wears the uniform of First Consul, Louis-Napoleon wears the presidential sash, and both point to a scroll stressing their role as lawmaker. The inference to be drawn is clear, that the post-coup Republic is to the Revolution of 1848 what the Consulate was to the Great Revolution (and, by further implication, as the Consulate led 'naturally' to the empire, so might the prince-presidency).

The line of continuity can be seen in the arrangement of the almanac: the opening references to Louis-Napoleon are followed by *Napoleon at the Invalides*,[36] *The Romance of the King of Rome*[37] and *The Romance of Queen Hortense, mother of Louis-Napoleon Bonaparte*.[38] In the first of these, the ghosts of Napoleon and old soldiers appear in the Invalides at midnight, with the final stanza containing the lines:

> One could believe that the triumphal era
> Was beginning once more its universal course.[39]

This link is reiterated in the decree itself, the preamble of which refers to a time when France 'can adopt openly the memories of the Empire and the symbols which recall its glory', and when 'the national flag need no longer be deprived of the renowned emblem which led our soldiers to victory in a hundred battles'.[40]

In the same way as the prophetic manuscripts of the Middle Ages used past achievements, represented as miraculous, as a guarantor of the promise of a glorious future, the implication here is clearly not only that these glories can be recalled under the new ruler, but that new glories will be experienced. Napoleonic propaganda during the Consulate and Empire had used the past in a similar way, constantly depicting Napoleon as the worthy heir to figures such as Alexander, Caesar and Charlemagne. Now it is the hereditary Bonaparte dynasty itself which is legitimated, not by the divine right which underpinned the Bourbon monarchy, but by its own achievements.

The way in which almanacs whose foundation shows no evidence of propagandistic intent were used to bolster the legitimacy of Louis-Napoleon's regime, in particular but not exclusively at the point at which he was seeking to replace the Republic he had been elected to head, can be seen if we examine two unusually long running publications, the *Almanach Impérial* (1846–55)[41] and the *Almanach de Napoléon* (1849–70).[42] Both these were associated with Emile Marco de Saint-Hilaire, a populariser of the Napoleonic legend who had already produced more than two dozen anecdotal histories by 1846.[43] The relationship between these two almanacs and the regime of Louis-Napoleon provides a fascinating insight into the interplay of politics and commercialism. As this chapter demonstrates, through a process of mutual reinforcement the almanac writers produced material which, directly or indirectly, contributed to the legitimising of Bonapartist rule, while at the same time playing on the renewed fashion that rule had created for *all* Napoleonic material, in order to boost their own reputation and sales. As the following chronological examination of each almanac reveals, variations in the orientation of the content from one issue to another were determined to a large extent by external factors relating to the development of the new Napoleonic state, often to specific events within that development.

The *Almanach Impérial* was founded explicitly as a piece of nostalgia. The introduction to the first number, having stressed that there is no expectation that the previous Imperial almanac of the first Napoleon will ever 'rise from the ashes', claims that the title has now become 'as innocent as it is inoffensive'.[44] Even allowing for the likely desire to reassure the July Monarchy censors, this approach is fully borne out by the first three numbers, which deal entirely with the kind of sentimental anecdotes for which Marco de Saint-Hilaire, whose participation is proclaimed by the publisher as a great honour,[45] was already well known. The 1848 number, after claiming sales of 40,000 for the previous year, continues to refer to the 'small monument which we have tried to raise to the most glorious period in our national history', in tones that clearly consign that glory to the past.[46]

However, the success of Louis-Napoleon in December 1848, while not discussed directly in the next issue, clearly had an impact on the producers of the 1849 almanac. Anecdotes of the past are still the main feature, but there is more contemporary comment, directed at discrediting the left (those who put down the revolt of June are praised)[47] and the Republic in general, portrayed in a satirical piece as the friend of crooked capitalists.[48] It is the opening story of the *Comet of 1849* which shows the most evident adopting of the cause of the new Bonaparte; it ends:

> Usually these stars announce the birth or death of a great man. Such cases are rare. One was seen when Mahomet came into the world; one was visible at Saint Helena on the eve of Napoleon's death. Perhaps this latest is announcing to us that France is about to produce a gr-r-r-r-eat citizen![49]

The following issue, the almanac for 1850, contains an editorial foreword in the form of an *avertissement de l'éditeur* (the style and content suggest it was almost certainly actually written by Marco de Saint-Hilaire himself), which confirms the support for Louis-Napoleon, significantly calling him the heir of Napoleon's name. First, the original goal of the *Almanach Impérial* is reaffirmed as being 'to entertain, and to awaken in the popular imagination noble and magnificent recollections of the Empire';[50] the foreword then continues: 'By a happy coincidence, this name of Napoleon which shines through almost every page of our almanac has produced political events which we had not predicted, but which we had always sensed and desired.'[51]

Finally, the *avertissement* confirms that Napoleon had always been 'the symbol of order within and of grandeur without', and asserts that 'if the heir of his name brings half of these benefits, we will render to the Napoleon of peace as complete homage as we have constantly rendered to the Napoleon of war'.[52] Although he does not directly say this will definitely happen, the implication is clear; the combination of order and grandeur is exactly what Louis-Napoleon highlighted in *Napoleonic Ideas* and in his election campaign, and the distancing of himself from war (which was necessary in Napoleon's time but is not any longer) was explicitly stressed in his election manifesto.[53]

As we have seen, there is nothing whatsoever in the almanacs prior to 1849 which would substantiate the claim to have 'always sensed and desired' Louis-Napoleon's election. Emile Marco de Saint-Hilaire himself did appear in 1848 to have espoused his cause, by collaborating with the Bonapartist newspaper *Le Petit Caporal*,[54] which was directed primarily at soldiers and which ran from June to December of that year. However, he in fact joined it in August, at precisely the moment when it lost its explicitly political character and became simply a 'historical journal of the new and old Army'.[55] It was only in the final few issues, during the electoral campaign for the presidency itself, that the newspaper began again to promote Louis-Napoleon's cause, calling him 'the heir of the sword of Austerlitz'[56] and 'the candidate of Marengo, Austerlitz, Wagram and Champaubert',[57] and claiming that the army would vote for him *en masse*.[58] As the production process of an almanac intended for use the following year did not allow for the embracing of the presidential candidacy at such a late stage, the allegiance could only be expressed retrospectively (and rather unconvincingly) as far as the *Almanach Impérial* was concerned.

The timing of the *avertissement* to the *Almanach Impérial* suggests that the producers of the manifesto were seeking to align themselves with the new order, but did not intend their almanac to become a regular vehicle for propaganda. This is confirmed by the fact that the next two issues returned to the staple diet of Napoleonic anecdotes, with nothing to link them to Louis-Napoleon. It is only with the next major political shift, after the 1851 coup and the imminent re-establishment of the empire, that a more explicitly political tone returned, with the 1853 issue once again being prefaced by a long statement by the publisher. In this the coup is said to have saved France from the anarchy which threatened it from all sides, exactly the way in which Napoleon's coup of 18 Brumaire 1799 had traditionally been represented by those sympathetic to him. More specifically, it shows the publisher assimilating the almanac's professed outlook directly to that adopted as his own by Louis-Napoleon himself; in *Napoleonic Ideas* he had written of Napoleon as the 'executor' of the Revolution, continuing:

> at length Napoleon appeared, cleared up the chaos of nothingness and glory, separated truths from passions and the elements of success from the seeds of death, and reduced to synthesis all those great principles which, contending together unceasingly, compromised the cause in which all were interested.[59]

The almanac goes on to provide a direct and enthusiastic justification of Louis-Napoleon's actions, together with a highly sympathetic pen-portrait of him, in which he is 'the man to whom France has entrusted her destiny',[60] who is 'following seriously and scrupulously the great mission which he has set for himself, to restore to France the prosperity of its great days'.[61]

The main body of the almanac, too, alongside the usual spate of recollections, contains a piece, *The Two Champs de Mars, 1815–1852*, which juxtaposes two ceremonies presided over by Napoleon and his nephew respectively, both of which stress the 'acclamations of the people'[62] and the way in which that people is celebrating its acknowledgement of the fact that the ruler is the incarnation of popular sovereignty.

None of the remaining issues have an *avertissement* in this manner, and indeed none contain such directly political material, which confirms the view that it is the immediacy of the new order which is the spur for this almanac. The 1854 number, however, does contain a slightly different form of promotion of Louis-Napoleon (now Napoleon III), in that he is regularly invoked in entries dealing primarily with material relating to the first Napoleon. Praise for Napoleon's rewarding of modest merit includes the statement that he knew the importance of this, 'as does his worthy successor, Napoleon III';[63] a veteran of the Imperial Guard has above his bed 'the imperial eagle . . . lit up by a double portrait of Napoleon I and Napoleon III – there is the cult of this man, there are his God and his idols';[64] finally, the story of a visit to Saint Helena opens with a reference to the people 'saluting the name of Napoleon III, the nephew, the heir, the worthy successor of Napoleon I'.[65]

The effect of these references is constantly to reinforce the claims made by Louis-Napoleon himself, claims regarding both his political legitimacy and his policies. The timing of the most overt support does suggest that the producers of the almanacs were seeking to ensure that they and their own publication would be assimilated to the new order. We may well here have a case in which propaganda derives not from genuinely held beliefs, nor from a specific desire to promote or maintain a political ruler or ruling group, but from motives which are essentially commercial, a point which will be developed more fully in the conclusion of this chapter.

A similar pattern can be seen if we examine the history of the *Almanach de Napoléon,* which first appeared in 1849, which used the already well-known Napoleonic illustrators Charlet and Raffet, and to which Marco de Saint-Hilaire's name was first publicly attached in 1852; priced at fifty centimes, a price which did not increase, this was clearly aimed at a popular market. Ménager describes it as an almanac in which 'the Napoleonic legend is combined with the cult of the new head of state, presented as the favourite nephew of Napoleon',[66] and the 1851 issue contains an illustration depicting Napoleon with the three-year-old Louis-Napoleon on his knee, saying he will be his father.[67]

The 1852 issue's foreword asserts that the almanac was originally inspired by the victory of 10 December, but that it is not just an almanac of Louis-Napoleon's period in power. Indeed, the issues before this date had concentrated very heavily on the 'glorious souvenirs of the Empire'[68] referred to in this same foreword. The links with the new regime are brief but persistent in these issues: 1849 has a portrait of Louis-Napoleon as president opposite the title page and ends with a biographical sketch of him. This sketch was included because his life had been 'deliberately and strangely distorted',[69] and it referred to the birth of a 'new heir to the Empire', of whom Napoleon said when he was seven, 'he is perhaps the hope of my race'.[70]

In 1850, when the almanac again has a portrait of Louis-Napoleon as its frontispiece, a large collection of anecdotes of the first Napoleon is interspersed with three entries dealing with actions of the prince-president, all of which have a thumbnail sketch of Napoleon I as illustration at the end. The link through illustration is continued in 1851, with (in addition to the drawing already noted of the infant Louis-Napoleon) a frontispiece in the form of a triple portrait of Napoleon I, Napoleon II and Louis-Napoleon, all on horseback; once again, it is dynastic continuity which is implied. This issue also reiterates the special role of the army as guarantor of Bonapartist sentiment and presents Louis-Napoleon as the legitimate object of its loyalty by ending a long description of the return of Napoleon's remains to Paris in 1840 with the claim that 'the population of the Hotel des Invalides voted *en masse* for the nephew of the Emperor'.[71]

It was, however, in 1852, with Louis-Napoleon's successful coup and the re-establishment of empire, that the almanac pronounced its allegiance most clearly and insistently. As already noted, this was the first time Marco de Saint-Hilaire chose to include his name on the title page, and this was the first time also that it was deemed necessary to include a publisher's foreword. This acclaims 'the prince Louis-Napoleon' and goes on to make the most direct statement yet of its goals:

> Now, if one part of our almanac must serve to perpetuate the memory of the great deeds which were accomplished in the time of the Empire, the other part will be employed to instruct France in the destinies of this family, which it will find always ready to perpetuate traditions which lead essentially to the prosperity and greatness of the nation.[72]

The dual purpose is then reinforced both verbally and pictorially in this issue; the frontispiece takes the form of a court scene depicting the Imperial family, but what it shows is that family across the generations, including Napoleon I, his son, both his wives, his brothers and sisters, Eugène and Hortense Beauharnais, as well as Louis-Napoleon; it is the clearest affirmation yet of dynastic solidarity and the new emperor's legitimacy.

The Napoleonic lineage, together with the element of the magical and miraculous seen in the *Comet of 1849*, is also evident in a piece about the so-called tree of 20 March. This is a tree in the Tuileries gardens 'known' to be covered in leaves on that date; it first appeared 'by magic'[73] in 1811 on the birth of Napoleon's son, 'as if this tree had wished, following the example of France, to offer in its turn its bouquet to the prestigious man in whose favour providence had never ceased giving birth to miracles'.[74] Struck by frost in 1812, and declining then disappearing after 1815, the phenomenon is reported as having been seen again in 1849.

Somewhat surprisingly after this change of tone, the almanac for 1853 reverts to an almost total reliance on Napoleonic anecdote (apart from a pen-portrait of the prince-president at the end), while the 1854 issue more or less alternates such entries with celebrations of the new empire (and particularly the emperor's marriage), without making any links between the two.

It is from 1855 that we see a new and decisive shift; the emphasis is now placed heavily on the achievements of the new empire, with anecdotes of the past confined to a *Napoleonic Album*, placed at the end and steadily diminishing in size from year to year, disappearing completely after 1859. Links were still made from time to time, such as the poem *Napoleon I at the Baptism of the Prince Imperial*[75] in 1857, where the continuation of the theme of dynastic legitimacy was once again evident. Such links were increasingly rare, however, and were related to specific aspects of the second empire (such as the birth of an heir): the narration of the Crimean war in the 1855 almanac has several references to the Napoleonic campaigns, with a frontispiece depicting an allegory of the war against Russia, which included the shade of Napoleon watching approvingly from the sky. Similarly, the victory parade on the Place Vendôme in 1857 was described as witnessed by 'the two great emperors, Napoleon I on the column and Napoleon III on horseback',[76] and the victory, it was claimed, is one which 'history will unhesitatingly set beside the old glories of Arcola and Austerlitz'.[77] Now that Napoleon III had proved himself a worthy emperor, the bolstering provided by references to the past was no longer so necessary.

The celebration of ten years of Louis-Napoleon, which formed almost the whole of the 1858 almanac, set the scene for the remaining issues; from now on the *only* references to Napoleon were related to contemporary events, such as the unveiling of statues, which were generally described in a sober reporting style. Even the obvious potential of the centenary of Napoleon's birth in 1869 was almost entirely overlooked; while it was anticipated briefly in an entry in 1867 which referred to the re-establishment of the festival of 15 August (Napoleon I's birthday and official saint's day), a day 'dedicated to the glory of France and of the Napoleons',[78] there was no mention whatsoever in either 1869 or 1870 of the centenary or of Napoleon I.[79] The only example in this whole period which recaptures in any way the tone of earlier Napoleonism related to the Italian war, and even here there was only one such entry in a volume (1860) devoted almost entirely to the campaign: *Magenta*, a poem by Méry (well known for poems celebrating French national glory), claimed 'the conqueror of Arcola is reborn in Napoleon'[80] and paralleled Magenta with Marengo, asserting 'we are returning to the days of illustrious renown'.[81] Even in this example, the emphasis was much more clearly on the actual achievements of Napoleon III, rather than simply his illustrious name or Napoleonic inheritance.

The evidence of these detailed surveys leads us to a number of conclusions demonstrating that a simple categorisation of the almanacs is misleading. First, they were clearly not simply a vehicle for Bonapartist propaganda; there were exceptions like the 1848 *Almanach de Louis-Napoléon Bonaparte* discussed earlier, but such deliberate electioneering only used the almanac form because it was already an established and familiar genre. Second, it would be simplistic to see the almanacs purely in terms of sentimental nostalgia for a glorious past. Although this is the avowed intention of most of those appearing in the 1840s, they succeeded in familiarising an audience with that past and thus provided the basis for the comparisons with the present which became evident at a later stage. Third, there was little evidence that the established almanacs produced propaganda in favour of Louis-Napoleon *before* his election to the presidency, in the sense of seeking 'to affect in a predetermined manner the attitudes and actions of large groups of people';[82] those that did operate in this way were founded specifically for the purpose and had, by their very nature, a limited and brief lifespan. And fourth, there was a tendency to link the established glorification of the past to the new head of state *after* that election, with considerable stress on his worthiness to bear the name of Napoleon and on the dynastic continuity of the Bonapartes. It was especially in the period surrounding his coup against the parliamentary republic and the subsequent re-establishment of empire that these links were made explicit (as in the 1852 and 1853 issues of *Almanach Impérial* and *Almanach de Napoléon*); once that empire was firmly established, it was more usual to celebrate the achievements of Napoleon III in his own right, which suggests that references to Napoleon I were no longer deemed necessary to boost the popularity and sales of the almanacs themselves.

What then does the examination of the almanacs and the shifts in their content tell us about the interplay of propaganda and free enterprise? For those which survived as long-term commercial ventures the most complex period in this respect is from 1849 to the mid-1850s. Before then the editors clearly believed that the market could best be exploited by reviving and developing the existing forms of Napoleonic material and embedding it within a longstanding almanac format. The high profile given to the names of writers and illustrators who had already acquired both reputation and popularity in this field further confirms this, and even the newly introduced *Almanach de Napoléon* of 1849 prominently advertised what was to be expected from it by including both Charlet's and Raffet's names in its full title.[83]

From the mid-1850s the situation was quite different. A large part of the appeal of the Napoleonic legend had lain in the nostalgia evoked for an age of colour, vitality and glory at a time when the culture of public life was dominated by the politics of the *juste milieu*. In this climate the market for all kinds of Napoleonic bric-a-brac had flourished, having been tolerated and even encouraged by the authorities as a useful safety valve. Once the second empire was well established, however, such contrasts between past and present were no longer appropriate. Any celebration of the Napoleonic past was incorporated into official policy[84] and was consequently of a style quite different from the popular sentimentality of the almanacs. These, in order to maintain the interest of readers, felt compelled to popularise the achievements of the new regime, playing up its triumphs and offering apparently intimate glimpses into the life of the court. Indeed, the most durable of the almanacs, the *Almanach de Napoléon*, came to adopt the tone of a quasi-official publication, including the Lists of the Imperial Household every year from 1854.[85] It is reasonable to assume that the position established in the market by this publication, the tone of whose last number is still buoyant, was only undermined by the sudden collapse of the empire itself; the complete discrediting of the entire Bonaparte dynasty, at least in the short term, by the disastrous war of 1870 meant that any further adaptation to circumstances, no matter how skilfully contrived, would have been out of the question.

As already stated, it was in that period when the new head of state was seeking to consolidate his power, and the producers of almanacs were seeking to respond to the changed commercial possibilities, that the relationship between enterprise and propaganda is at its most complex and revealing. Commercially produced almanacs would seek to make the most of specific events, but if their producers hoped to sustain publication over a period of years, they could not afford to be bound by, or dependent upon, one such event. For the same reason, they could only afford to allow their popularity to be dependent on that of Louis-Napoleon once his success was assured.

Thus, committed propaganda for his campaign in 1848 was only to be found, as has been shown, in a quite different kind of almanac, and even in 1849 the expressions of support and approval in both the established *Almanach Impérial* and the new *Almanach de Napoléon* were tentative and generalised. In both cases, references to Louis-Napoleon were in terms that suggested his electoral triumph had given new impetus to their own celebration of the past empire; in other words, they were simply using his success to raise the profile of their own kind of product. The *manner* in which the *Almanach de Napoléon* was introduced in 1849 bears this out, as does the general practice of Marco de Saint-Hilaire himself; his reputation and the popularity of his works were based strongly on his supposed familiarity with the Emperor's activities in his position as page, a position which he is now known never to have held.[86] He published in 1853 *Les deux Empereurs*, which appears at first sight to be a double biography, but which was in fact made up almost entirely of anecdotes relating to Napoleon I, virtually all of which were simply reprinted from his earlier works without acknowledgement – a clear piece of timely exploitation of circumstances.[87]

However opportunistic, the way in which the almanacs chose to bolster their anecdotes by intimating a cult of the new ruler undoubtedly did help underpin his claims to worth and legitimacy. The coup of December 1851, which simultaneously secured his position and led to the creation of a political system very similar to that of the first Napoleon, enabled and encouraged the producers of the almanacs to embrace his cause with more obvious enthusiasm. The marked increase in entries linking the two emperors suggests a conscious attempt to assimilate their products to the new regime, and the forewords included at this time (1852 for the *Almanach de Napoléon*,[88] 1853 for the *Almanach Impérial*[89]) represent the most *overt* form of propaganda in favour of Louis-Napoleon contained in either of these publications. The regime itself, concerned by the level of popular opposition to the coup,[90] was only too happy to welcome the adherence of publications directed at the lower classes. Thus, for a period of about three years, we witness the process of mutual reinforcement at its most intense; the means used by the almanac producers to raise their own profile did actually contribute to legitimising the regime, whose steady consolidation then made it even more imperative for those publishers and editors to be seen to be associated with it. Finally, as we have seen, by the mid-1850s the traditional nostalgic material had become redundant and the surviving almanacs now saw their future as lying simply in serving the present empire. So it does not seem that the propaganda, either direct or indirect, which served to reinforce the position of Louis-Napoleon in the early years of power was the product of an ideological commitment to political Bonapartism on the part of the producers or of a longstanding support for Louis-Napoleon as the man most fit to lead France. The almanacs were first and foremost commercial ventures, and their publishers and editors sought to exploit the situation created by Louis-Napoleon's success to raise the profile of their own products. The fact that these almanacs did not have propaganda as their prime and conscious motive does not mean, however, that they did not serve a propagandistic purpose. The new ruler's own claim to worth and legitimacy, together with his own frequent references to the heritage of the Napoleonic past undoubtedly were underpinned by the methods adopted, for their own ends, by the producers of the almanacs. Their products offer an excellent example of the way in which a political purpose can be served and the claims of a political regime reinforced by a genre, particularly a genre directed at a popular market, whose primary aim is to benefit from the apparent popularity of that cause and that regime.

Notes

1   R.B. Holtman, *The Napoleonic Revolution* (Baton Rouge, Louisiana State University Press, 1967), pp. 163–4. See also the same author's *Napoleonic Propaganda* (Baton Rouge, Louisiana State University Press, 1950).

2   For useful brief surveys of the use of these media by Napoleon, see M. Lyons, *Napoleon Bonaparte and the Legacy of the French Revolution* (London, Macmillan, 1994), ch. 13, pp. 178–94; and G. Ellis, *Napoleon* (London, Longman, 1997), ch. 6, pp. 155–88.

3   See, for instance, William Sheridan Allen, 'Die Wirkung der Propaganda', in D. Peukert and J. Reulecke (eds), *Die Reihen fest geschlossen: Beiträge zur Geschichte des Alltags unterm Nationalsozialismus* (Wuppertal, Hammer Verlag, 1981), p. 408: 'Propaganda can strengthen existing antipathies[. . .], but it cannot simply overturn popular convictions' (author's translation – unless otherwise indicated, all translations used in this chapter are the author's).

4   See, for instance, I. Kershaw, *The Hitler Myth* (Oxford University Press, 1987).

5   A typical example can be found in J.P.T. Bury, *France 1814–1940* (London, Methuen, 3rd edn,

1954): 'But these names spelt little to a nation which was by no means Republican at heart compared with another which had a meaning for the humblest peasant, a name known to all, a name covered with glory and which had gained such fresh popularity in recent years as a result of a romantic cult that it was capable of sweeping the country, almost regardless of the character and personality of its present bearer: the name of Napoleon.' p. 81.

6   See, for instance, Bernard Ménager, *Les Napoléon du Peuple* (Paris, Aubier, 1988), *passim*.

7   The oldest known example of such an almanac is claimed to be *Le Compost et calendrier des bergers* of 1493; see E. Kennedy, *A Cultural History of the French Revolution* (New Haven, Yale University Press, 1989), p. 43.

8   Kennedy, *Cultural History*, p. 44.

9   Figures from Kennedy, *Cultural History*, p. 47.

10   For example, popular boulevard theatre witnessed a spate of Napoleonic drama and tableaux, with 97 different plays to the glory of Napoleon being performed in Paris between 1831 and 1840; Ménager, *Peuple*, p. 81.

11   This tradition, frequently evoked in memoirs and autobiographies, was made familiar to readers through Goguelat, the enormously popular fictional storyteller created by Balzac in his novel *The Country Doctor*. The novel was first published late in 1833, but the Goguelat episode had been included in a magazine earlier in that year and was frequently reprinted separately over the subsequent decades; Honoré de Balzac, *Oeuvres* (12 vols, Gallimard, Paris, 1978), vol. IX, pp. 498–540; Ménager, *Peuple*, p. 81.

12   Alphonse de Lamartine describes in his memoirs the selling of such prints in his village by hawkers: 'Then the peasant would come out of his cottage and, with eyes shining in wonder, would see a display of heroic portraits, listen to tales of combat, and for one *sou* he would buy the history of these feats of arms. He nailed them to the walls of his house, or had his wife sew them to the serge curtain around his bed; for him and for his family, this was the whole history of France in great deeds.' Lyons, *Napoleon Bonaparte*, p. 153

13   Prints featuring the Napoleon saga had evidently escaped the censorship of the Bourbons, for it is estimated that over 100,000 *images d'Épinal*, the most popular form of cheap coloured print, had appeared on the subject even before 1830; Ménager, *Peuple*, p. 81; prints after 1830 are discussed by Barbara Ann Day in 'Napoleonic Art as a Vehicle for Government Propaganda and Political Resistance 1830–1836', *Proceedings of the Western Society for French History* (1993), and in her forthcoming book, provisionally entitled *Napoleonic Art: A Harbinger of Political Consciousness in Post-Revolutionary France*.

14   A. Dansette, *Louis-Napoléon à la conquête du pouvoir* (Paris, Hachette, 1961), p. 116.

15   A. Dansette, *Louis-Napoléon*, p. 156

16   Le Prince Napoléon-Louis (sic) Bonaparte, *Aux Mânes de L'Empereur* (Chez Bredolin, Paris, 1840).

17   *La Revue de l'Empire*, Bibliothèque Nationale (BN), Lc2.1540.

18   F. Bluche, *Le Bonapartisme* (Paris, Nouvelles Editions Latines, 1980), p. 253.

19   See R. Pimienta, *Le propagande bonapartiste en 1848* (Paris, Calmann-Levy, 1911), pp. 85–6.

20   *Le Neveu de l'Empereur*, BN, Ye 7185(307).

21   *La Voix du Peuple ou l'Ombre de Napoléon à son Neveu*, BN, Ye 7185(317).

22   *Louis-Napoléon au tombeau du Grand Homme*, BN, Ye 53445.

23 *L'Almanach constitutionnel de l'Empire Français*, BN, Lc.31.230.

24 *Le Triple Almanach Impérial*, BN, LC25.88.

25 In fact, the 'Imperial' element in the latter publication is limited to a few pages at the beginning of each volume and mentions in a 'summary of remarkable events' of the previous year, the bulk of the almanac being devoted to such general matters as agricultural and horticultural advice, tides and eclipses, and dates for annual fairs. The title seems to have been chosen primarily to give the appearance of official approval.

26 Further new almanacs of this kind appeared with greater frequency later in the second empire, such as the *Almanach historique, anectdotique et populaire de l'Empire Français* of 1867 (BN, Lc 22.340) and the *Almanach des Victoires de Napoléon III* of 1870 (BN, Lc 22.304), the latter rather ironically titled in the light of subsequent events of that year!

27 *Almanach des souvenirs de L'Empire, Bonapartiana*, BN, LC22.242.

28 *Almanach napoléonien de 1844*, BN, Lc22.138.

29 *Almanach napoléonien de 1844*, p. 150.

30 *Almanach napoléonien de 1844*, p. 152.

31 *Almanach napoléonien de 1844*, p. 154.

32 *L'Aigle Républicaine*, BN, Lc2.1872.

33 *Napoléon Républicain*, BN, Lc2.1879.

34 See n. 1.

35 *L'Aigle*, BN, Lc22.225.

36 *L'Aigle*, p. 3.

37 *L'Aigle*, p. 4.

38 *L'Aigle*, p. 5.

39 'On aurait cru que l'ère triomphale/Sur l'univers recommençait son cours', *L'Aigle*, p. 3.

40 *L'Aigle*, p. 6.

41 *Almanach Impérial*, BN, Lc22.144 (this file contains the complete run of the almanac from 1846 to 1855).

42 *Almanach de Napoléon illustré par Charlet et Raffet*, BN, Lc.22.165 (this file contains the complete run of the almanac, from 1849 to 1870).

43 In particular, his *Souvenirs intimes du temps de l'Empire*, first published in 1838, had already by this time run into several editions, and many more would follow.

44 *Almanach Impérial pour 1846*, p. 22.

45 *Almanach Impérial pour 1846*, p. 9.

46 *Almanach Impérial pour 1848*, p. 9.

47 *Almanach Impérial pour 1849*, p. 46.

48 *Almanach Impérial pour 1849*, p. 136.

49 *Almanach Impérial pour 1849*, p. 16.

50 *Almanach Impérial pour 1850*, p. 17.

51 *Almanach Impérial pour 1850*.

52 *Almanach Impérial pour 1850*, p. 18.

53 The manifesto, addressed to 'fellow citizens', was quite explicit on this point: 'With war we can have no relief to our ills. Peace, therefore, would be the dearest object of my desire.

France, at the time of her first revolution, was warlike, because others forced her to be so. Threatened with invasion, she replied by conquest. Now she is not threatened, she is free to concentrate all her resources to pacific measures of amelioration, without abandoning a loyal and resolute policy.'

54 *Le Petit Caporal*, BN Lc2.1887.

55 Pimienta, *Propagande*, p. 76.

56 *Caporal*, No. 20.

57 *Caporal*, No. 21.

58 *Caporal*, No. 20.

59 Louis-Napoleon Bonaparte, *Napoleonic Ideas*, ed. Brison D. Gooch (New York , Harper & Row, 1967), p. 33.

60 *Almanach Impérial pour 1853*, p. 24.

61 *Almanach Impérial pour 1853*, p. 24.

62 *Almanach Impérial pour 1853*, p. 67.

63 *Almanach Impérial pour 1854*, p. 136.

64 *Almanach Impérial pour 1854*, p. 148.

65 *Almanach Impérial pour 1854*, p. 159.

66 Ménager, *Peuple*, p. 107.

67 *Almanach de Napoléon pour 1851*, pp. 80–1.

68 *Almanach de Napoléon pour 1852*, p. 5.

69 *Almanach de Napoléon pour 1849*, p. 97.

70 *Almanach de Napoléon pour 1849*, p. 99.

71 *Almanach de Napoléon pour 1851*, p. 106.

72 *Almanach de Napoléon pour 1852*, p. 5.

73 *Almanach de Napoléon pour 1852*, p. 70.

74 *Almanach de Napoléon pour 1852*, p. 70.

75 *Almanach de Napoléon pour 1857*, pp. 58–61

76 *Almanach de Napoléon pour 1857*, p. 40.

77 *Almanach de Napoléon pour 1857*, p. 40.

78 *Almanach de Napoléon pour 1867*, pp. 62–3.

79 Similarly, an almanac which appeared for the first time in 1867, the *Almanach historique, anecdotique et populaire de l'Empire Français* (BN, Lc22.340), contains a substantial section on the activities of the current imperial family, but has no mention at all of Napoleon I or the first empire

80 *Almanach de Napoléon pour 1860*, p. 87.

81 *Almanach de Napoléon pour 1860*, p. 86.

82 Holtman, *Revolution*, p. 164.

83 See n. 42.

84 For example, the completion of the tomb in the Hotel des Invalides in 1861.

85 In addition, the names of Charlet and Raffet no longer appeared on the title page from 1858.

86 J. Tulard (ed.), *Le Dictionnaire Napoléon*, 2nd edn (Paris, Fayard, 1989), p. 1134. Unsurprisingly, many of his stories, and all those involving himself, are pure invention.

87 Never one to miss a chance for self-advertisement, Marco de Saint-Hilaire had included in

the 1853 edition of the *Almanach de Napoléon* a short extract from this book, under the heading *Portrait du Prince-Président*, the introduction to which proclaimed that it was drawn from 'an excellent recently published history'! (*Almanach de Napoléon pour 1853*, p. 110).

88   See n. 72.

89   See n. 60.

90   For the best study of the nature and extent of this opposition, see Ted. W. Margadant, *French Peasants in Revolt: the Insurrection of 1851* (Princeton University Press, 1979).

Part Three

GENDERING AND EMBODYING PROPAGANDA

This section contains three chapters dealing with forms of propaganda with social agenda. The first two chapters show how gender politics used propagandistic techniques to subvert organised political movements. Maire Cross explores the work of pioneer female French socialist Flora Tristan and shows how one individual could take on to promote gender politics and gender subversive schemes in radical circles and in the wider society of Orléanist France. She also demonstrates how Flora Tristan's whole being was propaganda and how propaganda activities shaped the identity of the propagandist. A similar point, albeit on a prosopographical scale, is made in the following chapter. In June Hannam and Karen Hunt's chapter devoted to women's columns in the socialist press, the authors show how suffragist and equal rights militants attempted to develop an original third way within socialism. The tensions between class and gender remained unresolved, but their propagandistic technique opened up the debate and was shaped by it. In all three chapters of this part we are looking at means of propaganda which address social and moral politics: the first two consider gender politics and women's rights; the third deals with the propaganda deployed in a moral health campaign which attempted to promote idealistic feminine values in order to combat the spread of sexually transmitted disease. Roger Davidson shows how Scottish health authorities used contemporary propaganda techniques to peddle a conservative message. In all three chapters we can see how propaganda becomes an essential element of the propagandist identity and how the rhetoric shapes the content of the message to a greater extent than the authors were ever aware.

9

FLORA TRISTAN'S SOCIALIST PROPAGANDA IN PROVINCIAL FRANCE, 1843–1844:

THE RELATIONSHIP BETWEEN PROPAGANDA, IDENTITY AND POLITICAL RHETORIC IN FLORA TRISTAN'S CAMPAIGN FOR A WORKERS' UNION

Máire F. Cross

On 4 February 1843 Flora Tristan began a journal with these words: 'Overworked as I am at the moment I can only jot down notes here – which later I shall be able to use in the work whose title I am using here. – First of all, all my letters from workers which are in order in the same packet – then events as they arise'.[1]

These events as they arose over the following months were faithfully recorded by her as she completely immersed herself in an all-out campaign of propaganda which ended abruptly with her death in Bordeaux in November 1844.

Her campaign was to organise the workers to form a union:

I come to you to propose a general union among working men and women, regardless of trade, who reside in the same region – a union which would have as its goal the CONSOLIDATION OF THE WORKING CLASS and the construction of several establishments (Workers' Union palaces), distributed evenly throughout France.[2]

At first sight her painstaking efforts may seem to have been to no avail. This union was not formed during her lifetime. It is possible, however, to assess the less obvious but more long-term impact of her short propaganda campaign thanks to the diary, correspondence[3] and other contemporary witnesses.[4] In her diary she provides a graphic account of meetings where she tried to win over well-established groups of workers who already had their own ideas about organising themselves:

Yesterday, 13th February. I went with Evrat and Rosenfeld at eight o'clock in the evening to the special committee meeting for the reading of my two chapters. It was in Rue Jean-Aubert, a dirty and muddy back street off the Rue Saint Martin, in an old hovel down a long dark alley, up a stairway which is a death trap, to the fourth storey where the committee meeting was held. – We went

into quite a clean room where about twenty people were already gathered. –
There, total silence reigned. – Not one person spoke to me, not even Vinçard
who knew me, and consequently, should have come to see me to excuse
himself for not coming to me about my work. – Nothing. – I was made to wait,
I who had announced I was bringing the salvation of the working class.[5]

Flora Tristan can be considered as a propagandist on three counts. The social
observer Flora Tristan wrote her own propaganda, putting forward her version of
the solution to poverty and ignorance. Having discovered the right solution to an
insurmountable problem, she then proceeded to prepare for and set out on a tour
of France to evangelise the working class and win them over to the idea which
she claimed as her own. The public role she claimed for herself during this time
was a far cry from the role expected of women in those days and, like other
women who wished to take part in the political process, she was ridiculed for this:

> While we were preoccupied with Ireland where important and significant events
> are about to take place through the dedication of O'Connell and the National
> Association, we scarcely imagined for one moment that we were about to be
> provided with a parody of all that: yet we are going to have our own Union, our
> O'Connell, our meetings, our cheering. . . . However, never let it be said that we
> would want to raise a storm in order to destroy Madame Flora Tristan's project
> . . . . Yes Madame Flora is perhaps our O'Connell, O'Connell in petticoats; . . .
> the O'Connell of France could well be Madame Flora. We would just love to see
> her up on the hustings platform, one hand across her chest, the other raised in a
> clenched fist with eyes ablaze, frowning and making us all cheer.[6]

To some extent this ridicule from other propagandists was very apt. Flora Tristan
took much of her inspiration from Daniel O'Connell's efforts to raise up the
dispossessed by creating a mass organisation, collecting very small sums to give a
sense of solidarity and to fund a defender to take up their cause in Parliament.
However, she was highly critical of O'Connell's demagogic style:

> Yesterday I got carried away and I said things worthy of an educated gathering.
> I saw that I was rising way above my audience . . . reduced to talking to the
> deaf. It's just not possible to talk to people about big social issues because
> people cannot understand. That would explain why poets and politicians who
> talk in such a beautiful manner without saying anything please the people so
> much. . . . it cannot understand the apostle. . . . I see now that I am on similar
> territory to O'Connell. . . . he only utters twaddle to the people – words in jest
> to produce laughter, and insults about the Saxon and the English Ministers.
> With that you could have a body of five hundred people around you. . . . It
> doesn't matter if there is no one educated among these bodies.[7]

During her tour of France she adopted quite a different tactic, shunning mass meetings, preferring to hold small sessions where she could really communicate her ideas to the workers capable of understanding and retaining her message:

> I must admit for my part, I am not satisfied with having a body of people in front of me. I prefer one mind to a million bodies. So I have to give up trying to get them to understand this first question of the formation of the working class. They don't even understand what 'the right to work' means. They will have to have that repeated over and over for the next ten years.[8]

Although she had had little experience of political activism, Flora Tristan plunged headlong into the task, only to realise its enormity:

> I am unfair to these poor creatures; I am asking more than they can give. . . . It is clear that seven or eight years will be needed for all my ideas in the little book to be spread and digested by the people, and I, blinded by the immense love which inflames me, I want the workers to take six months to find out what it took me twenty years to understand.[9]

Yet the vital qualities of faith, energy and enthusiasm that she displayed during her apostolic campaign ensured a measure of success for her tour and for her legacy. Propaganda therefore is a very important element of Flora Tristan's identity.

Her style was direct. From the outset she persuaded the workers that her scheme was the best.

To Working men and Women
Listen to me. For twenty-five years the most intelligent and devoted men have given their lives to defending your sacred cause. In their writings, speeches reports, memoirs, investigations and statistics, they have pointed out, observed and demonstrated to the government and the wealthy that the working class, in the current state of affairs, is morally and materially placed in an intolerable situation of poverty and grief. They have shown that, in this state of abandonment and suffering, most of the workers, inevitably embittered through misfortune and brutalised through ignorance, became dangerous to society. They have proven to the Government and the wealthy that not only justice and humanity call for the duty of aiding them through a law on labour organisation, but that even the public interest and security imperiously demand such a measure.[10]

This was a messenger conveying a sense of urgency as well as a sense of confidence to her audience. Where others had failed to act she would succeed:

Workers, put an end to twenty-five years of waiting for someone to intervene on your behalf. Experience and facts inform you well enough that the Government cannot or will not be concerned with your lot when its improvement is at issue. It is up to you alone, if you truly want it, to leave this labyrinth of misery, suffering and degradation in which you languish. Do you want to ensure good vocational education for your children and for yourselves, and certainty of rest in your old age? You can.[11]

Her propaganda was vibrant in its appeal but fraught with inner tensions. By transforming her analysis into a plan of action she chose to prioritise certain elements of her analysis at the cost of others. Furthermore, after writing her advice to the workers to redeem themselves, she insisted on showing them the 'right way' to their own salvation by instigating her missionary tour of France in the form of a programme of direct encounter with the targeted audience, the working class with whom she had little previous contact. In 1843, although she had already acquired a reputation as a minor Parisian literary figure, an exotic *femme fatale*, Flora Tristan had yet to prove herself as a skilful propagandist.[12] In this paper I suggest that any success of the political career of this early nineteenth-century socialist feminist was due largely to these skills she developed, albeit over a very short period.

PROPAGANDA

Political propaganda often has negative connotations of manipulation by the establishment, of dishonesty and deviation; it is a much used word and has a variety of meanings. To set the propaganda context in Tristan terms there are several aspects which we need to tease out. Although in Flora Tristan's case hers was a lone campaign, it was the product of a specific historical social setting. While she was against the establishment, her propaganda was far from negative. Overtly manipulative, her message was not intended to deceive. Propaganda in the Tristan sense was close to the original meaning; active transmission or propagation of the faith was an inherent part of it. In the French historic setting, propagation of ideas to the masses took on a new dimension in the early nineteenth century. Of course propaganda was not invented in the nineteenth century, but only since the French Revolution of 1789 has it been directed primarily at the masses.[13] Ever since then, popular support has been sought by all interest groups as a matter of course. This is especially true for the first half of the nineteenth century when France progressed from monarchy to republic to empire.

Revolutionary governments had begun the modernising process of manipulating wider audiences, a process continued by each successive regime thereafter. Winning over the opinion of the working class seemed to be more important for the authorities than wooing the peasant class, by far the most numerous class in nineteenth-century France. This was because the working class had revealed its potential destabilising power by the important part it had played in the overthrow of the Restoration monarchy in 1830, a fact that Flora Tristan herself recognised. Further uprisings in Paris and Lyons in 1831 and 1834 caused permanent anxiety among the ruling classes. Workers' discontent threatened property rights. This coincided with the prevalent view of the poor as pernicious threats to the values of order ascribed to by religion and society.[14] The monarchy was based on the notion of the king being the good father and leader of his people whose administration communicated the justice and wisdom of the ruler. The essence of good governing was controlling public opinion. With the growth of urban centres in the nineteenth century, the control of those who thought otherwise was an essential part of police work in the July Monarchy:

> The potential political strength of the working class and fear of its wrath led to two different propaganda messages for workers. On the one hand each of the dynasties, parties and ideologies contending for power in France disseminated its own propaganda message. And on the other, those groups satisfied with the social order often co-operated in the preparation and the distribution of propaganda defending it.[15]

Flora Tristan belongs to the former category, whose propaganda was less secretive than the latter kind, as Kulstein demonstrates with reference to Napoléon III. Yet this former category was seen as highly dangerous and was repressed by the latter. It was in the interest of the rulers not only to produce their own propaganda, but also to repress the opposition or at least deny it access to the means of producing its own propaganda. As Liz Curtis remarks with reference to a more recent context, 'Successive administrations have demonstrated that they are well aware that one way of keeping the people acquiescent is to keep them in ignorance.'[16] One of Flora Tristan's key messages in her propaganda was to break the cycle of ignorance which kept the masses acquiescent: 'The more I study the working class and research the *cause* of its abuses, the more convinced I remain that, in the moral as in the physical world, evil comes solely from *ignorance*. Therefore whatever the price, the working class must be extracted from this state of ignorance unless one wants to risk the country's future.'[17]

In many respects the French Revolution was a turning point in the modernisation of this 'evangelical' propaganda in French politics.[18] From that point onwards education of the masses became a political question. Who educated them into political awareness and how did this process develop? Among the many ideologies which developed during the July Monarchy each school of thought produced doctrines in pamphlets and books. The written word became essential for the spread of ideas, both for the rulers and those in opposition. As Flora Tristan discovered ignorance was shared by the working class and women of all classes. Access to political education was a great hindrance to their emancipation. This period also coincides with the beginning of the development of mass literacy. However, well before the advent of compulsory free schooling which was established by Jules Ferry's law in the 1880s, intellectuals played a privileged role in the dissemination of propaganda. Flora Tristan is a fine example, although a very minor player in a wider process of the spread of political ideas. From the early nineteenth century onwards, 'It was the small mass of the literate, the educated who were to hand on to the vast crowd of illiterates the new habits and the new opinions.'[19]

The role of intellectuals in instigating the education of the illiterate masses through propaganda has been studied at length in the twentieth-century context. Mass propaganda and socialism have negative connotations of brainwashing and severe punishment associated with Maoist China or with the Bolshevik experiment. Yet Lenin instigated the education of the illiterate Russian peasants for the same purpose as the politicians of the newly established Third Republic in the 1880s, to win support for the new regime seeking legitimacy. It is true that the more fragile the regime, the greater the need for an efficient propaganda machine, and the less tolerant it is towards opposition groups. In the case of Flora Tristan the July Monarchy was the fragile regime but socialism was in its infancy. Her propaganda was part of an emergent body of a new socialist ideal struggling to find new means of communication and a means to legitimise itself.

Flora Tristan's role as a socialist propagandist is also useful to highlight the rapport between intellectuals and the growth of new ideas. As far as the role of intellectuals in spreading propaganda is concerned, there is a question of the process of creation of new ideas. Where do they originate and when do they become propaganda? Are intellectuals responsible for creating these ideas or are they not the product themselves of the historical context from where the ideas have sprung? What made Flora Tristan play a part in what was in effect a middle-class leadership of the organisation of workers?

In claiming a unique place among the workers' organisations and in jostling for their affiliations, Flora Tristan acted like other intellectuals such as Proudhon, Cabet or Marx. Each one chose to have their own interpretation of the propaganda necessary and while the temptation was to claim originality it was also part of the act to denounce rival schemes. Mostly Flora Tristan acknowledged her debt to her contemporary fellow socialists. This in fact served her purpose. She believed one of the most important lessons she could get across to the workers was the shoddy way they were being treated by other groups or by the inadequacies of other schemes. She was rather high-handed and hurtful at times – in her dismissal of Perdiguier for instance:

> Agricol Perdiguier came to read my address to the workers. He has understood
> nothing. – The word 'to act' and 'the universal liaison of men and workers' did

not strike him as significant. The only thing which caught his attention is my trip around France. – 'Ah!' he cried, 'you too want to do a tour of France?' and he seemed to be jealous of this. I didn't take to him after this reading – I think it is because he has understood nothing.[20]

She also sometimes failed to mention key players who had put forward ideas very close to hers.[21]

According to Eyerman and Jamison, 'social movements provide the breeding ground for innovation in thought as well as the social organisation of thought'.[22] They argue that social movements which remain outside mainstream politics have a special role to play in the production of new ideas: 'Social movements which do not succeed provide a challenge to the dominant assumptions of the social order, provide spaces for new conceptualisations and organisational forms to develop, serving as social laboratories for experimenting with new forms of cognition.'[23] These new forms are absorbed and then transmitted by intellectuals who produce new identities and new propaganda. It is not the intellectuals who bring consciousness to the movement as Marxist-Leninists claimed for many years. There is a formative role of the social movements on intellectuals who feed on what is happening around them and then create new intellectual processes. Through her propaganda Flora Tristan created a new type of intellectual process and indeed a new type of professional intellectual. The Workers' Union was a new practice and it was certainly unique for a woman to campaign directly among the workers themselves and not over their heads. As a lone intellectual, however, she was not magically empowered through her propaganda to influence the formation of a powerful new working-class organisation. Her consciousness transformed into her message of propaganda was socially conditioned: it depended on her own conceptualisation of the problem but it was also bound by the concerns of equally historically situated actors and the reactions of their opponents. She was part of an intellectual process which centred on the working class and the part she played was in the construction of a collective political identity for a class of which she was not a part in origins but in intellectual contribution. Hence the importance of the role of propaganda in her political survival.

Political activists in France of the 1840s – republicans, socialists, feminists in particular – had a reforming zeal much in common with the religious committees of the Catholic church set up to oversee the propagation of the faith. Flora Tristan was typical of the new generation of political militants. Many others were to follow her example in the years that followed, again not always acknowledging her contribution. It has been pointed out that her work *Union Ouvrière* sold more copies than Marx's *Communist Manifesto* and Proudhon's *What is Property?*[24]

From the above contextualisation we have established that Flora Tristan was part of the opposition in late July-Monarchy France and that she developed her identity as a would-be political activist. In the next section we shall see that her skills as a propagandist were essential for her identity as a militant simply because she got no further than the propaganda stage. Therefore, although her programme was not put into effect immediately, the fact that her ideas survived at all was due to her propaganda work. This effort contributed to the evolution of the political education of the masses, which was a complex and intricate process.

IDENTITY

The context of Flora Tristan's propaganda is interesting for three reasons. First, the most obvious one is the way she operated while direct political propaganda had been banned by the authorities – the press was severely curtailed and public meetings of more than twelve people were banned. This gave her the identity of a subversive. Given the fragility of the regime anyone who set out to talk of mobilisation of the working class to take action to improve their material conditions was a quisling. This is therefore a very different setting from studies of propaganda designed to uphold the authority of the status quo as found for the later periods in the chapters of Peter Beck or Nicholas Cull. In this case Flora Tristan, herself a member of the enlightened bourgeoisie, wished to avoid any mention of reversing the political status quo. In a country which had just seen fifty years of upheavals of revolution, civil and international war and further political unrest, it is not surprising that the rules governing meetings, publications and collective movements were very strict. This was intended to protect the monarchy, but it affected the dispossessed and the uneducated the most whether they wanted the downfall of the Orleans monarchy or simply a rise in wages. The police had interventionist powers to observe and harass dangerous elements such as Flora Tristan, and exercise their powers they did, much to her chagrin, for she herself was very careful to steer away from revolutionary rhetoric in her propaganda.[25] In the event, police harassment only served to propagate her name among the workers. After she left Lyons, her reputation went before her.

Second, in the wider context of the growth of socialism and democracy in the early 1840s the state of left-wing propaganda was at a critical point. Broadly speaking the urban poor were being courted from two angles. On the one hand from the republicans and democrats the call for universal suffrage in the name of equality was being extended to the unenfranchised, and on the other hand also in the name of equality the call for unity in an organised working class was being made in order to gain strength to combat the ill effects of economic exploitation. Rivalry among these camps affected the form their propaganda was to take. Flora Tristan is a prime example of one caught up in the tensions of the opposition politics of the July Monarchy. She frequently expressed her disenchantment with republicans and democrats, and she was highly cynical about the nephew of Napoleon whom she denounced as a despot in no uncertain terms. For this reason she argued that the workers should rely on no one but themselves; she was contributing to the creation of a new legitimacy for socialism around the notion of a workers' self-contained organisation. She became identified with the socialists.

Third, she was a female exercising her skills in a male preserve of politics. Her female identity opened doors and enabled her to preach to those she would have had difficulty contacting otherwise. She used this to particular effect in her political rhetoric as we shall see in the following section. In doing so she avoided entering into a potentially antagonistic discourse of class war. Indeed, just as class conflict was becoming an integral part of socialist doctrine, Flora Tristan made full use of her identity as a sister or mother figure to preach union and fraternity.[26] For Flora Tristan this justified her own actions – the lone campaigner had been rejected by the workers' groups in Paris where she first tried out her ideas. They had a specific view of what public identity the working class should have and of what the family should be, and were not inclined to accept her dogmatic approach:

The chapter on women was read. – It was listened to with much less attention, that was to be expected. – The audience was tired, and besides, this chapter said relatively little compared with the other. – When the reading was finished Vinçard asked to speak again. – This time he wandered completely off the point. – He said that he was opposed to the inclusion of this chapter because it was said in it that the worker went to the cabaret, and that this was going to renew the attacks the bourgeois class made on the working class. – I tried in vain to tell him that I was only talking about husbands, that I wasn't questioning the existence of cabarets, that he was digressing from the question. – Impossible, he did not want to understand anything. – This time again everyone agreed with me – and said he was wrong. – Only one, the carpenter Roly asked to speak and said, with great anger, that he was strongly opposed to its inclusion because I insulted both men and women workers. I began a discussion with him, he admitted that workers went to the cabaret, but he said: 'among ourselves, we can admit our faults, but we mustn't have to put up with outsiders coming to take us to task – on the contrary we should hide them from the bourgeoisie; and we mustn't print in a workers' journal written by workers the painful and terrible things that Madame Flora has just thrown in our faces.' – 'So Sir you would like me to cure you without seeing your sores.' – 'Yes madam.' – Opinions were divided, several agreed with him, others, the majority, strongly disagreed. – Vinçard, two others and Miss Cecile Dufour said that I had mistreated women of the people too much – that they were not as rough as all that, – that they were tender towards their children and other sentimentalisms. – A woman as silly as a goose took the floor to say that I humiliated women by asking for rights for them, by saying that they had divine rights. – This poor woman was so inept that she couldn't go on. – The whole discussion was very heated. – The result of the ballot was 9 white with 3 black. It wasn't because of women's rights that there were three against but solely because of the cabaret issue etc., etc. – As I was leaving a woman came to me and said that she thought I hadn't demanded enough for women. – I exchanged a few words with her which confirmed my impression that she is very advanced.[27]

This also solved the problem of how to approach the working class as a complete stranger. The mother or sister figure suited very well. The question of propaganda in Flora Tristan's case is central to her identity as the lone campaigner that she became during the last year of her life in two ways. Although she was acting alone her identity is linked with that of a broader movement as she became known as a militant socialist during the utopian phase of French socialism. Through her contribution to socialism as a woman intellectual her story became more significant in the light of the subsequent development of the feminist movement. She holds an important place as a precursor to feminism. Indeed one of the most skilful aspects of her book *The Workers' Union* was the way she combined the cause of and solution to the oppression of women and the working class. It was to prove harder to get this message across to her audience. This aspect of her propaganda was to be the more enduring one nonetheless.

THE POLITICAL RHETORIC IN FLORA TRISTAN'S PROPAGANDA

In the latter years of her short life Flora Tristan willingly assumed the mantle of a propagandist; to be an apostle of a sacred mission was the highest form of socialist action. What inspired her to leave her comfortable position in Paris as an intellectual, to step outside the boundaries of gender norms and take up this cause?

Behind Flora Tristan's desire to act lay a complex set of motives. She was motivated to act on behalf of the most oppressed in society – women and the working class. In her propaganda however she argued also for the general good, for an all-inclusive well-being of class collaboration. She foresaw giving specific roles for each section of society according to their abilities to work towards bringing about change for the better. In *The Workers' Union* the message was directed towards several audiences and altered accordingly. There was a message to the enlightened bourgeois, to the king, to the church and to the workers, but always with the same targeted group in mind. The salvation of humanity was to be through redemption of one social class, with cooperation from others. In this respect she doctored her message considerably.

By suggesting that the whole of society would benefit from an improvement in the conditions of the working class and of women Flora Tristan was preaching the salvation of humanity. What comes across very strongly in her campaign is the strength of feeling about the need for a new moral order and a desire to improve society outside the formal political forum. *Votre soeur en l'humanité, Flora Tristan*, is how this intellectual women introduces herself to the workers of France. The trend was particularly strong among other thinkers who were concerned with regeneration of the whole of society through an assumption by the wealthier classes of the responsibility of the elimination of poverty and through a rehabilitation of womanly qualities as a vital contribution to society. The utopian socialists desired a new reign of peace and harmony through class collaboration. This was a far cry from the strident tones of the revolutionary rhetoric of the 1790s. Judt claims that the religious sentiment was very strong among socialists as it replaced the displaced established church which the Restoration monarchy had failed to reinstate to its former position of influence.[28] With Flora Tristan's propaganda, however, a link was maintained with 1789 through the desire to render more meaningful liberty, equality and fraternity. The year 1789 became an integral part of the socialist message of redemption.

In the nineteenth-century opposition groups 1789 developed slowly as a useful focus in political rhetoric. At first there were muted references to the 1789 Revolution because of its association with violent upheaval, but in Flora Tristan's generation the emphasis on the benefits of emulating the ideals of 1789 altered. The revolutionary principle of altering society for the better through conflict and violence was channelled into new forms of programmes for change through peaceful means, with the emphasis on the change and not on the violence and conflict. This was the case with the new theories of the Saint-Simonians, Fourierists, Owenites, and self-help worker groups. When socialism began to develop it was as a reaction to bourgeois individualistic values that social values were being proposed. There was a new emphasis on rights. The importance of work as a right enabled socialists to continue to use revolutionary rhetoric of eighteenth-century radicalism. There was a new interpretation of equality: economic equality.

Flora Tristan's optimism in her rhetoric in her book *The Workers' Union* (*Union Ouvrière*) compares starkly with her feeling of alienation from those she met during her tour of France. Provincial France was new territory for her. At first she was isolated because of lack of contacts, but the potentially subversive nature of her propaganda ensured this did not last. Her written message of propaganda had been based on several assumptions about the state of the working class in France. In this she was to be disappointed at first when she realised the extent of workers' exploitation and acquiescence. However, her opinions about the validity of her message were later vindicated. These visits to provincial towns enriched her experiences and were to be recorded in the book she never completed, but which was published posthumously as the *Tour de France*. What comes across in her notes is a sense of her belief in her ability, and her conviction that she was right. Her assumptions of superiority and authority enabled her to undertake a strenuous campaign. Her effrontery in challenging bishops, journalists, novelists, bourgeois and aristocratic women to rally round to her cause is matched only by the confidence which sustained her. The result was a canny ability to use every possible occasion to further her cause as a propagandist. In the battle for hearts and minds she was in competition with other socialists, republicans and democrats and she had to steer a narrow course between legality and illegality.

Her propaganda was directed towards economic rights, the right to work and associate, thus ignoring religious and political questions, which was not surprising given the censorship of the July Monarchy, particularly of anything which might smack of Republicanism. She carefully avoided this issue, even urged the workers to steer clear of the 'Robert Macaire' politicians who might contrive to seduce them into debates about democracy. Her critique of capitalism was watered down. In spite of what she had discovered her propaganda was not so much an attack on capitalism as an exhortation to the workers to act within the existing system, warts and all:

> Being capitalists, the bourgeois make laws with regard to the commodities they have to sell and thereby regulate as they will the price of wine, meat and even the people's bread. You see already more numerous and useful, the bourgeoisie has succeeded the nobility. The unification of the working class now remains to be accomplished. In turn the workers, the vital part of the nation, must create a huge union to assert their unity! Then the working class will be strong, then it will be able to make itself heard, to demand from the bourgeois gentlemen its right to work and organise.[29]

This raises questions as to the extent of her understanding of the workings of capitalism; there is a discrepancy between the rhetoric of her journal, wherein she condemned the effects of capitalist exploitation, and her public propaganda. The idea of having one paid defender to represent the workers in Parliament was useful in avoiding the question of political reform but was not to be realised. Tristan preferred a workers' union to demanding the right to equal political participation. Her warnings to the ruling classes of the imminent revolt of the outcasts of society imbibed with a sense of justice from 1789 went unheeded; the fragility of the political gains of the Second Republic and the tragedy of the June days bore out her original message.

At times, like many missionaries, Flora Tristan was blinded by her optimism; she overestimated the awareness of the working class. Yet less than four years after her death France was once more in the throes of revolution. This same call was taken up in political clubs in the February Revolution in 1848. The rallying cry of fraternity became official doctrine for a brief moment.[30] Indeed a measure of the success of this opposition propaganda in political education of the masses is the speed at which the political clubs and societies formed in February 1848. In a matter of weeks they were up and running whereas it had taken years for any committee to reach that stage in the 1790s.

CONCLUSION

Flora Tristan's propaganda was that of an impossible mission, doomed from the start according to Dijkstra,[31] but I would argue one with a delayed impact. For a long time considered a minor socialist figure,[32] her message achieved a new relevance with the growth of feminism; there was something of a delayed reaction to the relevance of her message and strength of her originality. Where traditional studies of class conflict concentrate on the results of struggles and gains of the working class she counts for very little. For the study of the spread of innovative political ideas she has been recognised.

The question of propaganda in Flora Tristan's case is central to her identity as the lone campaigner that she became during the last year of her life. Yet I have shown the context of her militancy: she was part of a wider movement of politicisation of the lower orders during the final years of the July Monarchy. Her work contributes to a corpus of ideas and networks of 'utopian' socialists, anxious to alleviate the sufferings inflicted by capitalism. Known as a militant socialist during the rich phase of early French socialism and for her contribution to socialism as a woman intellectual her story became more significant in the light of the development of the feminist movement. She holds an important place as a precursor to feminism in the heart of the utopian socialist movement. She succeeded in raising the profile of 'the woman question' in many circles hitherto ignorant of, or antagonistic to, women's emancipation. She left an important legacy for the socialist women of 1848, namely the task of incorporating the gender issue into socialist propaganda and the efforts required to find allies among the democrat and republican opposition activists in order to achieve notoriety for the cause.

In the study of her propaganda there is a hopelessness of both her aim and method. The aim was working for the salvation of the whole of humanity, the method was one woman touring France. The strenuous effort put into convincing her targeted audience was impossible to sustain. We could easily dismiss this case of Flora Tristan apparently struggling against all the odds as a fanatic who made no impact, until we realise that she did not disappear without trace. The force of her propaganda has gone beyond her short-lived campaign. It has been taken up by historians of feminism and given a new significance. Her evangelical spirit has endured.

Notes

1   Extract from Flora Tristan's Journal, in preparation for a work she intended to entitle *Le Tour de France. État actuel de la classe ouvrière sous l'aspect moral, intellectuel et matériel*, and published posthumously as *Le Tour de France. État actuel de la classe ouvrière sous l'aspect moral, intellectuel et matériel, Journal inédit de Flora Tristan*, ed. Michel Collinet and Jules Puech (Paris, Tête de Feuilles, 1973); new introduction Stéphane Michaud (2 vols, Paris, Maspéro, 1980, tr. Máire Cross (publication forthcoming) (Oxford, Berg, 1999), p. 27.

2   Flora Tristan, *The Workers' Union*, tr. with an Introduction by Beverly Livingston (Urbana, University of Illinois Press, 1983), p. 39.

3   See Stéphane Michaud (ed.), *Flora Tristan. Lettres* (Paris, Seuil, 1980); *Flora Tristan. La paria et son rêve* (Fontenay Saint-Cloud, ENS Editions, 1995).

4   The most comprehensive biography of Flora Tristan using contemporary sources is by Jules Puech, *La vie et l'oeuvre de Flora Tristan* (Paris, Marcel Rivière, 1925).

5   Tristan, *Le Tour de France*, vol.1, p. 28.

6   Cited in Máire Cross, 'Mary Wollstonecraft and Flora Tristan: One Pariah Redeems Another', in Clarissa Campbell-Orr (ed.), *Wollstonecraft's Daughters* (Manchester University Press, 1995), p. 124.

7   *Le Tour de France*, vol.1, pp. 115–16.

8   *Le Tour de France*, p. 116.

9   *Le Tour de France*, p. 117.

10   *The Workers' Union*, p. 37.

11   *The Workers' Union*, p. 38.

12   For the latest assessment of the many images of Flora Tristan, see Susan Grogan, *Flora Tristan, Life Stories* (London, Routledge, 1997).

13   David Kulstein, *Napoléon III and the Working Class: A Study of Government Propaganda under the Second Empire* (San José, The California State Colleges, 1969), pp. ix–x.

14   Howard M. Solomon, *Public Welfare, Science and Propaganda in Seventeenth-Century France: The Innovations of Théophraste Renaudot* (Princeton University Press, 1972), p. 23.

15   Kulstein, *Napoléon III and the Working Class*, p. x.

16   Liz Curtis, *Ireland: The Propaganda War* (London, Pluto Press, 1984), p. 1.

17   *The Workers' Union*, p. 150.

18   See Joan B. Landes, *Women and the Public Sphere in the Age of the Revolution* (Ithaca, Cornell University Press, 1988), ch. 2.

19   F.C. Bartlett, *Political Propaganda* (Cambridge University Press, 1940), p. 27.

20   *Le Tour de France*, vol. 1, p. 27.

21   This was the case for Pierre Moreau in particular who wrote a pamphlet entitled *De la réforme des abus de compagnonnage et de l'amélioration du sort des travilleurs*, 1843, of which extracts are reproduced in Jacques Rancière (ed.), *La parole ouvrière* (Paris, Union générale d'éditions, 1976), pp. 188–93. For background on her exchange of ideas with other activists see Puech, *La vie et l'oeuvre de Flora Tristan*; Jacques Rancière, *La nuit des prolétaires* (Paris, Fayard, 1981).

22   Ron Eyerman and Andrew Jamison, *Social Movements: A Cognitive Approach* (Cambridge, Polity Press, 1991), p. 3.

23   Eyerman and Jamison, *Social Movements*, pp. 165–6.

24   See Daniel Armogathe and Jacques Grandjonc, 'Introduction' to their edition of Flora Tristan, *Union Ouvrière* (Paris, Des femmes, 1986), p. 18.

25   For a discussion of her attitude to revolution and violence see Máire Cross, 'A Conflict of Interests: Gender, Class and Revolutionary Violence in Flora Tristan's Campaign 1843–44: The Polemics of Militancy', in Jan Windebank and Renate Gunther (eds), *Violence and Conflict in the Society of Modern France* (Lampeter, Mellen Press, 1995), pp. 21–35.

26   Grogan, *Flora Tristan. Life Stories*, ch. 7.

27   *Le Tour de France*, vol. 1, p. 30.

28   Tony Judt, *Marxism and the French Left: Studies in Labour and Politics in France 1830–1981* (Oxford University Press, 1981).

29   *The Workers' Union*, p. 58.

30   See Marcel David, *Le printemps de la fraternité* (Paris, Aubier, 1992), pp. 171–294.

31   Sandra Dijkstra, *Flora Tristan: Feminism in the Age of George Sand* (London, Pluto Press, 1992).

32   G.D.H Cole, *A History of Socialist Thought, Volume 1: 'The Forerunners 1789-1950'* (London, Macmiilan, 1953), ch. x, pp. 183–8.

10

PROPAGANDISING AS SOCIALIST WOMEN: THE CASE OF THE WOMEN'S COLUMNS IN BRITISH SOCIALIST NEWSPAPERS, 1884–1914

Karen Hunt and June Hannam

Dora Montefiore, a member of the executive of the Social Democratic Federation (SDF) and an active suffragist, wrote in the SDF newspaper *Justice* to complain about the tone adopted towards women in most professedly democratic publications:

> They are either written of by men in a tone of half humorous contempt or vulgar banter, or else a woman is engaged to write down to them of dress, cookery and chiffons; or else, coupled with children, they are trotted out as needing philanthropic legislation which workmen refuse to have applied to themselves. Scarcely ever are they written of, or treated as fellow workers with men, as an integral adult portion of the democracy which is to inspire the new order, to which the old order is daily giving way more and more.[1]

This quotation raises issues about women's political identity which were crucial for socialists in the period leading up to the First World War. The emphasis on class struggle at the workplace and the importance of the male worker meant that socialist rhetoric was masculinist in tone and content; the SDF, for example, referred constantly to the problem of the socialist's wife, a use of language which just assumed that the socialist was a male.[2] Women were viewed as a problem for socialists because they were thought to be steeped in domestic concerns which led to a conservative outlook – this was alarming in view of the influence that they had on children and even potentially on their husbands. For this reason it was accepted that it would be beneficial for the movement if women could be attracted to socialism. Nonetheless, the theory and practice of socialism tended to marginalise women and reduced its appeal to them.[3]

An influential group of socialist women propagandists, however, used their skills as speakers and writers to challenge the prevailing view of women's potential as political activists. The intention of this chapter is to focus on the journalism of these propagandists, in particular the women's columns which were published in the socialist press at a national level between 1890 and 1914, in order to explore the extent to which women journalists sought to modify the masculinist rhetoric and meaning of socialism.[4]

Most studies of propaganda concentrate on attempts by the state to exert hegemonic control, usually through the use of false or distorted information. The way in which oppositional groups use propaganda to 'propagate a belief, a position and a set of arguments' in order to persuade men and women to challenge the existing political system has received less attention.[5] Yet the socialist groups formed in the 1880s and 1890s saw propaganda as central to their main project of 'making socialists'.[6] It was assumed that socialism would not just happen because of the workings of impersonal forces. William Morris, for example, described the means to achieving socialism as 'First, educating people into desiring it, next organising them into claiming it effectively'.[7] For socialists, propaganda was essential if men and women were to be persuaded, both in their hearts as well as in their minds, to desire a world which could as yet only be imagined but which would come about if they would make it happen. To that end members of socialist groups involved themselves in actions which could touch hearts and minds, including trade union struggles, electoral politics and free speech campaigns, and were active as public speakers and writers.

Newspapers were thought to have a key role to play in spreading socialist propaganda. Between 1890 and 1910 '800 papers, half of them explicitly socialist, were published in the interests of labour'.[8] The most successful of these was the *Clarion*, edited by Robert Blatchford, which had a regular circulation of 30,000. It was not formally attached to a particular group, but sought to interest men, women and children in socialist and independent labour politics through *Clarion* van speaking tours and through 'cultural organisations', including cycling clubs and choirs, which often had a close relationship with the Independent Labour Party (ILP). Other newspapers were the official organs of particular groups, including *Commonweal* for the Socialist League and *Justice* for the SDF. The *Labour Leader* was in a more ambivalent position since it was owned and edited by an individual, Keir Hardie, but his role as one of the leaders of the ILP meant that his paper could be seen as expressing the views of the Party more generally. On the other hand he also used it to advance his own political strategies. After an initial rise in circulation to 50,000 the *Labour Leader* began to falter and by the time it was taken over officially by the ILP in 1904 circulation had fallen to just below 12,000. All of these national papers were published on a weekly basis. Many local SDF and ILP branches also had their own newspapers. Some of these were short-lived but others, such as the Glasgow ILP newspaper *Forward*, established in 1906, were influential and lasted beyond the First World War.[9]

Socialists believed that the press had an influence on political allegiances and behaviour, although the extent of this is difficult to determine, and they saw their own papers as providing an alternative voice to capitalist organs. Newspapers were aimed at men and women who were already members of socialist organisations and sought to elaborate and extend on existing beliefs, in some cases providing an organising focus. At the same time socialists were encouraged to sell newspapers on the streets in order to attract new members and to take the socialist message beyond a small group of party workers to influence a broader constituency.[10] A small but significant group of women journalists contributed to the socialist press. The majority came from middle-class backgrounds, although among those writing for *Justice* were Mary Gray who had been in service and whose husband was a victimised trade unionist, Amie Hicks who worked at different times as a ropemaker and a midwife, and her daughter Margaretta Hicks who was employed as a tailoress. Even among middle-class women there were considerable differences in their educational and financial circumstances. The ILP Quaker Isabella Ford who was born in 1855, the daughter of a Leeds solicitor and landowner, received a broad education at home and was unusual in being so well provided for by her parents that she did not need to engage in paid employment.[11] It was far more common for the slightly younger generation of propagandists, such as Enid Stacy and Katharine St John Conway, who were university educated and had given up employment as schoolteachers to become full-time activists in the socialist cause, to have to earn their own living from the fees they received through speaking and through journalism. They were similar to other 'new women' of the 1890s who sought a more independent life through paid employment and were interested in exploring new ways in which men and women could relate to each other both inside and outside marriage.[12] Female socialist propagandists believed that socialism would provide a route towards a more fulfilling life for women, and along with other 'new life' socialists tried to put some of their ideas into practice in their own lives.[13] Their activity as propagandists, therefore, was an integral part of their working lives and of their political identity.

Women conducted propaganda across a broad front and rarely worked just as journalists. Enid Stacy, Katharine Bruce Glasier and Dora Montefiore, for example, were also inspiring speakers, while Isabella Ford helped to organise tailoresses and textile workers in Leeds during the 1890s. Women's writing was also more varied than the term journalism might imply. Eleanor Marx wrote literary articles and reviews and translated texts such as *Madame Bovary*. Dora Montefiore also undertook translations and wrote poetry, while Katharine Bruce Glasier and Isabella Ford wrote short stories and novels. It was in their novels that women were most likely to imagine a world in which women's lives were no longer restricted and to discuss the relationship between personal and political life. Male socialists tended to view such questions as 'bourgeois' or individualistic and therefore it was more acceptable for women socialists to explore them in novels.[14]

As journalists women concentrated on the general project of 'making socialists'. They explored the meaning of socialism and how a socialist future would lead to a broad transformation in the lives of men, women and children. In common with their male colleagues they used their own activities and interests as the basis for much of their journalism. The ILP propagandist Margaret McMillan, for example, used her articles, which were submitted to a variety of socialist and labour papers, to develop a theoretical basis for her schemes to improve child education and welfare which arose from her work as a member of the Bradford School Board. She also saw her journalism as a means to publicise, and to gain support for, specific campaigns in which she was engaged, such as the feeding of schoolchildren.[15] Women journalists were more likely than men to make the social and economic conditions of working-class women's lives the subject of their articles. They also raised issues about women's role in socialist politics and explored how socialism related to women's emancipation. On the other hand, such articles did not appear very frequently in *Justice* and the *Labour Leader*, the two papers most closely associated with specific socialist organisations. *Justice*, for example, provided very little space for signed articles, although current events could lead to a debate on women's social position; for example the Edith Lanchester case prompted a discussion about marriage and free love in the 1890s. The revival of the women's suffrage campaign after 1905 also led to an increase in articles in the socialist press which discussed both the specific issue of the terms on which the franchise should be given and also the more general question of women's role in socialist politics. This interest was not sustained, however, at least in the *Labour Leader*. Many ILP suffragists gave a full-time commitment to suffrage campaigning after 1907 and their perspective was absent from the *Labour Leader* until the alliance between the Labour Party and the National Union of Women's Suffrage Societies brought them back into the centre of socialist politics. It was in this context that the development of women's columns must be seen as important in giving women their own space within socialist newspapers, although the purpose of the columns and, indeed, whether they should exist at all, was hotly debated.

WOMEN'S COLUMNS

For the purposes of this chapter a women's column is defined as one which had a specific author or editor, appeared on a regular basis and covered a variety of issues relating to women, usually in a way which involved analysis and discussion. It is difficult to draw a hard and fast line between a women's column and other specific space for women. After 1909, for example, the *Labour Leader* set aside space for a women's page – this contained an article each week on a different topic, such as 'The Sundholm Workhouse' by Marion Coates Hansen or 'International Women at Work' by Margaret MacDonald, or else provided space for a short story. However, the absence of a regular editor meant that the page lacked a distinctive point of view and there was little continuity of approach from week to week. Also included in the women's page was a regular column, written by Margaret MacDonald, about the activities of the Women's Labour League. Margaretta Hicks wrote a similar column in *Justice* after 1913 which covered the work of the Women's Council of the British Socialist Party.[16] Despite their single authorship these have not been included as women's columns in this chapter. Their emphasis on reporting the activities of a specific organisation of women meant that they did not discuss the same broad range of issues relating to women's social, economic and political position which can be found in the other women's columns.

Women's columns proliferated in the socialist and labour press in this period. Some were written by women who worked mainly as journalists, whereas others were compiled by women who were active in the socialist movement in more varied ways. The *Clarion* had one of the longest lasting women's columns which provided an important and consistent space for socialist women to express their views when other socialist newspapers did not have a women's column. Entitled 'Our Woman's Letter', it first appeared in February 1895. For two months it was written by Eleanor Keeling, a member of the Liverpool Fabian Society and secretary of the Labour Church Pioneers, but it was soon taken over by Julia Dawson, the pen name of Mrs D. Middleton Worrall who had been a religious journalist for eight years.[17] She continued in this position until 1911. Julia Dawson also wrote in the *Women's Trade Union Review* and in 1909 edited the *Woman Worker* which was established by the *Clarion* editor, Robert Blatchford.

Two women's columns appeared in the *Labour Leader*. The first, entitled 'Matrons and Maidens', was written by Lily Bell and appeared between March 1894 and December 1898. There was then a gap until 'Our Women's Outlook', written by Iona between 1906 and 1909. Lily Bell was the pseudonym of Isabella Bream Pearce, president of the Glasgow Women's Labour Party, vice-president of the Glasgow Labour Party and a member of the Cathcart School Board. Both Isabella and her husband Charles, a wine merchant for an American organisation, the Brotherhood of the New Life, who was adopted as an ILP candidate for the parliamentary seat of Camlachie in the early 1890s, were close friends of Keir Hardie.[18] It appears likely that Iona was the pseudonym of Katharine Bruce Glasier, although there were times when she wrote under her own name and claimed that she was substituting for Iona.[19]

Justice was the one major socialist newspaper which did not have a women's column until after the turn of the century. When this was first established in 1907 it was written by Jill, but its most important editor was Dora Montefiore who took over in March 1909.[20] She had lived for nearly two decades in Australia where she had helped to form the key suffragist group, the Womanhood Suffrage League of New South Wales, before returning to England in 1892. Here she continued with her suffrage work but became increasingly interested in labour and socialist issues. She was a propagandist with the *Clarion* van in 1898 and joined the SDF some time after, being elected to the executive for the first time in 1903.

Dora Montefiore was unusual among women's columnists at a national level for signing her column with her own name. Most of the others, in common with many male socialist journalists, used a pseudonym. There was a greater variety of practice, however, in the local socialist press where women's columns also proliferated. Isabella Ford always signed her column in the *Leeds Forward* with her initials, IOF, and Mary Phillips, a suffragette and socialist, signed her column for the Glasgow *Forward* with her own name. Lily Bell, however, continued to use her old pseudonym when she also wrote a column for a brief period in *Forward*. It is difficult to see any pattern in this use of pseudonyms as against actual names – in no case did it seem to make a difference in terms of freedom of expression or in the content of the columns. One could speculate, however, that the use of a pseudonym separated off journalism from the other activities pursued by the columnists, whereas those who wrote under their own names self-consciously adopted a more integrated political identity.

The columns looked very different from one another. At the beginning 'Matrons and Maidens' was headed by a line drawing which represented Lily Bell in an idealised way, sitting thoughtfully with pen in hand and looking distinctly feminine. This was later replaced by a variety of small illustrations. The banner heading to 'Our Women's Circle' in *Justice* was the most elaborate – this may have been one of the conditions imposed by Dora Montefiore in agreeing to provide a regular column. The appearance of the page was certainly useful in drawing attention to women's circles and in attracting female readers. A.A. Watts of the SDF said 'he had often sold *Justice* to some woman in the crowd by opening the paper at the Woman's Column'.[21] The fears of some female socialists about whether a column would marginalise women seemed to be confirmed in those papers such as the *Labour Leader* where the women's column was placed next to the children's corner. The importance of women as consumers, which was recognised in the press more generally in this period, is also evident in these pages which are full of advertisements for goods related to women's needs.[22]

There was considerable ambivalence, especially among active women socialists, about whether there should be a separate column for women and what this implied about women's role as political activists within the broader socialist project. These debates mirrored the more general discussion within the Second International as a whole about whether women should organise separately alongside or as part of socialist groups. In Britain, women's groups attached to the main socialist organisations did develop in an ad hoc way at local level, but there was no attempt to organise systematically throughout the country until after the turn of the century. Both the SDF and the ILP were reluctant to pursue women's self-organisation because it raised the issue of whether the identification of a group by sex was compatible with a class analysis. As women became more vocal in expressing their own demands, however, in particular for the vote, socialist groups began to take the question of women's organisation more seriously. The SDF responded by organising Women's Socialist Circles after 1904, while female members of the ILP were responsible for establishing the Women's Labour League in 1906 in order to gain working women's allegiance for the Labour Party and to draw them away from the suffrage movement.

Underlying the debate about whether women should organise separately or should have their own column in the socialist press was the issue of whether women, because of their specific social and economic position, had different interests and needs from men. For those who hoped to see women as active and equal participants alongside men in the development of socialist politics it was feared that a designated separate space would imply marginality. Ethel Snowden, an ILP member, suffragist and well-known speaker for socialism, objected to the establishment of Iona's column on the grounds that although men and women had 'different tastes and desires in many cases . . . in matters of citizenship and on questions of reform there need be nothing in the way of specialisation for either of the sexes . . . for whose benefit is the remainder of the *Labour Leader*? If for men only, why so much more space for men than for women? If for both men and women, why a special column for women?'[23] Isabella Ford echoed these views, arguing that 'I thought the day had gone by for the separate treatment of men and women's interests', although a decade before she had edited her own women's column in the *Leeds Forward*.[24] Her position may have changed because, in the context of a revived suffrage movement, she hoped that the ILP would give its full and active backing to the women's cause and would see the demand for the vote as an integral part of its own political agenda.

It was not uncommon for women propagandists to change their views about women's columns. Dora Montefiore edited a women's column in the radical paper *New Age*, but just before she was about to take over the editorship of the women's column in *Justice* expressed similar ideas to those of Ethel Snowden and Isabella Ford about the desirability of separate space for women in the newspaper of a mixed-sex socialist group:

> It's rather against my principles to write for a Woman's Column just because I don't think it's the woman's fair share of the paper . . . instead of being poked away in a corner, they should have at least a fair half share in every paper that is working for the cause of humanity. . . . When we have a real women's paper of our own, as we shall have some day, we will be generous and let the men have a corner all to themselves, just to let them know what it is like and we will get a man who knows all about it to write on the latest thing in cravats and how to 'do up' offices and smoking rooms in 'Liberty muslin' and giving the latest recipe for baldness. etc. etc. but until then. . . .[25]

For many women socialists, therefore, the question of women's columns was a complex one. Their opinions could be affected by the more general political context, including the extent to which socialist groups were giving weight to women's needs, and the relationship between socialism and the women's movement. They could also be influenced by the proposed content and purpose of specific women's columns.

There was a general fear that women's columns might mirror those which were already prevalent in the mainstream press and some labour papers. Margaret Pease thought that Isabella Ford's objection to Iona's column might have been prompted by the fact that hitherto women's columns were 'filled up with pudding recipes and frivolous chatter about fashions' and the dread that this might appear in the *Leader* was 'natural and excusable'.[26] Iona replied in a humorous vein: 'Well, I haven't given any pudding recipes and I haven't really said anything about fashions as yet . . . but if ever a really good and wholesome recipe comes my way I shall plump it into my column without a blush.'[27] Iona's attitude can be contrasted with that of Dora Montefiore who was bitterly opposed to including anything on such topics. Nonetheless, despite their differences none of the women's columns in the socialist press gave very much space to recipes, fashion or household hints. They all covered a wide variety of issues including the suffrage movement, rational dress, sweated work conditions, women explorers, the socialist movement internationally, women authored books, responses to readers' letters and women's role on elected public bodies. They also gave publicity to women's organisation in the branches. Although the creation of a women's organisation was not the primary function of these columns and they never took on a coordinating role, at least they drew the attention of their readers to the possibilities of women organising together. The writers of women's columns not only gave information about activities and events, they also discussed issues such as women's suffrage or rational dress in a more theoretical way and debated women's role within socialist politics.

Underlying these similarities, however, were fundamental disagreements over two closely related issues: which women should be the target audience and what was the best way to attract them to socialism. A crucial area for debate was how far women's different social and economic position, and their interest in domestic issues, should be recognised in the columns and used as the basis to engage them in socialist politics. The approach to such issues affected the way in which the writers of women's columns engaged in a more theoretical discussion about women's political identity and the relationship between class and gender politics. Julia Dawson and Iona emphasised the importance of women's role as wives and mothers and it was the woman in the home that they hoped to attract to socialism. They recognised that the model of politicisation which informed the action of socialist groups, which assumed that socialists were either 'converted' through the power of a speaker, or else were influenced by the experience of work or by taking part in strikes, was a gendered one.[28] The SDF, for instance, assumed that political propaganda would have its greatest effect on individuals who were already discontented and who had some experience of collective action in a strike or in a political campaign. Their education then needed to continue long after the initial conversion so that through party membership they could become class-conscious socialists.[29] Women were far less likely than men, however, to have engaged in such collective actions or to have had the time to attend meetings. When she reflected on what was to happen to women's organisations in the new party, the BSP, Margaretta Hicks, its first woman organiser, commented that:

> The difficulty is that most of the propaganda of Socialism has been carried on in terms of political economy or political action, both of which are far more used by men than by women, and, besides that, we must all recognise that women who have young children find it very difficult to attend evening meetings, or meetings of any kind, if it means travelling any distance. So we must needs find other ways of propaganda. It is sure to be difficult, and there will be many comrades conservative enough to dislike variations from the regularly accepted methods of public meetings, which are considered good enough for men, and therefore should be good enough for women. We must consider, however, that the circumstances are different.[30]

These difficulties were recognised by those who argued in favour of women's columns. A separate column was a way of reaching women who had little access to other forms of propaganda and whose interests were rarely catered for in the main body of the socialist press. Implicit within this was the view that women found it more difficult than men to make time to read socialist papers. Sarah Burgess, who had written a column in the *Workman's Times*, a paper edited by her husband, later supported the introduction of Iona's column because 'there are thousands of wives in the Labour movement who have time only to skim the political part of the paper . . . and who will be thankful for the wee column all their own'.[31] Julia Dawson justified including some household tips in her column because 'if I can show women an easier method of performing their daily tasks in the house I shall be helping on Socialism. When women get the leisure they ought to have for reading, thinking and resting, Socialism will be within close reach.'[32]

In seeking to attract housewives and mothers to socialist politics it was assumed that domestic questions needed to be given emphasis. In Germany, for example, the highly successful socialist women's paper, *Die Gleichheit*, edited by Clara Zetkin, which was officially a magazine for women workers, began to include regular supplements for mothers and children after 1905 and circulation increased sharply. Recruitment of women to the SPD also increased and they were overwhelmingly the wives of men already in the party.[33] For Iona this was also a class issue. On several occasions she referred to the different outlook of middle-class and working-class women socialists and declared that she rarely heard complaints from the latter about covering domestic issues. 'These tiresome sayings usually come from those who place upon others the drudgery of cooking and looking after babies, but themselves wear the fine dresses and jewels.'[34]

The intention of Julia Dawson and Iona in addressing household questions was to look at domestic and family concerns from a socialist perspective. In a discussion of spring-cleaning, for example, Iona wrote:

> And so, these very fingers that each week will write about politics and books and all things that interest the mind, will soon be busy as bees in every corner and cranny of the home. . . . And how tired and sometimes cross many of us will be! But what makes women's home work and men's outdoor work so songless today is not its hardness, but its thanklessness and sense of drudgery. How different it becomes directly men and women feel that work is in itself good and of real avail for those they love. But work altogether today has become such a matter of work for masters and for profit, and not for our own use and joy, that nearly every kind of work has fallen under the common curse of capitalism.[35]

Julia Dawson and Iona emphasised that women could use the experiences they had gained in the home to inform campaigns for better housing, educational reform and for humanising institutions such as the Poor Law. By asserting that home life was an important site of politicisation for socialists and that the values fostered there meant that women could make a special contribution to public life, women columnists raised the possibility of redefining the meaning of socialism and making it appear more relevant for women. On the other hand this posed little challenge to the Victorian ideology of separate spheres and enabled the authors to sidestep issues which highlighted gender as well as class inequalities in the socialist movement and which raised the potential for women to act together as women across political boundaries.

Lily Bell and later Dora Montefiore addressed their columns to a far wider range of women, including waged workers. Dora Montefiore claimed that she wanted 'news from the factory, and the workshop . . . news from the underpaid post office and telephone girls; news from the sweated East End workers and news from the domestic servants, the waitresses, the barmaids, and from any women workers who have a grievance against society as at present organised . . . .'[36] She hoped to use her column to 'concentrate on the special side of Socialist propaganda, as it affects women, and interpret everyday events from the standpoint of Social Democracy', since the bourgeois press misinterpreted all the vital questions. Her own interest in international affairs meant that she wanted her column to educate women socialists in Britain about what was happening in the rest of the world and to 'be a means of spreading information that will link up the endeavours of class conscious working women in every country, realising as we do, that in helping forward the development of women we are helping forward the development of the race'.[37]

Both Lily Bell and Dora Montefiore were remarkably similar in wanting women to feel actively involved in their columns. Lily Bell said: 'I want you all to have a feeling of proprietorship in this column, and not to look on it as simply a place for airing my own particular views on matters in general . . . I invite confidences. I mean this column to be a real help to women in the movement.'[38] Dora Montefiore agreed with her editor's view that as many women as possible should write into the column for 'I am the last person to wish to "spoonfeed" the women who read this column, I am only here to provide some sort of nourishment until they are producing and distributing for themselves.' She hoped the column would 'voice the demands and aspirations of socialist women'.[39]

In the view of these columnists, therefore, propaganda was a complex process which, to be effective, needed the active participation of readers who would help to shape the content of what was written. This reflected the dual purpose of the columns. They not only intended to politicise women and to make socialists, but they also hoped to express the views of women who had few other outlets to put forward their opinions and thereby to modify the nature of socialism itself.

Although her outlook was in many ways similar to Lily Bell, in one respect Dora Montefiore was much closer to the views of Iona. This was over the question of the relationship between gender and class when addressing socialist women's political identity. Lily Bell tried to keep her socialism and her feminism inextricably linked, and was determined not to put one before the other. She was willing to raise issues of male power over women, in particular when discussing domestic questions; for example, in urging the need for sex education for girls she argued that 'ignorance has been the main point men have relied on to keep women in subjection to them'.[40] She criticised socialists for not taking women's emancipation seriously enough and for viewing it as a side issue rather than as central to the socialist project.

> I hope our socialist women will never forget that they are 'women first and Socialists afterwards', being Socialists simply because through Socialism they hope to find fuller outlet for their womanhood; and as womanhood cannot evolve truly except in freedom, therefore it is our *first* duty to see that its man made barriers are removed.[41]

Both Dora Montefiore and Iona, however, were anxious to emphasise the importance of socialism for working women and the need for them to associate with their class rather than with their sex. This is partly related to their ideological position, but also must be seen in the context of the revival of the suffrage movement after 1905 which threatened to divert women away from the socialist cause. Thus, Dora Montefiore claimed that 'the working woman is too often either apathetic because she has no knowledge of the economic and other forces which have shaped her lot, or, if she has a glimmering of better possibilities she listens to the voice of her middle-class sister, and believes that she can improve her lot by joining forces with a sex instead of with a class'.[42] In similar vein, Iona, in debating with a suffragist, argued that men had had votes for a long time but had not used them wisely: 'nor will we women when we get them unless we are taught the truth of socialism. This is why I stick by the ILP.'[43]

Overall, therefore, there were considerable differences in the way in which women columnists constructed the socialist woman and explored her political identity. Nonetheless, they all emphasised that women, whether in the workplace or in the home, had the potential to take an interest in, and to become involved in, socialist politics. They believed that it was important for women to think for themselves about political issues and were eager to give examples of women taking action in progressive causes around the world. Despite her reservations about the outlook and tactics of women's suffrage activists in the prewar years, Iona still praised them for 'stirring women of all classes to think for themselves'.[44] In varying degrees the columnists accepted that women did have different interests from men (as well as sharing some concerns in common) and argued that socialists needed to address these if they were to gain women's support. At the same time socialism needed to be redefined so that it held out the promise of a transformation in those areas of life which most affected women. While most of the columns accepted that family life and domestic concerns were of key importance to women, they all argued that women's lives should not be bounded by these. Lily Bell, for instance, claimed that 'judging from my own feelings in the matter it is only because men have tried to *limit* us to domestic affairs that we are inclined to rebel against them more than we should otherwise do'.[45]

In a context in which they were rarely in positions of power, either in socialist organisations or in their associated newspapers, and where socialists continued to express concern about any emphasis on gender, women's columnists found it difficult to express their views with complete openness or to guarantee a particular amount of space in socialist newspapers. There were only a small number of women who owned and edited their own newspapers, including Annie Besant who published *The Link* in the late 1880s and Florence Grove, a member of the Chelsea ILP, who produced the *Chelsea Pick and Shovel*. Florence Grove used her paper to publicise campaigns over inadequate housing and other issues which arose from her work on the local Board of Guardians. In 1911 Margaretta Hicks edited a 'socialist home paper' which was also called *The Link*. This was not to be a women's paper as such, but was intended to be 'written with the idea that it was especially for women to read and understand'. It ran into difficulties because the editor was unable to advertise it widely enough. 'When the tailor's strike was on, and I had no work, "The Link" had to stop for a month.'[46]

It was more usual, therefore, for women to have to take account of the views of their male editors. It is significant that when Iona was asked by correspondents whether she favoured the Women's Social and Political Union or the Women's Labour League she prefaced her remarks with: 'The Editor has quite generously allowed me a free hand on the question. . . .'[47] It is difficult to know whether women were chosen to write particular columns because their ideas seemed to 'fit' the general tone of the paper. Robert Blatchford of the *Clarion* and John Bluce Glasier, who edited the *Labour Leader* from 1905 to 1909, both emphasised the important role that women played in the home and this was reflected in their respective women's columns. It is likely that Lily Bell was employed by Keir Hardie because she was a personal friend and because her husband had subsidised the paper. She was able to put forward a hard-hitting feminist analysis and criticism of socialist men because in the 1890s this had few immediate political implications. It was much more difficult for women's columnists to do this after 1905 when the women's suffrage movement posed difficult questions about political loyalties. It is significant that the only socialist paper which introduced a women's column which expressed similar views to those of Lily Bell, and indeed was written by her for a while, was the Glasgow *Forward* whose editor, Tom Johnston, was sympathetic to militant suffragettes. This meant that the paper had a very different tone and contained many more articles which explored the relationship between class and gender politics than the *Labour Leader*.

The space allotted to women's columns changed over time: Dora Montefiore's column started off as a whole page in *Justice*, including advertisements. Six months later, although the heading stretched across the whole page, the column and advertisements occupied only half the page. The vulnerability of women journalists can be seen when they fell out with their editors which meant that they usually left the newspaper. Lily Bell was dismissed in 1898 because Hardie claimed that she was 'hopeless', although it is unclear whether he was referring to her opinions or to her journalistic skills.[48] Julia Dawson was willing to criticise the editor on various occasions, in particular when a man was appointed to edit the *Woman Worker*, but she eventually left the *Clarion* in 1911 because she disagreed with Blatchford's anti-Germanism and hostility to the ILP.[49] When the German women's paper *Die Gleichheit* was taken over by the SPD, Clara Zetkin was obliged to change its format and character, including far more articles on cooking and fashion, although she disapproved of this development.[50]

Despite all the difficulties, women's columns did provide one of the few ways in which readers could find out about what other women were doing in the movement, both at home and abroad, and could bring women in touch with each other. They also contributed towards discussions on the 'woman question' which took place in the branches. It is difficult to say with any certainty how widely they were read. It has been suggested that the *Clarion* had a large female readership and that this could partly be explained by Julia Dawson's column.[51]

Letters sent into the women's columns also implied that they struck a chord with female readers and Iona claimed that the advent of her column 'has aroused as much interest in what I, whoever I may be, will say in the *Leader* as in what Philip Snowden or John Hodge will say in Parliament'.[52] This seems, however, to be a rather exaggerated claim and was not shared by members of the National Administrative Council who grumbled that the column was not read.[53]

What the columns provided, however, was a regular space in which one woman could put forward a consistent view of the importance of socialist politics for women and the need for women to be active in the movement. Unlike regular columns which reported on the activities of groups such as the Women's Labour League, the women's columns were able to discuss issues related to socialist women's politics rather than just providing information about events. Although many of them contributed to the mainstream socialist view of the family, in particular in the ILP, in which women had the main responsibility for domestic affairs and childcare, they were consistent in arguing that this should not limit women's horizons and that they should play their part in forwarding socialist politics. The columns, therefore, were a key space in which a woman-focused socialism could be articulated.

Propaganda was one of the few areas in which women could make a substantial public contribution to furthering the cause of socialism. When the ILP began to focus on electioneering and on building an alliance with trade unions after the mid-1890s rather than on making socialists, this development was deplored by leading propagandists such as Katharine Bruce Glasier and Margaret McMillan who believed that women would become marginalised still further.[54] Although female propagandists aimed to attract both men and women to socialism, they also drew attention to the need to appeal specifically to women and through the women's columns developed a style of propaganda which addressed this constituency. The nature of the audience and the way in which class and gender questions were conceptualised differed from column to column, but they all emphasised women's potential for political activism. They may have had difficulties in pursuing their claims, but they made sure that the masculine rhetoric of socialism did not remain unchallenged and that there was space in which 'to voice the demands and aspirations of socialist women'.[55]

Notes

1   *Justice* (4/05/1903).

2   K. Hunt, 'Fractured Universality: The Language of British Socialism before the First World War', in J. Belchem and N. Kirk (eds), *Languages of Labour* (Aldershot, Ashgate, 1997), pp. 3–4.

3   For a full discussion of this, see K. Hunt, *Equivocal Feminists: The Social Democratic Federation and the Woman Question, 1884–1911* (Cambridge University Press, 1996); J. Hannam, 'Women and the ILP, 1890–1914', in D. James, T. Jowitt and K. Laybourn (eds), *The Centennial History of the Independent Labour Party* (Halifax, Ryburn, 1992).

4   The chapter will focus on women journalists in the Social Democratic Federation, a group

influenced by Marxism and formed in 1884, and the Independent Labour Party, established in 1893, and often characterised as espousing a more pragmatic socialism.

5   For a discussion of the different definitions of propaganda, see L. Tickner, *The Spectacle of Women: Imagery of the Suffrage Campaign, 1907–1914* (London, Chatto & Windus, 1987), prologue.

6   For example, S. Yeo, 'A New Life: The Religion of Socialism in Britain, 1883–1896', *History Workshop Journal*, 4 (1977) and Hunt, *Equivocal Feminists*, pp. 197–200.

7   Quoted in E.P. Thompson, *William Morris: Romantic to Revolutionary* (London, Merlin, 1977), p. 325.

8   D. Hopkin, 'The Socialist Press in Britain, 1890–1910', in D. Boyce, J. Curran and P. Wingate (eds), *Newspaper History: From the 17th Century to the Present Day* (London, Constable, 1978), p. 294.

9   Hopkin, 'The Socialist Press'; D. Hopkin, 'The Newspapers of the Independent Labour Party, 1893–1906' (unpublished Ph.D. thesis, University of Aberystwyth, 1981); L Barrow, 'The Socialism of Robert Blatchford and the *Clarion* Newspaper, 1889–1918' (unpublished Ph.D. thesis, University of London, 1975); F. Reid, 'Keir Hardie and the *Labour Leader*, 1893–1903', in J. Winter (ed.), *The Working Class in Modern British History* (Cambridge University Press, 1983).

10   C. Steedman, *Childhood, Culture and Class in Britain: Margaret McMillan, 1860–1931* (London, Virago, 1990), p. 150; J. Smith, 'Taking the Leadership of the Labour Movement: The ILP in Glasgow, 1906–14', in A. Mckinlay and R.J. Morris (eds), *The ILP on Clydeside, 1893–1932: From Foundation to Disintegration* (Manchester University Press, 1991), p. 73.

11   J. Hannam, *Isabella Ford, 1855–1924* (Oxford, Blackwell, 1989).

12   For a discussion of the 'new woman', see D. Rubinstein, *Before the Suffragettes: Women's Emancipation in the 1890s* (Brighton, Harvester, 1986); S. Ledger, *The New Woman: Fiction and Feminism at the Fin de Siècle* (Manchester University Press, 1997); A. Ardis, *New Women, New Novels: Feminism and Early Modernism* (New Brunswick, Rutgers University Press, 1990).

13   For new life socialism, see S. Yeo, 'A New Life'; S. Rowbotham and J. Weeks, *Socialism and the New Life: The Personal and Sexual Politics of Edward Carpenter and Havelock Ellis* (London, Pluto Press, 1977).

14   C. Waters, 'New Women and Socialist-Feminist Fiction: The Novels of Isabella Ford and Katharine Bruce Glasier', in A. Ingram and D. Patai (eds), *Discovering Forgotten Radicals: British Women Writers, 1859–1939* (Chapel Hill, University of North Carolina Press, 1993). See also C. Wheedon, 'The Limits of Patriarchy: German Feminist Writers', in H. Forsas Scott (ed.), *Textual Liberation: European Feminist Writing in the Twentieth Century* (London, Routledge, 1991).

15   Steedman, *Childhood, Culture and Class*.

16   In 1911, as part of a push for socialist unity, the SDF, now called the Social Democratic Party, joined with some ILP members and non-aligned socialists to form the British Socialist Party (BSP). The SDF were the dominant grouping within the new party and generally the BSP was read as being the old SDF under a new name.

17   For Keeling, see *Labour Leader* (21/04/1894); for Julia Dawson, see the portrait in *Woman Worker* (31/07/1908).

18   H. Lintell, 'Lily Bell: Socialist and Feminist, 1894–1898'(unpublished MA thesis, Bristol Polytechnic, 1990); *Labour Leader* (27/04/1895).

19   The style and content of the column make it difficult to see who else but Katharine Bruce Glasier could have written it. While her husband was editing the paper she was very involved in its affairs more generally. See John Bruce Glasier, *Diary*, 1905–9, Sidney Jones Library, Liverpool.

20   Dora Montefiore edited the women's column between 20 March 1909 and 26 November 1911.

21   *Justice* (10/04/1909).

22   M. Beetham, *A Magazine of Her Own: Domesticity and Desire in the Woman's Magazine, 1800–1914* (London, Routledge, 1996), ch. 10.

23   *Labour Leader* (23/03/1906).

24   *Labour Leader*, (2/03/1906).

25   *Justice* (8/10/1908).

26   *Labour Leader* (16/03/1906).

27   *Labour Leader* (16/03/1906).

28   Series on 'How I Became a Socialist', in *Forward* (13/07/1907; 20/08/1907); Yeo, 'A New Life', pp. 9–16.

29   Hunt, *Equivocal Feminists*, pp. 198–200.

30   *Justice* (27/01/1912).

31   *Labour Leader* (30/03/1906).

32   *Clarion* (24/04/1897).

33   R.J. Evans, *The Feminist Movement in Germany, 1894–1933* (London, 1976); K.Honeycutt, 'Clara Zetkin', in M.J. Boxer and J.H. Quataert (eds), *Socialist Women: European Socialist Feminism in the Nineteenth and Early Twentieth Centuries* (New York, 1978).

34   *Labour Leader* (23/03/1906).

35   *Labour Leader* (23/03/1906).

36   *Justice* (27/03/1909).

37   *Justice* (20/03/1909).

38   *Labour Leader* (03/1894).

39   *Justice* (27/03/1909).

40   *Labour Leader* (30/05/1894).

41   *Labour Leader*, (13/04/1895).

42   *Justice* (20/03/1909).

43   *Labour Leader* (5/06/1908).

44   *Labour Leader*.

45   *Labour Leader* (4/08/1894).

46   *Justice* (23/01/1912).

47   *Labour Leader* (6/04/1906).

48   Lintell, 'Lily Bell'.

49   Barrow, 'The Socialism of Robert Blatchford', p. 55; Lintell, 'Lily Bell'.

50   Honeycutt, 'Clara Zetkin', pp. 294–7.

51   Logie Barrow *pace* Steedman, and Lidd and Norris.

52   *Labour Leader* (5/06/1908).

53   John Bruce Glasier, *Diary* (22/01/1909).

54   C. Collins, 'Women and Labour Politics in Britain, 1893–1932' (unpublished Ph.D. thesis, London School of Economics, 1991), p. 81.

55   *Justice*, 'Our Women's Circle' (27/03/1909).

11

VD PROPAGANDA, SEXUAL HYGIENE AND THE STATE IN INTERWAR SCOTLAND

Roger Davidson

During the late nineteenth and early twentieth centuries, VD became in many countries a metaphor for physical and moral decay, for the forces of pollution and contamination that appeared to threaten the institutions of social order and racial progress. Alarm over the issue of VD therefore offered an opportunity to express concern about the moral direction of society. Given the supposedly wilful nature of its diffusion and its threat to social hygiene, it also provided a powerful justification for the social construction and proscription of dangerous sexualities. Well into the twentieth century, Scottish debate and administration relating to VD conflated issues of public order, public health and public morality and the discourse surrounding VD was fuelled and shaped by general community concerns to regulate sexual norms and behaviour. This paper aims to show how VD propaganda materials both reflected and reinforced this process and how fears of the 'Great Scourge' were used to define moral identities and socially desirable boundaries of sexual behaviour.

THE ORGANISATION OF PROPAGANDA

According to the Royal Commission on Venereal Diseases, reporting in 1916, 'the evils which [led] to the spread of venereal diseases [were], in great part, due to want of control, ignorance and inexperience'. To combat the 'Great Scourge', medical strategies would have to be complemented by an upgrading of public awareness and of 'the moral standards and practice of the community'.[1] Accordingly, as the main strategy of prevention, the VD Regulations of 1916 empowered Scottish health authorities to liaise with the police, with medical and educational authorities, and with social hygiene agencies, in the provision of 'instructional lectures' and 'the diffusion of information' on questions relating to venereal diseases. The regulations laid particular stress on the need to highlight their 'far-reaching and disastrous effects on the social efficiency of the family'.[2]

Scottish health officials fully endorsed the views of the Royal Commission and continued to regard moral hygiene and education as a fundamental aim of VD policy and a precondition of any effective medical advance against the 'social evil'.[3] A major constraint upon the success of the new VD services was perceived to be ignorance: ignorance of the prevalence of VD, of its 'incalculable ravages' upon family and racial health, of the medical facilities available and the vital importance of early and professional treatment and, above all, of the moral and sexual conduct conducive to its transmission and elimination. Accordingly, administrators and clinicians welcomed the efforts of social hygiene agencies to 'educate for chastity' and to preach the importance of sexual continence for physical and racial health. For David Lees, Medical Officer in charge of Edinburgh's VD Scheme, propaganda was a vital adjunct to medical science in furthering the cause of public health and optimising the use of the clinics, while for medical officers of health such as A.K. Chalmers and W.L. Burgess, who perceived the First World War as having fractured sexual norms, education in sexual hygiene was imperative to counter 'the lower moral code sapping the vigour of our youth' and to alert the young of 'the moral and physical dangers which imperilled them'.[4]

The organisation and content of propaganda were shaped by a variety of social forces and ideologies and could often be contentious. As recommended by the Royal Commission on Venereal Diseases, the prime responsibility for the preparation and dissemination of materials rested with local health authorities in collaboration with local branches of the National Council for Combating Venereal Diseases (subsequently the British Social Hygiene Council), which enjoyed accredited status with the Scottish Board of Health for funding out of the Venereal Diseases Grant.[5] During the period of postwar demobilisation, the National Council in London played an extremely proactive role in trying to pump-prime and coordinate the educational work of Scottish local authorities, but after the establishment of a Scottish Committee in 1921, responsibility for propaganda was formally devolved upon its local branches.[6]

Within each branch, the medical officer of health and VD medical officer were decisive in determining policy with respect to the content and targeting of information, often on the basis of the pattern of attendance at the clinics.[7] Nonetheless, other medics, educationalists, social workers, church leaders, and social hygiene and purity activists making up the NCCVD/BSHC local executive committees also shaped VD propaganda, as did members of local Public Health and National Health Insurance Committees.[8] Purity organisations, such as the purity department of the British Women's Temperance Association, which supplemented the NCCVD's literature with their own tracts, were particularly vocal on the issue.[9] In Scotland, the Alliance of Honour was especially concerned to ensure that VD literature and lectures addressed ethical aspects of the question. Founded in 1903 as an interdenominational youth purity organisation devoted to the inculcation of a high and single standard of chastity, the Alliance was strongly represented in the east of Scotland, where it launched a series of educational campaigns in liaison with the NCCVD, with whom it often shared the patronage of local civic leaders.[10]

On issues of social hygiene education, the newfound social authority of the public health professions had also to be shared with the older authority exercised by the Scottish clergy. The Scottish churches viewed VD propaganda as part of a broader campaign for moral reform to counter the spiritual debilitation of war and postwar shifts in social mores, and were highly influential in validating the content and format of local educational initiatives.

According to the Scottish Board of Health, by 1925 a comprehensive programme of 'propaganda work' was under way. This included 'meetings, lectures, and exhibitions of films, both for laymen and for the medical profession; conferences with local health authorities, education authorities, and other public bodies; lectures at large public works and to social organisations; exhibition of suitable posters; advertisements and articles in newspapers, trade union journals and women's periodicals, and distribution of appropriate literature, including leaflets for foreign seamen printed in most continental languages'.[11] Despite the best efforts of the NCCVD/BSHC to standardise procedures, the mix and format and targeting of propaganda varied widely across the country, with considerable deference to local sentiment. Thus, some local health authorities preferred to issue their own VD posters rather than the more explicit posters of the Council, fearing that the latter might offend public opinion and purity activists.[12] For similar reasons, the issue of where VD posters might appropriately be displayed was often contentious. Glasgow Corporation's Sub-Committee on VD agonised over the issue for years, and was extremely reluctant to sanction their display other than in the men's toilets at railway stations.[13] Indeed, even this limited distribution of posters encountered opposition.[14]

The format of public meetings and lectures was also shaped by a mix of medico-moral and professional agendas, with particular regard to the need to control the access and response of working-class audiences to information on VD, and to ensure that sexual propriety was observed and that individual issues of sexual hygiene were firmly located within broader obligations to public morality and racial health.

Overarching the propaganda work of the NCCVD/BSHC in the 1920s were a series of public meetings held in collaboration with the major health authorities. These were a means of raising Scottish public consciousness of the incidence and effects of venereal infection and of networking the voluntary and governmental agencies dealing with the disease.[15] The meetings were carefully orchestrated to manufacture civic consensus on the issue and to represent both the medical and moral strands of social hygiene discourse. Typically, meetings would be chaired by a local civic or church dignitary with contributions from the medical officer of health, a leading clinician, a representative of the executive committee of the NCCVD, a local minister, and a social purity activist.

Lecture programmes were similarly arranged so as to ensure that information on VD was appropriately disseminated and contextualised. In the early years, there was concern to focus lectures on 'responsible people', on the moral gatekeepers in local society such as teachers, purity activists, social workers and community nurses.[16] Thus, in 1919, lectures in Edinburgh were reserved for groups such as the local branches of the National Vigilance and Women Citizens' Association, the Matrons' Association, voluntary health visitors, and dispensary and poorhouse nurses.[17] A professional monopoly on the dissemination of medical knowledge was strictly adhered to, and specialist lectures were normally delivered by either a venereologist or infectious diseases officer. Where medical slides were used to illustrate talks, they had to be approved by the medical officer of health.[18] Lectures on the medical aspects of VD were differentiated according to the sex of the audience, partly for reasons of propriety but also in recognition of prevailing gendered perceptions of health.

Lectures and slide-shows to wider public audiences, which in the West of Scotland frequently numbered in excess of eight hundred people, were also often gender specific, especially in the early part of the interwar period, and normally subject to an age restriction. Talks to male and female adolescent groups were always conducted separately. It was customary for lectures to be chaired either by a local minister or medical officer of health, reflecting the professional power structure within the social hygiene movement, and for the lectures to provide a focal point for the supervised and 'appropriate' distribution of literature, whose promiscuous distribution among uninformed members of the public was viewed as an incitement to prurience.[19] As the dissemination of medical information was perceived as part of a broader process of social and moral regeneration, typically, a series of lectures was grouped so as to provide an ethical and biological framework for the discussion of VD. Precedence was given to the evolutionary aspects of sex in animals and plants and to the health 'responsibility of citizenship' and its implications for national efficiency.[20]

From the start, Scottish local health authorities were alive to the potential of the cinema as a medium for VD propaganda. As early as 1917, Dundee Public Health Committee arranged with the proprietors of its cinema theatres to screen public announcements relating to its VD campaign. Subsequently, both documentary films and fictional propaganda films such as *The End of the Road*, *Flaw*, *Damaged Goods* and *John Smith and Son* were widely used as a means of popular education in social hygiene.[21] In the 1920s, attendances at cinema performances at times exceeded three thousand,[22] and this level of public interest was sustained into the 1930s. For example, an estimated twenty-six thousand people attended VD propaganda films in Scotland in the four months ending 30 January 1932, with an average attendance of 665.[23] Even in the more remote areas, VD films were widely exhibited with the aid of mobile 'cinemotors'.[24]

However, significant constraints were imposed by the authorities on the exhibition of VD propaganda films in Scotland. Some Scottish Board of Health officials shared the reservations of several medical officers of health about the value and appropriateness of the message being projected in some of the dramatised documentary films. For example, the Board's medical member, Sir Leslie Mackenzie, feared their 'confusion of two orders of ethical values – the treatment of a person for disease as disease, and the treatment of a person for moral delinquency as moral delinquency'.[25] In general, the Board favoured instructional films that focused upon 'the natural history of the infective micro-organisms . . . and upon the demonstrated facility of destroying those germs so long as they remain[ed] on the surface'.[26]

In addition, as in England, the social purity movement in Scotland had reservations about the content and venue of the propaganda films exhibited. As Kuhn has revealed, a crucial problem for social purity organisations, such as the National Vigilance Association and National Council for Public Morals, was 'the instability of propaganda films as bearers of meaning' and of ensuring that the films would be read for their social hygiene content and not be of pornographic interest to their audiences. Additional concerns related to the conditions in which such films were viewed, with the darkness and intimate seating of the cinema being viewed as a risk to public morality.[27] In many instances, social hygiene organisations negotiated with the commercial distributors over the conditions under which VD propaganda films would be shown. Even when this was not the case, Scottish local authorities strictly regulated performances in terms of the age, gender and social composition of the audience, according to the perceived suitability of each film.[28] Normally, films were screened as part of a longer meeting organised by social hygiene and purity agencies and were customarily introduced by medical officers of health or local VD medical officers.[29]

SOCIAL HYGIENE EDUCATION IN SCHOOLS

The Royal Commission on Venereal Diseases had considered specific instruction on sex hygiene to be 'undesirable' for the elementary school curriculum. However, it had strongly recommended that such instruction be introduced in evening continuation schools, in public and secondary schools, and in all teachers' training colleges,[30] and these proposals attracted substantial support in postwar Scotland. The Scottish Committee of the NCCVD campaigned widely for instruction on 'hygiene' to be accorded 'an adequate place in all permanent educational arrangements' and lobbied the Scottish Education Department accordingly. It established local committees to liaise with educational leaders and pressure groups and concentrated many of its early lecture programmes on schoolteachers.[31] Various purity organisations were also active in promoting the cause of sex education as a means of combating VD. The East of Scotland

Branch of the National Vigilance Association mounted a hard-fought campaign to introduce moral hygiene instruction into secondary and continuation schools, as did the Dundee and Glasgow branches of the Alliance of Honour.[32] Meanwhile, in Aberdeenshire, the Scottish Band of Hope secured permission to lecture on hygiene and temperance in the local authority schools.[33]

Health officials and clinicians, often inspired by eugenics, were also extremely active in canvassing the need for sexual issues to be addressed in schools as part of more general education on personal hygiene and racial health.[34] Similarly, while reserving specific instruction on VD for infectious diseases courses for adolescents over 16, the Scottish Association of Medical Women advocated systematic training in biology and physiology including reproduction 'and their moral and racial significance, for all young people of all classes by specially qualified teachers'.[35]

At the same time, as Mort has indicated, the issue of sex education, especially in elementary schools, became the 'sharp focus for disagreement' within the medico-moral alliances of the social hygiene movement.[36] A considerable body of Scottish public opinion, including many teachers and some leading educationalists, were fearful of a policy of 'sexual enlightenment in youth'. In the view of Sir Henry Keith, President of the Scottish Education Authorities' Association, addressing a conference on 'The Social Evil' in Glasgow in 1921, 'it was a moot point whether they did not do more harm by giving information at an early age which otherwise would not occur to the young mind'.[37] Similarly, receiving evidence in 1925, a Scottish Office Committee encountered a commonly held opinion that, in the absence of properly trained teachers, sex education would lead 'to the very precocity and malpractice which it [was] designed to prevent', and that 'a second-hand familiarity with the facts of sexual vice [could not] fail to be injurious to youth'.[38]

At a local level, there was often tension between medics and purity groups over the control and content of hygiene instruction. In particular, purity groups, along with church leaders, were concerned that in conveying information on VD, moral issues and ideals should remain to the fore and that the 'whole subject' should be lifted 'to a higher sphere by purifying the thoughts of the rising generation'.[39] For their part, many teachers and education authorities in working-class areas of Scotland feared that such instruction might prove disruptive with pupils and raise sectarian issues.[40] Thus, Glasgow's Local Education Authority decided to discontinue the teaching of sex hygiene in its schools in 1920 and subsequently resisted all attempts by the Public Health Committee to reverse the decision.[41]

The Departmental Committee on Sexual Offences Against Children and Young Persons in Scotland did recommend in 1926 that parental guidance on sexual hygiene should be subsequently followed up by instruction by doctors and teachers in the schools as part of more general physical training.[42] In addition, a number of joint VD committees continued to lobby the educational and medical establishment, but given a continuing lack of professional and public consensus on the issue, and the reluctance of English authorities to introduce new provisions, the Scottish Education Department (SED) was forced in 1929 to leave the matter 'to the discretion of individual authorities'.[43]

In the 1930s, the Scottish Committee of the BSHC collaborated with the Salvation Army and the Church of Scotland in providing illustrated lectures to juveniles in residential schools and children's homes.[44] It also sought to upgrade the provision of biology in schools as a basis for dispelling ignorance on matters of social hygiene, and initiated discussions between venereologists, public health officers, the SED, the Educational Institute for Scotland and the teachers' training colleges. Evidence was submitted to the Committee on the Scottish Health Services stressing the medical benefits to be gained from health education initiatives but evidence would suggest that, as in England, the school curriculum in Scotland remained largely impervious to the propaganda of the social hygiene movement.[45]

THE MESSAGE OF VD PROPAGANDA

The language of VD propaganda in interwar Scotland was clearly shaped by eugenics and the politics of national efficiency with its demonology of racial poisons and degeneration. As Kuhn has observed, such propaganda was not merely an effect of the moral panic produced by the Report of the Royal Commission on Venereal Diseases. It actively participated in it by 'constructing, reconstructing and circulating discourses' in which the moral and spiritual state of the nation was conflated with its physical health, with VD the focus of and metaphor for broader fears surrounding the degenerative effects of atavistic, 'uncontained sexuality', allegedly induced by the impact of war and postwar social change upon conventional moral controls.[46] VD propaganda commonly highlighted the impact of 'The Deadly Peril' on industrial and racial efficiency and the disgenic effects of immoral (i.e. extramarital) intercourse upon infant mortality and disablement.[47] Private sexual practices were defined as an issue of public and racial health to be regulated by the sexual health 'responsibilities of citizenship'.[48]

A prime responsibility was 'enlightenment'. According to the materials distributed and exhibited by the Scottish Committee of the NCCVD/BSHC, the high incidence of VD was primarily a function of 'ignorance rather than barbarity'. Central to the iconography of its posters and literature was the identification of 'ignorance' with moral corruptibility and 'disease', in juxtaposition to 'knowledge and health'. 'Ignorance the Great Enemy' featured prominently in the social epidemiology of VD articulated in pamphlets and films, and public awareness of the salient facts about VD was identified as pivotal to its control.[49] There was, therefore, a 'Duty of Knowledge' and 'it was a matter of honour for all who [had] at heart the welfare of the human race and of their kith and kin . . . to familiarise themselves with the facts', so that 'the dark menace of venereal diseases [might] be dispelled before the sunshine of enlightenment'.[50] Above all, in order 'to stamp out the scourge', and to protect future generations, it was imperative that information on social hygiene should be disseminated to the youth of the nation.

It was equally imperative that such knowledge should be 'correct knowledge', authoritative knowledge enunciated, on the one hand, by properly qualified medical practitioners, and on the other, by professionals whose brief was public morality. In VD literature, documentary films and allegorical cartoons, such as *The Road to Health*, it was medical expertise that formed the bridge from the gloomy depths of depravity and disease to the enlightened paths of racial health and national efficiency. In all types of VD propaganda, the practitioner was allocated a pivotal role in articulating the medico-moral prescriptions of the social hygiene movement. In films such as *Damaged Goods*, the doctor was either depicted 'as part of a setting (surgery, laboratory) connoting status and specialised knowledge', or positioned in relation to other characters as the dispenser of wisdom. As Kuhn observes: 'Everything about this man's appearance and expression convey[ed] rectitude, sternness, strictness and rigorously unbending correctness. From this elevated position, his enunciation of information – "the facts" about VD – acquire[d] a peculiarly authoritative quality, as [did] his instructions and injunctions to other characters.'[51] Significantly, medication was never illustrated independently of the physician, as it was his personal authority which symbolised the power of modern healing. This presentation of professional expertise and authority was heavily gendered. The power of medical science was personified by male doctors, and nurses and midwives never figured alone.

Within VD propaganda materials, there was a vigorous representation of the penalties of non-compliance with professional advice and of recourse to herbalists and other quacks.[52] Such penalties, central to the narrative of films such as *Deferred Payment*, *The Gift of Life* and *John Smith and Son*, and to many of the NCCVD/BSHC's leaflets, were most commonly illustrated by a caricature of the archetypal 'syphilitic runt' destined for either premature death or degeneration or of the sightless victim of gonorrheal ophthalmia. In such images, the sins of self-indulgent parents who failed to defer to the new 'heroic' therapies of medical science were visibly visited upon the next generation. Similarly, defaulters from treatment were depicted as 'condemning themselves to live under the shadow of a great peril, a peril as ominous as the menace of Vesuvius – liable to burst at any moment into terrible activity'. Their only salvation was 'to continue treatment until given a clean bill of health by the doctor, and to dismiss all thoughts of marriage until a cure [had] been definitely pronounced'.[53]

Although educational in content, VD propaganda materials were expressly circulated as a form of 'moral inspiration' towards a 'higher moral standard'. As with the public health reports of the period, pamphlets, posters, and film and lecture scripts subscribed to an aetiology and epidemiology of VD that recognised an explicit taxonomy of guilt and blame. VD was represented not just as a physical disease but as the penalty for moral turpitude and sexual intemperance. It was as much the immorality as the infectivity of 'impure sexual intercourse' that threatened racial health and the integrity of the family in society and which in films such as *Trial for Marriage* stood to be condemned. Social hygiene propagandists did avoid the more negative proscriptions on sexuality of the purity movement, but they continued to identify social health and evolution with moral self-restraint and 'a noble sex life' within the confines of responsible parenthood. Similarly, curative regimes of treatment and follow-up were commonly presented as involving a moral as well as physical process of rehabilitation with the rewards of medical science and adherence to qualified treatment predicated upon compliance with a moral regime of sexual abstention and reform. There was a clear ideological conflation of moral redemption ('salvation' was the metaphor commonly employed in propaganda material) with submission to professional treatment, in which 'the power of Science and the rewards of moral virtue [were] constituted as mutually dependent'.[54]

It was precisely this need for a moral as well as medical response to the threat of VD that persuaded Scottish public health authorities to reject the propaganda literature of the Society for the Prevention of VD whose leaflets, while advocating abstention from 'irregular sexual intercourse', focused primarily on the use of medical prophylaxis in the form of packets of potassium permanganate and calomel ointment.[55]

The moral dimension of VD propaganda was, however, firmly shaped by a male-produced discourse and both echoed and reinforced prevailing double standards of sexual morality. As in other countries, Scottish propaganda materials were acutely gendered in their representation of the causes and spread of venereal infection. They commonly represented sexually active women as the major source and vector of infection, albeit with a strong shift in focus from professional prostitutes to so-called 'amateurs': young women who had casual sex on a non-pecuniary basis and whose alleged indifference to health precautions rendered them the more virulently infectious.[56]

In contrast, men were typically represented as the recipients of disease. Sometimes, in leaflets such as *The Seafarer's Chart of Healthy Manhood*, or films such as *Deferred Payment*, men's sexual indiscretions were clearly identified as a threat to family and racial health, but even where male culpability was emphasised, the prostitute or casual good-time girl remained the constant point of reference as the root source of VD. Men were rarely depicted as wilfully evil vectors of infection. More usually, propaganda portrayed the contraction of VD by men as a function of ignorance and misguided susceptibility to the attentions of predatory women, especially when their moral inhibitions were loosened by alcohol. Even where the demoralisation of a woman had been caused by male exploitation, it was the loss of female chastity that was held to be central to the spread of disease.[57]

Within this presentation of the causes and diffusion of VD, social hygiene propaganda both reflected and reaffirmed powerful assumptions about the nature and socially desirable boundaries of female sexuality. Women were accorded a strictly limited set of sexual roles. They could either opt for the passive sexuality of the wife and mother, or, as sexual initiator, be stigmatised as a prostitute and the reservoir of disease. There was no acceptable sphere for non-marital female sexual activity, which was clearly defined by social hygienists as diseased and pathological. Healthy female sexuality was identified with reproduction and, within VD propaganda, positive depictions of women as sexual participants were always accompanied by images of children and motherhood.

Similarly, it was conformity by women to the ideals of chastity and maternity that, according to the social hygiene movement, was critical in the containment of VD and the preservation of racial health, and it was upon women that the responsibility for maintaining the moral integrity of society was primarily devolved. Typical was the injunction of Mary Scarlieb, in her lectures for the NCCVD and Alliance of Honour, that: 'The men are what the women make them and unless the wives and mothers of the country do their duty, and uphold the standard of purity, the nation . . . and our magnificent empire must follow the empires of olden days into utter ruin.'[58] Such sentiments, perpetuating the assumption that male self-control was problematic, and that their moral behaviour was ultimately the responsibility of their female partners, were frequently aired in social hygiene leaflets such as *How Girls Can Help*, and films such as *The End of the Road*. Significantly, NCCVD/BSHC lecturers were recommended to close with a slide of the Madonna and 'a few words on the power of womanhood to save the next generation through the purity and good of woman's life'.[59]

The experience of VD was also expressed in gender-specific terms. While male sickness was often represented in the context of manpower needs and racial efficiency, it was also portrayed as an individual disaster on its own terms. In contrast, women's venereal illnesses were always linked to maternity, either by reference to sterility or to the presence of congenitally ill children. The emotional appeal of the propaganda was directed not at the disabilities of the mother but at the sickness of the child and especially the degeneration of the family.[60] The sexual health of the single woman was only accorded a separate identity as a source and carrier of venereal disease, or as a function of 'moral imbecility'.[61] Similarly, while information leaflets for men stressed their responsibility for their own 'physical and mental efficiency' and for the health of their families (including their faithfully chaste future brides), no reference was made to the health of their sexually active girlfriends or consorts. Moreover, while men might rehabilitate themselves by compliance with professional treatment, single women remained permanently tainted by their sexual initiation, notwithstanding their medical cure.

THE IMPACT OF VD PROPAGANDA

It is impossible to estimate with any precision the impact of propaganda on the incidence and effects of VD in interwar Scotland. There were indications that VD propaganda was securing a higher and earlier take-up of qualified medical advice and treatment. In particular, both the rising proportion of new cases at the clinics found to be non-infectious, increasing from 11 per cent in 1922 to 28 per cent in 1932, and the rising ratio of gonorrhoea to syphilis cases, were widely regarded as indicators of an increasing public awareness of the gravity of venereal infections and their sequelae.[62]

From the standpoint of VD clinicians, perhaps the most valuable effect of propaganda was to encourage a growing proportion of patients to report in the early stages of their disease when the condition was more readily amenable to treatment, the duration of treatment lessened and the period of likely infectivity within the family and community minimised.[63] Systematic evidence for this is lacking. Nonetheless, scattered data do suggest that the critical importance of early treatment was gradually appreciated by those at risk, although significant variance is evident in the behaviour of male and female patients.[64] Evidence of increases in the number of average attendances per case was also viewed as reflecting the impact of propaganda on patient compliance, although this could equally have reflected shifts in the pattern of therapy and the availability of resources.[65]

Yet, the propaganda work of the Scottish Committee of the BSHC and local public health committees was clearly only partially successful in raising public awareness of the nature of VD. As the Medical Officer of Health for Aberdeen lamented in 1935, 'ignorance' was still 'amongst the greatest factors that one has to contend with in dealing with venereal diseases'.[66] Well into the late 1920s, much of the public was oblivious of the existence of the VD clinics.[67] Venereal infection was often trivialised. In particular, gonorrhoea was frequently dismissed 'as a cold in the pipe' and, in some districts of Scotland, the discharge was 'considered a good thing for the patient, "running off" in some mysterious way, disordered or unhealthy blood'.[68] Popular myths and stereotypes surrounding the origins and transmission of the disease survived until after the Second World War, including the fear that it could be readily caught from toilet seats and eating utensils, and 'the appalling and unwarranted belief' that it could be cured by intercourse with a virgin.[69] According to medical and police authorities, this notion inspired many sexual offences against children and the communication of

VD continued to feature as an aggravating offence in many High Court indictments for sexual assault on young girls.[70]

Nor was the social hygiene movement successful in reducing the moral stigma surrounding VD in Scotland. By emphasising the role of individual conduct and perpetuating its association with infidelity, immorality and promiscuity, it failed to eradicate the 'popular stigma which consign[ed] all venereally infected individuals . . . to the same social category of moral outcasts'.[71] Public opinion continued to view those afflicted with VD as 'moral lepers' rather than as cases of infectious disease, with the inevitable avoidance of professional treatment and recourse to quacks. Jessie Kesson's autobiographical novel, *The White Bird Passes*, vividly captures contemporary prejudice surrounding venereal infection, with the matron of Skene children's home in Aberdeenshire refusing to release her to attend to her dying syphilitic mother.[72]

However, the primary concern of venereologists and local health authorities in interwar Scotland was the apparent failure of VD propaganda to change the sexual behaviour of patients and to secure their compliance with treatment regimes. Clinicians reported a disturbingly high incidence of reinfection. For example, in 1927, it was reported that at the Broomielaw Municipal Clinic in Glasgow 'more than half the total number of cases treated (both syphilis and gonorrhoea) had formerly undergone a course of treatment, followed by cessation of symptoms, and had returned, after an interval, for treatment of fresh symptoms, which they attributed to re-exposure to infection'.[73] In the opinion of Glasgow's Medical Officer of Health, such evidence of venereal recidivism clearly indicated the cynical exploitation of the clinics by 'libertines'.[74] Unfortunately, the detailed case notes for patients at the Edinburgh clinics have been destroyed, but the surviving summary registers for the period convey a very similar story.

The continuing high level of default from treatment, despite the best efforts of social hygiene propaganda, was also perceived by the Scottish medical establishment as severely compromising the efficiency of the VD services and as the major factor determining the 'stubborn' level of infection within the community.[75] Around one-third of patients attending Scottish VD clinics during the 1920s failed to complete their course of treatment, while another quarter withdrew before 'final tests for cure' had been conducted. Levels of default varied markedly with Glasgow clinics having the highest default rate, averaging some 65 per cent for the period 1921–9 as compared with the national average of 56 per cent.[76] Even in Edinburgh, which was recognised as having the best compliance record, a default rate for the 1920s of 34 per cent was recorded. As a result of more developed 'follow-up' procedures, levels of default did decline in the 1930s but the national annual average for the period 1930–7 was still 46 per cent.

CONCLUSION

The development of the VD services in interwar Scotland was shaped by a powerful set of moral fears, assumptions and objectives. Despite the assertion of some politicians and medical practitioners that VD should be treated as purely a medical issue, the provision of a comprehensive system of state-funded diagnostic and treatment facilities did not 'mean the end of moralistic service or the demystification of the diseases'.[77] On the contrary, moral issues and taxonomies continued to inform the aetiology and epidemiology of VD as represented in propaganda leaflets, posters and films. The ideology of social hygiene viewed medical treatment and moral instruction as mutually interdependent solutions to the 'hideous scourge', with both strands heavily defined by prevailing concerns over the apparent breakdown in social and sexual controls.

Equally, the evidence suggests that in Scotland, as in many other countries,[78] the articulation of VD as a public health issue provided a powerful legitimation for the social construction and regulation of 'dangerous sexualities'. One witnesses in propaganda materials the same stereotyping and proscription of risk groups such as 'defaulters' and 'problem girls', the same confusion of clinical aetiology and moral accountability in confronting sexually transmitted diseases, and a similar use of a judgemental epidemiology to define and reform unhygienic habits that endangered fertility and racial health. Certainly, the ideology of VD propaganda in interwar Scotland conforms with the Foucauldian view of the rise of a medico-sexual regime, advancing a pathology of 'unproductive' sexual practices and a discourse in which the implications of the private world of sexuality for social health and efficiency sanctioned new forms of surveillances and controls.[79]

Notes

1   Final Report of the Royal Commission on Venereal Diseases, P.[arliamentary] P.[apers] 1916 (Cmd 8189) *XVI*, p. 60.

2   Local Government Board for Scotland, Public Health (Venereal Diseases) Regulations and Memorandum on Schemes for the Diagnosis, Treatment and Prevention of Venereal Diseases (Edinburgh, HMSO, 1916), pp. 4, 7, 10. For an overview of the government's general strategy towards health education between the wars, see M. Grant, *Propaganda and the Role of the State in Interwar Britain* (Oxford, Clarendon Press, 1994), ch. 5.

3   Scottish Board of Health [hereinafter SBH] Sixth Annual Report (1924), PP 1924–5 (Cmd 2416) *XIII*, p. 63. For an analysis of the social and medical ideology of the public health administrators and clinicians dealing with VD, see R. Davidson, 'Venereal Disease, Sexual Morality, and Public Health in Interwar Scotland', *Journal of the History of Sexuality*, 5 (1994), 267–94, at pp. 270–3.

4   D. Lees, 'VD in City Life', *Journal of State Medicine*, 40 (1932), 85–95, at pp. 92–3; *Glasgow MOH Annual Report* (1921), p. 8; *Dundee MOH. Annual Report* (1920), p. 46.

5   On the social politics of the NCCVD's propaganda work, see especially B. Towers, 'Health Education Policy 1916–26: Venereal Disease and the Prophylactic Dilemma', *Medical History*, 24 (1980), 70–87.

6   Edinburgh City Archives, File 15, Box 34, DRT 14, Edinburgh Corporation Town Clerk's Department, VD General File.

7   ECA, File 15/11, Box 36, DRT 14, Minutes of Scottish Committee of the BSHC, 20 Oct. 1933; *Royal Commission on National Health Insurance, Minutes of Evidence*, (London, HMSO, 1926), q. 20847.

8   See e.g. ECA, File 15, Box 34, DRT 14; Files 15(1) and 15(2) Box 8, DRT 14; Glasgow City Archives, Public Health Department newscuttings; Dundee City Archives, Town Clerk's Papers, File 344, NCCVD. 1918 and 1919.

9   GCA, Glasgow Public Health Department newscuttings, 1921–2.

10   See e.g. *Dundee MOH Annual Report* (1920), p. 45; ECA, File 15, Box 34, DRT 14, Edinburgh Branch, Alliance of Honour to Edinburgh Branch, NCCVD, 2 Feb. 1918; Northern Health Services Archive, Aberdeen Public Health Committee Minutes, 15 Dec. 1919.

11   *SBH Seventh Annual Report, PP 1926* (Cmd 2674) *XI*, p. 84.

12   See e.g. GCA, Glasgow Corporation Minutes, Sub-Committee on VD, 21 Oct. 1929, Fife County Archives, Fife and Kinross Joint VD Committee, Minutes, 2 May 1927.

13   GCA, Glasgow Corporation Minutes, Sub-Committee on VD, 17 Sept. 1919, 16 June 1921, 21 March 1923, 18 Feb. 1925.

14   J. Weeks, *Sex, Politics and Society, The Regulation of Sexuality since 1800*, 2nd edn (Harlow, Longman, 1989), p. 216. In part, this stemmed from a concern that posters might be just a first step towards the introduction of prophylactic ablution centres in men's toilets.

15   Between 1921 and 1929, the Scottish Committee of the NCCVD/BSHC organised 400 public meetings, with an attendance of over 175,000 people. See *Glasgow Herald*, 19 Oct. 1929.

16   See e.g. DCA, Dundee Public Health Committee Minutes, 28 Aug. 1917.

17   ECA, File 15/1 Box 34, DRT 14, Report of Edinburgh Branch of NCCVD to Local Government Board for Scotland, Oct. 1919.

18   See DCA, Town Clerk's Correspondence, File 344, NCCVD 1919.

19   For accounts of typical meetings, see e.g. *Glasgow Herald* (13/03/1917, 3/12/ 1921).

20   See eg. GCA, Glasgow Public Health Department newscuttings; *Dundee MOH Annual Report* (1920), pp. 45–6; (1921), pp. 36–7. Broader lecture titles such as 'Sex and Heredity' were also found to avoid the stigma that many people attached to attending advertised talks on VD. See ECA, File 15/2, Box 8, DRT 14, A. Chalmers Watson to Town Clerk, 4 July 1919.

21   See e.g. *Glasgow MOH Annual Report (1926)*, p. 154; ECA, Public Health Department Papers, Files 15/5,15/11, Box 36, DRT 14. On the social politics surrounding the emergence of a new cinematic genre of propaganda films, see especially, A. Kuhn, *Cinema, Censorship and Sexuality 1909–25* (London, Routledge, 1988).

22   Contemporary Medical Archives Centre, SA/BSH, A2/7, extract from minutes of Scottish Committee of the NCCVD, 22 Jan. 1923.

23   *Glasgow MOH Annual Report (1925)*, p. 141; editorial, 'The Social Evil', *Glasgow Herald*, 24 Nov. 1922, p. 11; ECA, Public Health Department Files, 15/11, Box 36 DRT 14, SCBSHC minutes.

24   Thus, in the autumn of 1925, the cinemotors travelled extensively in the rural areas of Lanarkshire and Wigtownshire, with an average attendance of 125. CMAC, SA/BSH, A2/9, extract from minutes of Executive Committee of SCBSHC, 2 Dec. 1925.

25   *Glasgow Herald*, 3 Dec. 1921; W.E. Whyte, 'Place of the Local Authority in the VD Campaign (Scotland)', in *Proceedings of the Imperial Social Hygiene Congress* (1924), p. 103.

26   *SBH Ninth Annual Report, PP 1928* (Cmd 3112) *X*, p. 109. The Ministry of Health also censored VD propaganda films. For example, it refused to sanction *Social Hygiene for Women* for exhibition other than to select audiences of nurses, midwives, health visitors and teachers. Similarly, it refused permission for *Whatsoever a Man Soweth* to be on general release for mixed audiences. Limited exhibition to single-sex audiences was permitted as long as this was approved by the medical officer of health and 'the bedroom scene omitted' (CMAC, SA/BSH/ C1/5, minutes of NCCVD Propaganda Committee, 17 Nov. 1924, 15 Dec. 1924).

27   A. Kuhn, *The Power of the Image: Essays on Representation and Sexuality* (London, Routledge and Kegan Paul, 1985), pp. 123–7; Kuhn, *Cinema, Censorship and Sexuality*, pp. 42, 112–13, 120. The more general efforts of the social purity movement to censor film material and to regulate access to cinemas in Scotland is discussed in V.E. Cree, *From Public Streets to Private Life: The Changing Task of Social Work* (Aldershot, Avebury,1995), p. 26.

28   DCA, Town Clerk's Papers, File 344, A.C. Gotto to Secretary, Dundee Branch NCCVD, 11 June 1920.

29   See e.g. ECA, File 15/11, Box 36, DRT 14, SCBSHC minutes; *Royal Commission on National Health Insurance, Mins of Ev.* (London, HMSO, 1926), q. 20847.

30   *Final Report of the Royal Commission on Venereal Diseases, PP 1916* (Cd 8189) *XVI*, p. 60.

31   See e.g. ECA, File 15 (2) Box 8, DRT 14, Public Health Department, VD.

32   Cree, *From Public Streets to Private Life*, p. 29; DCA, Town Clerk's Papers, File 344, NCCVD 1918, minutes of meeting between Dundee Educational Authorities and Joint Committee of NCCVD and Alliance of Honour, 1 Nov. 1918.

33   NHSA, E2/6/1, E2/6/5, E2/6/10, Education Authority for County of Aberdeen, minutes of proceedings, (1919–20), p. 194; (1923–4), p. 77; (1928–9), p. 76

34   See e.g. the views of Edinburgh's Medical Officer of Health, ECA, File 15/1, Box 34, DRT 14, Conference Minutes, p. 9.

35   CMAC, SA/MWF Uncat.56, Scottish Association of Medical Women, Memorandum 1919.

36   F. Mort, *Dangerous Sexualities: Medico-Moral Politics in England since 1830* (London, Routledge and Kegan Paul, 1987), pp. 196–7.

37   *Glasgow Herald*, 3 Dec. 1921, p. 10.

38   *Report of Departmental Committee on Sexual Offences against Children and Young Persons in Scotland, PP 1926* (Cmd 2592) *XV*, p. 36.

39   See e.g. *Glasgow Medical Journal*, 90 (1918), 44–6.

40   For similar fears elsewhere, see Mort, *Dangerous Sexualities*, p. 197.

41   GCA, Glasgow Corporation Public Health Sub-Committee on VD, minutes, 21 Jan. 1920, 19 May 1926. On the contest between various discourses over the appropriate source of ' "proper" knowledge about the body and its sexuality' in interwar Britain, see Kuhn, *Cinema, Censorship and Sexuality*, pp. 110–13.

42   *Departmental Committee Report, PP 1926* (Cmd 2592) *XV*, p. 36.

43   CMAC, SA/BSH, A2/9, A2/10, extracts from minutes of SCBSHC, 2 Dec. 1925, 4 July 1927, 6 Dec. 1928; Scottish Record Office, HH 60/278, *Scottish Education Department Circular No. 79* (16/01/1929).

44   CMAC, SA/BSH, A2/12, A2/14, extracts from minutes of SCBSHC, 2 March 1931, 7 Dec. 1933.

45   ECA, 15/11, Box 36, DRT 14, SCBSHC minutes, 10 June 1932, 23 Feb. 1933; CMAC, SA/BSH, F8, minutes of BSHC Educational Advisory Board, 20 June 1934; *Training for Citizenship: A Report of the Advisory Council on Education in Scotland, PP 1943–44* (Cmd 6495) *III*, p. 12. On England, see Mort, *Dangerous Sexualities*, pp. 196–8.

46   Kuhn, *The Power of the Image*, pp. 129–30.

47   These were frequently juxtaposed in slide-shows with the beauty and sanctity of procreative reproduction in nature.

48   For similar discourses in continental VD propaganda, see A. Mooij, *Out of Otherness: Characters and Narrators in the Dutch Venereal Disease Debates 1850–1990* (Amsterdam, Rodopi, 1998), ch. 2; F.L. Bernstein, 'Envisioning Health in Revolutionary Russia: Gender and Politics in Anti-Venereal Disease Posters of the 1920s', *Russian Review*, 57, no. 2 (April 1998), 191–217.

49   *The Tragedy of Ignorance* was one of the most widely exhibited films in Scotland in the late 1920s. On the broader significance of 'ignorance' in the narrative interpretation of VD propaganda films, see Kuhn, *The Power of the Image*, p. 105.

50   ECA, File15, Box 34, DRT 14, Public Health Department Files, *The Deadly Peril of Venereal Diseases*, p. 3; GCA, Glasgow Public Health Department, newscuttings; Kuhn, *Cinema, Censorship and Sexuality*, pp. 106, 109.

51   Kuhn, *The Power of the Image*, pp. 109–10.

52   See e.g. DCA, Town Clerk's Papers, File 344, NCCVD 1918, NCCVD. Warning leaflet, 'Some Perils of Venereal Disease: No.3, The Folly of Self-Drugging'; File 344, NCCVD 1919, NCCVD leaflet, 'Quackery and Venereal Disease'.

53   DCA, Town Clerk's papers, NCCVD 1919, NCCVD Warning leaflet, 'Living Beneath Vesuvius'.

54   Kuhn, *The Power of the Image*, pp. 111–12.

55   See e.g. GCA, Glasgow Public Health Committee minutes, 20 April 1920; Sub-Committee on Clinical Services, 21 Nov. 1930, 7 Aug. 1931, 19 May 1933. On the battle over 'appropriate' propaganda strategies between the NCCVD/BSHC and the SPVD, see R. Davenport Hines, *Sex, Death and Punishment: Attitudes to Sex and Sexuality in Britain since the Renaissance* (London, William Collins, 1990), ch. 6.

56   See e.g. the role of Hermani in *Trial for Marriage* and Doris, the bridesmaid, in *John Smith and Son*.

57   Thus, in the film *Damaged Goods*, it is the girl who has resorted to prostitution who according to the doctor sums up 'the whole problem' of VD, rather than the employer who has sexually assaulted her, or her male clients.

58   M. Scarlieb, 'Purity and the Nation's Welfare', in *Facing the Problem: A Call to Womanhood* (London, Alliance of Honour, 1925), p. 8.

59 ECA, Public Health Department 15/1, Box 34, DRT 14, text for slide-show, 'Love-Marriage-Parenthood'.

60 See e.g. the plots of *John Smith and Son* and *Deferred Payment*, National Film and Television Archive, shotlists and viewing copies.

61 See e.g. DCA, Town Clerk's Papers. File 344, NCCVD 1918, A.F. Tredgold, *Mental Deficiency in Relation to Venereal Disease* (NCCVD Pamphlet).

62 *SBH Ninth Annual Report, PP 1928* (Cmd 3112) *X*, p. 121; *Tenth Annual Report, PP 1928–29* (Cmd 3304) *VII*, p. 219; *Dundee MOH Annual Report* (1928), p. 133; *Glasgow MOH Annual Reports* (1925), p. 144; (1926), p. 154.

63 See e.g. *Dundee MOH Annual Report (1936)*, p. 109; *EPHD Annual Report (1925)*, p. 54; (1935), p. 74; *Glasgow MOH Annual Report (1928)*, pp. 110–11.

64 *GMOH Annual Reports (1925)*, p. 149; (1934), p. 138; (1937), p. 131.

65 Average attendances at Glasgow clinics increased from 24.8 in 1924 to 34.3 in 1933. *Glasgow MOH Annual Reports*.

66 *Aberdeen MOH Annual Report (1935)*, p. 51.

67 *SBH Ninth Annual Report, PP 1928* (Cmd 3112) *X*, p. 108.

68 M. Archibald [Assistant Surgeon, Glasgow Lock Hospital], 'The Position of the General Practitioner in Anti-Venereal Disease Schemes', *Proceedings of the Imperial Social Hygiene Congress* (1924), 186–96, at p. 188.

69 *Glasgow MOH Annual Report (1922)*, p. 86; Mass Observation Archives, University of Sussex, Box DR 59, File 478, Glasgow Respondent 2554, November 1942.

70 *Report of Departmental Committee on Sexual Offences against Children and Young Persons in Scotland. PP 1926* (Cmd 2592) *XV*, p. 15.

71 See e.g. *Aberdeen MOH Annual Report (1935)*, p. 51.

72 J. Kesson, *The White Bird Passes* (Edinburgh, B & W Publishing, 1996 edn), p. 124.

73 *Glasgow MOH Annual Report (1927)*, p. 155.

74 *Glasgow MOH Annual Report (1925)*, p. 150.

75 *EPHD Annual Report (1926)*, pp. vi–vii; *Glasgow MOH Annual Reports (1922)*, p. 10; (1923), pp. 20–1; (1928), p. 155.

76 *SBH/SDH Annual Reports*; *Glasgow MOH Annual Report (1929)*, p. 151.

77 Weeks, *Sex, Politics and Society*, p. 228.

78 See especially A. Brandt, *No Magic Bullet: A Social History of Venereal Disease in the United States since 1880* (Oxford University Press, 1985); P. Fleming, 'Fighting the "Red Plague": Observations on the Response to Venereal Disease in New Zealand, 1910–1945', *New Zealand Journal of History*, 22 (1988), 56–64, at pp. 59–61; J. Cassel, *The Secret Plague: Venereal Disease in Canada, 1838–1939* (University of Toronto Press, 1987), ch. 9.

79 M. Foucault, *The History of Sexuality*, Vol.1, *An Introduction* (London, Allen Lane, 1979), pp. 26, 36, 41–2, 145.

Part Four

WAR AND PROPAGANDA

As mentioned in the Introduction, wars and propaganda go hand-in-hand. Never is the need for urgent communication and total adhesion greater; never is the demand on a sense of identity stronger. The three papers in this section cover the three major European wars of the last 130 years. The Franco-Prussian War has been described as perhaps the first instance of a total war in the Clauswitzian sense. Bertrand Taithe's paper demonstrates, however, the singular ineptitude of the French government in propagandistic matters. Given propaganda's role as more than simply communication, this failure to be credible affected the war effort and chances of victory. In a paradoxical evolution, non-governmental propaganda deployed after the conflict proved successful in shaping the historiographical accounts of Franco-German relations. The First World War, which was perhaps a result of this successful propaganda, saw the development of extensive recruitment campaigns, particularly in countries which did not adopt conscription. Tim Bowman's paper shows how complex these recruitment drives could be, and how propaganda needed to rely on local politics and identity to be effective. The English-led fiasco in Ireland demonstrated how amateurish many such campaigns were, even in total war. It also shows how the state could be hijacked by competing sectarian interests, and how the war propaganda could be manipulated to serve long-term political aims. Margaretta Jolly's chapter shows a degree of refinement of propaganda techniques in the Second World War, avoiding the crudities of First World War campaigning in America. Letter-writing and the publication of letter-books enabled private citizens to enlist their American contacts in the British campaigning to take the United States into the war. These letters also demonstrate how a gender agenda could serve war propaganda. Jolly studies particularly women's letters and last letters, two sub-categories of this literary genre. This is perhaps a progress narrative, but it is importantly not a state-led progress narrative.

12

RHETORIC, PROPAGANDA AND MEMORY: FRAMING THE FRANCO-PRUSSIAN WAR

Bertrand Taithe

Propaganda has been associated with many negative connotations; the term inspires harsh judgements on callous manipulators and it seems significant that the adjective most often associated with propaganda is 'crude'. There are many more subtle definitions of the term as this book demonstrates. In this chapter the term will be used as an umbrella to cover the many practices of communication and make-believe used during the Franco-Prussian war of 1870–1. In fact the term propaganda was hardly if at all used during the conflict: communication, rhetoric, preaches and pleads were words more commonly used to define what the people and their governments attempted to do. Rhetoric in the sense of the art of persuasion defined by Thomas de Quincey, including the art of eloquence, was part of the political culture and language of all major figures of French politics in 1870.[1] In this sense their use of propagandistic techniques could be simultaneously calculated and natural, the result of carefully planned tactical action and the fruit of a flow of passionate eloquence.[2] Eloquence rather than rhetoric was the major quality universally recognised in leading figures of the 4 September Republican government: Jules Favre was deemed to be one the best speakers of his generation,[3] Trochu was deemed a good speaker while Gambetta's entire fame rested on a few major speeches against Napoleon III's regime.[4] Good speeches and texts make for good propaganda which is never made of outright lies and always builds on strong convictions and skewed evidence.

A war is particularly interesting as an opportunity for propaganda because it puts modes of representation at the centre-stage in an attempt to enthuse many normally peaceful citizens to make them act with more brutality than they would ever do spontaneously, focusing attention on the necessity of the conflict and on its real meanings. In this sense propaganda serves as a way of excluding competing understandings of the same events. It is, as seen in other chapters of this book, a dual process involving the intended audience and the producers in equal and reciprocal measure. Propaganda is thus a rhetorical device taking many shapes and forms. In this chapter I will suggest that there are many layers to the Franco-French propaganda, i.e. the propaganda aimed by the French at the French people, and I will narrow down this study to the 'people's war'[5] fought by the Republican government proclaimed on 4 September 1870 after the capture of the French emperor Napoleon III.[6] As a brief reminder, the French went to war over the obscure question of the Hohenzollern candidacy to the throne of Spain in July 1870.[7] The imperial regime was immediately rendered more fragile and suffered a series of crushing military defeats in August. Two governments fell in succession and the regime collapsed after the battle of Sedan. On 4 September 1870 a government composed of the Republican deputies of Paris and led by a Catholic general proclaimed the Republic and endeavoured to free the national territory.[8] The Republican war lasted from September to early February 1871. During that period the *gouvernement de la défense nationale* had to organise new armies to resist the German invaders and try to liberate Paris, while maintaining morale in a number of besieged cities including Paris.[9]

There were therefore three different political spaces in which the government and its agents had to deploy propaganda: a closed space, within besieged cities,[10] an occupied space and a free space. The division between urban and rural space prevailed throughout as did the more blurred border between civilian and military.[11] To act on these various areas the government depended on various means of communication; it fragmented itself into two governments, a fully constituted government which remained in Paris and a dictatorial deputation led by the Belleville deputy, Gambetta, settled in Tours.[12] The choice of Tours was made because of its relative proximity to the western front of the occupying armies and because it was at the heart of train connections and enabled the rapid transportation of troops and news.[13] The government had at its disposal a diversity of means of communication well established by previous authoritarian governments: official newspapers, proclamations to be published in the independent press,[14] censorship administration and a network of informers and administrators led in each of the departments (regional and administrative subdivisions) by the prefects. After the collapse of the second empire, the order not to print any military information was no longer enforced except through self-censorship and sheer lack of information.[15] To communicate between the two geographical spaces still under French government control was more difficult in the sense that the French had few means of access through enemy lines: balloons, pigeons and emissaries who risked their lives to cross the lines were the only means available. In this context it was often easier to communicate from the besieged cities to the provinces than the other way round. The messages to the public were thus different because the government was split geographically and, relatively soon afterwards, ideologically.

To add to the confusion a little, other forms of government also appeared in France after 4 September 1870. Municipalities which had been repressed for the duration of the empire created their own self-government and chose to promote their own vision of the national defence.[16] In each area these municipal powers controlled adequate media of communication ranging from placards, spectacles and petitions to their own troops, the sedentary national guards who acted as the ultimate reserve of the nation at arms.[17] These municipal governments are worth mentioning because of the relative autonomy that many enjoyed and because the war propaganda they promoted differed somewhat from that of the government. Here we have a conflict in space and ideology which meant that no official propaganda ever managed to exclude diverging ways of representing the same evidence. The first part of this chapter will study this official propaganda and consider the intellectual tools in use; it will conclude on its failure. In January 1871 the French capital city, starved of food and news, surrendered and put an end to the conflict in three-quarters of the territory.[18] The hyperbolic rhetoric used so far to maintain morale suddenly backfired and damaged the chances of the government's political survival in defeat.

The second part of the article will look at the production of war narratives explaining the necessity of the war to the French people themselves. These narratives came from a diversity of agencies, closely associated with the government or a specific political party for the most part. These narratives produced during and immediately after the war can also be considered as propaganda in the sense that they answered to immediate needs by filling a vacuum of meaning in explaining the defeat, the war and the will to regroup around a number of political values constitutive of a national spirit.[19] In many respects this type of literature, which remained more limited in the sense that each political sector or party catered for its own partisans, was the most successful and, though it largely contained criticisms of the government's action and words, it aimed at serving a national purpose.

The final section will look at the international implications of this conflict, considering the impact of French representations of the war on foreign powers. Here again the initial communication strategy adopted by the government failed to have a significant impact on the foreign powers while that developed by other agencies, such as the Red Cross or other groups, was far more successful in reversing the perception of the French as trouble-makers and in attracting a large amount of compassion and practical help from abroad. Taking into account the last two sections of this chapter I wish to suggest that the war propaganda and rhetoric originating from so many different sources managed to win the peace in the sense that the French historiography found it extremely difficult to free itself from its fundamental paradigms and tenets. Though this language was not of the kind that leads to ultimate victory on the battlefield it was still of the stuff that makes national legends and helps crystallise historical identity.[20]

GOVERNMENTS, LOCALITIES AND OFFICIAL PROPAGANDA

The siege of Paris started around 19 September when the railway lines were cut by the encircling German forces. The French government had chosen to remain with the people which had acclaimed it to power and remained thus a virtual prisoner to the Parisians and the Germans encircling them.[21] Paris was surrounded by enemy forces and had to live off its food reserves for as long as it would take for the provincial armies to organise themselves and break the siege. In other words, the situation was critical, especially considering the dearth of any substantial provincial army on the open field. The need to communicate an upbeat war message was therefore tempered from the start by the fear that expectations might rise too high and make an eventual surrender difficult. Contested by the more radical elements of the population, the government had to rely on an army largely composed of volunteers to maintain law and order and protect the city.[22]

The major tools of communications at that time were official proclamations read to the troops and pasted on the walls of the city. These were then used by newspapers starved of any first-hand information and analysed in detail to the point of turning into urban myth. The art of proclamation had been most prevalent under the second empire when Napoléon III imitated his uncle's poetic rhetoric.[23] The government of 1870 chose to use the phrases and the tone of the volunteers of 1792. This rhetoric contained an element of risk in the sense that the first foreign policy dispatch contained all the elements of a revolutionary pamphlet likely to make provincial conservatives and foreign powers wary of the new Parisian leadership. Within Paris the government, staffed with lawyers and headed by the most eloquent but also prolix general of the French army, did not spare its words. Announcing battles, major attacks, in turn calling for revolutionary enthusiasm to fire the army and calling for calm, describing the prosperous state of the food supply while discreetly trying to establish the real needs and prepare rationing,[24] the government was soon perceived to be torn between various imperatives and its discourse did not seem to match its political conservatism.[25] In the words of a sceptical observer: 'what it wanted, it was said, was to create (in their own words and to serve the interests of the Government) a radical popularity for themselves in the hope to absorb the riotous elements [of the population]'.[26] It is thus hard to identify clearly when the government lost control of the street since it soon became obvious that the Parisian people perceived the government to be theirs and in their control.[27] Constantly receiving deputations and petitions, the government had to lend an ear to any demonstrator able to summon a crowd in arms. The defeat of the Bourget and the surrender of the largest remaining imperial army at Metz led to a direct confrontation on 31 October, which, while bloodless, marked the end of a soft consensualism of national defence.[28] The oratory skills of Favre or Trochu became increasingly powerless against a virulent and blossoming press and the multitude of pamphlets and placards.[29] Even some successful areas of the government's policy failed to impress.

The long siege, which only started really to bite in December and January, proved that the government had indeed managed food rationing reasonably well considering the immense difficulties. The communication of food-rationing information nevertheless proved too difficult for Jules Ferry's limited political skills.[30] The rumour of rationing was enough to create a crisis, the rations fixed at generous but unsustainable rates proved impossible to sustain in the long term and soon the real problem of the government was its lack of credibility among the Parisians. Within the army composed of soldiers, conscripts (mobiles) and reserves (gardes nationales), the fervent military language was rapidly eroded by a series of scandalous defeats, defections on the battlefield and gross incompetence on the commanders' side. When the volunteers of Belleville ran away shouting 'treason' the revolutionary credentials of the extreme-left were dented and the value of *levée en masse* was severely undermined.[31] The officers then hesitated to use such unreliable troops in their miscalculated and disorderly offensives.

When the French did make some advance against the besiegers, the units found themselves isolated, without fresh supplies and soon having to withdraw, salvaging a defeat from the jaws of victory. When a general proclaimed that he would come back 'dead or victorious' like Ducrot and, two days later, the same man returned unharmed and defeated, Parisians learned to read between the lines and to take omissions as lies and silence as the evidence of defeat.[32] During the whole siege the government failed to be proactive and did not manage its propaganda in a responsible way. In some respects it could be argued that the government was the victim of its own make-believe and lack of information. When the Germans wanted to undermine Parisian confidence they simply released a certain amount of information on the conduct of the war in the provinces.[33] The American embassy and the anglophone community had also access to the largely francophobe *The Times*. German propaganda never lied but always selected the latest defeats to encourage the Parisian people in the conviction of their isolation.[34] The Germans were generally more proactive and attempted to shape French public opinion. Within occupied territories, however, the German papers produced in French lacked any credentials of truth,[35] yet their columns were generally richer in actual facts and evidence than the French's own.[36] These titles were only published after the German authorities had failed to obtain the verbatim reporting of their news and messages by French titles. *Le Nouvelliste de Versailles*, a daily newspaper, was thus published after the French local press refused to cooperate or to agree to the strictest censorship. The German prefect of Versailles then had it pasted on the walls to make sure that it would be read. This backfired when the graffiti 'Lies by Bismarck and Co.' defaced many posters.[37]

To return to the French government's mismanagement of war propaganda we can stress that there were a number of crude errors. By making the press entirely free it encouraged challenges to its monopoly on war news and failed to direct war enthusiasm in a specific manner, so that it soon became the scapegoat of the military defeat. The original mobilisation of enthusiasm remained to a large extent in Paris, but it became associated with a deep-seated defiance of the government. Soldiers and guardsmen believed that they had been betrayed and that the government's propaganda acted as a smokescreen for pacifist and traitorous plots. This acceptance of the necessity for war therefore seems to imply that the government's propaganda might have been more successful than expected; in fact it seems that the government formulated a response to war enthusiasm, rather than convincing a reluctant crowd of the necessity of war. A nice metaphor of this discrepancy and delayed reaction is the snow statue of the resistance built by the sculptor Falguière, which, like the government's resolve, melted well before the Parisians were tired of visiting it. It remained the sole war monument to symbolise the siege.[38]

In the provinces, the situation was very different. Gambetta became the republican dictator in charge of the military reorganisation of the army and promoter of the war to the last doctrine. In direct contrast with Paris, which needed little convincing for the continuation of the war which would relieve the siege, provincial Frenchmen were less enthusiastic as Audoin-Rouzeau and Roth have shown.[39] To stimulate an invaded country to wage a war of attrition is not a mean feat and Gambetta proved the best writer of calls to arms and dispatches. His proclamations addressed to the prefects of the unoccupied departments were reprinted in the local newspapers and even in foreign border broadsheets.[40] The language was rich with revolutionary allusions and borrowed heavily from the great military myth of the nation in arms[41] developed by historians and popular writers, from Michelet to Béranger, since 1815.[42] The following dispatch published on 1 December after the reconquest of Orléans shows some of the qualities and weaknesses of this style:

1 December
The Genius of France, damaged [other meaning of the word, *raped*] for a while, comes back, through the effort of the whole nation.

Victory reappears, and, as if to show the long series of our misfortunes, she now favours us on every side.

Thus our Loire army has taken the Prussians by surprise and has fought back all their attacks. Their tactic has been powerless against our solid troops, on the right and the left. . . . The Prussians can now measure today the difference between a despotic regime fighting for its whims and a people in arms which does not want to die.

It will be the eternal honour of the Republic to have brought back the sentiment of France to herself, to have found her wounded, degraded, betrayed, occupied, to have brought her honour back to her, her discipline, her armies and her victories.

The invaders are now on the roads where our people in arms will shoot them.

This is, Citizens, what a great nation can do to maintain untouched the glory of its past, which only wants to let blood, its own or that of the enemy to see the triumph of right and justice.

The call to images of great historical destiny and to major achievements of the past to back present efforts had an important echo and few dared like Edmond About to voice publicly their doubts about the continuation of the war.[43] Gambetta was successful in organising and arming perhaps 600,000 men in less than four months; his armies were nevertheless improvised and under-equipped.[44] In a fatal reading of a Parisian telegram informing him of an advance on the Marne, Gambetta misread the map, confusing two Épinay and thought that the German lines had been crossed. A few days later this blunder became public and severely undermined the credibility of Gambetta's information and judgement. Similarly, the military information was increasingly challenged and contested.

Foreign newspapers soon replaced French sources as the best providers of information and trustworthy news.[45] Even though English titles were held as being pro-German, Belgian and Swiss articles enabled a cross-referencing proving that they did not lie even though their analysis might be debatable.[46] In some respects what remained of the governmental propaganda was its analysis of the war effort while much of the information became discredited. By extension the analysis could be challenged too. Major localities like Lyons, Marseilles, Toulouse and Bordeaux also developed their own war propaganda to serve their own purpose.[47] Many of these radical cities had recovered rights to self-government unheard of since the 1789 Revolution and Lyons made it known that the Republic was proclaimed in the old capital of the Gaul before Paris had made up its mind.[48] When you add to this the fact that each municipality had to equip and arm their volunteers you obtain a very fragmented political patchwork in which each city created its own army, buying weapons abroad, raising taxes and exceptional loans to sustain the war effort.[49] In that situation, the local government could promote war for the defence of freshly acquired political rights and social policies.[50] Local newspapers could carry the message of the municipal powers and help the localities to root their war effort in local public opinion. This was greatly helped by a multiplicity of representative echelons which enabled a constant dialogue between governing and governed. The national guard, in itself a democratic institution since the officers were elected rather than nominated, petitioned widely and passed on information while simultaneously safeguarding law and order or, alternatively, presenting the most dangerous revolutionary threat.[51] The clubs also fed a radical war propaganda which meant that urban areas always had a hard-core of war supporters who attempted to promote war and political reform.[52] This latter point is particularly relevant here.

One of the great problems of the war effort and the revolutionary language used to promote it was precisely that the defenders of war seemed to promote a far from consensual political system: the Republic, and for some of them the 'social' Republic stolen by Napoleon III in 1851.[53] The suspicion that the war prolonged and, if victorious, would impose a debated political system was reinforced by Gambetta's radical reputation and his style of propaganda. While Gambetta accepted any volunteers from the most ultramontane soldiers[54] to Garibaldi's red shirts,[55] his speeches always insisted on the Republic as the only guarantor of a victorious people in arms. Unlike many regimes which use war propaganda to occlude political and social divisions, the Republic of 1870 was the fruit of war and its propaganda called for the continuation of a conflict which was its only source of legitimacy. Only too late in the conflict did Gambetta perceive clearly this danger and his penultimate official dispatch bears witness of his anxieties at the time when Parisian ministers had signed an armistice for most of France excluding the eastern departments:[56]

Frenchmen!
Think of our fathers who have left a compact and indivisible France; let us not betray our history, let us not give away our traditional property to the Barbarians. Who will sign? It cannot be you, legitimists, who are fighting so valiantly under the republican flag to defend the land of the old French kingdom; nor you sons of the bourgeois of 1789, whose masterpiece was to weld together the old provinces in a permanent pact of unity; it cannot be you, urban workers, whose intelligent and generous patriotism always represents France in its strength and unity, like the initiative of a people with modern freedoms; nor you, at last, landowners workers of the countryside who have never bartered your blood in the defence of the Revolution to which you owe your ownership of the land and your title of citizen!

No there will not be one Frenchman to sign this infamous pact; the foreigners will be disappointed; they will have to renounce the mutilation of France, because, all together in our love of the fatherland, we would become strong again and we would hunt them out.

To achieve this sacred aim, we must devote everything, our hearts, our wills, our lives and sacrifice even more difficult perhaps, forget our preferences.

We need to unite around the Republic, let us stay cool headed and strong; let us have no passion, weakness; let us swear to defend against all France and the Republic.

To Arms!
Vive la France!
Vive la République!

                                                            Léon Gambetta.

Gambetta's call to unite around the Republic which could somehow guarantee so many different 'preferences' and aspirations smacks of desperation and somewhat backfired, in the sense that Republicanism and war became so closely associated that a tired nation elected a party of peace at the national elections of 8 February 1871, which contained a large majority of anti-Republican figures, Royalists and conservatives who would probably not have been elected under their true colours. Some good examples of this are the constituencies of Lyons and its neighbourhood which voted for the candidates of the conservative press in favour of peace although it was traditionally a very Republican area. It would take years for this warmongering propaganda to subside in the electoral games.

This does not mean that all war propaganda failed or backfired on its instigators. To cope with defeat most contemporary French historians structured the narratives of the war in a manner which reversed the order of the conflict. From being the aggressor the French became the victims, instead of being losers they became moral victors. The historiography of the war also transformed geographic locations into landmarks of collective memory. Sedan the town and Sedan the defeat became irretrievably associated. The perception of the national territory, of history in space involved this controversial political assimilation: Sedan, Metz, Alsace-Lorraine, Bazeilles. . . .

A simple survey of a handful of towns or villages where some killing happened turns into a survey of the failures of the imperial regime and of the French army. Unlike Dunkirk for the English reader, they do not imply an understanding of the rationale of the conflict and a positive collective experience. They mapped a geography of resentment and loss. By 1871 most had if not forgotten at least minimised the relevance of the Spanish succession crisis of July 1870 which had led France to such a disaster. The confusion that remained about the real causes of the war also left more scope for interpretative licence. This lack of clarity made possible illuminating but contradictory narratives of the war which sought to make sense of the events and the sequence in which they took place. Conspiracy theories mixed with either Republican or religious exaltation provided explanations for everything. Those authors found in the anecdotes the proof that the whole picture did not reflect individual efforts. The sum of individual merits was well above the final collective result. Witnesses especially stressed the importance of individual experience and the validity of their subjective and narrow view. 'The war in its brutal reality, such as a doctor sees it, the war as it is.'[57] No meta-narrative gained prominence during the war or even after the war – no imaginary narrative, no structured form of storytelling.[58] The complexity of the situation on the fast-moving front and on static siege lines around key towns and fortresses meant that such meta-narrative was impossible.

Make-believe narratives on the other hand were not only possible but useful tools of political propaganda. Louis Veuillot, ultramontane editor of *L'Univers* and legitimist campaigner, could thus write in a private letter to Mrs Charlotte de

Gramont: 'If you know it, please tell me in the detail, the story of the flag of the [pontifical] zouaves? We need such salubrious episodes. They help us withstand the peace.'[59] The precise anecdote Veuillot referred to was the sacrifice of ultra-Catholic soldiers who, refusing to drop the 'sacred heart of Jesus Christ' flag, passed it on from one dying soldier to another. While Veuillot was carefully constructing a whole network of Catholic media he also insisted on propagating war stories which would cast the war in a religious light. Veuillot and his legitimist friends were not alone in using fragments of warfare to carve a postwar political victory. Similar anecdotes could be found for Garibaldian volunteers, franc-tireurs, children, women, old civil servants, the cities of Belfort and Bitche which were besieged from November 1870 until February 1871 and refused to surrender until the government forced them to.[60] Each anecdote could then be invested with a heroic message serving a precise political purpose. The army recast its disastrous performance through the careful use of some ludicrous gallant charges or meaningless defence. Some of these stories were excessively naive and amused the readers like that of 'when fifty Uhlans were flying before seven Sappers (!). . .' or when 'a wounded Turco [native North African soldier] and four boys armed with flint muskets putting a cloud of Uhlans to flight'.[61] The church produced its own list of martyrs to the national defence. The bishop of Angers made a very public statement asking trainee priests of his bishopric to serve as nurses in war hospitals, so that either they 'will fall martyrs of the nation or serve religion in the best possible manner'.[62] The Republicans easily hijacked the Gambetta legend, escaping Paris in a balloon to raise France and be denied the means of victory by the royalists and conservatives.[63] Only the partisans of Napoléon III found it difficult to salvage anything from the national disaster.[64]

During the war itself a whole set of images were produced specifically to support some more or less spurious religious allegations. A good example of propaganda could be the use of religious images and prophecies. Apart from a multitude of religious allegories on sin and retribution spread throughout the conservative press, some specific examples of religious supernatural received an inordinate amount of attention. The prophecies of a long-dead nun of Blois, named Marianne like the French Republic, and maintained by oral tradition in her convent, provided a clear sign of divine intervention.[65] As the oracle included an imminent victory, conservative newspapers found it worth the page space. Other instances of pagan prophecy, such as a Provençal prophecy from Avignon, received a more derisory attention, as did the ever ready Nostradamus:[66] 'we wanted to make this prophecy public first of all for curiosity's sake and then to tell clearly to the good people of Avignon how stupid are those who believe in such twaddle'.[67] The Virgin Mary also obligingly appeared a few times in 1870 in the wake of Lourdes. Other more worldly virgins were said to be travelling through occupied France and German lines to deliver a mysterious message to the government, visit Orléans like Joan of Arc and then return home peacefully.

While some of these stories obviously stretched the credulity of the middle-class readers one cannot underestimate the importance of the Virgin Mary in the Catholic church, the dogma of the immaculate conception being still very recent, or the political role of the Noviah cult during and after the war.[68] At the occasion of the celebration of the immaculate conception of Mary, the archbishop of Lyons, primate of the Gauls, declared in his episcopal message read in all churches:

> Our race is not abandoned by God, our ancient strength has not degenerated in absolute powerlessness . . . prayer too is a struggle; a struggle against divine retribution through a constant and humble call to his misericord. As God seems to answer our calls we must insist further through our charitable work . . . . These are patriotic actions that we can all achieve, nobody can avoid this service.[69]

The building of a number of redemptive churches, such as Montmartre or the basilica in Fourvière at Lyons, aimed at placing France under the special protection of the mother of Christ.[70]

The return to a messianic language was perhaps crude propaganda for the unbeliever, but it was also a powerful reinforcing of a more commonly held feeling of doom and stunned anxiety at the extent of French powerlessness. While the Academy of Medicine isolated tuberculosis, alcohol and hereditary diseases as the hidden causes of the French collapse, the church could just as legitimately argue that a moral and religious decline was the visible source of divisive struggles and defeat.[71] The same events could be presented just as powerfully to sustain other types of political propaganda. The clubs as mentioned above soon took the mantel of warmongers to the last, promoting the revolution of 1793 as the objective to achieve instead of the example of 1792 more generally favoured by moderate Republicans.[72] A good instance of this would be a national guardsmen petition which referred explicitly to the revolution of 1793, only for the last digit to be turned into a two on around two-thirds of the remaining petition sheets. In this case a reading of history prevailed to explain the future.

The 1870 war also saw the European development of the Red Cross and the use of a humanitarian logic to explain neutral intervention on the battlefield. Some foreigners used their philanthropic efforts as a cloak to cover their own specific agenda. The Quakers thus attempted a breakthrough in a traditionally hostile country[73] while the Irish nationalists used their humanitarian expedition as a ploy to help the French army directly and remind everyone of the 'year of the French' (1798), the last major armed rebellion against the British.[74] Within France the Red Cross was divided between two different organisations which catered for different needs and served different constituencies. The *société de secours*, composed of the original humanitarian activists, used international aristocratic connections and was led by a cluster of major conservative figures such as the vicomte de Melun. The *Presse* organisation, sponsored by major conservative newspapers, split from the former over a number of issues ranging from personality differences to more fundamental disputes on patriotism.[75] Both organisations remained independent from the state until 31 December 1870, a month before the surrender. They both served as morale boosters during the siege, collection boxes were found in all shops of Paris, the red and white flag became second-best after the national tricolour and before the radical red flag used in some quarters. Red Cross ambulances were protected by the terms of the Geneva Convention which sheltered doctors and patients and guaranteed that their lives would not be threatened. The word 'ambulance' in 1870 described something very different from the modern vehicle and usually referred to a makeshift hospital organised behind the front lines to cater for the most urgent needs. In due time the French lines demonstrated a propensity for moving backwards and thus turned the makeshift hospitals into front-line forts. An occasional shot from a window would then lead to the massacre of all in the ambulance. A few incidents of that kind took place in the provinces: an ambulance was destroyed near Sedan, later the Saône-et-Loire ambulance was executed in cold blood,[76] and Le Mans was savagely occupied and its ambulances were not respected.[77] Most of the time these incidents were not premeditated and took place in the heat of the action, but the French humanitarian movement could still use them for national purposes and denounce the barbarity of the invaders.[78]

In rhetorical terms the murder of a defenceless doctor became a trope of war narratives. Most books denouncing German barbarity (and therefore vindicating the French aggression) contained a scene, or occasionally a picture, describing the slaughter of French humanitarian staff. A multitude of pamphlets came to light in France and francophone Europe: Hector de Condé's *La Prusse au pilori de la civilisation (crimes et forfaits des prussiens en France)* (1871); C.A. Daubant, *La Guerre comme la font les Prussiens* (1871); Amédée Marteau, *Le Droit prime la force, page d'histoire de l'Empire d'Allemagne* (1876); *Recueil de documents sur les exactions, vols. et cruautés des armées prussiennes en France* (1871); A. Vavasseur, *La Paix honteuse ou le droit des gens selon les prussiens* (1871); Némésis, *Crimes, forfaits, atrocités et viols commis par les prussiens sur le sol de la France* (1871); comte Alfred de la Guéronnière, *La Prusse devant l'Europe* (1870).[79] These few titles do not represent an exhaustive list and their ephemeral nature may mean that they had a transient effect on public opinion. Most French-biased books will however use the same stories, usually in the same terms and often referring back to the same Red Cross evidence. This propaganda was so obviously effective that the Prussian government had to react publicly with its own pamphlet published in French, German and English and made freely available to the international media and organisations: *Comment les français font la guerre. Recueil de faits pour servir à l'histoire des moeurs et de la civilisation au xixème siècle* (1871).

To undermine internal investigations launched by French-speaking Swiss Red Cross authorities, the prize of the Empress Augusta was presented to Carl Lüder's violently anti-French book of 1876 on the Geneva Convention which countered most French accusations of malpractice.[80] International claims were also made by French surgeons who claimed to have witnessed wounds which could only be explained by the use of forbidden weapons such as the infamous explosive bullets.[81] The shelling of Paris also enabled superb French propaganda:

The Barbarians
Arson is a duty prescribed to soldiers by their leaders. They have even made it a legal punishment . . . pillage is coming instinctively to the Teutonic race so is a limitless greed and a revolting grubbiness. As to their bloodthirsty cruelty it will remain proverbial in this war of extermination. How many innocent throats were slit that the press has to report every day . . .'[82]

The war victims were graphically depicted as being children and women, innocent bystanders and hospitals, especially in January 1871 when German guns started shelling Paris. The medical petitions sent by doctors and eminent scientists to the German high command were certainly not effective in stopping the German fire, but they had an international impact which made uneasy the doves led by the Kronprintz at Versailles.[83] This type of propaganda, based on visual evidence and using international legislation, made a rational case for French powerlessness and was extremely successful in changing public images of the conflict abroad. The British press seems to have taken a more positive stance towards the French when the full extent of war atrocities and starvation reached it in January 1871.[84] Nationally, the Red Cross served a conservative agenda, in so far as it supported established figures fighting for survival in the war turmoil and defended traditional French values of gallantry, generosity, charity and self-sacrifice against the barbaric enemy and the subversive socialists.

These values were of the sort required by the imperatives of childhood literature and many titles published in France and the francophone world were matched by English books on the same themes.[85] French propaganda cashed in on the romance of the beautiful losers. This enduring imagery found many outlets in the postwar literary production. It ranges from high literature to the penny dreadful and the pedagogic stories. Jules Michelet's widely advertised *La France devant l'Europe* cast the myth of French civilisation defeated by barbaric violence and ungrateful international indifference in a properly historical vein.[86] Alphonse Daudet's sickly sentimental short stories,[87] Maupassant's brutal naturalist novellas and Émile Zola's *Débâcle* contributed to transcend defeat into art. Victor Hugo, in his *L'Année Terrible*, even managed to turn the invasion into a victory for France:

For Whom the Final Victory?
We must teach you Teutons, you must learn
No, you will not take Alsace and Lorrain,
and it is us who will take Germany. Listen
To cross the borders, to enter our cities
see minds work here, read our books
breathe deeply the air that inspires our thinkers
is to give back its sword to progress,
it is to drink at our chalice, accept our regrets,
our sorrows, our pregnant ills, our hopes, our dreams
it is to cry our tears, it is to wish for our sufferings
it is to want this great wind, the Revolution; . . .
. . . Brothers you will hand back our flame made larger
we are the torch, you will be the fire.

December 1870[88]

Successive generations of French citizens learned to be more sceptical on the immediate returns of this lesson of civilisation to the German hordes. The huge literature which appeared after the war made increasingly less charitable comments on the invaders and this multi-layered literary and pictorial production eventually penetrated at all levels the French national consciousness.[89] The school teaching of the need for a revenge, which took some innocent-looking forms such as *Le Tour de France par deux enfants*, used all the rhetorical tropes developed during and immediately after the war in the propaganda effort.[90] The more aggressive and openly revenge-seeking literary production of talented authors such as Déroulède built on this propaganda and assumed its historical validity and its timeless relevance to the readers.[91]

In a sense the propaganda that mattered was less the governmental rhetoric which missed the mark too often in promising impossible reversals of fortune, than the crude, yet documented, characterisation of the enemy as a race of envious barbarians eager to penetrate France to plunder her natural wealth of civilisation and 'amputate its national territory'.[92] The fall of the Roman empire provided a natural reference and each 'German aggression' of the past was reinterpreted in school manuals in this light. Even though many French intellectuals had felt some unease with the rise of Prussia in Germany before 1870, many only abandoned more recent romantic representations of Germans and Germany in 1870 but this break was real and deep-reaching.[93] In this sense the creation of a basic propagandistic historiography was successful beyond the hopes of any government or power.[94] Its greatest achievement was to become such a universally shared tenet of French historiography that the few who dared to think in contradiction to these paradigms appeared suspect of anti-French activities to the majority. It seems significant that even avowed pacifists like

Edmond About, mentioned earlier, had to reconsider their own position in the aftermath of the peace settlement, stating, 'to think that in the Spring 1870, merely 18 months ago, the old tirades on the national flag made us smile!'[95] It is only with the rise of a specifically internationalist and usually socialist historiography that the nationalistic paradigms were eventually challenged. Jaurès' history of the war, published in 1907, in itself a chapter of the socialist history of France, is thus a remarkable analysis of the political causes of the conflict and a denunciation of this dark German legend at the time when the Moroccan crisis made another war against Germany a strong possibility. His untimely death on the eve of the First World War, at the hands of a nationalistic assassin who then walked free a few years later, should still remind us how risky such an enterprise could be.[96]

Notes

1   See Kenneth Cmiel, *Democratic Eloquence: The Fight over Popular Speech in Nineteenth-Century America* (Berkeley, University of California Press, 1990), pp. 55–93; French democrat speakers were still adepts of the Grand Style and of rich and elevated figures of speech.

2   Thomas de Quincey, *Critical Suggestions on Style and Rhetoric* (London, James Hogg & Sons, c. 1826), pp. 21–78.

3   Theodore Zeldin, *Emile Ollivier and the Liberal Empire* (Oxford, Clarendon Press, 1963).

4   E.B. Washburne, *Recollections of a Minister to France, 1869–1877* (2 vols, London, Sampson Low, 1887), vol. 1, p. 183; J.P.T. Bury, *Gambetta and the Making of the Third Republic* (London, Longman, 1973), p. 4.

5   Col. Lonsdale Hale, *The "People's War" in France 1870–1871* (London, Hugh Rees, 1904), pp. 1–32; François Roth, *La Guerre de 1870* (Paris, Fayard, 1990), pp. 411–51.

6   Richard Holmes, *The Road to Sedan: The French Army 1866–1870* (London, Royal Historical Society, 1984); Michael Howard, *The Franco–Prussian War: The German Invasion of France, 1870–1871* (New York, Dorset Press, 1961, repr. 1990); Stéphane Audoin-Rouzeau, *1870, La France dans la guerre* (Paris, Armand Colin, 1989), pp. 16–17.

7   Albert Sorel, *Histoire Diplomatique de la Guerre Franco-Allemande* (2 vols, Paris, Plon, 1875); E. Ollivier, *The Franco-Prussian War and its Hidden Causes* (London, Isaac Pitman and Sons, 1913); Howard, *The Franco-Prussian War*, pp. 48–56. L. Steefel, *Bismarck, the Hohenzollern Candidacy and the Origins of the Franco-German War of 1870* (Cambridge, MA, Harvard University Press, 1962).

8   Philip A Bertocci, *Jules Simon: Republican Anticlericalism and Cultural Politics in France, 1848–1886* (Columbia, University of Missouri Press, 1978).

9   General Ducrot, *La Défense de Paris (1870–1871)* (4 vols, Paris, Dentu, 1875); Baron Von der Goltz, *Gambetta et ses armées* (Paris, Sandoz & Fischbacher, 1877), pp. 12, 26, 342.

10   See for instance Strasburg: G. Fischbach, *Guerre de 1870, le siège et le bombardement de Strasbourg* (Paris, Cherbuliez, 1871); Jacques Flach, *Strasbourg après le bombardement, 2 octobre 1870–30 septembre 1872, rapports sur les travaux du comité de secours strasbourgeois pour les victimes du bombardement* (Strasburg, Imprimerie de Fischbach, 1873).

11   Yves Lequin, *Les Ouvriers de la région lyonnaise (1848–1914), les intérêts de classe et la république* (2 vols, Presses Universitaires de Lyon, 1977), vol. 2, p. 212.

12   *Rapport sur les actes de la délégation du gouvernment de la défense nationale à Tours et à Bordeaux* (Versailles, Cerf, 1876); *Bulletin officiel du ministère de l'intérieur, délégation de Tours et de Bordeaux* (Poitiers, A. Dupré, 1871). For a very negative assessment see Léonce Dupont, *Tours et Bordeaux, souvenirs de la république à outrance* (Paris, E. Dentu, 1877); Alphonse Glais-Bizoin, *Dictature de cinq mois, mémoires pour servir à l'histoire du Gouvernement de la Défense Nationale à Tours et à Bordeaux* (Paris, Dentu, 1873).

13   Alfred Auguste Ernouf, *Histoire des chemins de fer français pendant la guerre franco-prussienne* (Paris, Librairie Générale, 1874); F. Jacqmin, *Les chemins de fer pendant la guerre de 1870–1871* (Paris, Hachette, 1872).

14   Lynn M. Case, *French Opinion on War and Diplomacy during the Second Empire* (New York, Octagon Books, 1972), pp. 1–13.

15   Claude Bellanger, Pierre Guiral and Fernand Terrou, *Histoire générale de la presse française* (Paris, Presses Universitaires de France, 1969), pp. 364–9.

16   Joannès Guetton, *Six mois de drapeau rouge à Lyon* (Paris, P.N. Josserand, 1871); Alphonse V. Roche, *Provençal Regionalism* (Evanston, Northwestern University Press, 1954), p. 62; Louis M. Greenberg, *Sisters of Liberty: Marseille, Lyon, Paris and the Reaction to a Centralized State, 1868–1871* (Cambridge, MA, Harvard University Press, 1971), p. 48. The Lyons experience had much to do with rebuilding municipal government after eighteen years of direct autocratic rule.

17   Bertrand Taithe, 'Reliving the Revolution: War and Political Identity during the Franco-Prussian War', in B. Taithe and T. Thornton (eds), *War: Identities in Conflict 1300–2000*, Themes in History (Stroud, Sutton Publishing, 1998), pp. 141–58.

18   Francisque Sarcey, *Le Siège de Paris* (Paris, Nelson Editeurs, *c.* 1935), pp. 140–1.

19   Brian Jenkins, *Nationalism in France: Class and Nation Since 1789* (London, Routledge, 1990), pp. 75–122.

20   Henry Contamine, *La Revanche, 1871–1914* (Paris, Berger-Levrault, 1957); A. Dupuy, *Sedan et l'enseignement de la revanche* (Paris, Institut National de Recherche et de Documentation Pédagogique, 1975); Henri Guillemin, *Nationalistes et nationaux (1870–1940)* (Paris, Gallimard, idée, 1974).

21   Jules Favre, *Gouvernement de la Défense Nationale du 30 juin au 31 octobre 1870* (Paris, Plon, 1871).

22   The recent reforms following the Prussian victory of Sadowa against Austria had led the French army to create two types of reserves, the better trained mobile and the *garde nationale*, an often sedentary force with little or no training and equipment but a revolutionary symbol dating from Lafayette. Jean Casevitz, *Une Loi manquée: la loi Niel 1866–1868, l'armée française à la veille de la guerre de 1870* (Paris, Presses Universitaires de France, 1959); Laurent Llopez, 'La Garde Mobile de l'Hérault: défendre le territoire nationale de Paris à l'Algérie', *Histoire et Défense*, 33:1 (1996), 31–62; Charles Dolivet, *Histoire de la garde nationale et des bataillons mobilisés du IXème arrondissement* (Paris, 1872); Georges Carrot, 'La Garde Nationale 1789–1871, une institution de la Nation' (Thèse de Doctorat de 3ième cycle, Université de Nice, 1979).

23   Geoff Watkins in his chapter rightly stresses the continuity of rhetoric and language between the two Bonapartes.

24   P.C. Joubert and Arnauld de Vresse, *De la défense de Paris pendant le siège au point de vue de l'alimentation* (Paris, Arnauld de Vresse, 1871); A. Legoyt, 'L'Alimentation et les prix pendant le siège de Paris', *Journal des Économistes*, 66 (mai 1871), 331–47; Fernand Papillon, 'Hygiène et alimentation de Paris pendant le siège de 1870', *Revue des Deux Mondes* (1/10/1870), 575–84; Adolphe Morillon, *L'Approvisionnement de Paris en temps de guerre, souvenirs et prévisions* (Paris, Didier, 1888).

25   This rich but vacuous prose can be found in the various decrees and announcements

catalogued in *Recueil officiel des actes du Gouvernement de la Défense Nationale pendant le siège de Paris* (Paris, Bibliothèque administrative Paul Dupont, 1871).

26   Morillon, *L'Approvisionnement de Paris*, p. 68.

27   Martial Delpit, *Rapport fait au nom de la commission d'enquête chargée au termes de la loi du 17 juin 1871, de rechercher les causes de l'insurrection du 18 mars et de constater les faits qui s'y rattachent* (3 vols, Versailles, CERF, 1872).

28   Edmond Bapst, *Le siège de Metz en 1870* (Paris, Lahure, 1926), pp. 364–415; *Rapports du conseil d'enquête sur les capitulations des places fortes* (Paris, Librairie Centrale, 1872); *Extrait des causes célèbres de tous les peuples, le maréchal Bazaine, relation complète* (Paris, Lebrun, 1874), tomes 7 and 8, esp. tome 8, pp. 155–71, 173.

29   The volume of this literature is huge and struck contemporaries by its richness and diversity; see Firmin Maillard, *Les Publications de la rue pendant le siège et la Commune* (Paris, Auguste Aubry, 1874) and *Élections des 26 mars et avril 1871, Affiches, professions de foi, documents officiels, clubs et comités pendant la Commune* (Paris, E. Dentu, 1871).

30   Jules Ferry's legend has grown with the rise of the Third Republic's golden legend of compulsory education. It is refreshing to read contemporaries like Louis Fiaux, *Jules Ferry, un malfaiteur public* (Paris, Librairie Internationale Achille Le Rey, 1886), p. 37.

31   Gustave Flourens, *Paris livré* (Paris, A. Lacroix, Verboeckhaven et Cie., 1871), p. 103.

32   Alistair Horne, *The Fall of Paris: The Siege and the Commune 1870–1* (London, The Reprint Society, 2nd edn, 1967), p. 150.

33   Michael Howard, *The Franco-Prussian War: The German Invasion of France, 1870–1871* (New York, Dorset Press, 1961), p. 351.

34   Louis Marchant (trans.), *La Bourgogne pendant la guerre et l'occupation allemande (1870–1871) d'après la gazette officielle de Carlsruhe* (Dijon, Marchand & Maniere-loquin, 1875), pp. 231–3.

35   *Le Salut Public* (Lyons): this denounced all German publications as lies (05/11/1870).

36   *The Times* correspondent in Berlin, *Letters on International Relations before and during the war of 1870* (2 vols, London, Tinsley Brothers, 1871), vol. 2, pp. 350–1.

37   E. Delerot, *Versailles pendant l'occupation allemande 1870–1871* (Versailles, L. Bernard, 1900), pp. 165–74.

38   *La Guerre Illustrée* (7/01/1871), 48: 384.

39   François Roth, *La Guerre de 1870* (Paris, Fayard, 1990); *La Lorraine dans la guerre de 1870* (Nancy, Presses Universitaires de Nancy, 1984); Audoin-Rouzeau, *La France dans la guerre*.

40   *Salut Public* (Lyons). The first Gambetta proclamation of 8 October was thus published in Lyons on 11/10/1870.

41   Richard D. Challener, *The French Theory of the Nation in Arms, 1866–1939* (New York, Columbia University Press, 1965); Thomas J. Adriance, *The Last Gaiter Button: A Study of the Mobilisation and Concentration of the French Army in the War of 1870* (Westport, The Greenwood Press, 1987); Holmes, *The Road to Sedan*.

42   Sorel, *Histoire Diplomatique de la Guerre Franco-Allemande*, vol. 2, pp. 384–5.

43   About was a journalist of *Le Soir*, a daily newspaper, and his article published after 31 October 1870 was much debated: Francisque Sarcey, *Le Siège de Paris* (Paris, Nelson Editeurs, n.d. 1930s), p. 169.

44   Many scandals marred this improvised war effort, see for Lyons: Louis Philippe de Ségur, *Les Marchés de la guerre à Lyon et à l'armée de Garibaldi* (Paris, H. Plon, 1873).

45   See Sarcey, *Siège de Paris*, p. 144.

46   The news of the surrender of Paris came to Lyons through the *Journal de Genève*, for instance. *Le Salut Public* (Lyons) (29/01/1871).

47   Jacques Girault, *La Commune et Bordeaux (1870–1871)* (Paris, Éditions Sociales, 1971).

48   Archives du Rhône [AR] 1 M 118. Demandes de la Commune de Lyon à la délégation de Tours.

49   Not mentioning the federative movements led from Marseilles or Lyons. See Archives Municipales de Montpellier [AMM] Conseil Municipal de Montpellier, délibérations, 57 D1, 20/09/1870.

50   The political developments of the provinces have not been looked at in much detail yet: see Jeanne Gaillard, *Communes de province, commune de Paris 1870–1871* (Paris, Flammarion, 1971).

51   In Lyons the guardsmen were very actively petitioning in an organised manner with preprinted petition sheets. I have counted 100 sheets left representing *c.* 7,000 signatures. AR, 1 M 118.

52   Propaganda material varied from speeches to handmade fliers. AR, 1 M 118, fly leaflet, 6 × 4 inches, to specific newspapers such as *L'Antéchrist* published in Lyons, 16 Brumaire 79 (16/11/1870), AR 4 M 223.

53   Katherine Auspitz, *The Radical Bourgeoisie: The 'Ligue de l'Enseignement' and the Origins of the Third Republic, 1866–1885* (Cambridge University Press, 1982); Philip A. Bertocci, *Jules Simon: Republican Anticlericalism and Cultural Politics in France, 1848–1886* (Columbia, University of Missouri Press, 1978); Pamela M. Pilbeam, *Republicanism in Nineteenth-Century France, 1814–1871* (Basingstoke, Macmillan, 1995).

54   Colonel D'Albiousse, *Le Drapeau du Sacré-Coeur, campagne de France (zouaves pontificaux)* (Rennes, Hauvespre, 1873); Abbot J.S. Allard, *Les Zouaves pontificaux, ou journal de Mgr. Daniel, aumônier des zouaves* (Paris, Hugny, 1880); Henri d'Arsac, *Les Mercenaires ou les zouaves pontificaux en France* (Reims, imprimerie coopérative, 1873).

55   Robert Middleton, *Garibaldi, ses opérations à l'armée des Vosges* (Paris, Garnier Frères, 1872), pp. 249–77; Ségur, *Les Marchés de la guerre*; Riciotti Garibaldi, *Souvenirs de la campagne de France 1870–71* (Nice, La Semaine Niçoise, 1899), pp. 118–19; P.A. Dormoy, *Les Trois Batailles de Dijon, 30 octobre, 26 novembre, 21 janvier* (Paris, Librairie Militaire Dubois, 1894), pp. 370–3; also SHAT, Lg1 correspondence of the Vosges Army.

56   General Joachim Ambert, *Gaulois et Germains, récits militaires. I l'invasion; II après Sedan; III la Loire et l'Est; IV le siège de Paris* (4 vols, Paris, Blond et Barral, 1883–5).

57   Henri Étienne Beaunis, *Impressions de campagne, siège de Strasbourg, campagne de la Loire, campagne de l'Est* (Paris, Felix Alcan & Berger Levrault et cie, 1887, reprinted from the *Gazette médicale de Paris*), p. vi.

58   Lloyd S. Kramer, 'Literature and Historical Imagination', in Lynn Hunt (ed.), *The New Cultural History* (Berkeley, University of California Press, 1989), pp. 97–130.

59   Louis Veuillot, *Oeuvres complètes*, ed. François Veuillot (deuxième série, 22 vols, Paris, Lethielleux Libraire, 1932), vol. 10, p. 321.

60   Léon Belin, *Le Siège de Belfort (siège et bombardement)* (Paris and Nancy, Berger Levrault, 1871).

61 D. Bingham, *Recollections of Paris* (2 vols, London, Chapman and Hall, 1896), vol. 1, p. 177.

62 *Le Salut Public* (Lyons) (22/11/1870).

63 Charles de Freycinet, *Souvenirs, 1848–1878* (Paris, Delagrave, 1912).

64 John Rothney, *Bonapartism after Sedan* (New York, Cornell University Press, 1969).

65 *Le Salut Public* (Lyons) (1/11/1870).

66 *Le Salut Public* (Lyons) (2/11/1870).

67 *La Marseillaise* (Marseilles) (30/10/1870).

68 John McManners, *The Church and State in France, 1870–1914* (London, SPCK Church Historical Society, 1972).

69 AR, V 21 /0. J.M.A. Ginoulhiac, archevêque de Lyon et Vienne, Primat des Gaules, *Mandements à l'occasion de la fête de l'immaculée conception de la sainte Vierge* (np, 21 November 1870), pp. 2–4.

70 David Harvey, *Consciousness and the Urban Experience: Studies in the History and Theory of Capitalist Urbanization* (2 vols, Oxford, Basil Blackwell, 1992), vol. 1, pp. 221–49.

71 *Bulletin de l'Académie Nationale de Médecine*, vol. xxxvi, (Paris: J.B. Baillière et fils, 1870), p. 56; William H. Schneider, *Quality and Quantity: The Quest for Biological Regeneration in Twentieth Century France* (Cambridge University Press, 1989), pp. 20–7.

72 Martin Philip Johnson, *The Paradise of Association: Political Culture and Popular Agitation in the Paris Commune of 1871* (University of Michigan Press, 1996), p. 133.

73 William K. Sessions, *They Chose the Star: Quaker War Relief Work in France, 1870–1875* (York, The Ebor Press, 1991).

74 *Report of the Irish Ambulance Committee of Dublin, Irish Ambulance Corp for the Service of the French Wounded* (Dublin, Browne and Nobu, 1871), pp. 5–27 ; John Fleetwood, 'An Irish Field-Ambulance in the Franco-Prussian War', *The Irish Sword* (1964), 137–48.

75 J.M. Félix Christot, *Le massacre de l'ambulance de Saône-et-Loire, 21 Janvier 1871. Rapport du comité médical de secours aux blessés le 7 juillet 1871* (Lyons, A. Vingtrinier, 1871).

76 *Le Salut Public* (Lyons) (25/01/1871).

77 Ambroise Eusèbe Mordret, *Rapport sur le service militaire de santé (Guerre de 1870–1871) dans la ville du Mans, du 19 août 1870 au 20 avril 1871, adressé à M le Ministre de la Guerre le 11 juin 1871* (Le Mans, Monnoyer, 1872); Louis Joseph Charpignon, *Souvenirs de l'occupation d'Orléans par les Allemands en 1870-1871, théorie de l'invasion; les effets, les assassinats, les blessés* (Orléans, H. Herluison, 1872).

78 *Le Salut Public* (Lyons) (08/10/1870).

79 Hector de Condé, *La Prusse au pilori de la civilisation (crimes et forfaits des prussiens en France)* (Brussels, Devillé, 1871); Anon., *Comment les français font la guerre. Recueil de faits pour servir à l'histoire des moeurs et de la civilisation au xixème siècle* (Berlin, C. Duncker, 1871) (simultaneously published in German and English usually attributed to the Prussian Foreign Office); C.A. Daubant, *La Guerre comme la font les Prussiens* (Paris, Plon, 1871); Amédée Marteau, *Le Droit prime la force, page d'histoire de l'Empire d'Allemagne* (Paris, Librairie Internationale, 1876); *Recueil de documents sur les exactions, vols et cruautés des armées prussiennes en France* (Bordeaux, Férot et Fils, 1871); A. Vavasseur, *La Paix honteuse ou le droit des gens selon les prussiens* (Paris, Lacroix, Verboeckhoven et Cie., 1871); Némésis, *Crimes, forfaits, atrocités et viols commis par les prussiens sur le sol de la France* (Paris, André Sagnier, 1871); comte Alfred de la Guéronnière, *La Prusse devant l'Europe* (Brussels, Office de Publicité, 1870).

80   C. Lüder, *La Convention de Genève au point de vue historique, critique et dogmatique* (Erlangen, Besold, 1876).

81   *The Times* correspondent in Berlin, *Letters on International Relations before and during the war of 1870* (2 vols, London, Tinsley Brothers, 1871), vol. 1, pp. 669–70.

82   *Le Salut Public (Lyons)*, leader (18/01/1871); *Le Salut Public (Lyons)* was a moderate conservative newspaper.

83   A.R. Allinson (ed.), *The War Diary of the Emperor Frederick III, 1870–1871* (Westport, Greenwood Press, 1971), p. 240; Major H. de Sarrepont, *Le Bombardement de Paris par les prussiens en janvier 1871* (Paris, Firmin Didot frères, 1872).

84   Archibald Forbes, *My Experiences of the War between France and Germany* (2 vols, London, Hurst and Blackett, 1871).

85   Captain F. S. Brereton, *A Hero of Sedan: A Tale of the Franco-Prussian War* (London, Blackie and Son Ltd, 1910); G.A. Henty, *The Young Franc-Tireurs* (London, Griffith and Farran, 1872); James Nisbet, *Wounded in War: A Tale of August 1870* (London, n.p., 1870).

86   Jules Michelet, *La France devant l'Europe* (Florence, Hachette, Le Monnier, Feb. 1871), pp. 7–25.

87   Alphonse Daudet, *Les Contes du lundi* (Paris (1873), Maxi Poche Classiques Français, 1995).

88   Victor Hugo, *L'Année terrible* (Paris, Gallimard, 1985), pp. 82–6.

89   Amédée Chassagne, *Contre le Prussien: I Hier . . . , II aujourd'hui . . ., III demain* (Paris and Limoges, Henri Charles Lavauzelle, 1896).

90   A. Dupuy, *Sedan et l'enseignement de la revanche* (Paris, Institut National de Recherche et de Documentation Pédagogique, 1975).

91   Paul Déroulède, author of *Les Chants du Soldat*, regularly started his books with a violent open letter to his 'enemy readers or more simply Prussian readers': *Pages françaises* (Paris, Bloud, 1909); *1870, feuilles de route, des bois de Verrières à la forteresse de Breslau* (Paris, F. Juven, 31 edn, 1907); *Nouvelles feuilles de Route de la forteresse de Breslau aux allées de Tourny* (Paris, F. Juven, 1907), p. vii.

92   Juliette Adam, *Mes Angoisses et nos luttes, 1871–1873* (Paris, Alphonse Lemerre, 1907), p. 42.

93   René Bourgeois, 'De la Germanophilie à la Teutophobie', in Simone Bernard-Griffiths and Paul Viallaneix (eds), *Edgar Quinet ce Juif Errant* (Clermont Ferrand, Clermont Ferrand University Press, 1978), pp. 251–62.

94   Claude Digeon, *La Crise allemande de la pensée française* (Paris, Presses Universitaires de France, 1959).

95   E. About, *Alsace, 1871–1872* (11th edn, Paris, Hachette, 1906), p. 25.

96   Henri Guillemin, *Nationalistes et nationaux (1870–1940)* (Paris, Gallimard, 1974), pp. 149–50; Jean Rabaut, *Jaurès et son assassin* (2nd edn, Paris, Cercle du Bibliophile, 1971), pp. 44, 187.

13

THE IRISH RECRUITING AND
ANTI-RECRUITING CAMPAIGNS, 1914–1918

Tim Bowman

In Ireland, unlike in the rest of the United Kingdom, the First World War
has always been seen as a politically divisive issue. While in Britain appeals
to king and country and posters bearing the grizzled features of F.M. Lord
Kitchener were utilised to attract recruits, in Ireland recruiting propaganda
had to be much more subtle. Another key difference between recruiting
propaganda in Britain and Ireland was that when recruits were not
forthcoming in Britain, conscription was introduced in January 1916. In
Ireland, however, the political situation prevented the implementation of this
measure and, instead, a diverse set of propaganda materials were utilised in the
entire 1914–18 period.

In terms of propaganda, army recruitment in Ireland during the First World
War was used by a number of groups. First, Irish politicians, both Unionist and
Nationalist, aided the recruitment campaign for selfish political motives. Thus, in
the sphere of propaganda, each political grouping claimed to be able to provide a
large number of troops, if its political demands were met. Second, the British
government clearly had to use very different forms of propaganda in Ireland to
gain recruits, in comparison with that used in Great Britain. This was often
influenced by political pressure from the Irish Parliamentary Party and Ulster
Unionists. Third, the British government could use recruiting propaganda to
solve other embarrassing political problems: for example, it was used to prevent
Col. Arthur Lynch expressing pro-Sinn Fein sentiments.

Finally, anti-recruiting propaganda must be considered in this period. This
policy, built on Republican opposition to recruitment, was first aired in 1842 and
reached its height during the South African War of 1899–1902.[1] Anti-recruiting
was widely supported by Republicans and advanced Nationalists as it was one of
the few policies on which they could agree. It encompassed all advanced
Nationalist political groupings: Republicans and Dual-monarchists, militarists
and non-militarists, and socialists and conservatives. In addition to this, following
the Easter Rising of 1916, recruiting activities provided the only legal public
meetings where Sinn Fein members could make their voices heard.

In July 1914 Ireland had appeared to be on the very brink of civil war between
the Ulster Volunteer Force and Irish National Volunteers, and the cabinet feared
that, in the event of British participation in the European war, the small British

Expeditionary Force would have to be employed in Ireland rather than France. As Myles Dungan comments however:

> In the world of paranoid alliances which existed in Europe in 1914 it was not at all illogical that the shot fired by a Serbian nationalist which killed an Austro-Hungarian potentate in modern day Bosnia should have forestalled a possible Irish civil war. That shot reverberated in Ireland like a loud bang which distracts two men involved in a squabble of their own. It was as if a neighbour's house was on fire. Both ran to join the chain gang. Neither did so from the purest of motives. They wanted to be seen with buckets in their hands dousing the flames. Both expected the neighbour would reward them once the fire was extinguished.[2]

Thus both Irish political groupings offered their support to the British government during the war. Sir Edward Carson 'on the 1. August 1914 made it clear that, in the event of war, the Ulster Volunteer Force would not only be available for home defence, but would be in a position to send a unit overseas'.[3]

John Redmond's response was somewhat more complicated. On the outbreak of war he supported British policy and pledged that the defence of Southern Ireland could safely be left to the Irish National Volunteers.[4] Only in his 'Manifesto on the War' published in *Freeman's Journal* on 17 September 1914 and, later, in his Woodenbridge speech on 20 September did Redmond urge his supporters to enlist in the British armed forces.[5] Even in this speech there was some ambiguity. David Fitzpatrick suggests that 'Redmond's speech of 20th September alarmed more Volunteers than it inspirited',[6] while this speech can also be interpreted as one recruiting for the Irish National Volunteers rather than the British Army.

Both Carson's and Redmond's stances had, obviously, much to do with the Third Home Rule Bill. This measure was placed on the statute book in September 1914, with the proviso that it would not actually be introduced until the end of the war and that provision for the exclusion of Ulster, or at least parts of north-eastern Ulster would be made before its implementation. This legislation offered Sir Edward Carson and the Ulster Unionists very little room for manoeuvre. While clearly taking up arms against the British government in 1913 and 1914, Unionists had always claimed to be acting in the spirit of the constitution and to be patriotically defending the empire. Thus, with the advent of war, they could hardly refuse to place the Ulster Volunteer Force at the government's disposal and encourage Unionists to join the British Army. The clause relating to future Ulster exclusion meant, however, that from August 1914 Ulster Unionists began a skilful propaganda campaign which suggested that, in Ireland, only Unionists were really prepared to help Britain in her hour of need.

As early as August 1914, therefore, Carson, and his chief lieutenant, Sir James Craig, met Lord Kitchener at the War Office. Carson proposed that if Home Rule was put in cold storage, then at least one division drawn from the Ulster Volunteer Force would be available for overseas service. This interview was inconclusive; Carson's desire for an 'Ulster' division to be formed was vetoed by Kitchener, who also made some ill-advised comments on partition.[7]

John Redmond's policy relating to his support for the war was very different. While, in August 1914 the Irish National Volunteers numbered around 140,000 men and were still recruiting, they desperately lacked trained officers and NCOs and equipment. Redmond realised that if, after the war, Home Rule was to be enforced throughout Ireland, an efficient Irish National Army would be required to enforce it.[8] He thus hoped that the Irish National Volunteers would be employed by the War Office in a home defence role in a manner similar to that envisaged for the Territorial Force in Great Britain, under the 1908 army reforms. At the same time, Redmond wanted an 'Irish Brigade' formed from Irish Nationalist Volunteers to serve overseas. This would mean that, in propaganda terms, the Nationalists would not be outdone by the Unionists in their sacrifice for the empire. Many leading IPP figures also felt that joint military service overseas would break down some of the barriers between Nationalists and Unionists. As David Fitzpatrick has pointed out: 'In urging Home Rulers to participate in the war, John Redmond had hoped to eradicate lingering national and religious hostilities through the agency of personal contact. If Ulstermen, Home Rulers, Englishmen and Scotsmen fought together, their growing comradeship and mutual admiration would allay their mutual suspicions and those of politicians at home.'[9]

Initially the British government had little time for either Carson's or Redmond's proposals to regularise their prewar paramilitary organisations. Poor recruiting for the 10th (Irish) Division, however, made it clear that political backing was required if Irish recruiting was to be at all satisfactory. As a result the 36th (Ulster) Division was formed, which aimed to draw Unionist recruits, while the 16th (Irish) Division aimed to capitalise on Nationalist recruitment. The creation of these 'political divisions' had serious implications for recruiting propaganda in Ireland. Both groups promised large numbers of recruits if their demands were met. For example, John Dillon, a leading figure in the IPP, noted in November 1914 that

Had it not been for the perversity of the War Office in treating with contempt any suggestion we made a *very large* [number] of Nationalists would have entered the New Army before now.

There is a considerable movement in favour of recruiting since the Irish Brigades were really put in working order – and I think that movement could be largely strengthened by other measures – if the War Office could be induced to adopt them.[10]

Both political groupings insisted on certain measures to make their divisions more marketable. Divisional symbols, unit names and the choice of officers were all seen as ways in which recruitment could be increased. Thus the 36th Division was given the prefix 'Ulster', a title unknown in the British Army before 1914, and the Red Hand of Ulster as its divisional badge. In addition, large numbers of UVF officers were given commissions in the new division.

For the 16th Division, these concessions were offered grudgingly. This would appear to be for a number of reasons. First, the INV were not seen as a particularly efficient military force.[11] In particular, given that no Catholic school or university in Ireland possessed an officer training corps unit there were few competent officers. This was in sharp contrast to the UVF where 62 per cent of officers were retired British Army officers[12] and most officers had at least limited military experience in an OTC or militia unit. Second, the commanding officer of the 16th Division, Lt-Gen. Sir Lawrence Parsons, had little regard for anything but regular soldiers. This meant that Parsons had many bitter clashes with John Redmond over the division. One of the earliest was over the question of badges. While Redmond felt that a divisional badge of a harp with the word 'Ireland' underneath it would be a useful propaganda device, attracting many recruits, Parsons opposed:

> I have always been opposed to any special Badge being stuck to the 16th Division . . . [members of new units are in battalions of] old Irish Regts. whose honours and badges they have a right to + should be proud to wear. . . . These old Battns. are all wearing their old badges, why should their new brothers in arms require a new badge?
>
> The only reason I can see is that the Ulster Divn. has a silly badge replacing the time honoured badges of the Regiments they belong to. I am not in favour of copying the Ulster Divn.
>
> Remember I view the question entirely with a soldier's eyes. I have spent 44 years in the Army + know its traditions, history + sentiment + share with all other old soldiers a dislike of 'Fancy' Corps + an intense love and admiration for our old Regimental institution.[13]

Eventually Kitchener overruled Parsons and decreed that the divisional symbol was to be a shamrock.[14] Parsons' attitude to commissioning INV officers was equally unhelpful. The few such officers who were commissioned generally brought in large numbers of recruits: for example, John Wray, an officer of the Enniskillen INV, brought 200 recruits with him into the 6th Battalion of the Connaught Rangers.[15] Parsons, however, refused to exploit the propaganda value of employing such officers. In November 1914, Parsons wrote of men applying for commissions in the 16th Division: 'Many of the Candidates are quite socially impossible as Officers – men who write their applications in red or green ink on a blank bill-head of a village shop.'[16] Parsons insisted that all potential officers had to enlist as ordinary privates into a special cadet company in the 7th Battalion, Leinster Regiment. W.A. Redmond, MP (John Redmond's son) sought a direct commission into the division, a not unreasonable request given that any well-connected young man in Britain could expect to enter an officer's mess at this time. Parsons refused to allow this and indeed described W.A. Redmond as 'a perfectly poisonous bounder'.[17] This refusal not only, naturally, offended John Redmond, but was proved to be a great error in retrospect. W. A. Redmond not only won a Military Cross while serving as a captain in the Irish Guards, but was one of the handful of IPP MPs to retain his seat in the Sinn Fein landslide of 1918. This suggests not only a high level of personal courage but also a charisma which could have been well used in recruiting for the 16th (Irish) Division.

Lastly, an area of Irish recruits which Parsons refused to tap were Irishmen living in Great Britain. Indeed he was to describe such men as 'slum birds' and 'corner boys'.[18] This meant that the Tyneside Irish Brigade was allocated to the 34th Division, when Redmond had made it clear that he wanted it to serve as a component of the 16th Division. Significantly, Parsons was relieved of the command of the 16th Division before it left for overseas service. While the War Office had questioned some of Parson's decisions as early as February 1915, by December it was clear that if he continued in command, recruiting in Ireland would be adversely affected.

Ulster Unionists managed a slick propaganda campaign around the 36th Division both during its formation and after the war.[19] Behind this façade, however, lurked a number of recruiting problems. Especially in rural areas battalions found recruiting very slow. The 16th Battalion, Royal Irish Rifles, recruiting mainly in County Down, as late as January 1915 had a strength of 666 all ranks when its establishment was 1,139. Eventually this battalion was only made up to its full strength in June 1915 by a draft of 200 men from the 14th Battalion, Royal Irish Rifles, a unit which had recruited heavily in Belfast.[20] Thus, as early as October 1914, Lt-Col. Ambrose Ricardo of the 9th Battalion, Royal Inniskilling Fusiliers had a handbill circulated among County Tyrone UVF members which stated that his unit was still 300 men under strength and, more ominously, 'If the Ballot Act [i.e. conscription] is put into force you will not be able to choose your regiment.'[21] Equally, the Ulster Division was actively recruiting men in England.[22]

Interestingly, contemporaries realised that recruiting figures quoted by leading Ulster Unionists were fraudulent and, indeed, adversely affected recruiting. Lord Wimborne, the lord lieutenant of Ireland, noted: 'I think there has been too much [of] this [sic] wild claims of Belfast and Ulster to have contributed an absurd percentage to the forces. This is injurious to recruiting.'[23]

An even more strident criticism of Ulster's recruiting record came from a very unexpected quarter – namely Maj.-Gen. Sir Oliver Nugent, General Officer

Commanding the 36th (Ulster) Division, and prewar commander of the County
Cavan UVF. When asked by the Unionist *Belfast Newsletter* to provide a 1916
Christmas message, Nugent wrote:

> A message to the people of Ulster from Ulster's Division must contain besides
> greetings and good wishes, some hard truths.
>
> For this is the position as it stands today between the Ulster Division and
> those of its own kin at home.
>
> When the people of Ulster in 1914 promised a Division to the service of
> King and Country, no finer body of men than those who redeemed the
> promise were raised in any portion of the King's Dominions. . . .The morning
> of the 1st July will be one of the glories of the Province as long as men love to
> think of gallant deeds.
>
> Will there be an element of shame in the memory among the thousands of
> lusty young Ulstermen at home?
>
> They have no part as yet in the honour of the real manhood of Ulster. They
> will have no part in the future when the Ulster Division comes home to enjoy
> the respect and esteem earned by those who have seen the path of duty and
> have followed it even to the end.[24]

Despite this, in retrospect, the 36th Ulster Division has long been seen as an
entirely Protestant and Unionist unit, as exemplified by the Orange Order's
elaborate wreath-laying ceremonies to the fallen and the frequent use of the
divisional symbols in Loyalist wall murals.[25]

Ultimately, Irish politicians proved themselves unable to deliver on their
promises over recruitment. Of the 100,000 UVF personnel in 1914, only 31,000
had joined the British Army by the Armistice; meanwhile the INV record was
even less impressive, only 31,000 of their 180,000 members enlisting.[26] As
outlined above, politics did influence the recruiting propaganda used in Ireland
in terms of the new units formed, symbols utilised and officers appointed. Now,
the issue of the propaganda actually used in recruiting campaigns must be
considered. As David Fitzpatrick remarks, 'The sluggishness of enlistment in
many parts of Ireland had more to do with inadequate market research than
political alienation. The responsibility for that failure of mobilisation lay with
British administrators rather than Irish rebels.'[27]

During the First World War a wide range of recruitment propaganda was used
in Ireland. Unfortunately, given the fact that the civilian Central Committee for
the Organisation of Recruiting in Ireland (CCORI) never kept centralised
records and that administrative records of the British Army in Ireland did not
survive the British withdrawal from Southern Ireland in 1922, it is impossible to
deduce what market research went into British recruiting propaganda in Ireland
or even how it was organised throughout the island.[28] Perhaps the best examples

were used in Hedley Le Bas' model scheme used in Waterford from 19 March to 10 April 1915. In this highly ambitious campaign, advertisements in the local press, a large number of attractive posters, the use of a prominent building as a recruiting office, performances by a military band and speeches by prominent local and national political figures, all combined to ensure success.[29]

Le Bas' campaign was not repeated elsewhere, and indeed, the choice of Waterford rather than Dublin, Belfast or Cork for such a trial does seem rather strange. Nevertheless, while rarely as well coordinated as in this Waterford example, recruiting propaganda was widely used in Ireland between 1914 and 1918 and it is worth examining the problems encountered with some aspects of it. The poster campaign in Ireland was initially very poorly organised and insensitive to Irish opinion. During 1914 copies of posters used elsewhere in Britain were simply utilised in Ireland.[30] These, in many areas, did little to encourage recruiting, as Sir Francis Vane, a major in the 9th Battalion, Royal Munster Fusiliers noted, in September 1914:

> On arrival in Cork by motor, the first thing I observed was that the walls of that hot bed of Home Rule were plastered over by posters on which the Union Jack was displayed with the words underneath: 'Come and fight for your flag'. This seemed to me a particularly inadvisable method of obtaining recruits in a city which was markedly opposed to the political union between England and Ireland. So after consultation with the permanent recruiting officer there – a very amicable officer, we had these superposed, and the Irish Harp substituted with the same words: 'Come and fight for your flag'.[31]

Recruiting posters in Ireland, as in the rest of the United Kingdom, relied on a number of diverse themes. In Ireland posters depicting women, sporting analogies and German atrocities predominated. However, the poster campaign failed to coordinate with recruiting speeches and while speakers urged their audiences to join the 16th (Irish) or 36th (Ulster) Division, only one poster actually mentioned these units.[32] Equally, one contemporary noted that many Ulstermen did not appreciate being appealed to as 'Irishmen' in recruiting literature.[33]

The buildings used as recruiting offices were another important piece of recruiting propaganda. If magnificently designed and situated in a prominent place they could act as an impressive advertisement both for civic pride and the British Army. In Belfast, the buildings available for recruitment were badly misused. The resplendent City Hall, completed in 1906, was a monument to the prosperity of early twentieth-century Belfast. Yet, at a time when politicians in the city were urging their constituents to join local units and all recruiting posters carried the message, 'Join an Irish Regiment Today', this building was designated as a general recruiting office. This meant that non-Irish units, for example, the

Royal Artillery, Scottish Highland Territorial Force units and the Canadian Expeditionary Force recruited from it. The Old Town Hall was a relatively spacious building; however, its prewar use as UVF Headquarters and its role as the main recruiting office for the 36th (Ulster) Division did little to attract Catholic recruits. Recruits for the 16th (Irish) Division were expected to enlist at one of two tenement houses. One of these was so small that Maj. Kinsman, DSO, Assistant Inspector of Recruiting noted, 'it is necessary for recruits to stand on the stairs leading up to this room to have their eyes tested. These premises are entirely unsuitable for Medical Recruiting purposes.'[34]

The choice of public speakers for recruiting platforms also often left a great deal to be desired. For example, at a major meeting at the Mansion House, Dublin, on 5 September 1915, William Martin Murphy was a member of the platform party.[35] Given that Murphy had led the employers in the 1913 Dublin lock-out, his presence can have done little to encourage urban working-class men to enlist.

These problems conceal more fundamental difficulties with the use of recruiting propaganda in Ireland. First, as Fitzpatrick notes, there was very poor market research. This was fundamental as it failed to identify regional variations in Irish recruiting. Belfast possibly contributed as many as 46,000 recruits out of an Irish total of 146,000,[36] and appears to have followed a typical (if there is such a thing) British recruiting pattern into late 1915. Meanwhile, recruitment in south-western Ireland remained sluggish throughout the war and, unlike the general British pattern, this area's recruitment figures peaked in 1915.[37]

The occupational background of recruits also varied regionally. One local study suggests that up to 86 per cent of recruits in Wexford were labourers before enlistment.[38] By contrast, it would appear that a substantial percentage of lower middle-class and skilled workers enlisted in Belfast.[39]

The ultimate hallmark of the poor research endemic in the Irish recruitment campaign is shown by the various estimates of available manpower. In August 1914, John Redmond was promising Lord Kitchener 100,000 to 200,000 men, while Sir Edward Carson offered two complete UVF divisions for overseas service.[40] In January 1916 Joseph Brennan believed that 72,000 men were available[41] while the official Report on Recruiting in Ireland gave an estimate of 100,000 available men.[42] Surprisingly, Gen. Sir John Maxwell, the General Officer Commanding in Ireland, actually agreed with the latter figure.[43] In early 1917, H.E. Duke believed there were around 161,000 Irishmen avaliable for military service,[44] while, in June 1918, the Irish Recruiting Committee believed that 20,000 recruits could still be obtained by October, a figure which Lloyd George increased to 50,000.[45]

This unreality meant that few of the innovative schemes used successfully in Britain to obtain lower middle-class and skilled working-class recruits were tried in Ireland. For example 'Pals Battalions', which, in England, had enabled men from the same social group, class and locality to serve together, were almost non-existent in Ireland (although, arguably, some units of the 36th (Ulster) Division fulfilled this role), 'D' company of the 7th Battalion, Royal Dublin Fusiliers being a rare exception. Plans to make the 5th Battalion, Royal Dublin Fusiliers a 'Commercial' battalion; the 5th Battalion, Leinster Regiment, a 'farmers' battalion; and the 10th battalion, Royal Dublin Fusiliers, a 'clerical' battalion[46] were doomed to failure as these were draft-finding units and therefore unable to offer the guarantee of joint service implicit in a 'Pals' unit.

Bizarrely, in a complete *volte-face* in August 1915 serious proposals were made to attract members of the 'commercial' classes into the army, not by the formation of a 'Pals' unit on the British pattern, but by forming a new regiment to be called the Irish Light Infantry. The unit was to be made more marketable to potential middle-class recruits by the adoption of a saffron kilt, the establishment of an officer training unit in its first battalion and the appointment of Lord Frederick Fitzgerald as its commanding officer. While this scheme was supported by both the Central Committee for the Organisation of Recruitment in Ireland (CCORI) and Maj.-Gen. Friend, the GOC in Ireland, it did not come to fruition.[47]

Interestingly, while most Irish recruits to the British Army were drawn from the urban working class, both during the war, and indeed, in the 1911–14 period, the CCORI, as shown above, devoted much of its energy to schemes for attracting middle-class recruits. Meanwhile both Lt-Gen. Sir Lawrence Parsons and Maj.-Gen. Sir Oliver Nugent both sought ways to attract rural recruits. Parsons sought 'the clean, fine, strong, temperate, hurley-playing country fellows such as we used to get in the Munsters, Royal Irish [and] Connaught Rangers'.[48] Meanwhile, Nugent had serious reservations about the military prowess of the Belfast-raised units in his division.[49]

In addition to this, the organisation of recruiting in Ireland was somewhat shambolic. While a Dublin recruiting committee was established in September 1914, a Cork recruiting committee in April 1915 and a Belfast Businessmen's recruiting committee, also at that time, it was only in April 1915 that the CCORI was formed.[50] Significantly, while Belfast was the largest single provider of recruits, no Belfast representative was a member of the central committee of the CCORI. Indeed, of the twenty-two members of this body, seventeen were from Dublin.[51] Even more surprisingly, of the 208 members of the general council of the CCORI, only one, John Burke, was from Belfast.[52]

This organisation was dissolved in October 1915, largely, it would appear, because the Dublin recruiting committee had taken over many of its functions and also because the honorary director, Henry Mc Laughlin, felt that the Derby Scheme (which introduced a form of conscription in Great Britain) should be extended to Ireland. Mc Laughlin also complained that the CCORI, by merging with the Dublin committee, led by the earl of Meath, would lose all Nationalist support.[53]

In October 1915 the Department of Recruiting in Ireland was formed which, like its predecessor, appears to have been an overly Dublin-based body. In addition to this, its links with the Department of National Service in London appear to have been very poor. Its replacement by the Irish Recruiting Committee in April 1918 was a forlorn attempt to boost recruiting following the conscription crisis. This change was only notable as, for the first time, full responsibility for recruiting in Ireland was transferred from the General Officer Commanding in Ireland to a civilian body in June 1918.[54]

These 'central bodies' suffered from a number of problems. Their relations not only with local agencies, but also with their British counterparts were unstable. Also, these bodies were chronically underfunded. For example, in August 1918 the government refused to provide the finance required to enable the Irish Recruiting Committee to purchase two motor cars, even though it had been found impossible to rent any.[55] In addition, these bodies managed to appoint a vast number of political non-entities as civilian recruiters. Incredibly, pitifully few of these appointees were influential figures in either the IPP or Ulster Unionist parties.

Lastly, the recruiting campaign was decidedly low-tech and up until mid-1918 portrayed an anachronistic image of war. Callan notes: 'The silver screen could not disguise the drudgery and monotony of life at the front. A mud banked terrain, bordered with barbed wire, did not nestle comfortably with the idealism inherent in the recruiting drive.'[56] However, there was very little imagination shown in the official film *The Irish at the Somme*.

Rather less information is available on the anti-recruiting campaign of 1914. Its resources were, obviously, much more limited than the government's and depended on a number of regional factors. Also the results of anti-recruiting propaganda are difficult to discern.

The main propaganda techniques used by those opposed to recruiting were to interrupt recruiting meetings and to circulate pamphlets. As early as October 1914 anti-recruiting pamphlets had been circulated in Wexford and Dublin.[57] However, it is impossible to estimate both the circulation and impact which these notices made.

Perhaps the most widely circulated and influential anti-recruiting pamphlet was that issued by the National Executive of the Irish Trades Union Congress and Labour Party. This *Manifesto to the Workers of Ireland* suggested that the war was merely 'for the aggrandisement of the capitalistic class' and that famine prices would soon come into effect as a result of the war. It concluded by urging men to stay at home and resist the temptation to enlist.[58] The labour movement, at least in Dublin, continued its campaign through the pages of the *Irish Worker*, *Irish Freedom* and *The Leader*. In many ways the Dublin labour movement was using its anti-recruiting campaign to refight the lock-out of 1913. When major employers, such as William Martin Murphy, supported the recruiting campaign, it was in no way surprising that the labour movement should oppose it.

A persistent claim, made especially by Dublin labour, was that a policy of unofficial conscription was being operated in Ireland; employers were effectively refusing to employ men of military age in an attempt to force them into the army.[59] It does appear that at least some of these allegations were well-founded. Alfred Byrne, MP, alleged that the General Post Office in Ireland had made forty men redundant to force them into the army. Meanwhile, both the North Dublin Union and Belfast Corporation refused to employ men of military age.[60]

Another tactic used by anti-recruiting agents was the interruption of recruiting meetings. Callan suggests that most recruiters were 'lacklustre speakers',[61] and few responded well to hecklers. In May 1915, in Wexford, Henry Mc Laughlin, faced by a heckler, simply stated, 'There is a man who ought to be with the Germans cutting off little babies' hands.'[62] Meanwhile, confronted by a heckler in Enniscorthy, in March 1915, Capt W.A. Redmond, MP, simply walked out of the meeting.[63]

The recruiting meetings which provided the best forum for Sinn Fein agitation were those held by Col. Lynch in his attempt to raise an 'Irish Brigade'. FM Lord French complained that Lynch invited all local Sinn Feiners to his meetings, 'in which the Sinn Feiners are to be allowed to express their views on every conceivable subject, and have them reported in every newspaper in the country. Now that is exactly what we have been doing our utmost to prevent.'[64] Walter Long's comments on Lynch's activities demonstrate the uses to which recruiting propaganda in Ireland was being put in 1918:

> As for Lynch I hope you will forgive me if I venture to suggest that your Excellency is looking at him + his vagaries from the point of a soldier + that possibly you ignore the two facts,
> 1) That it is better he should be recruiting in some form in Ireland than preaching Republicanism in England.
> 2) That the Irish have a new toy + this move on his part might easily sap the foundations of S.[inn] F.[ein].[65]

The anti-recruitment campaign probably had its finest hour during the conscription crisis of 1918. Unionists had always spoken in support of conscription; Southern Unionists felt that as an ideological issue Ireland should be treated in the same manner as the rest of the United Kingdom.[66] Ulster Unionists supported conscription for other reasons. First, with the munitions and shipbuilding industries in Belfast it was unlikely that many of their supporters would be affected by this measure. Second, if conscription, or at least a national register was introduced into Ulster, then this would be a strong argument and, indeed, basis for partition when Home Rule was finally introduced.

On 23 April 1918 a general strike against conscription occurred in Ireland which was almost totally successful outside Belfast.[67] At the same time, IPP MPs withdrew from the House of Commons, thereby following the policy advocated by Sinn Fein since its formation. In propaganda terms it was this event, rather than the 1918 general election which established Sinn Fein as the premier political party in Ireland.

To conclude, it is rather difficult to reach a balanced assessment of the Irish recruiting and anti-recruiting campaigns during the First World War. In British terms, Irish recruiting figures were disappointing. However, that should hardly surprise us. Being largely rural and with an ageing population and medical rejection rates of recruits at up to 74 per cent, Ireland could hardly be expected to compare favourably with the United Kingdom as a whole.[68] Equally, it may not be getting too far into the realms of fantasy to suggest that if conscription had not been introduced in Britain in 1916, the Irish recruitment figures may have been consistent with wider British trends. Therefore, it would appear fair to conclude that a system of propaganda which continued to draw in recruits, not only after the Curragh Incident of March 1914 and Bachelor's Walk shootings of 1914, but the Easter Rising of 1916 and the attempt to introduce conscription in 1918, was reasonably successful.

The anti-recruiting campaign appears to have been less successful. From 1899 to 1913 anti-recruiting activities had little apparent impact and this would appear to have been the case during the First World War. The fact that recruitment increased from September to November 1918, at the very time when Sinn Fein was growing in popularity, would appear to support this. The non-effectiveness of the anti-recruiting campaign is perhaps shown by the fact that while the Irish Transport and General Workers' Union was one of the largest opponents of recruiting, by May 1915, 2,700 former members of this union were serving in the British Army.[69] This would suggest that the decision to enlist in Ireland, both before and during the war, was influenced more by economic than political considerations. In Irish political terms, support for the British war effort probably hastened the demise of the IPP. The loss of young and effective MPs and constituency workers to the Western Front caused irreparable damage to the party at a local level. Meanwhile, Redmond's inability to receive government recognition for the INV caused a severe dent to the party's prestige.

Equally, the Dublin labour movement's support for the anti-recruitment campaign served to split labour supporters even further along Nationalist/ Unionist lines. Many workers in Belfast heavy industry benefited greatly from the war, while the Dublin economy during the 1914–18 period was virtually the only part of the United Kingdom to be in recession.[70] These conflicting economic experiences of the war had already sharply divided the attitude of labour activists in the two cities, but the recruitment issue provided the basis for an irreconcilable split between those, mainly working in Belfast, who were affiliated to British trade unions and those affiliated to Irish unions which backed the anti-recruitment policy. This split effectively prevented the development of labour as a significant independent force in Irish politics. In the South, labour increasingly appeared to be following a Sinn Fein agenda and, indeed, refused to field candidates against the party in the 1918 general election. By contrast, many labour supporters in Belfast became active supporters of the Ulster Unionist party.

The Ulster Unionists probably benefited most from the war. Their effective propaganda campaign, extolling the Ulster Division as entirely Protestant and Unionist, meant that a postwar debt of honour could be redeemed. Ironically, however, it was the Ulstermen who stayed at home, rather than those who died in the trenches, who ensured partition. Bloated by war contracts, Belfast industry appeared buoyant and more than self-sufficient when partition was discussed in 1920.

Notes

1   See T. Denman, ' "The Red Livery of Shame": The Campaign against Army Recruitment in Ireland 1899–1914', *Irish Historical Studies*, XXIX (1994), 208–33.

2   M. Dungan, *Irish Voices from the Great War* (Dublin, Irish Academic Press, 1995), p. 15.

3   D. and J. Howie, 'Irish Recruiting and the Home Rule Crisis of August–September 1914', in M. Dockrill and D. French (eds), *Strategy and Intelligence: British Policy during the First World War* (London, Hambledon Press, 1996), p. 4.

4   P. Bew, *John Redmond* (Dublin, The Historical Association of Ireland, 1996), p. 37.

5   The texts of Redmond's statements are reproduced in full in A. Mitchell and P. O Snodaigh (eds), *Irish Political Documents 1869–1916* (Dublin, Irish Academic Press, 1989), pp. 171–3.

6   D. Fitzpatrick, *Politics and Irish Life, 1913–21: Provincial Experience of War and Revolution* (Dublin, Gill and Macmillan, 1977), p. 110.

7   H. Montgomery Hyde, *Carson: The Life of Sir Edward Carson, Lord Carson of Duncairn* (London, William Heinemann, 1953, repr. Constable, 1987), pp. 377–9.

8   T.P. Dooley, ' "Politics, Bands and Marketing": Army Recruitment in Waterford City 1914–15', *The Irish Sword*, 72 (1991), 209.

9   D. Fitzpatrick, ' "The Overflow of the Deluge": Anglo-Irish Relationships, 1914–22', in O. MacDonagh and W.F. Mandle, *Ireland and Irish Australia: Studies in Cultural and Political History* (London, Croom Helm, 1986), p. 83.

10   Bodleian Library, Nathan Papers, MS 451: Letter, Dillon to Sir Mathew Nathan, 28/11/14.

11   T. Denman, *Ireland's Unknown Soldiers: The 16th (Irish) Division in the Great War* (Dublin, Irish Academic Press, 1992), p. 41.

12   H. Strachan, *The Politics of the British Army* (Oxford, Clarendon Press, 1997), p. 112.

13   National Library of Ireland, Redmond Papers, MS.15,519; Letter, Parsons to Redmond, 12/12/14.

14   NLI, Redmond Papers, MS.15,519; Letter, Parsons to Redmond, 27/6/15.

15   Denman, *Ireland's Unknown Soldiers*, pp. 43–4.

16   NLI, MS.21,278, Correspondence of Lieutenant-General Sir Lawrence W. Parsons, 1914–18; Letter, Parsons to The Secretary, War Office, 29/11/14.

17   NLI, MS.21,524, Parsons' diary entry for 24/2/15.

18   T. Johnstone, *Orange, Green and Khaki: The Story of the Irish Regiments in the Great War, 1914–18* (Dublin, Gill and Macmillan,1992), p. 196.

19   Perhaps the best immediate postwar example of this was; C. Falls, *A History of the 36th (Ulster) Division* (Belfast, McCaw, Stevenson and Orr, 1922).

20   S.N. White, *The Terrors, 16th (Pioneer) Battalion Royal Irish Rifles* (Belfast, The Somme Association, 1996), pp. 11 and 21.

21   Royal Inniskilling Fusiliers' Museum Archives, box 12. Letter Ricardo to Mr Robinson, 10/11/14.

22   See F.P. Crozier, *A Brass Hat in No Man's Land* (London, Michael Joseph Ltd., 1930, repr. Bath, Chivers, 1968), pp. 29–33, and P. Simkins, *Kitchener's Army: The Raising of the New Armies, 1914–16* (Manchester University Press, 1988), p. 71.

23   Bodleian Library, MS448, Nathan Papers; Letter Wimborne to Nathan, 8/1/16.

24   Public Record Office of Northern Ireland, MIC/571/10; Letter, Nugent to The Editor of the *Belfast Newsletter*, 19/12/16. Surprisingly, given Nugent's strong views on recruitment, which conflicted sharply with those of Ulster Unionist politicians, these criticisms were published in full.

25   An excellent example of the latter can be seen on the Newtownards Road in Belfast, where the members of the Ulster Division are heralded, along with Cuchulain, the 'B' Specials, the Ulster Defence Regiment and various Loyalist paramilitary groups, as 'Ulster's Defenders'.

26   Figures taken from D. Fitzpatrick, ' "The Logic of Collective Sacrifice": Ireland and the British Army, 1914–18', *Historical Journal*, 38 (1995), 1028–9.

27   Fitzpatrick, ' "Logic of Collective Sacrifice" ', p. 1030.

28   P. Callan, 'Voluntary Recruiting for the British Army in Ireland during the First World War' (Unpublished Ph.D. thesis, University College Dublin, 1984), p. 6.

29   Details taken from T.P. Dooley, 'Politics, Bands and Marketing', pp. 212–15.

30   M. Tierney, P. Bowen and D. Fitzpatrick, 'Recruiting Posters', in D. Fitzpatrick (ed.), *Ireland and the First World War* (Dublin, Trinity History Workshop, 1988), p. 48.

31   F. Vane, *Agin the Governments* (London, Samson Low and Marston, 1928), p. 251.

32   Vane, *Agin the Governments*, p. 251.

33   G.A. Birmingham, 'Ireland in Two Wars II; Recruiting in Ireland To-Day', *The Nineteenth Century and After*, 79 (1916), p. 175.

34   Report on Bridge End, Ballymacarrett in Public Record Office, NATS1/191, file relating to recruiting offices in Ireland.

35   T. Morrissey, *William Martin Murphy* (Dublin, Historical Association of Ireland, 1997), p. 61.

36   *Belfast Newsletter* (16/11/18). I am indebted to Mr Eric Mercer for this reference and would like to thank him for letting me read a draft version of his MA dissertation, 'Recruiting in Belfast during the First World War', which is due to be submitted to The Queen's University of Belfast shortly. By 15 October 1916, 38,543 men had enlisted in Belfast. 'Statement giving Particulars regarding Men of Military Age in Ireland', *Parliamentary Papers*, vol. XVII, Cmd. 8390 (London, HMSO, 1916), p. 583.

37   D. Fitzpatrick, *Politics and Irish Life*, pp. 110–11.

38   P. Codd, 'Recruiting and Responses to the War in Wexford', in D. Fitzpatrick (ed.), *Ireland and the First World War*, p. 15. Interestingly, the pattern in County Clare appears to have been similar: M.

Staunton, 'Kilrush, Co. Clare and the Royal Munster Fusiliers: The Experience of an Irish Town in the First World War', *The Irish Sword*, vol. XVI, no. 65 (1987), 269.

39   E. Mercer, 'Recruiting in Belfast during the First World War'.

40   D. and J. Howie, 'Irish Recruiting and the Home Rule Crisis', pp. 11, 13.

41   NLI, J. Brennan papers, MS.26,191.

42   'Report on Recruiting in Ireland', *Parliamentary Papers*, vol. 39, p. 525, Cmd. 8168 (1914–16).

43   Cabinet paper entitled, 'Recruiting in Ireland', Oct. 1916, David Lloyd-George Papers, House of Lords Record Office, E/9/4/16.

44   A.J. Ward, 'Lloyd George and the 1918 Irish Conscription Crisis', *Historical Journal*, XVII (1974), 108.

45   P. Callan, '"The Irish Soldier": A Propaganda Paper for Ireland, September to December 1918', *The Irish Sword*, XV, no. 59 (1982), p. 67.

46   NLI, MS.21,278, Letter, General Hammond to Lieutenant General Sir Lawrence Parsons, 26/11/15.

47   PRONI, Henry Mc Laughlin papers, D/3809/67/2, Letters: E. A. Aston to Henry Mc Laughlin, 11/8/15 and Friend to Aston, 26/8/15.

48   T. Denman, *Ireland's Unknown Soldiers*, p. 41, citing D. Gwynn, *The Life of John Redmond* (London, George G. Harrup, 1932), p. 400.

49   PRONI, D/3835/E/2/5/20A, Letter, Nugent to his wife, 26/10/15; and PRONI, MIC/571/10, Letter, Nugent to the Adjutant General, 11/12/17.

50   Callan, 'Voluntary Recruiting for the British Army', pp. 63–4.

51   Callan, 'Voluntary Recruiting for the British Army', pp. 106–9.

52   PRONI, Henry Mc Laughlin papers, D/3808/67/2.

53   PRONI, Henry Mc Laughlin papers, D/3808/67/2, Letters, Maj.-Gen. Friend to Mc Laughlin, 7/10/15 and to Mc Laughlin, 8/10/15.

54   Callan, 'Voluntary Recruiting for the British Army', p. 4.

55   PRO, NATS1/40, Letter, J.R. Hyde to W. Vaughan, Ministry of National Service 28/8/18.

56   Callan, 'Voluntary Recruiting for the British Army', p. 121.

57   PRONI, D1507/A/8/22, Nathan papers and Carson papers.

58   I am grateful to Ms Theresa Moriarty of the Irish Labour History Museum and Archive for providing me with a copy of this document.

59   P. Murray, 'The First World War and a Dublin Distillery Workforce: Recruiting and Redundancy at John Power & Son, 1915–1917', *Saothar*, 15 (1990), 50.

60   Callan, 'Voluntary Recruiting for the British Army', pp. 178–80.

61   Callan, 'Voluntary Recruiting for the British Army', p. 119.

62   Callan, 'Voluntary Recruiting for the British Army', p. 118.

63   Codd, 'Recruiting and Responses to the War in Wexford', pp. 24–5.

64   Imperial War Museum, French papers, 75/46/1, Letter to David Lloyd George from French, 2/9/18.

65   IWM, French papers 75/46/13, Letter, Long to French, 4/9/18.

66   D. Fitzpatrick, *Politics and Irish Life*, p. 65.

67   A. Mitchell, *Labour in Irish Politics, 1890–1930* (Dublin, Irish Universities Press, 1974), p. 88.

68   T.P. Dooley, 'Politics, Bands and Marketing', p. 216.

69   D. Fitzpatrick, 'Strikes in Ireland, 1914–21', *Saothar*, 6 (1980), 28.

70   T. Dooley, 'Southern Ireland, Historians and the First World War', *Irish Studies Review*, 4 (Autumn 1993), 8–9.

14

BETWEEN OURSELVES: THE LETTER AS PROPAGANDA

Margaretta Jolly

Dear Son J.   Birmingham, 20 Nov., 1940
Its my Birthday today 64 my Second war. We have no windows in one room, no gas, and a beautifull Shower Bath is waiting outside. But we all went to Bed Cheerfull. and got up thankfull. a Bomb dropped in B— St. made us *all* turn over. heart included. J. was on guard at the mint they missed it and Hit next door we are all O.K. dont worry I am packing some things today in the large traveling case and having it put in the celler. Things were certainly very bad here last night everyone had to be evacuated from B— Street. But Belive me, every one *man woman* and *children* too are never heard say, *Stop it,* all they clamer for is more action, all ask the Chance to *fight*.[1]

This chapter examines some of the letters and letter-books published during the Second World War, to argue that they constitute an unusual, hitherto unconsidered, form of propaganda. This was not organised state propaganda, though of course letters were censored for security purposes. Rather, the sudden fashion for publishing patriotic letters in pamphlets, newspaper columns, published correspondences, anthologies and on radio programmes, exemplified a much more diffuse form of persuasion which resulted from the willing cooperation of the media and literati with the Allied governments. Well outside the direct policies of the Ministry of Information, editors, writers and publishers supported the government stance that the war was not only inevitable but just. The letters that they published took this as their central theme.

Publishing personal letters was a particularly opportune form of such persuasion. Editors introduced them as private and unprompted expressions of patriotism, embedded in the simple function of keeping in touch across difficult wartime separations. Moreover, because the war had prompted everyone into letter-writing, letters could be represented as a democratic form appropriate to the literature of a 'People's War'. The first section of this chapter explores a number of letter-books that were published as part of the British campaign to combat American isolationism and gain its military support from 1939 until Pearl Harbor in 1941, when the United States entered the war. We will see how editors and publishers sought out writers from varying backgrounds, and enhanced themes of social unity across class, region and gender in order to convince

American readers not only that 'Britain could take it', but that Britain was a sister democracy worth fighting for.

The second section considers specifically the prominent role of women in this public use of letters. In the new reach of total war, women's economic and military contributions were crucial, and positive letters were valuable evidence of their embrace of their new roles as warworkers, servicewomen or military targets. While they are used as the gauge of new popular engagement as a whole, women's letters were also used more conservatively as a resource to keep up male military morale, most famously and symbolically in Vera Lynn's BBC radio show for the British troops, *Sincerely Yours*, which was set up in the form of a 'letter from home to the men in the forces'. I suggest not only that women's letters were a complex representation of fidelity and solidarity between the sexes, but that in published form they represented the nation as a faithful family. In this way, women's social and literary institutionalisation as letter-writers comes together with ideologies of women as reproducers of national and racial identity.

The final section concerns one of the saddest and most characteristic genres of wartime letter, the 'last letter'. These self-consciously rhetorical texts were often the forum for the most explicit attempts to unify public and private roles and were, arguably ironically, particularly used for propagandistic purposes. Once again, the different responsibilities ascribed to men and women in wartime defined this as a highly gendered genre. However, the last letter most literally displayed the enforced individual sacrifice in all sectors of wartime society. In this sense, it epitomised all the letters considered in this chapter.

It is difficult to assess how much such letters were read and how effective they were in their aims of winning over an isolationist American public, encouraging civilian women to join the war effort, or to raise the morale of servicemen. What they do show clearly is the extent to which the private was co-opted by the public in this war, as perhaps in all wars. Much has been written about the unprecedented development of state propaganda by both the British and American governments in this period, despite deep suspicion of the practice in both countries after the First World War and refusal for the most part to acknowledge it as such. This chapter attempts a rather different and more literary study of the parallel spread of polemic both in cultural organs and even personal communications, at the point where overt propaganda meets with longer term ideologies. The dramatic limitation of expression even in personal letters is ironic given the Allied governments' great and arguably justified pride in retaining, as much as possible, the ideal of a free press in the exigencies of total war.

LETTERS FROM 'THE PEOPLE'S WAR'

Perhaps the most ingenious exploitation of letters as tools of propaganda took place as part of the British government's highly orchestrated campaign to obtain the United States' military support and, after the fall of France, its entry into the war. Powerful factions in the United States were not only strongly isolationist and anti-British, but anti-propaganda, to which the British Ministry of Information responded by maintaining an official policy of 'no propaganda'.[2] The MoI strategically circumvented this, however, by using not only film, literature, documentary and journalism, but also private letters to portray the British perspective, in an early move in the 'ideological' war.[3] Nicholas Cull describes how the MoI's American Division enlisted ordinary men and women in their campaign:

> Numerous Britons who regularly corresponded with people in the United States sought the ministry's advice on how they might treat political subjects in their letters. The division replied with regular broadsheets outlining topics that might profitably be discussed; and seemingly innocent British pen-pals joined the propaganda war.[4]

It was presumably from correspondences like these that a significant number of books, pamphlets, open letters and literary correspondences were published throughout the first three years of the war: Fryn Tennyson-Jesse and her husband Harold Harwood's correspondence to American friends, *London Front* (1940), and its sequel, *While London Burns* (1942); Beatrice Curtis Brown and 'Mrs Miniver' in Jan Struther's edition of *Women of Britain: Letters from England* (1941); Diana Forbes-Robertson and Roger W. Strauss's *War Letters from Britain* (1941); the anonymous collection of letters from a London cook to her evacuated employers, *Respectfully Yours, Annie*; and the letters of Hilda Silberman that she duplicated for American friends as 'a general news-letter from England in wartime', later collected as *Unimportant Letters of Important Years 1941–1951* – missives such as these joined BBC broadcasts of J.B. Priestley, Churchill, the king and queen, and Humphrey Jennings' documentary *London Can Take It* (1940) to bring the day-to-day experiences of the phoney war, the battle of Britain and the blitz home to the American public. Americans also corresponded on behalf of the British. While Edward Murrow and other journalists were pioneering war radio and film in the cause of interventionism and good media, the British-born *New Yorker* correspondent Mollie Panter-Downes published her war pieces as *Letter from England* and American women's magazine writer Margaret Culkin Banning wrote *Letters from England* (1942) on the theme that Britain was no longer the cold, imperialist and overblown little country Americans could be forgiven for thinking it was, but a newly 'living and articulate' democracy (p. 103). Cull argues that in America the 'the best-sellers of 1941 were either by anglophile Americans or by British writers themselves. American reportage and comment jostled with British polemics, letters, fact, and fiction for a place in the booksellers' windows.'[5]

These early letter-collections are therefore defined by a particular political alliance featuring British socialists, American anti-fascists and anglophiles, and a media driven by a professional interest in saleable forms of war reporting. They chart the transformation of a 1930s' discourse of popular struggle into a patriotic rhetoric of cross-class and Anglo-American friendship and resistance. British journalist and novelist Fryn Tennyson-Jesse expressed typical sentiments when she advised her American friends: 'This war is not one between nations – it is the greatest civil war history has known.'[6] Her playwright husband Harold Harwood's inflammatory opening letter of 3 September 1939 makes explicit allusion to the English Civil War as a precedent for 'just' violence in a war as much internal as international:

> This is not to be a war engineered by bankers, the city or the propertied classes. The leaders of public opinion in this matter are the 'little people', led by such Press as *The Manchester Guardian* and *Yorkshire Post*. We are not even afraid of our own Government now; they are doing what they have to. The people the Germans are up against are not international bankers anxious still to look on Germany as a potential customer – they are the descendants of the people who cut off King Charles's head and who have been out of business now for 300 years.
>
> I hope the U.S. will keep out of it.[7]

This conclusion, effectively absolving American neutrality, signals one of the most intriguing aspects of personal letters published as propaganda. For inevitably the context of personal friendships allowed a softened debate about American responsibility towards the British. Fryn reassures her guilty American correspondents that 'I was never one of those people who like to know that other people were unhappy because I was.'[8] This is a model for an Anglo-American relationship that is confidential yet not demanding, instructive yet not needy, in line with the MoI propaganda policy pre-1941, that Britain wanted not intervention but aid, not America's self-sacrifice but its understanding.

Although this upper-class, elderly, London literary couple are hardly typical of the population, their self-construction in relation to the war, the appeasing government and internal social reform suggests that they were published as representative of Britain at war. *London Front* fulfils the demands of a new style of propoganda defined by realism and the quietly heroic. Gill Plain has described this realism as centring on civilian imagery, cheerfulness, understatement, and deliberately rejecting the genre of heroic romance associated with the First World War, as well as counterpointing the more obvious escapist strains of Hollywood. We can certainly see this borne out in Fryn's novelistic anecdotes and reflections (all the occasions on which she has met dictators; the worrisome virtue of uniform architecture when 'uniformity of style in *thought* is . . . what we are now fighting against';[9] their runaway cat; her anxieties about 'Tottie's' need to feel useful although too old for military service) and 'Tottie's' punctuating invectives. The alternating voices of the married couple themselves represent the new sense of war as cutting across traditional, gendered lines of home and front. Such domestic articulations of belligerence symbolise a war that depended upon the retired, the Home Guard and the Women's Voluntary Services. For the American reader, furthermore, the letter form set up the private correspondent as national mediator, making unofficial diplomatic interventions in what one American writer characterised as 'a very small, insignificant act of deliberate friendliness'. Once collected and published, this function becomes symbolic of the democratisation of the war correspondent, historian or diplomat in 'the people's war'.

Herbert Davis, reviewing *London Front, Women of Britain* and *War Letters from Britain* for the *Yale Review* in 1940, shows us that many Americans couldn't help but read all British writing as a letter of appeal, a letter that was extremely difficult to answer:

> It is as difficult to write about these volumes of private letters, and of news by journalists and radio commentators, as it is to write to friends in England. Since September 1939, in spite of all their cheerful and courageous assurances, first the threat and then the reality have carried them beyond our reach; and we wonder whether we shall be able to recognize one another again when that day comes that will bring us together once more. In the meantime, we gaze astonished at them walking in the midst of a burning fiery furnace, and we turn doubtfully to books and letters such as these to try to get some understanding of what it is like to live in England now.[10]

In this sense, the American journalist Margaret Culkin Banning was strategic in turning to the personal letter-form as a deliberate device. Banning, a well-known author of women's fiction and feature stories for women's magazines, adopts the ruse of writing to her daughter in *Letters from England*. Written over June 1942 and published the following year by Harper Collins, the book is structured around Banning's trip from New York to London and its surrounds, where she visits hotels, shops, factories, and interviews people such as Harold Laski, Dorothy Elliott of the Transport Workers Union, Constance Spry, Noel Streatfeild, Storm Jameson, the Labour MP Jennie Lee, and Lady Reading, the founder and chairwoman of the Women's Voluntary Services. Her ostensible reader, 'Mary', allows Banning to focus on the changes in civilian, particularly women's lives, and to identify herself as an 'ordinary person', able to record the 'ordinary British', on a mission as personal as it is political:

> The statesmen and the generals will make important trips back and forth. Churchill comes one way, and General Marshall and Harry Hopkins go the

other, and the air and sea ferries are full of people who are on vital diplomatic and military errands. . . . But if the ordinary people in their countries are drifting into antagonism, or maybe being beguiled into mutual distrust, we shall get nothing more out of this war than a military victory and maybe not that. . . . So perhaps people should come even without portfolio and see what good they can do by bringing home a picture of ordinary British life in wartime.[11]

The implication that individuals should hijack the planning process for a social rather than merely 'military victory' establishes her interest in representing 'the people's war' in similar terms to Jesse and Harwood. But Banning does not only follow public policy in bringing the causes of war and democracy together. She ingeniously exploits the attributes of the travel letter to relativise national identity.[12] Counterpointing England's new war-engendered democracy with America's complacent nominal one, she inverts familiar and foreign to question the American reader's national identity against the new Britain:

There is something else, hardly more than an impression but it struck me as soon as I arrived in London. A great deal of pompousness and most of the signs of social distinction have been stripped from the city. No doubt it is due in part to the fact that there are hardly any big or shining cars in the streets, very few displays of luxuries in the shop windows. The taxis are old and rattling and shabby. I keep thinking back to New York, and it seems very luxurious. And every time I see a long queue of people waiting for a bus and know that there are undoubtedly titled people, housemaids, and mechanics standing in line together in the drizzle of rain, I feel that I've come into a democracy that is just now more realistic than our own. But we've only been at war for seven months.[13]

Thus the 'innocent' rhetoric of the letter permits a more politically sensitive challenge to American sexual and social inequality as well as to American prejudice against the British. Again, setting up the surrogate reader as daughter naturalises discussion of the particular opportunities that the war could bring women:

The most important women in England today are not the few whose names I may happen to mention. Those are well-known and useful women. But the important ones are the many who are proving that women are stronger than they were believed to be, hard of muscle and mechanically apt, diligent and patient to the amazement of those men who work with them, whether it's in the Services or the factories. Woman history is actually being made. The organization of homes is being modernized. I don't believe that the community nursery in industrial districts, or the community restaurants for largescale, inexpensive feeding, will ever be given up. They will be improved and kept.

The English woman is more than a cut ahead of us in the United States at the present moment in personal independence, self-reliance and realism. And I hope we can catch up.

I came back to the hotel feeling pretty damned incompetent. I can't even run a typewriter accurately. But I thought a good deal about you and am glad that you are completely *au courant* with your own times. Look after your health, and there is no limit to your usefulness in the future.[14]

This last drop to the personal note gives an idea of her general epistolary strategy, as it permits her to parade those qualities she admires in the English woman, 'personal independence, self-reliance, realism', while also claiming the vulnerability of the ordinary worried mother and technologically incapable woman. Thus, she smokes cigarettes in the air raid and is sarcastic about British puddings, but carries a 'monstrously large travelling purse' and appreciates the efforts of factory women to maintain their appearance. In effect, the letter's mediation between Britain and the States also conceals a mediation between old and new woman. These two functions are symbolically brought closer by her leaving behind her evening dress, extra clothes and cosmetics, for needy Englishwomen, on her departure. She does not push self-sacrifice as far as her daughter, however. 'I'm still glad you aren't here. I'm glad that you've skipped this in your life, and I hope that you'll continue to skip it.'[15]

Despite such admissions, it is striking how little real sense of the precariousness of this role of mediator we have. *Letters from England* shows how easily the travel letter lends itself to political use, in which the letter-writer's 'little public' blurs to the homogeneous national addressee.

We have thus far considered professional writers turned amateur diplomats through epistolary form. Non-professional writers also play a part in this epistolary propaganda, via the edited anthology. Two collections of private letters from writers across the social spectrum were solicited through a press appeal and published in 1941 in the States to raise money for air raid victims and the British-American Ambulance Corps: Diana Forbes-Robertson and Roger W. Strauss' *War Letters from Britain* and Beatrice Curtis Brown and Jan Struther's *Women of Britain*. Both books claimed the literary as well as social interest of 'ordinary' people's writing. This demonstrated an editorial aesthetic not only of sincerity but of pluralism, literally embodied in the cumulative effect of many voices united by historical theme rather than narrative. At the same time, the editor is crucial as the mediator and authoriser of 'the people's voice'. In the foreword to *War Letters from Britain* Forbes-Robertson and Strauss clearly state their criterion for selection as 'letters representative of many types and classes written at all stages of the war'. Most valued are 'unfeigned and unvarnished expressions'. The editors identify with their authors by implication, as 'the like-minded' in a war of ideas not nations:

> The letters assembled in this book give an idea of the indomitable spirit which sustained [the English people]. The editors have tried to choose letters representative of many types and classes, written at all stages of the war since its relatively inactive early phases. Some of these may have been written with an eye to publication – it is not impossible, even in the most personal of letters – but most are obviously the unfeigned and unvarnished expressions of what their writers felt as the world reeled on to catastrophe. I suggest that such letters could not have been written in 1914–1918, when a simple nationalistic conflict on an immense scale engaged the energies and darkened the minds of Europe. There is, in this way, a consciousness of the international value of all ideas, an awareness of the like-minded in all countries. Neither the Nazi nor the democratic Weltanschauung is restricted to the inhabitants of any one country. . . . One system or the other must conquer: there is no middle ground, no possibility of compromise.

Beatrice Curtis Brown's typological rather than chronological editing of *Women of Britain* goes further to present the letters as a sampling of the different strands of the nation's people:

> Some of them give a connected story of external events, others throw an interesting light on the changes in spirit and mental outlook which took place during succeeding phases of the war. Except for these series, the letters in each section of the book are in chronological order, but the book as a whole is not arranged chronologically. We thought it more interesting to divide the writers in various ways, sometimes according to age, sometimes according to habitat, sometimes according to social background – in order to illustrate the impact of the war upon different groups of people in a highly intricate modern civilisation.[16]

Jan Struther's introduction further distances the book from suspicions of organised propaganda, in stressing the authenticity and creativity of a 'miraculous revival of the custom of letter-writing', produced out of the conditions of wartime separation, boredom and disappointment:

> I should dearly love to know some statistics about the number and length of private letters which were written in Great Britain during the first nine months of the war. And the habit, once begun, was kept up even after the Blitzkrieg began. All this, perhaps is fairly natural: but what is remarkable is the style in which most of the letters are written. The British are supposed to be, in

general, an inarticulate race, shy of expressing emotion, shyer still of putting their beliefs and theories into words. Yet read through these letters, and you will find not only scattered sentences which move the heart 'more than a trumpet', but whole paragraphs of the acutest perception, the frankest self-analysis, and when you have read them all you will find that from these sentences, these paragraphs, has emerged the whole philosophy of a nation. It is not a portrait, painted by one artist, but a mosaic picture, made up by many hands out of small chippings from dozens of different lives. That is what makes it so poignant and revealing.[17]

I will consider *Women of Britain* in the next section, but Struther's model of the 'mosaic. . . made up by many hands' equally describes the aesthetics of *War Letters*. Robertson and Strauss's anthology creates not only a temporal dynamic of the population's growing patriotism throughout the first year of the war, but a synchronic theme of a new 'friendship' among the English across the individual Anglo-American friendships referred to by the letters. This friendship united classes, sexes, regions and even ages. The letters ranged from a ten-year-old's plea to the *New York Herald Tribune* for American foster parents, to those of artists and writers such as Myra Hess and John Gielgud, to political letters such as between Bevin, the Minister of Labour and National Service, and Spencer Miller, Jnr, the Director of the Workers Educational Bureau of America. More than half the letters are from women, who often make self-conscious appeals to be included in the real business of the war. The unification of the sexes again typifies the combination of critical demand for a more democratic warfare, and a pledge to popular unity in total war, no longer 'waged only on one's front' but 'behind one, and on the flanks, from above and from beneath'.[18] In one example, 'an English Author to her literary agent' rejects the code of sexual chivalry and its 'gooey romance' as part of the new kind of war:

We have now had almost a week of real war, and curiously enough I don't feel any different. We have new ways to continue to sleep and transport to our jobs, but there is not a gloss of pretence over it, we aren't pretending that it's a romantic picnic. I never felt so much reality about me before. I never saw girls and women look so tired, nor men so satisfied. Society can say what it likes, but man likes to have his woman beside him, even in, *especially* in danger. If she can rally and support him with her courage, he doesn't go all gooey and romantic and want to have the women and children first, willy nilly, he grows to the responsibility in toughness as well as spiritual zeal. Besides, there never was a war before in which everyone had something to do – well, not never. In the days of the pioneers, it was like this – and how I've longed to belong to them![19]

This view of the war as 'real' rather than 'romantic' suggests the way such letters worked as newly realist war writing. But the image of the 'days of the pioneers', loaded with its appeal to a specifically American form of sexual democracy, points to the rhetorical frame of the letter, which ultimately makes it such a convenient form of propaganda.

These letter-books are illuminated by Paul Fussell's remark that the Second World War was 'the age of anthologies'. This was, he suggests, not simply because bite-sized reading was more practical for a public of troops and warworkers on the move, nor because of the contemporary cult of guided readings by popular 'men of letters'. It also reflected an important ideological 'desire in both anthologist and reader to survey "the heritage" as a way of seeking an answer to the pressing question, what are we fighting for?:'

> The war forced everyone back onto traditional cultural possessions and responses and forced people to consider which things were valuable enough to be preserved and enjoyed over and over again. If the enemy insisted on the principle *Ein Volk, Ein Reich*, the principle of variety honored by the anthologies was a way of taking an anti-totalitarian, anti-uniformitarian stance, a way of honoring the pluralism and exuberance of the 'democratic' Allied cause.[20]

Letter-books demonstrated this principle of 'variety' and 'pluralism', not through the canons of the 'heritage' but through proclaiming the new or potential literatures of the ordinary 'man or woman in the street'. The *Times Literary Supplement*'s review of *War Letters* suggests precisely this:

> Those who are making a collection of war literature should not miss this collection of letters from people in Great Britain. . . . What strikes the reader most, apart from the almost universal absence of complaint and fear, is the extraordinarily high standard of literary excellence throughout the book; it is very difficult, opening at random, to guess which pages are the work of the professional and which come from the pens of the man or woman in the street.[21]

The wartime letter-anthology exemplifies a democratic aesthetics, but it also demonstrates how an already rhetorical form is pushed further into propaganda.[22] Indeed, Nicholas Cull concludes that the MoI's use of such indirect forms of propaganda was crucial to the eventual entry of the United States into the war.[23] But in the longer term, we must question the representativeness of such texts. The 'history' that the 'people' are celebrated as making, in wartime anthologies, now looks far more homogenised than various, and suffers from its disembodiment from the individual story. In many ways, this is particularly ironic in the case of women's letters, which gained newly public status precisely for their ostensibly private and personal expression. It is this irony that I explore in the next section.

WRITING TO THE NATIONAL FAMILY: WOMEN'S OPEN LETTERS

If letters could become a medium by which people naturally began to express their participation in political debate or public reporting, they also became a means of knitting the domestic into the public sphere. Women's letters, especially as they represented the civilian home, gain a new public importance. On the home front, letter-writing circles, serial letters, epistolary columns in local newspapers and pamphlets in letter-form became common popular forms of women's writing and publishing. Jenny Hartley, in her extensive survey of British women's wartime writing, argues that:

> Women's particular skills as letter-writers were recognized in the practice which spread among servicemen abroad of asking visiting female celebrities to write home for them. Elsie and Doris Waters ('Gert and Daisy'), Joyce Grenfell, Eleanor Roosevelt and Adele Astaire were all inundated with requests and complied good-naturedly. Joyce Grenfell tried 'hard to make each one different and try to imagine the homes the letters are going to. But it takes time. However, it seems, mysteriously, to give pleasure.'[24]

This blurring of professional and private writing once again has particular significance for women letter-writers, who have typically been praised for their letters but as 'natural' communicators rather than authors. Hartley continues:

> With personal letters written to strangers, the traditional categories of letters (written to others you know), books (written to others you do not know) and diaries (written for yourself) started to blur. The movement seemed to have been towards the public . . . It was the effects rather than the deeds of war which interested women writers. War was forcing new conjunctions between public and private in their own lives, and these conjunctions called for expression. New hybrids emerged as women writers blended previously discrete genres such as journalism, fiction and autobiography. . . . Vera Brittain's success with her First World War *Testament of Youth* had shown how a 'new type of autobiography', as she called it, could do justice to women's experience of war. This autobiographical impulse combined with women's traditional propensity towards the novel, and with the documentary styles of the 1930s, to initiate some strikingly apt innovations.[25]

In my following discussion of several of these 'new hybrids', however, we will see that this did not necessarily mean they did 'justice to women's experience of war'. Part of this may be precisely the difference between an 'autobiographical' and an 'epistolary' impulse, that Hartley does not acknowledge here, particularly as personal writing was institutionalised and published. Yet it was also clear that women's writing was largely valued in the limited terms of sexual and national fidelity to absent men. Rather than change women's relationship to the public sphere, the publicising of women's letters expressed the ideological value of civilian women's letters embodying the idea of home as nation. One token of this is the way that women's open letters, or editors of women's letters, describe the public readership as an extended family.[26] This pattern is true of British and American women's letters, but the far greater thrust of British women into the forefront of the war sharpened the strategy and its contradictions, in their writing. I will therefore focus my discussion through Beatrice Curtis Brown and Jan Struther's collection *Women of Britain: Letters from England* (1941) and two fictional letters by Struther's 'Mrs Miniver' (1939).

Beatrice Curtis Brown and Jan Struther's collection *Women of Britain: Letters from England*, is exemplary in its assertion of civilian women's perspectives as both the gauge of total war and maintainers of the social fabric. 'Business just has to go on',[27] writes an ex-governess to an ex-pupil now evacuated to the States, and the letters are largely about the continuity of the 'business' of daily life at home as their writers repeatedly assert their attempts to cook, sleep, organise childcare, wash in the midst of evacuation, rationing, refugees billeting, the blackout and the blitz. But women's letters are designated not as passively keeping the homefires burning, but as actively creating an idea of home in its absence. One writer literally asserts that she does not mind being evacuated from her flat because she realises she has a deeper idea of home. Another creates home in a public shelter, and another has adopted 'a nomadic life'. Having sent her children to the country, she buys a 'strong bicycle with a big luggage grid on the back and a sort of butcher boy's rack on front' so that 'if the railroads get bombed or get jammed with refugees, I am still mobile, and can get back to the children somehow'.[28]

Struther's rousing introduction implies that there is a big difference between this and women's traditional role. This is crucially effected through contrasting the chaos of women's private lives in England with the peaceful domestic routines in a Brooklyn suburb, from where she herself writes in confessional safety. In her terms, the epistolary format is related explicitly to the perception of women's new historical agency – and we see the familiar motif of the people's war return:

> An American philosopher, after going right through the manuscript of this book in complete silence, laid it down and made one brief comment. 'These people,' he said, 'are not only making history: they are writing history.'[29]

However, if the letters' domestication of destruction embodies women's defiance, they easily slide into caricature. Even curling one's hair gains national significance:

> The Germans were busy last night, and it really don't give one's curls a chance. I had just washed my hair and set it into a beautiful page boy bob and I had to take the curlers out before it was dry because I had to go down to the basement and did not know who else might be there.[30]

The several letters by children that are included perhaps demonstrate most clearly the reduction of private to public sphere, as they confidently joke about air raids and the nasty 'Jerry's'. Furthermore, the egalitarian mood sits uneasily with the highly class-conscious Miniveresque views of many of the upper middle-class letter-writers. Despite Struther's claim for the literary and autobiographical value of such a group portrait, the editor Curtis Brown overtly asserts that 'young-middle-aged, upper middle-class London women's' perspectives are the truest voice of civilian England, 'because this kind of woman in England, as in every country, is articulate and reflective and expresses a general view – a view held by many who do not or cannot put it into words'.[31]

Struther herself, perhaps the epitome of the upper middle-class woman propagandist, adopted the letter-form in the last two columns of her infamous soap opera *Mrs Miniver*, written in the lead-up to war. Although these are not real letters, they are closely linked to *Women of Britain* – not only through Struther, but because they pre-empt it in constructing a citizens' propaganda through epistolary form. Alison Light comments that Struther's shift from her polished essay form to letters 'allows [her] a more personal and more immediate style'.[32] However, as a signal of the war's disruption of private life, this move to the letter is more significant as an early transformation of the Miniveresque ideology of home and hearth into the ideology of national home. Light has shown how the Miniver column in the prewar years worked as a model for publicly celebrating the domestic and ordinary, in a new form of understated, personal national identity, that she calls 'a patriotism of private life'. She contends that the essay format, the detached, indirect, archness, as well as the small-scale content, all create a literature of 'Eternity framed in domesticity'. The outbreak of war is clearly the moment when domesticity must now encompass not eternity but temporality, the crashing in of history. In the first of Mrs Miniver's letters to her 'sister-in-law', she urges:

> So write all the letters you can, Susan, please (to me, if you feel like it, but at any rate to somebody), and keep all the ones you get, and put down somewhere, too, everything you see or hear which will help later on to recapture the spirit of this tragic, marvellous and eye-opening time: so that, having recaptured it, we can use it for better ends.[33]

These records of the moment represent the ability of the ordinary citizen to write, and to make history, creating what she terms a 'non-material war museum'.

Unlike the indirect voice of the essay which appeals to the reader through example, the letter-writer actively exhorts and tugs in a much more urgent form of education. The change to the letter-form thus signifies the arrival of debate into national – and, by implication, class – consensus. Yet it immediately contains this debate within a model of family and sisterly networking that reassures us national unity is never really in question:

> Everything that really matters always does go on being the same: the fun of thinking things out and delight in awareness for its own sake, and, above all, the unending fascination of personal relationships. To say nothing of such trifles as love and courage and kindness and integrity and the quite astonishing resilience of the human spirit.[34]

Struther's turn to the letter is thus a small measure of the transformation of the patriotism of private life, that emerged in the 1930s, into the patriotism of the people's war. On the transformation of the English *Mrs Miniver* column into the Hollywood film of 1942, Light argues:

> Neither the film nor the book form of *Mrs Miniver* has worn well, and on the face of it they might seem to have little in common. The film belongs as clearly to the more romantic Toryism of the Churchillian mood as the original does to the less resounding conservatisms of 'appeasement'. Yet under the impress of war it seems that it was easy for the one to build upon and transform the other; those same retiring virtues of 1938 could themselves, in a larger theatre, paradoxically come to seem the stuff of a nation in arms. The war inflated and magnified Jan Struther's domestic sentiments into something far grander, and provided a new heroic stage for a British people seen, not as a race of empire builders or natural warriors, but rather as an essentially unassuming nation, peaceable by temperament, who wanted nothing better than a quiet life. At the heart of it was a powerful and new sense of national history, not as the doings of the great and the good, but as that which was made by the little, ordinary people at home, 'muddling through'. Well before the bombing a patriotism of private life was being felt and expressed.[35]

Just as the move from text to film adapted private to public citizenship, the public use of letters in the war revealed the reach of such ideologies in their prewar private form.[36] More generally, such close readings of women's letters show that the forcible invasion of the private sphere does not so much encourage self-expression as, paradoxically, dissolve it into the rhetoric of the public citizen.

Nowhere is this clearer than in letters written to be read in the event of death, where the letter must bear the weight of severing relationships forever, and more often than not turns to patriotic discourses of the most traditional kind to do so.

LAST LETTERS: THE TRAGEDY OF CITIZENSHIP

'One of the lessons of war is how to say goodbye, though few attempted to learn it,' Ronald Blythe has commented in his excellent anthology *Private Words: Letters and Diaries of the Second World War* (1993). Although he considers that 'deliberated last words were comparatively rare', the number of letters people prepared to be sent in the event of their death to loved ones represents a significant 'lesson' in writing, and certainly a genre that was and still is a classic form of wartime literature.[37] It is somewhat ironic that it has also been a staple of wartime propaganda.

The defining text of the genre must be the letter from 'an airman to his mother', as *The Times* published it on 18 June 1940, under the caption 'The Fight with Evil: "My Earthly Mission is fulfilled"'.[38] A stock-exchange clerk and only son of a widow, Vivian Rosewarne was shot down on 31 May. Although this letter was hardly typical in the extent of its publicity, its very success demonstrates some of the aesthetic as well as ideological issues involved in the public consumption of the genre, and how dramatically they can contrast with the extremely personal intentions of the writer. *The Times* reprinted the letter as a leaflet (12 for 7*d*; 250 for 8*s* 6*d*; postage free); *The Times* readers wrote in, suggesting it be read to boys in schools, broadcast, left on church pews. The letter was displayed at the fund-raising 'Wings for Victory' rallies and Frank Salisbury painted the 'airman's' posthumous portrait. Lord Wakefield wished he were not too old to make a similar sacrifice, praising the airman's mother as the letter's indirect author, in having 'given to the world a message of such rare power and beauty'.[39] Eleanor Rathbone argued the sacrifice was not all in vain,[40] and the editor of *The New World*, D.H. Barber, even renounced his pacifism on the strength of reading the letter. He attributes this to the letter's literary power: 'I . . . cannot hold out any longer in face of the unstudied eloquence of your dead and anonymous contributor':[41]

Dearest Mother,

Though I feel no premonition at all, events are moving rapidly and I have instructed that this letter be forwarded to you should I fail to return from one of the raids which we shall shortly be called upon to undertake. . . .

I have always admired your amazing courage in the face of continual setbacks; in the way you have given me as good an education and background as anyone in the country; and always kept up appearances without ever losing faith in the future. My death would not mean that your struggle has been in vain. Far from it. It means that your sacrifice is as great as mine. Those who serve England must expect nothing from her; we debase ourselves if we regard our country as merely a place in which to eat and sleep.[42]

('The Fight with Evil')

The airman's repeated call on his mother to accept and take pride in his death as sacrifice forms the core of his letter. To do this, he has to justify not only his death but, far more difficult, her loss. He does this by aligning her sacrifice with his, rhetorically drawing her into battle, too, as she who trained the warrior. 'Your sacrifice is as great as mine,' he argues, ingenuously, continuing, 'Yet there is more work for you to do,' as representative of the home front, and finally: 'You must not grieve for me, for if you really believe in religion and all that it entails that would be hypocrisy.' Here, he suddenly swells out of his immediate address to an almost euphoric vision of war as the essence of what it means to be human: 'Those who just eat and sleep, prosper and procreate, are no better than animals if all their lives they are at peace.' While this belief may inspire him, the real issue is his unification of the interests of mothers and nations, and it is for this that the letter was so immediately useful as propaganda. The young officer's station commander is quoted as saying:

This letter was perhaps the most amazing one I have ever read; simple and direct in its wording but splendid and uplifting in its outlook. . . . It was inevitable that I should read it – in fact he must have intended this, for it was left open in order that I might be certain that no prohibited information was disclosed.

I sent the letter to the bereaved mother, and asked her whether I might publish it anonymously, as I feel its contents may bring comfort to other mothers, and that every one in our country may feel proud to read of the sentiments which support 'an average airman' in the execution of his present arduous duties. I have received the mother's permission, and I hope this letter may be read by the greatest possible number of our countrymen at home and abroad.[43]

Clearly, letters from servicemen to mothers, girlfriends, wives or daughters, had obvious propagandic value in terms of transcending the sexual division of labour in war, which has historically so often aligned women, particularly mothers, with pacifism. We have seen how the patriotic letters of civilian women were particularly publicised for similar reasons.

The gender politics of securing popular consensus clearly underlie one unusual letter-collection, which represents a rare example of a civilian woman's 'last letters'. Simpkin Marshall in 1942 published in pamphlet form *Letters to Libya*, the letters of an ordinary housewife from February to April 1942, to her husband, an anti-tank gunner in the Eighth Army.[44] The anonymous writer had unexpectedly been killed in an air raid, shortly before her husband received the letters. It is puzzling to today's reader that this story, according to the distributor at least, should be considered comforting or inspiring. Indeed, on the inside back cover we are informed that 'Because of the necessity for economy in paper, only a limited number of copies of the booklet have been printed. When you have read it, please pass it on to a friend, or leave it at a Post Office so that it may be sent to the men and women in the Services.' Was it ever really sent to the troops? Why would those at the front wish to read about the death of their loved ones at home? And what made the letter-collection seem to be an appropriate form in which to tell it? The preface gives us the editor's answers:

> A Member of Parliament to whom these letters were shown before publication remarked, 'I had been anxious about the effect of the fourth war winter on our people. I am now ashamed of my fears. We are too apt to deprecate ourselves and to listen to small minorities with grumbles and criticisms – to forget that a woman like this can write, "We know that we can take it, and are proud to know it."'
>
> The husband was persuaded that the letters express the thoughts, feelings and faith of the many thousands of women, who, separated from their menfolk and usually with children to care for, are still cheerfully carrying on. It is to these women that this little book is dedicated.[45]

Clearly the letters were valued as representative of 'thousands of women': even the quote from the housewife is expressed in the plural. This is also borne out in the fact that the letters are anonymous – all we know is that she is 'the wife of an anti-tank gunner'. While the editorial preface explicitly underlines their authenticity, the particular authority of the writer is downplayed. Letters, once again, are used to represent the unity of individual and collective, the more valuable for being those of an ordinary housewife. But the fact that these are 'last letters' also functions as a kind of 'reason' for publication, as the dramatic 'ending' of her sudden death gives them that 'aesthetic' unity valued in all last letters. It may be that this sombre aesthetic fulfilment is what counteracts the potential subversiveness of last letters as statements of people not ready to die. It certainly makes publishable her otherwise humdrum accounts of the children, household tasks and family news. The irony is that she herself considers the literary elevation of suffering unconvincing. After her father's death, she writes:

> A whole lot of silly annoying little things have happened this week. Gladys went off with a pair of my stockings which she won't remember to send back, and Tommy has broken my hair comb. It is all so trivial when you have just

been through a real tragedy. You ought not to notice them, but it doesn't work that way. You seem to take them more to heart. I can't say I find sorrow uplifting the way they say it is in books.[46]

The disparity between trivia and tragedy is a struggle inherent in wartime correspondences between the protected and the unprotected, yet this self-deprecating language points out the gendered dimension to her judgement that her daily life is trivial. The letters chart not only her growing patriotism but a tension over her role as a wife, in which she wishes to join the ATS but reassures her husband:

Don't worry, I know I can't leave the children, and we've been told that housewives are doing as good work as anybody, and I wouldn't be much use at anything else.[47]

Her new engagement with politics and the state is invariably couched in negative, passive terms. After the war, she says:

I personally, shan't mind cutting off the frills, and I don't think many other wives and mothers will either.

Still, we have got to win the old war first. It will be a dreary job. I shall get sick to death of working in the evening as well as all day, and you will get browned off when there is nothing doing in your bit of the desert, but we must stick it. This isn't a war to end war, but to end our fear of war so that never again will we hesitate to fight for the life we believe is right, because we are afraid of losing our lives, or security or comfort.

I know it is not like me to be bothering my head over things like that, but these last few weeks of worry about you have made me think a bit. When I was terribly depressed I was tempted to wonder if it was all worth while, and now my darling, I know it is even if we should never meet on this earth again.[48]

It is notable that after this unprecedented venture into a Churchillian rhetoric, she abruptly drops in register and begins a new paragraph in her normal self-conscious format: 'I know it is not like me to be bothering my head. . . .' Personal engagement in public consciousness is articulated in terms of sacrifice alone, in the most vague and circular of political ideals: 'the life we believe is right', which in terms of her relationship only affirms her wish to 'start all over again' when he comes back, despite the perspective undoubtedly gained. Thus as last letters they struggle to unite the state demand for private sacrifice in a different way to male soldiers, not just in the absence of the sexualised rhetoric of nation as mother or mistress, but in their lack of a heroic stance or structure.

Most obviously, of course, her death is unanticipated. It is the unfinishedness of the letters which most powerfully represents that invisibility of women's sacrifices. That they were published as propaganda, therefore, only suggests the institution of women's sacrifices as continuous with life. Pathos rather than tragedy is the genre of a housewife's death, in a reworking of the classic function of epistolary literature to record a version of female suffering as passive and cloistered.

In this chapter I have shown that epistolary publication during the war constituted an unusual recognition of the eloquence and efficacy of the private letter as a form of nationalist literature. It was an effective form of propaganda, precisely because it was making use of personal and unprompted expressions of patriotism and the instincts both to preach and to reassure inherent in letter-writing. More specifically, the letter form was a natural forum in which to debate and represent the new forms of social and sexual democracy advanced as part of 'the people's war'. Yet, as I have suggested, the circularity between the personal patriotism expressed in private letters, the media's discourses of class, gender and nation, and state policy does not testify to the genuine unification of personal with public interest. Rather, it should be read as evidence of the difficulty in articulating dissenting views.

In some senses, these letters do dramatise a strong sense of individual participation in political life, particularly novel in the case of women. In hindsight, it is clear that the letters that were published offered only limited insight into people's actual feelings about the war. Certainly, the war letters published in the last twenty years disrupt the homogenising discourses of patriotism with admissions of fear, depression, lack of conviction and anger or boredom.[49] More telling still are the differences between letters and other forms of account such as diaries, oral histories or contemporary verbal accounts.[50] The real interest of wartime epistolary publications is that nationalist propaganda so ingeniously exploited the genre's inherent characteristics as private polemic.

Notes

1   'A Birmingham mother to her son in the Royal Air Force, who enclosed it in a letter to a friend in the U.S.A.', Beatrice Curtis Brown (ed.) and Jan Struther (Intro.), *Women of Britain: Letters from England* (New York, Harcourt, 1941).

2   The MoI was responsible for propaganda in the Allied states; the Foreign Office for that in the Axis countries. On the complex innovations in the use and conceptions of propaganda during the war, see Nicholas John Cull, *Selling War: The British Propaganda Campaign Against American 'Neutrality' in World War II* (New York, Oxford University Press, 1995) and Ian McLaine, *Ministry of Morale: Home Front Morale and the Ministry of Information in World War II* (London, Allen and Unwin, 1979). For the representation of women in propaganda, see Maureen Honey, *Creating Rosie the Riveter: Class, Gender and Propaganda during World War II* (Amherst, MA, University of Massachusetts Press; 1984), Michael

Renov, *Hollywood's Wartime Women: Representation and Ideology* (Ann Arbour, UMI Research Press, 1988), and Leila Rupp, *Mobilizing Women for War: German and American Propaganda 1939–1945* (Princeton, NJ, Princeton University Press, 1978).

3   In September 1939, the Ministry of Information set up a Books Committee which commissioned literature according to the political needs of the hour and fed the completed manuscripts to independent commercial publishing houses such as Penguin, Macmillan, Harcourt, Doubleday and Oxford University Press. The author list of the MoI Literary and Editorial Unit included Harold Laski, E.M. Forster, Howard Spring, Vernon Bartlett, Harold Nicolson and Graham Greene. For the American audience in particular, Norman Angell wrote *For What Do We Fight?* and the Labour MP Josiah Wedgewood wrote *Forever Freedom*. See Cull, *Selling War*.

4   Cull, *Selling War*, p. 57.

5   Cull, *Selling War*, p. 176. Cull, however, also notes that British non-fiction never matched the sales of the United States' own offerings, although British fiction did – including *Mrs Miniver* and *Random Harvest* by James Hilton (author of *Good-bye Mr Chips*) and *This Above All* by Eric Knight, p. 178.

6   Fryn Tennyson Jesse and Harold Harwood, *London Front: Letters Written to America* (August 1939–July 1940) (London, Constable, 1940), p. 459. Their correspondents were the astronomer Edwin Hubble and his wife Grace, Mr and Mrs Carl Hovey and the playwright Sam Behrman.

7   Jesse and Harwood, *London Front*, p. 2.

8   Jesse and Harwood, *London Front*, p. 226.

9   Jesse and Harwood, *London Front*, p. 12.

10   Herbert Davis, 'In England, Now', *Yale Review* (1940), 825–8. Davis was also reviewing: Vera Brittain, *England's Hour*; Allan Michie and Walter Graebner, *Their Finest Hour*; A.P. Herbert, *England Speaks*; Phyllis Bottome, *Mansion House of Liberty*; and Edward Murrow, *This is London*.

11   Margaret Culkin Banning, *Letters from England, Summer 1942* (New York, Harper, 1943), p. 5.

12   Another letter-book worth considering in this light is the Communist writer Clive Branson's *British Soldier in India: The Letters of Clive Branson* (London, Communist Party, 1944), which goes much further in undercutting racial and national stereotypes. At the other end of the spectrum is a 1945 British publication of some German letters and diaries, pointedly titled *True to Type: A Selection from Letters and Diaries of German Soldiers and Civilians Collected on the Soviet–German Front* (London, Hutchinson, 1945). The extracts from 38 diarists and 429 letter-writers are organised under headings reminiscent of the seven deadly sins, from 'Swaggerers and Adventurers' to 'Slave-Owners', and tell a Faustian story of the fall from crude jubilant pride in the launch of the German offensive on Moscow to snivelling despair at its crushing defeat in the summer of 1943. Although the typecasting is lurid, the contents are fascinating, suggesting everything repressed from the good Allied soldier and faithful wife's letters.

13   Banning, *Letters from England*, p. 25.

14   Banning, *Letters from England*, pp. 111–12.

15   Banning, *Letters from England*, p. 170.

16   Brown, *Women of Britain*, p. 12.

17   Brown, *Women of Britain*, pp. 24–5.

18   This phrase is the author Alec Waugh's, from a letter dated June 1940, to his friend and

publisher John Farrar in New York, 'after his Return with the BEF from Flanders', in Diana Forbes-Robertson and Roger W. Strauss (eds), *War Letters from Britain* (London, Jarrolds, 1942), p. 26.

19   Forbes-Robertson and Strauss, *War Letters*, p. 84.

20   Paul Fussell, *Wartime: Understanding and Behaviour in the Second World War* (New York, Oxford University Press, 1989), p. 245.

21   'Review of *War Letters from Britain*', *Times Literary Supplement* (9 May 1942), p. 23.

22   An interesting comparison is the American interest in and use of letters. Without the immediate propagandistic interest of early Anglo-American correspondences, letter-books such as Harry E. Maule (ed.), *A Book of War Letters* (New York, 1943); Mina Curtiss (ed.), *Letters Home* (Boston, Little, 1944); James Waterman Wise (ed.), *Very Truly Ours: Letters from America's Fighting Men* (New York, Dial, 1943); and Alma Lutz (ed.), *With Love, Jane: Letters from American Women in the War Fronts* (New York, Day, 1945) also demonstrate a self-consciously democratic and pluralist aesthetic, that pays tribute to the literary ability of the 'common' man and woman. Curtiss most explicitly hails her letters as following in the 'oldest and simplest pioneer tradition of American writing . . . which Ring Lardner and Mark Twain would have been proud to have written'. A notable difference from British collections is their (limited) interest in racial equality, both in the writers represented and their rhetorical linking of the war against Nazism with combating American racial segregation and anti-Semitism. The weekly epistolary column by ex-school teacher Keith Frazier Somerville to her 'boys' in the services provides a particularly interesting example of the way that a woman exploited the public letter to create a vision of an inter-racial national 'family'. This has been republished and edited by Judy Barrett Litoff and David C. Smith as *Dear Boys: World War II Letters from a Woman Back Home* (Jackson, University of Mississippi, 1991).

23   Cull, *Selling War*, pp. 198–202.

24   Jenny Hartley, *Hearts Undefeated: Women's Writing of the Second World War* (London, Virago, 1995), p. 2.

25   Hartley, *Hearts Undefeated*, pp. 2–3, 5–6.

26   Kathleen McPherson, for example, wrote a fortnightly column for the *Highland News* in the form of letters to her Army nurse daughter, reissued in pamphlet form in 1941 as *Letters to My Daughter* (London, Hodge, 1941). Another pamphlet, by Angela Kelf, *Letters Between Aunt Jane and Tabitha* (London, Stockwell, 1940), puts different generations of upper-class women in dialogue, to point out the end of their sheltered life. James Waterman Wise revealingly introduces the American collection *Very Truly Ours* thus: 'In one sense these letters, though personal and intimate, are public domain. For there is hardly an American who has neither relative nor friend in the fighting forces. Thus the comradeship of the men who wrote these letters is here extended to us at home. We, who read them will be justified in feeling that they might have been written by our own fathers and husbands and sons and brothers.'

27   Brown, *Women of Britain*, p. 293.

28   Brown, *Women of Britain*, p. 264.

29   Brown, *Women of Britain*, p. 26.

30   Brown, *Women of Britain*, p. 153.

31   Brown, *Women of Britain*, p. 37.

32   Alison Light, *Forever England: Femininity, Literature and Conservatism* (London, Routledge, 1991), p. 152.

33   Jan Struther, *Mrs Miniver* (London, Virago, 1989), p. 123.

34   Struther, *Mrs Miniver*, p. 140.

35   Light, *Forever England*, p. 154.

36   Vera Brittain's use of the family letter for pacifist polemic in *Humiliation with Honour* (London, Dakers, 1942) is an interesting parallel to the pro-war epistolary propaganda, in which she writes to her evacuee son to justify her pacifism. The pamphlet sold ten thousand copies by February 1943 (Hartley, *Hearts Undefeated*, p. 237). Despite her critique of nationalism and militarism, in many ways the letters' expression of a mother forced to sacrifice her son for her cause duplicates rather than challenges the conservative gender relations in Struther and Curtis Brown. She also used the epistolary form in her 'open letters to Peace-Lovers', which she wrote weekly to private subscribers. These have been reissued and edited by Winifred and Alan Eden-Grech (eds), *Testament of a Peace Lover: Letters from Vera Brittain* (London, Virago, 1988).

37   Joanna Lumley's coffee-table anthology, *Forces Sweethearts*, commissioned by the Imperial War Museum (London, Bloomsbury, 1993), contains several such letters, as do Annette Tapert (ed.), *Despatches from the Heart: An Anthology of Letters from the Front during the First and Second World Wars* (London, Hamilton, 1984); Annette Tapert (ed.), *Lines of Battle: An Anthology of Letters by American Servicemen in World War II* (New York, Times Books, 1987); and Judy Barrett Litoff and David C. Smith (eds), *We're in This War, Too: World War II Letters from American Women in Uniform* (New York, Oxford University Press, 1994). A particularly interesting example is the letter by a young man to his fiancée published in *The Spectator*, 1 June 1945, which was introduced by Fryn Tennyson Jesse as exemplary not for its patriotism but for its beautiful style. See P. Tennyson Jesse, 'Death and Love', in Fiona Glass and Philip Marsden-Smedley (eds), *Articles of War: The Spectator Book of World War II* (London, Grafton, 1989), p. 375.

38   It is reprinted in Ronald Blythe, *Private Words: Letters and Diaries of the Second World War* (London, Penguin, 1993), p. 305.

39   Lord Wakefield, 'Letter', *The Times* (21 June 1940), p. 7.

40   Eleanor Rathbone, 'Letter', *The Times* (24 June 1940), p. 4.

41   D.H. Barber, 'Letter', *The Times* (19 June 1940), p. 7.

42   Blythe, *Private Words*, pp. 306–7.

43   'The Fight with Evil: "My Earthly Mission is Fulfilled"', *The Times* (18 June 1940), p. 7.

44   Although I have found no evidence that they were a hoax, one extremely popular 'diary' of a Dutch boy and refugee, the 1941 *My Sister and I*, was exposed as a fake by Paul Fussell in the course of researching *Wartime*, published in 1989. Fussell: *Wartime*, p. 166.

45   Anon., *Letters to Libya* (London, Simpkin Marshall, 1942), Preface.

46   Anon., *Letters to Libya*, p. 5.

47   Anon., *Letters to Libya*, p. 12.

48   Anon., *Letters to Libya*, p. 35.

49   See Mirren Barford and Lieutenant Jock Lewes, *Joy Street: A Wartime Romance in Letters*, ed. Michael T. Wise (London, Little, 1995); Eva Figes (ed.), *Women's Letters in Wartime* (London, Pandora, 1994); Margaretta Jolly (ed.), *Dear Laughing Motorbyke: Letters from Women Welders in the Second World War* (London, Scarlet Press, 1997); Judy Barrett Litoff and David C. Smith (eds), *Since You Went Away: World War Two Letters from American Women on the Home Front* (Oxford University Press, 1991); Jocelyn Statler

(ed.), *Special Relations: Transatlantic Letters Linking Three English Evacuees and their Families, 1940–45* (London, Imperial War Museum, 1990); Keith Winston, PFC, *V-Mail: Letters of a World War II Combat Medic*, ed. Sarah Winston (Chapel Hill, Algonquin, 1985).

50 See Blythe, *Private Words*; Angus Calder and Dorothy Sheridan (eds), *Speak for Yourself: A Mass-Observation Anthology 1937–49* (Oxford University Press, 1985); Angus Calder, *The Myth of the Blitz* (London, Cape, 1991); Tom Harrison, *Living Through the Blitz* (New York, Simon and Schuster, 1989); Naomi Mitchison, *Among You Taking Notes . . . : The Wartime Diary of Naomi Mitchison 1939–45*, ed. Dorothy Sheridan (London, Gollancz, 1985).

Part Five

INTERWAR AND IDEOLOGY

The post-Bolshevik period saw the rise of extreme ideologies such as Nazism and Communism. These two chapters deal not with the more obvious and better-known examples of these ideological extremes, but with their impact on liberal pluralistic democratic societies. Peter Beck shows well how the British Foreign Office could harness sporting events to convey an idealised vision of Britain abroad. Sport, with its ideologically neutral ethos, has proved to be a most permeable medium of propaganda in the twentieth century. By looking at a global sport such as association football (soccer), Beck shows that sporting behaviour and the quality of the play could fulfil a crucial diplomatic role in a tense international environment. The ideological content of propaganda can be over-read and Graham Barnfield shows that the radical writings of American novelists of the 1930s might not have been dictated from Moscow but partook of a wider radical subculture. In fact, the very resistance of these authors to any kind of direct party line which would lack an aesthetic grounding shows that propaganda may well be found most concerted in liberal literary critiques. For the historian of propaganda, ideologies present the problem of being part of our own mindset, and literary critics who chose to denounce, as impartially as they thought they might be, the flaws of proletarian novels did not reflect on their own ideological baggage. This is the problem of mirror representations, where each side's credibility is undermined by the suspicion of propaganda.

15

PROJECTING AN IMAGE OF A GREAT NATION ON THE WORLD SCREEN THROUGH FOOTBALL

BRITISH CULTURAL PROPAGANDA BETWEEN THE WARS

Peter J. Beck

Traditionally, state interference in sport has been associated with the Nazi, Fascist and Soviet regimes between the wars or in post-1945 Communist states. In general, this feature was perceived as something alien to the British scene, particularly during the interwar period. Even in recent decades, after British governments first appointed a Minister of Sport (currently, this post, first created in 1963, is part of the Department for Culture, Media and Sport), Richard Tracey, one holder of the office (1985–7) during the Thatcher years, claimed: 'Of course, in Britain we have no political control of sport, unlike other countries.'[1] For Tony Mason, one of our leading sports historians, a chapter on sport and politics, though central to his book on South America, 'would probably not exist in a book on British football'.[2]

Of course, this preferred non-interference strategy has not prevented British politicians from taking a close interest in the game and linking themselves to the fortunes of specific clubs, even if this trend only became more common after the 1960s, when Harold Wilson (Prime Minister, 1964–70, 1974–6), a keen supporter of Huddersfield, presided over England's 1966 World Cup success. Reportedly, Wilson, who liked to claim that he knew more about football than politics, identified an interest in the game as 'the mark of a leader'.[3] Other politicians closely associated with individual clubs either today or in recent decades include Tony Banks, the current Minister for Sport (Chelsea), Kenneth Clarke (Nottingham Forest), Roy Hattersley (Sheffield Wednesday) and John Major (Chelsea). Tony Blair, who supports Newcastle United, has proved no exception, even if one of his more interesting contributions occurred in January 1995, that is, before he became prime minister; thus, Blair, addressing the Football Writers' Association, articulated his longstanding interest in the game, most notably, his admiration of the sporting values epitomised by Stanley Matthews.[4] By contrast, Margaret Thatcher (Prime Minister, 1979–90), as recorded by Kenneth Clarke, 'found it difficult to understand why any one would want to go to a football match at all', even if one of her visits to Liverpool (1976) had commenced significantly at Anfield.[5]

Despite the challenge of rival sports and its relative lack of impact on the USA, association football has proved, and remains, the world's major sport in terms of participation, spectators and popular interest. However, to quote Christopher Andrew, 'Of all popular movements in modern history, the most popular, though not among historians, is surely football.'[6] Like many people, historians might turn first to the sports pages of their daily newspaper, but even today – Andrew was writing over a decade ago – their academic horizons often stop short of taking account of the sporting dimension. Admittedly, there has occurred a growth in the serious study of sport by a range of academic disciplines, not excluding history, but the history of sport has yet to be regarded by the historical profession, at least in Britain, as being on a par with, say, the historical study of high politics. For most historians, Bastin, Hapgood and Matthews have yet to equal Baldwin, Chamberlain and Ramsay MacDonald in terms of their historical significance. Against this background, this chapter, illuminating the historical insights arising from its study, identifies international sport as a missing dimension in the history of British foreign policy between the wars, with specific reference to football's potential as a less elitist form of national projection and insidious propaganda.[7]

After all, following the inimitable late Bill Shankly in a phrase used also in Peter Clarke's recently published history of Britain, for some people football is not only more important than life or death but also often interpreted as, to quote George Orwell's comments about a 1945 British tour conducted by a Moscow football team, 'war minus the shooting'.[8] More recently, in July 1995, John Major (Prime Minister, 1990–7), echoing some of the views advanced by Tony Blair six months earlier, launched his government's 'Raising the Game' initiative by pressing sport's policy importance: 'Some people say that sport is a peripheral and minor concern. I profoundly disagree. Sport is a binding force between generations and across borders. But, by a miraculous paradox, it is at the same time one of the defining characteristics of nationhood and of local pride. We should cherish it for both these reasons.'[9] What he failed to mention was the fact that, by implication, international sport, a competitive activity undertaken in a world of nation states, was equally capable of becoming a divisive force 'across borders', especially as national football teams, perceived as 'primary expressions of their imagined communities', are often perceived as visible expressions of 'national struggle'.[10]

During the interwar period, a growing number of European governments intervened in sport in pursuit of their respective foreign policy, totalitarian and other aspirations. German sport, though subject already during the Weimar regime to a reasonable degree of politicisation, was no exception to Hitler's process of *Gleichschaltung* (coordination). Sir Eric Phipps, the British ambassador in Berlin, reported the 'tightening' Nazi control over sport through the *Deutscher*

Reichsbund für Leibesübungen (German Federal Association for Physical Culture), German sport's increasingly 'political' character, and the influential role performed by the *Reichsports Führer* (leader of German Sport), Captain Hans von Tschammer und Osten.[11] In 1935, a manual for political education, entitled *Deutschkunde über Volk, Staat, Leibesübungen* ('*Deutschkunde*' has no obvious English equivalent, but a possible translation is *German Culture – People, Nation and Physical Exercise*), left readers, including Sir Robert Vansittart (Permanent Under-Secretary of State, Foreign Office), with little doubt about sport's political role: 'Gymnastics and sport are thus an institution for the education of the body and a school of the political will in the service of the State. Unpolitical, so-called neutral gymnasts and sportsmen are unthinkable in Hitler's state.'[12]

Soon afterwards, the 1936 winter and summer Olympics, held at Garmisch-Partenkirchen and Berlin respectively, reaffirmed sport's prominent place in the German propaganda machine during mid- to late 1930s, when, to quote Nevile Henderson, Phipps' successor at the Berlin embassy, 'the Nazis are looking for victories to boost their regime. It is their way of claiming a super-race.'[13] Football's popularity, in conjunction with the media visibility attracted by international matches, meant that results were capable of presentation by Hitler's government through the officially controlled media as a reflection of the quality of far more than German football, as evidenced by the frequent exploitation of victories achieved on the football field to boost national prestige at home and abroad through a focus on the regime's strengths and other countries' weaknesses, even decadence. Nor was Germany alone in this practice, for the Italian government, helped by victories in the 1934 and 1938 World Cup tournaments as well as the 1936 Olympic football tournament, used sport to impress both domestic and external audiences with the qualities forged through Mussolini's hold over power.

Despite its relatively isolationist course in the world of international sport between the wars, the same was true of the Soviet Union, where sport was integrated into the all-pervasive socialist state in order to meet its varying needs, whether these be 'health, hygiene, defence, patriotism, integration, productivity, international recognition, even nation-building'.[14] As happened in Germany and Italy, this 'functionalised' approach rendered physical culture and sport far too important to be left to non-political bodies, as stated in July 1925, when the Communist party offered its first authoritative pronouncement on the subject:

Physical culture must be considered not only from the standpoint of public health and physical education but should also be utilised as a means to rally the broad working masses around various Party, Government and trade union organisations through which the masses of workers and peasants are drawn into social and political life. . . . Physical culture must play an integral part in the general political and cultural training and education of the masses.[15]

In turn, 'On the Tasks of the Party in Physical Culture', offering 'the definitive statement on the role of sport in Soviet society to which all subsequent policy statements were to refer', paved the way for the eventual establishment of a kind of *de facto* ministry of sport, as expressed after 1930 through the All-Union Physical Culture and Sports Council.[16]

For the Soviet Union, international sporting contacts were severely limited in terms of frequency, countries involved and type of contact.[17] Inevitably, western domination of international sports organisations meant that Soviet non-membership of, say, FIFA (Fédération Internationale de Football Association) and the IOC (International Olympic Committee) was an inevitable consequence of its difficult relationship with the major powers during the period following the 1917 Bolshevik Revolution, even if there existed also a self-imposed exclusion arising from an alleged preference to fortify 'the international workers' front' through alternative 'contacts between worker-athletes of the Soviet Union and other countries'.[18] Despite continuing controversy about, say, the place of competitive sport in a socialist regime, association football survived, even prospered, as the country's leading sport.[19] Non-membership of FIFA, emphasising Soviet isolation from the world of international football, explained the virtual absence of recognised international matches, excepting occasional 'internationals' against Turkey.[20] External footballing contacts largely operated within the framework of Communist internationalism, as evidenced by foreign tours conducted by Soviet factory sides or occasional Soviet visits by teams representing the British Workers' Sports Federation (BWSF) and other left-wing organisations.

The growing politicisation of sport in continental Europe meant that other countries, even Britain, where sporting bodies, like the Football Association (FA), operated as non-governmental organisations, could not remain untouched by this trend, particularly when engaged in the Olympic Games or football internationals against a country like Germany. Pressures to follow suit were reinforced by international sport's contribution to propaganda in a period characterised as one of 'European Civil War' between Communism, Fascism and Liberal Democracy. Propaganda established itself as a 'fact of modern political and diplomatic life' in the 1930s, as acknowledged in May 1938 by Richard Butler, the Parliamentary Under-Secretary of State at the Foreign Office (1938–40): 'Propaganda, as practised by the totalitarian states, is not only part of the new technique of government, but is used as a potent instrument . . . to make known the achievements of the regime both at home and abroad. Mass production of news and opinion accompanies the mass production of armaments. This is a new and important phenomenon in modern life and it would be foolish to underestimate it.'[21] Within this context, British governments were forced to concede the policy potential of a programme of 'national advertisement' or 'projection' – these terms were preferred to the 'unBritish' term 'propaganda' – conducted principally through the Foreign Office news department and, after 1934/5, also the newly established British Council.

The writings of Philip Taylor, among others, have illuminated the nature, development and achievements of British 'cultural propaganda', defined to mean 'the dissemination of British ideals and beliefs in a general rather than specifically political form', in the context of what Lord Lloyd, the British Council's chairman, described as the 'fierce war of ideas' dividing Europe.[22] Confronted by a wide-ranging, escalating, well-funded and state-directed propaganda challenge from overseas, British policy-makers realised that abstention was no longer a profitable policy: 'In the last resort, like can only be met with like, and propaganda with propaganda.'[23] In many respects, Britain became, to quote one member of the British Council, 'an unwilling participant in the cultural struggle' conducted on the broad European, even global, stage.[24] Britain's great power status in the postwar world could not be taken for granted: 'Modern conditions require something more than a mere negative complacency. Sound policy cannot usefully speak without an opportunity to be heard.'[25] British interests and values had to be protected and promoted overseas, foreign policy explained, and misrepresentations corrected in an increasingly tense and divided world. Sir Arthur Willert, one-time head of the Foreign Office news department, pressed the need to confront contemporary realities: 'It is obviously difficult for a school of statesmanship so long inculcated with the idea of the inevitable and automatic supremacy of Great Britain in world affairs to realise how things have changed in that respect and how thoroughly the present precariousness of our position, both political and economic, justifies the growing demand for an adequate system of national advertisement.'[26]

Cultural diplomacy, avoiding the self-defeating consequences of more blatant forms of propaganda, was deemed to provide intangible, but real, benefits for Britain's interests in the wider world. In December 1937 Anthony Eden, the Foreign Secretary (1935–8), and Neville Chamberlain, the Prime Minister (1937–40), echoed Lord Lloyd's remarks about the supportive role performed by cultural propaganda for British diplomacy, trade and influence.[27] Politically, the objective was to project a favourable image of Britain as a 'great nation' espousing liberal democracy, justice and fair play, among other values and principles, as an alternative to rival doctrines propagated by Communist and Fascist governments. Thus, the aim was to persuade other states and peoples to look towards Britain, rather than to, say, Germany, Italy or the Soviet Union. There was also an economic dimension, as stressed in November 1935 by Sir Samuel Hoare, Eden's predecessor at the Foreign Office:

> The commercial arguments in favour of intensifying the work of British cultural propaganda are no less strong than the political arguments. In all the danger of German cultural and commercial penetration, which may be expected to increase as the power and wealth of Germany revive, make it particularly desirable for British cultural propaganda to secure as firm a hold as possible in the minds of the population.[28]

Generally speaking, British cultural propaganda concentrated on more elitist activities, like drama, fine arts, literature and music, as emphasised by Taylor's writings. However, it operated also in a limited manner at the more popular level, most notably through sport, which proved capable of reaching both a large and extremely responsive overseas audience. Football, like other sports 'invented' in Britain, emerged as one way of promoting and disseminating British ideals, values and achievements in the wider world, as argued by Sir Stephen Tallents in *The Projection of England* (1932).[29] 'If we want to know what material England should project, it is wise to ask ourselves what are the English characteristics in which the outside world is most interested. It is an entertaining pursuit – this breaking up of the fame of England into its primary colours. At one end of the spectrum are to be found, I suppose, such national institutions and virtues, as: the monarchy . . . parliamentary institutions . . . Shakespeare, and Dickens.'[30] Tallents' influence upon official thinking, and particularly upon the events resulting in the creation of the British Council, imparts relevance to his coverage of sporting aspects suitable for national projection: 'In sport – a reputation for fair play. At the other end of the spectrum might be found such events as the Derby and the Grand National . . . the Boat Race, Henley, Wimbledon, the Test Matches, and the Cup Final.' Between these two extremes, he identified a 'medley of institutions and excellencies', including 'Oxford and St Andrews' and 'football and foxhunting'. 'Of some such elements as these is the standing raw material of England's esteem in the world composed. There should be added to them all those achievements which by a sudden stroke place England from time to time on the world's screen and win her there a favourable reflection.' References to, say, St Andrews highlighted the common official tendency to conflate 'England' and 'Britain'.

From this perspective, the England football team, like its counterparts from the other home countries, was in a strong position to secure 'a favourable reflection' on the 'world's screen', as depicted by the press, radio and newsreels. Moreover, victories over teams representing countries adjudged responsible for conducting anti-British propaganda, as well as for treating sport in a highly politicised manner, would serve not only to contain the impact of such hostile messages but also enhance British prestige within these states. Of course, there were two sides to the story, for international football was equally capable of conveying negative images to the wider world through defeats and/or unsporting play. In this vein, any sport, like football, capable of contributing to national projection became also an essentially political activity supporting or working against policy-makers, regardless of the British government's *laissez faire* preferences.

During the 1920s, and even more so during the 1930s, Britain could not isolate itself from what was happening in the wider world, where international sport in general and football matches between teams representing the major powers in particular were viewed increasingly through political spectacles. In particular,

British governments were not immune to external pressures arising from the way in which the great importance attached to propaganda compelled countries to prove themselves in all spheres of activity, not excluding sport. Regardless of their pronouncements about the separation of politics and sport, they were unable to prevent any football international from being interpreted by foreign governments, media and opinion as a gauge of national power, values, prestige, influence and vitality.[31]

During the early 1920s, Britain's international sporting contacts operated within an international political framework defined largely by wartime attitudes and peacemaking. Initially, Germany, like other defeated countries, was ostracised in both politico-economic (e.g. exclusion from the League of Nations and major postwar conferences) and sporting terms; thus, it was invited to neither the 1920 nor the 1924 Olympic Games. In addition, during 1919/20 the four British footballing associations decided against playing German teams at either club or international level. Politically and economically, things began to improve for Germany in the mid-1920s through, say, the Dawes Plan (1924), the Treaty of Locarno (1925) and entry to the League (1926). Participation in the 1928 Amsterdam Olympics, signalling Germany's return to the Olympic movement, soon followed these advances. Meanwhile, British football clubs began to visit Germany more regularly in a series of close season tours, thereby providing the foundation for full internationals versus Scotland and England at Berlin in 1929 and 1930 respectively.

Paradoxically, despite football's global spread and status as 'the world game', British football remained a relatively 'insular game'.[32] For James Walvin, this feature derived from a fundamental conservatism prompting an arrogant belief in the continued superiority of the British game, as highlighted by the priority assigned to both the Football League programme and the home international championship. In turn, the resulting unquestioned belief in an inherited national footballing superiority was reinforced by a somewhat myopic attitude regarding advances elsewhere in terms of both the standard of play and attitude towards coaching and tactics.[33] Unsurprisingly, the four British football associations experienced a difficult relationship with FIFA. The British associations, having refused to participate in the founding meeting held at Paris in 1904, joined late (i.e. between 1906 and 1911), withdrew *en bloc* (1920), rejoined (1924), soon left again (1928), but did not return until 1946. Fundamentally, British football's problems with FIFA, though focused on specific issues concerning postwar matches against ex-enemy countries and then the amateur–professional divide, indicated resentment regarding any external interference in 'their game' because of a strong preference to continue doing their own thing in the same old way.

The four British football associations, feeling that they had little to learn from others, let alone to prove, refused repeated invitations to participate in FIFA's World Cup competitions held in 1930, 1934 and 1938. For them, the home international tournament, accounting for the large proportion of their full (as opposed to amateur) international matches (Table 1, Fig. 1), represented the premier global football competition. During the 1920s neither Northern Ireland nor Wales played a single foreign team. Nor did Scotland until a continental tour undertaken in 1929. England proved more adventurous both before and after the First World War, but still played the majority of its fixtures against the home countries. Excepting Northern Ireland, the 1930s witnessed a slightly more outgoing British attitude, even if Wales still crossed the Channel only twice (to France) and continental opposition accounted for less than one-third of Scotland's games. Once again, England led the way, with half its matches arranged now against non-British sides. No full internationals were played against a national team from Latin America, the game's other stronghold, let alone any other part of the world, even if occasional club and representative (e.g. by FA teams) tours were undertaken to Latin America and the empire, with visits to Canada often including the USA.

TABLE 1 THE INSULAR NATURE OF BRITISH FOOTBALL, 1900–1939

	TOTAL GAMES PLAYED	NO. AGAINST NON-BRITISH TEAMS	% AGAINST NON-BRITISH TEAMS
England			
1900–19	54	7	13%
1920–29	49	18	37%
1930–39	56	28	50%
Northern Ireland			
1900–19	46	0	0%
1920–29	30	0	0%
1930–39	29	0	0%
Scotland			
1900–19	45	0	0%
1920–29	34	3	9%
1930–39	41	12	29%
Wales			
1900–19	45	0	0%
1920–29	32	0	0%
1930–39	30	2	7%

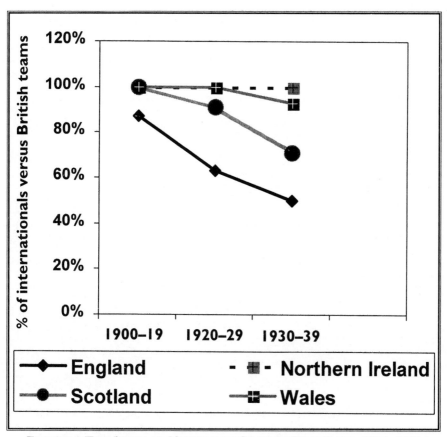

FIGURE 1 THE INSULAR NATURE OF BRITISH FOOTBALL, 1900–1939

During the 1920s the British government's non-interference strategy regarding sport, including the associated stress on the autonomy of the responsible sporting bodies, was qualified nonetheless by a concern to protect and enhance Britain's image abroad. Diplomats, particularly those in the Foreign Office news department, increasingly identified international football as a 'problem' because of the way in which the national image was frequently damaged by poor performances and player misbehaviour on and off the field. Clubs engaged on close season overseas tours proved the main culprits. The problem was less pronounced at national team level, since England, the only home country facing foreign teams until 1928, had a good record in such matches; indeed, its first defeat by continental opposition did not occur until September 1929, when Spain triumphed 4–3 in Madrid (Fig. 2).

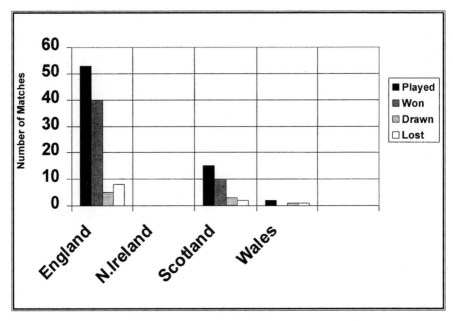

FIGURE 2 RESULTS AGAINST NON-BRITISH TEAMS, 1900–1939

Complaints and representations flowed in to the Foreign and War Offices on a regular basis from British diplomats, consular officials and others (e.g. Lord Kilmarnock, the Inter-Allied Rhineland High Commissioner at Koblenz) stationed throughout Europe. As a result, a strong official reluctance to intervene in sport, or so to appear, was countered increasingly by a belief that something should be done, for the situation seemed to be deteriorating rather than improving: 'the evil is apparently becoming a serious one'.[34] Ideally, football, like any other activity undertaken by Britons abroad, should promote a positive image supportive of British policy and interests in the wider world, especially once it was realised that the outcome of international sporting contests was interpreted in other countries in far more than sporting terms. For example, in November 1928, Thomas Preston, the British consul in Turin, reminded London about the 'enormous interest' and the 'different mental angle' of continental countries towards football: 'It might be argued that sport is sport and that it does not matter so much who wins; this is all very well with matches with our colonial teams, but not so with continental teams.'[35] For Italy, an international football match was far more than a mere game: 'it is an event of international importance'. According to Lord Kilmarnock, the same applied in Germany: 'The significance is wider (than the occupation) and affects British prestige in general. The Germans have always looked up to us as leaders in sport, and now that they themselves are beginning to attach importance to prowess in games, the maintenance of our prestige is perhaps of even more interest than before.'[36] Officials, noting the 'harm of sending inferior teams abroad', appreciated the value of playing to win, for in any sphere of activity – to quote Arthur Yencken – 'it is still true that success is by far the best form of propaganda'.[37] Victories were adjudged important, especially if achieved with style and fair play. The worst scenario was to lose, while performing in an unsporting manner on and off the field.

The Foreign Office, albeit uncertain about the appropriate corrective strategy, believed that it possessed a reasonable understanding of the causes and nature of the problem: 'the basis of the trouble lies in the professionalism, which has overtaken sporting effort in this country'.[38] Moreover, the alleged greed of clubs – they did 'not seem to care so long as they can make money' – was adjudged to render them unreceptive to arguments centred on national prestige. Officials, imbued with the amateur ethic through public school and university, complained also about the 'unsatisfactory composition' and other shortcomings (e.g. tiredness, preference for socialising, tendency towards excessive drinking) characteristic of club teams undertaking close season overseas tours at the end of a long and arduous league season. Nor was the national team neglected, given British football's alleged tendency to place club before country.

Eventually, in December 1928, the Foreign Office, opting for a low-key, clandestine approach, despatched a semi-official letter to the FA apprising it of the high quality of many overseas teams, most notably Italy, alongside the importance of sending abroad only good quality, well-balanced teams.[39] Despite departmental hopes of remaining in the background to avoid charges of political intervention, this move, prompted by Preston's reports about a rumoured Italy–England fixture and the reputed high quality of Italian football, was soon picked up by the media, even if the resulting press flurry, centred on the *Daily Express* and *The Times*, failed to disturb traditional images regarding the fundamental separation of politics and sport in Britain. Indeed, the episode's main consequence was to heighten government sensitivity about being seen to intervene in sporting questions. Meanwhile, the basic problem remained. Throughout the 1930s, both the Foreign Office and the British Council (created 1934–5) received a steady stream of complaints from British diplomatic representatives overseas about the adverse impacts exerted upon national prestige by British footballers on and off the field in overseas matches. One of the more frequent complainants was Sir Howard Kennard, who was particularly incensed by the unsporting display of Chelsea on their 1936 Polish tour.[40] In this regard, one football match was adjudged capable within ninety minutes of undermining, even reversing, the impact of ongoing propaganda activities designed 'to disseminate among foreigners an appreciation of the glories of British culture'.[41]

As happened in 1928, the rare cases of political intervention occurred behind the scenes because of the government's reluctance to draw attention to any bridges built between the allegedly separate worlds of politics and sport. From this perspective, 1930 offered an exceptional case, which not only became the subject of parliamentary and media attention but also went beyond the usual official preoccupation with results and player behaviour. More significantly, given the more sympathetic attitude displayed towards the Soviet Union by the Labour party as compared with its Conservative counterpart, the resulting ban on the entry of a Soviet football team came at the time of a Labour government (1929–31) led by Ramsay MacDonald. Already, in 1927, the preceding Conservative government, led by Stanley Baldwin, had become involved in a proposed Soviet tour by a BWSF football team. Inevitably, exchanges between the Foreign, Home and Passport Offices, pointing to the BWSF's communist affiliations, focused on the tour's propaganda implications.[42] In the event, the Passport Office, advised by the Foreign and Home Offices as well as Scotland Yard, issued passports for everyone, excepting two 'known communists', for a tour which – to quote the late Stephen Jones – 'gave ordinary workers – railwaymen, woodworkers, and furniture workers – as *Young Worker* (27 August 1927) wrote, "the opportunity to see the Workers' State for themselves"'.[43]

However, the British government intervened more decisively and publicly in 1930, when the BWSF requested entry visas for a Soviet factory football team. Despite their departure from FIFA in 1928, the British associations continued to refuse permission for fixtures against foreign teams from non-FIFA members, like the USSR. But the FA lacked jurisdiction over the BWSF, and hence this case was dealt with by the government primarily as a political question, with particular reference to the problematic course of diplomatic relations between the two countries. Anglo-Soviet links, having been disrupted by the 1917 Revolution, were resumed in 1924, only to be broken off again in 1927 until December 1929. Subsequently, British governments strictly controlled bilateral exchanges, and in 1930 entry visas were being issued only for Soviet citizens involved in activities adjudged likely to benefit British trade in the wake of the recently concluded Anglo-Soviet Commercial Agreement (April 1930).[44] The Home Office, which took the lead in visa-related matters, concluded that the tour promised no benefits for either sport or trade: 'the main object of the proposed visit of the Russian football team was propaganda, not sport'.[45] Even worse, departmental fears about serious disorder at match locations were fuelled by the involvement of the British Communist Party as well as by reports of Communist-inspired disturbances during the course of a Soviet team's visit to France.[46] As a result, on 1 May 1930, Samuel Clynes, the Home Secretary, justified the refusal of visas in Parliament in terms of the overt politicisation of Soviet sport alongside the BWSF's affiliation to the sports section of *Communist International*: 'In the absence of any evidence that the object of the proposed tour was for the purpose of genuine sport, I could not see my way to accede to the application.'[47]

This episode provided perhaps the clearest and most public example of government intervention in British football between 1900 and 1939. In effect, MacDonald's Labour government prevented a sporting event on political grounds, even if some might quibble with the description of the proposed tour as a 'sporting event'. The rejection of visa applications enabled the British government to take a strong anti-Communist stand in a relatively risk-free manner, for the Soviet government, though irritated, was unlikely to regard the ban as grounds for a serious rift or conflict, especially as diplomatic relations had been resumed only recently. At the same time, for a country espousing liberal values on the world stage, the British response might be interpreted not only as a gross over-reaction but also as evidence that in Britain 'the state and its governing institutions viewed sport as an expression of political values and allegiances'.[48] If nothing else, the affair, highlighting official sensitivities about the propaganda consequences of any form of Anglo-Soviet contact, emphasised the Soviet Union's status as an international sporting recluse, and, at a time when the Olympic movement and international football were sweeping the world, Philip Noel-Baker, among others, regretted that the Soviet Union remained 'a gap not being filled'.[49] George Sinfield, a Communist active in the BWSF's affairs during the late 1920s, summarised the position clearly and concisely: 'no official British sporting organisation was prepared to touch Russia with a barge-pole'.[50] Subsequently, British governments retained considerable reservations respecting the Soviet Union, as highlighted during 1938 and 1939 by the latter's absence from the Munich Conference (September 1938) and the tardy progress of the Anglo-French-Soviet alliance negotiations in 1939. For British football, these political reservations were reinforced by the Soviet Union's continued non-membership of FIFA.

By contrast, during the 1930s, the improvement of Britain's relations with Germany represented a major, increasingly the major, foreign policy goal, as epitomised by Neville Chamberlain's determined pursuit of appeasement and seeming acceptance of the 'Better Hitler than Stalin' view.[51] Inevitably, England's fixtures with Germany (1930, 1935, 1938), though presented by British governments as purely footballing occasions, possessed a significant international political dimension. Two England–Germany games will be treated as case studies, even if no more than an outline can be provided here.[52] Following the drawn match played at Berlin in 1930 – this represented the first England–Germany game since the First World War – the FA and Deutscher Fussball Bund (DFB) arranged a return fixture for Tottenham Hotspur's ground in December 1935. Of course, by this time Hitler's advent to power had transformed German politics and sport in the manner described by Phipps, among other observers. As a result, the closing months of 1935 witnessed an active debate within Britain about the fixture's merits, particularly given the determined efforts to ban the match and the ongoing campaign for a boycott of the forthcoming 1936 Olympic Games to be hosted by Germany. Protests against the fixture derived from a range of British groups (e.g. trade unions, anti-Fascist and Jewish organisations) opposed to contacts with a regime adjudged responsible for not only the control of German sport but also the persecution of Jews, political parties and trade unions. Fears of disorder arising from the predicted presence of some 10,000 German supporters, or 'Nazis' as they were contemptuously described by the fixture's critics, were compounded by official concern about the manner in which the match promised to provide a useful opportunity for Nazi propaganda.

Regardless of its wishes and electoral concerns (General Election, November 1935), the British government was drawn into the debate and forced to take the issue seriously. Both Sir Samuel Hoare, the Foreign Secretary, and Sir John Simon, the Home Secretary, became involved from an early stage. Regular exchanges, guided by the Metropolitan Police Commissioner and Special Branch representatives, took place between the Foreign and Home Offices at both ministerial and official levels, while the Foreign Office maintained regular contact with the German embassy, the British embassy at Berlin and the FA, where Stanley Rous, the recently appointed Secretary, proved extremely cooperative.

By implication, these exchanges raised the question of government responsibility for sport. Despite a strong desire to avoid appearing to encroach on sporting matters as well as to 'say as little as possible and intervene as little as possible' (Hoare), the government found it impossible to stay on the sidelines.[53] Significantly, the Foreign and Home Offices, seeking to push responsibility on to each other, adopted varying views about the central issue: was it primarily a matter of law and order, falling within the Home Office's jurisdiction, or a Foreign Office question because of its implications for Anglo-German relations? The British government, confronted by the FA and DFB with the fixture as a *fait accompli*, referred to the former's autonomy in arranging fixtures; thus, Simon, reminding the TUC, a major advocate of a ban, that the FA was 'independent of government', asserted that 'Wednesday's match has no political significance whatever . . . it is a game of football, which nobody need attend unless he wishes'.[54] Neither department saw any reason to stop the match, especially as the Home Office's confidence in the Metropolitan Police's ability to preserve order was reinforced by the Foreign Office's reluctance to appear responsible for preventing a meaningful Anglo-German contact, particularly given the German government's responsibility for German sport.

In the event, the match, prompting the largest one-day foreign invasion of Britain to date, passed off without serious incident. There were few arrests, and none of the feared disturbances materialised. More importantly for the British government, England won 3–0 in a sporting game, which compared favourably with the 'Battle of Highbury' one year earlier when England and Italy fought out a bad-tempered affair. Nor was the officially controlled

German media – the match received widespread press and radio coverage in Germany – too displeased by the outcome, given its team's performance against the acknowledged 'masters of the game'. According to *Börsen Zeitung*, 'the German invasion has turned into a complete and gratifying success in every way'.[55]

The next match between the two countries, arranged in November 1937 as part of a two-match home-and-away package, was scheduled for Berlin in May 1938, with the return match being pencilled in for the 1939/40 season! This time the German authorities and media appeared more confident of a good result from a team undefeated in fourteen matches played since late 1936, especially as the *Anschluss* (March 1938) rendered Austrian players – their national side, boasting a recent 2–1 win over England (May 1936), had proved one of the strongest during the 1930s – eligible for selection by the DFB. The fixture, though arranged once again by the FA without consulting the government, was in line with British foreign policy towards Germany. Indeed, in May 1937, Neville Chamberlain's accession as Prime Minister gave renewed impetus to the policy of appeasing Germany, even if irritation at Hitler's methods in annexing Austria (March 1938), the resulting German threat to Czechoslovakia, and the ever-closer Axis relationship prompted a continuing reappraisal of British policy. Of course, Chamberlain's continued search for improved Anglo-German relations, in conjunction with a strong reluctance to antagonise Hitler, meant that the British government saw no reason to stop the game. On the contrary, there seemed every reason to allow the match to go ahead as a highly visible and meaningful bilateral contact.

Contrary to public images of non-interference, the Chamberlain government did intervene behind the scenes in order to make the best use of the opportunity's propaganda potential. Vansittart, whose new post as Chief Diplomatic Adviser included the coordination of British publicity abroad, pressed the 'great importance' of the match on the FA. Informal conversations, reinforced by a 'semi-official' letter, 'instructed' the FA that 'it is really important for our prestige that the British team should put up a really first class performance. I hope that every possible effort will be made to ensure this.'[56] In the event, the FA, albeit arranging no special pre-tour training on the German model (German players received a fortnight's training in the Black Forest), reassured the Foreign Office that 'every member of the team will do his utmost to uphold the prestige of his country'.[57]

As a result, upon their arrival in Berlin, players were made fully aware of the match's extra-footballing importance by the officials in charge of the England tour party. More controversially, they were instructed to give the Nazi salute while the German national anthem was being played prior to kick-off. This controversial decision, guided by Henderson's desire to secure the sympathy of the crowd and government, was influenced also by Rous's recall of Hitler's reputed annoyance at the apparent failure of the British team to acknowledge his presence at the opening ceremony of the 1936 Berlin Olympics.[58] Hitler, having just returned from a state visit to Rome, was absent, but the match was watched by Joseph Goebbels (Minister for Propaganda), Rudolf Hess (Deputy Führer), Joachim von Ribbentrop (Foreign Minister), Tschammer und Osten and Henderson, among others. They witnessed a very impressive England performance. England, having led 4–2 at the break, finished with a stunning 6–3 win. Henderson, who expressed his satisfaction personally to the team for having played 'for England', informed the Foreign Office that the result, in conjunction with the players' sportsmanship and performance of the Nazi salute, 'undoubtedly revived in Germany British sporting prestige'.[59] He anticipated that the promise of future cordial relations would extend beyond sport. England played two more games – a defeat in Switzerland was followed by victory in France – but the German match remained the most significant tour fixture in both the political and footballing senses. Indeed, in June 1938, the FA, responding to favourable Foreign Office feedback, recorded its 'special appreciation' of the players' performance and behaviour in Berlin. Each player, having received the usual match fees of £8 per international, received a special gift comprising a canteen of cutlery![60]

In the event, any foreign policy benefits were soon qualified by the 'May crisis' (20–21 May 1938), which erupted during the following weekend while the England team continued its tour in Switzerland. But Chamberlain persisted in his search for detente with Germany, as evidenced by the Munich agreement concluded in September 1938. Significantly, one of the numerous post-Munich congratulatory messages received by the prime minister derived from the FA. But the international situation continued to deteriorate, so that by the 1939/40 season, when the next England–Germany match was scheduled, Anglo-German rivalry had already been transferred to the battlefield. War delayed the return match until 1954, when paradoxically Germany, or rather the Federal Republic of Germany (West Germany), came to Wembley as recently crowned World Cup champions. Stanley Matthews, having played in both the 1935 and 1938 matches, was the only player involved in all three games. England won again (3–1), but subsequently, excepting the 1966 World Cup, Germany has possessed a superior international, particularly World Cup, record. Meanwhile, Hitler's legacy lives on, as evidenced in 1994 when the Germany–England game scheduled to be played on what transpired to be his birthday (20 April) was cancelled for fear of its exploitation for propaganda purposes by right-wing and other groups.

During the interwar period, international football took place in a competitive nationalistic context in which several governments interpreted sport as extending their diplomatic repertoire, such as in terms of fostering bilateral relations, creating goodwill, indicating disapproval of other regimes or demonstrating a favourable national image *vis-à-vis* other countries. In Britain, where it was viewed traditionally as largely peripheral to international politics, there was never any conscious decision to make international sport a tool of foreign policy. Instead, the government's position developed pragmatically within the overall policy framework, as individual events raised issues perceived as too important to be left to sporting bodies. Even so, there emerged no monolithic government position, given both the lack of any clear departmental responsibility for sport and the varying positions assumed by individual departments towards any event.

Case studies based on the 1930 Soviet tour proposal and the 1935 and 1938 England–Germany internationals qualify the usual impression cultivated and publicised by successive governments that, in Britain at least, sport and politics have always been independent of each other. Admittedly, the scale of political intervention therein between the wars was of a far lesser order than in, say, Germany, Italy or the USSR, but even a decision not to intervene to stop an international fixture, as happened in 1935, was made primarily on political grounds. Despite carefully cultivated *laissez faire* images, British governments, feeling unable to stand aside, adopted an interventionist strategy from time to time, most notably to fine-tune the process through the exertion of pressure in support of good results and behaviour or to undertake damage limitation exercises. As a result, British football, reaching a mass audience even in countries difficult to penetrate by other forms of propaganda, became an important part of the government's cultural propaganda strategy in terms of both projecting a favourable image of Britain as a great nation characterised by an ability to win well in a fair and sporting manner and countering the detrimental effects of foreign propaganda (Fig. 2).

Writing about British propaganda in the First World War, Andrew Steed briefly considered the postwar situation: 'The propagandists were closed down, and through the interwar years little was done to counter the anti-liberal propaganda spread by the dictators. The result of this was that when Britain went to war in 1939, a new MoI had to relearn the principles of managing official propaganda that had already been discovered by an earlier generation.'[61] Despite this somewhat sweeping assertion, the writings of Philip Taylor and others have established that the policy contribution of British cultural propaganda between the wars should not be underestimated. Nor should the propaganda role of international sport be overlooked, even if it proves difficult, if not impossible, to assess accurately the precise impact of football or any other form of propaganda. In their recent survey of British foreign policy past, present and future, Laurence Martin and John Garnett, having acknowledged cultural diplomacy's depiction as 'soft power' as compared with the 'hard power' embodied in military and economic strength, offered a sound appraisal of its contribution: 'Although it is impossible to put a value on cultural diplomacy or to pinpoint specific examples of instances where it has made a difference, common sense suggests that it is valuable.'[62]

Within this context, this chapter has sought to illuminate the way in which international sport represents a missing dimension in the historiography of British foreign relations between the wars. Respecting, for instance, Anglo-German relations, international football constituted a contributory factor at both the official and popular levels to the policy of appeasement. For a British government, anxious to maintain good relations with Germany and to avoid antagonising Hitler by blatant propaganda (nor was the British Council allowed to operate in Germany), a high-profile football match offered a low-cost, seemingly apolitical, way of pushing British interests in Germany through the projection of positive images of footballing hegemony and fair play. Moreover, it bypassed the usual obstacles to British propaganda therein, and provided a means of scoring diplomatic points as well as goals at Germany's expense.

Notes

I am grateful to the Hon. Francis Noel-Baker and the Masters and Fellows of Trinity College, Cambridge, for permission to quote from the papers of Lord Noel-Baker and Lord Butler respectively.

1   R. Tracey, *Today* programme, BBC, Radio Four, 23 September 1986.

2   Tony Mason, *Passion of the People? Football in South America* (London, Verso, 1995), p. ix.

3   David Bull, 'Politicians as Football Fans – Incredible!', in D. Bull and A. Campbell (eds), *Football and the Common People* (Sheffield, Juma, 1994), p. 7.

4   Tony Blair, 'Stan's my man', *New Statesman and Society* (20/01/1995), 9.

5   Quoted, *Sunday Times* (18/09/1994).

6   Christopher Andrew, '1883 Cup Final: "Patricians" v. "Plebeians"', *History Today*, 33 (1983), 21.

7   Peter J. Beck, 'England versus Germany, 1938', *History Today*, 32 (June 1982), 29–34; Peter J. Beck, 'To Play or Not to Play?: That is the Anglo-Argentine Question', *Contemporary Review*, 245 (1984), 70–4; Dave Russell, *Football and the English: A Social History of Association Football in England, 1863–1995* (Preston, Carnegie, 1997), pp. 122–3; Peter J. Beck, *Scoring for Britain: International Football and International Politics, 1900–1939* (London, Frank Cass, 1999), pp. 10–13, 33–6.

8   Peter Clarke, *Hope and Glory: Britain, 1900–1990* (London, Allen Lane, 1996), p. 53; George Orwell, 'The Sporting Spirit', *Tribune* (14/12/1945).

9   John Major, *Sport: Raising the Game*, foreword (London, Dept. of National Heritage, 1995), p. 2; *Daily Telegraph* (15/07/1995).

10   Eric Hobsbawm, *Nations and Nationalism Since 1780: Programme, Myth, Reality* (Cambridge, University Press, 1990), p. 143. For a more critical perspective on this linkage, see Grant Jarvie, 'Giving the Game Away', *Sports Historian*, 17 (1997), 212; Martin Polley, *Moving the Goalposts: A History of Sport and Society since 1945* (London, Routledge, 1998), pp. 35–41.

11   Public Record Office (hereafter PRO), Sir Eric Phipps to S. Hoare, 16/12/1935, FO371/18884, C8362/7175/18.

12   PRO, minute, R. Vansittart, 31 Dec. 1935, FO371/18884, C8362/7175/18.

13   Quoted, Ivan Sharpe, *Forty Years of Football* (London, Hutchinson, 1952), p. 73.

14   Samuel S. Shipman, 'Sports in the Soviet Union', *Current History*, XLVII (1937), 81; James

Riordan, *Soviet Sport: Background to the Olympics* (Oxford, Blackwell, 1980), pp. 3–4; Henry W. Morton, *Soviet Sport* (New York, Collier, 1963), pp. 17–18.

15   James Riordan, 'The USSR', in J. Riordan (ed.), *Sport under Communism: The USSR, Czechoslovakia, the GDR, Cuba* (London, Hurst, 1978), p. 18; Riordan, *Soviet Sport*, pp. 30–3, 42; Morton, *Soviet Sport*, pp. 20, 22; John N. Washburn, 'Sport as a Soviet Tool', *Foreign Affairs*, 34 (1956), 496; James Riordan, 'Worker Sport Within a Worker State: the Soviet Union', in A. Krüger and J. Riordan (eds), *The Story of Worker Sport* (Leeds, Human Kinetics, 1996), pp. 46–64.

16   Riordan, *The USSR*, p. 21.

17   Riordan, *Soviet Sport*, p. 115; Victor Peppard and James Riordan, *Playing Politics: Soviet Sport Diplomacy to 1992* (Greenwood, Conn., JAI Press, 1993), pp. 27–43.

18   Riordan, *The USSR*, p. 21; Riordan, *Worker Sport*, pp. 62–3.

19   Riordan, *Soviet Sport*, pp. 113–18.

20   Peppard and Riordan, *Playing Politics*, pp. 38–40, 100–1.

21   Library, Trinity College, Cambridge University, Lord Butler of Saffron Walden Papers (RAB), speech by Richard Butler, 23 May 1938, RAB K4/8; Sir Arthur Willert, 'National Advertisement', *The Fortnightly* (January 1939), 7; Philip Taylor, *The Projection of Britain: British Overseas Publicity and Propaganda, 1914–1939* (Cambridge University Press, 1981), p. 292.

22   Lord Lloyd, chairman of British Council, to A. Eden, 22 December 1937, quoted Taylor, *Projection of Britain*, p. 168.

23   Taylor, *Projection of Britain*, p. 84; PRO, memorandum, K. Johnstone, 10 Oct. 1936, BW2/85; Sterling Memorial Library, Yale University, minute, Willert, 2 Jan. 1934, Sir Arthur Willert papers (MG), MG 720/14/56.

24   PRO, memorandum, K. Johnstone, 10/10/1936, BW2/85.

25   PRO, memorandum, A. Yencken, 17/09/1927, FO395/423/P995.

26   Willert, *National Advertisement*, pp. 3–4.

27   Eden to Lloyd, 22/12/1937, quoted Taylor, *Projection of Britain*, p. 168.

28   PRO, Hoare to Kennard, 8 Nov. 1935, FO395/529, P3900/267/150.

29   Sir Stephen Tallents, *The Projection of England* (London, Faber, 1932). See also, PRO, 'The Projection of Britain', 1946, encl. FO953/1216/P1011.

30   Tallents, *Projection of England*, pp. 14–15, 40.

31   See *Evening Standard* (29/11/1935).

32   James Walvin, *The People's Game: A Social History of British Football* (Edinburgh, Mainstream, 1994 revised edn), pp. 118–43.

33   Author's interview with Sir Stanley Rous, 28 March 1980.

34   PRO, minute, R. Kenney, 14/07/1927, FO395/423, P689/689/150.

35   PRO, Thomas Preston, Turin, to Consular dept., 30/11/1928, FO370/289, L7516/7516/405.

36   PRO Lord Kilmarnock to War Office, 6/07/1927, FO395/423, P689/689/150.

37   PRO, minute, C.J. Norton, 2/01/1929, FO395/434, P4/4/150; memorandum, A. Yencken, 17/09/1927, FO395/423, P995/993/150.

38   PRO, minute, L. Collier, 21/07/1927, FO395/423, P689/689/150.

39   PRO, S. Gaselee to F. Wall, FA, 7/12/1928, FO370/289, L7516/7516/405.

40 PRO, Sir Howard Kennard, British ambassador in Warsaw, to Leeper, 26/05/1936, FO371/20642, W5343/542/50.

41 PRO, C. Bridge, British Council, to R. Leeper, 12/07/1938, FO395/568, P2241/28/150.

42 PRO, minute, Gascoigne, 8/08/1927, FO371/12606/N3771.

43 Stephen Jones, 'The British Workers' Sports Federation: 1923–1935', in A. Krüger and J. Riordan (eds), *The Story of Worker Sport* (Leeds, Human Kinetics, 1996), p. 105.

44 PRO, minute, F. Newsam, 3/11/1935, HO45/16425/688144; Hansard (Commons), 5th. series CCXXXVIII, 349–50, 1/05/1930.

45 PRO, minute, Newsam, 3/11/1935, HO45/16425/688144.

46 PRO, minute, L. Baggalley, 28/04/1930, FO371/14883/N2923.

47 Hansard (Commons), 5th. series CCXXXVIII, 349–50, 1/05/1930.

48 Stephen G. Jones, 'State Intervention in Sport and Leisure in Britain Between the Wars', *Journal of Contemporary History*, 22 (1987), 172.

49 Cambridge University, Churchill Archives Centre, Churchill College, extracts from SCR (probably LSE Senior Common Room) talk by Noel-Baker, 'Russia and Sport', 12/02/1928, pp. 1, 8, Lord Noel-Baker (NBKR) papers, NBKR 8/7/2. The file has only an incomplete copy.

50 George Sinfield, 'When our British Players Gave the Russians a Shock', *Daily Worker* (13/11/1954).

51 See R.A.C. Parker, *Chamberlain and Appeasement: British Policy and the Coming of the Second World War* (Macmillan, London, 1993); John W. Young, *Britain and the World in the Twentieth Century* (London, Arnold, 1997), pp. 114–27.

52 Beck, *Scoring for Britain*, pp. 1–10, 173–205; Hans Joachim Teichler, *Internationale Sportpolitik im Dritten Reich* (Schorndorf, Hofmann, 1991), pp. 154–7, 186.

53 PRO, minute, S. Hoare, 24/11/1935, FO371/18884, C7757/7175/18.

54 PRO, J. Simon to Citrine, 29/11/1935, FO371/18884, C7975/7175/18.

55 *Börsen Zeitung* (7/12/1935).

56 PRO, Vansittart to Rous, 6/05/1938, FO395/568, P1718/28/150.

57 PRO, Rous to Vansittart, 10/05/1938, FO395/568, P1718/28/150.

58 Author's interview with Sir Stanley Rous, 28/03/1980.

59 PRO, N. Henderson to Foreign Office, 9/06/1938 and Consul-General, Berlin, to Henderson, n/d (May 1938), FO395/568, P2054/28/150; author's interview with Rous, 28/03/1980.

60 Library, Football Association, minutes of International Selection Committee, 24/06/1938. At this time, £12 was the maximum weekly wage of players.

61 Andrew Steed, 'British Propaganda in the First World War', in I. Stewart and S.L. Carruthers (eds), *War, Culture and the Media: Representations of the Military in 20th Century Britain* (Trowbridge, Flicks Books, 1996), p. 36.

62 Laurence Martin and John Garnett, *British Foreign Policy: Challenges and Choices for the 21st Century* (London, Royal Institute of International Affairs/Pinter, 1997), pp. 46–7.

16

THE NOVEL AS PROPAGANDA: REVISITING THE DEBATE[1]

Graham Barnfield

P*artisan Review* editor Philip Rahv's essay, 'Proletarian Literature: A Political Autopsy', appeared in 1939. It welcomed the demise of 'the literature of a party disguised as the literature of a class'.[2] Subsequently, this phrase was widely cited to show that the 'proletarian novels' of 1930s America existed solely to fulfil the propaganda objectives of the US Communist Party (CPUSA) and, by implication, of the Soviet Union itself. During the Cold War this interpretation proved highly influential.

Discussing Communist 'propaganda' in the context of 1930s America invites confusion. The Bolsheviks originally used the term to denote the patient explanation of a complex programme to a militant yet politically sophisticated minority. Agitation, on the other hand, could convey a platform of immediate, often minimal demands to a mass audience.[3] The term itself was initially neutral in its connotations, regardless of whether or not one agreed with the content of the propaganda.[4] Although Lenin once formulated an emergency resolution on the post-1917 relationship between the People's Commissariat of Education and the Proletcult Congress,[5] he did not advocate propagandising in the realm of aesthetic production (unlike the Proletcult, a short-lived Soviet artists' group).

Proletcult inspired a handful of US writers; prominent among them was Michael Gold. Gold's interpretation of propagandist activity – like that of the CPUSA more broadly – had far more in common with the methods of agitation. Such confusion among American Communists was closely related to broad political developments, outlined in the schema below:

- Under Stalin, the remains of Lenin's organisation became the privileged administrators of the Soviet state (the *nomenklatura*). Dogma and repression ensued, both within the international Communist movement and cultural policy alike.[6]
- The Comintern's 'Third Period' – here summarised as its instructing national sections to prepare for imminent revolution, regardless of the specific conditions they operated in – obliterated Lenin's insistence on a careful distinction between propaganda and agitation.[7]

- In Russia, aesthetic activity was subject to political supervision.[8] Once characterised by the rivalries between the Proletcult and other organisations, cultural policy ossified into rigid controls and an official policy of Socialist Realism.
- Given the experiences of Fascist and Stalinist terror, the term 'propaganda' itself was to acquire increasingly sinister connotations in the 1940s, even further removed from its use by the Bolsheviks to mean selective persuasion.

Against this backdrop, it was asserted that a parallel process had afflicted the United States in the same period. Hence this chapter's key concern: did the CPUSA attempt to transform the novel into 'propaganda' in the 1930s, as is widely alleged? More specifically, how can we disentangle the idea of the propaganda novel in its interwar context from the interpretation prevalent in later years?

The first part of my investigation retraces the 'propaganda' narrative, while demonstrating its contemporary forms. The second considers the organisations which formed the backbone of the 1930s literary left. The third examines the notion of 'the party line in literature', focusing on Michael Gold, the individual most frequently blamed for American fiction's darkest days. The final part discusses the contribution of literary criticism in the Communist press to the perception of a propaganda campaign in literary and popular fiction.

Until recently, a consensus existed that the proletarian novel, 'the Communist Party's favoured term for the radical novel in the early Depression',[9] was the primary form of left-wing literary activity in 1930s America. In part, this was a consequence of the way most if not all such writing was recast as 'propaganda' in the postwar period. What precisely constituted a proletarian novel was widely debated. A useful summary appeared in the influential 1935 anthology *Proletarian Literature in the United States*, championing the 'emergence of a galaxy of young novelists [who have discovered] that art is more than a parlour game to amuse soulful parasites, that the American workers, farmers, and professionals are the true nation, and that the only major theme of our time is the fate of these people'.[10] More specific generic elements were also apparent, like the strike novel and political poetry, both written with an agitational tone. Titles like *Parched Earth, Strike!* and *The Disinherited* indicate the prevalent themes.

At a societal level, a mass working-class readership seemed a distant hope. The proletarian novel's disproportionate impact was among book reviewers, literary critics and the readers of liberal publications like *Nation* and *New Republic*. The genre's almost uniformly low sales did little to prevent this influence. Poor sales were to some extent attributable to the Depression rather than the novels themselves, while low circulation was also slightly offset by library borrowing. The 'little magazines' of the early 1930s went some way to providing an outlet for writers from a working-class background, given the suitability of the poem and short story form for magazines and other more ephemeral publications. On balance, the true extent of a popular readership for proletarian literature was certainly greater than sales figures would suggest.

Regardless of these nuances of content and circulation, such writing has been largely represented as a homogeneous bloc produced according to Soviet demands. Proletcult had, however, virtually disappeared off the Soviet scene by the time the *New Masses* magazine was advocating it in the USA. As James Murphy shows, the Russian cultural groups who sought to create from scratch a culture made by workers, for workers or about workers – or some combination of the three – were sidelined prior to the 'proletarian' infatuation taking off in America.[11] US proletcult stemmed from its advocacy by CPUSA-affiliated critics like Michael Gold, Edwin Seaver, Joshua Kunitz and V.J. Jerome, who were inspired by events in Russia, such as the Soviet Writers Congress at Kharkov. It is hard to quantify the extent to which Soviet trends had a specifically literary impact. Wall newspapers and the collective novel were a failure in America, with Gold finding the latter 'too tough' to write.[12] Socialist realism, the Soviet successor to proletcult, was well received in the pages of the *New Masses*,[13] but there was no attempt to promote or anthologise a US equivalent.

Textual analysis of the American fiction labelled as 'proletarian literature' also suggests continuity with earlier naturalistic writing, notably that of Jack London and Upton Sinclair. Such connections with the radical past were further reinforced by the subject matter of a number of pivotal 1930s radical novels, such as *Jews Without Money* and *Call It Sleep*, which consisted of immigrant experiences drawn from the first two decades of the twentieth century. In terms of style, there is also much to highlight commonalities at the level of narrative and generic conventions with the hard-boiled writing of magazines like *Black Mask*. Thus, far from following Soviet orders, US proletarian writers developed their own, sometimes derivative genre, which some then theorised as a contribution to a wider political project. To some extent this process was codified in the anthology *Proletarian Literature in the United States*.[14]

In the 1990s, revisionist dissent from Cold War orthodoxy has become the norm in scholarly literature, stressing the 'history from below' of left-wing authors. In this vein, Barbara Foley's *Radical Representations* presents a devastating challenge to the idea that the novel was used as propaganda by the CPUSA in the 1930s. Her comprehensive account of the proletarian fiction movement debunks the misrepresentation that has dogged it almost since its inception. Foley's concerns include the 'legacy of anti-communism', which informed a largely hostile reconstruction of 'the Thirties', close readings of dozens of actual proletarian novels (a process absent from most Cold War accounts and sadly, for reasons of space, from the present essay), and a consideration of the political worldview that informed such writing. She demonstrates that writers were animated by a commitment to social justice and curious as to their capacity to inspire others, while maintaining a theory that was 'almost exclusively cognitive and reflectionist rather than agitational and hortatory.'[15] Moreover, unlike Soviet socialist realists, US writers never allowed their chosen genre to be overshadowed by set topoi, which made literature adhere to precise rhetorical standards – regardless of reality – in order to be accepted as legitimate.[16] Foley's treatment of the specific debate over whether literature could function as propaganda shows that almost every *New Masses* critic of any note opposed an instrumentalist conception of the novel's role.[17]

If Foley is correct, then surely no further comment is necessary: there was no party line that said novels should be used propagandistically. Furthermore, a wide range of more practical tools were at hand, including newspapers like the *Daily Worker*, pamphlets, handbills and, to a lesser extent, agit prop theatre. So why return to this issue? In part because monographs like Foley's seem to occupy a separate world from that in which the 'novel as propaganda' narrative is perpetuated. Although logically undermined by revisionist accounts, this myth is nevertheless a perennial feature of memoirs, textbooks and journalistic shorthand. In effect, the uncommunicative character of these divergent discourses allows Rahv's caricature to live on, regardless of the archival evidence.[18]

The critics taking a lead from Rahv often draw on editorial statements in the Communist press to support their arguments, e.g. *New Masses* editor Joseph Freeman, who declared that 'the Communist says frankly: art, an instrument in the class struggle, must be developed by the proletariat as one of its weapons'.[19] Many have concluded from this, and the many like-minded quotations that litter the archives, that the party sought to determine the content of radical writing, transforming it into propaganda. Indeed, Freeman himself sensed that this charge was gaining ground, claiming, 'if you were to take a worker gifted with a creative imagination and ask him to set down his experience honestly, it would be an experience so remote from that of the bourgeois that the Man in White would, as usual, raise the cry of "propaganda"'.[20] Such comments follow a declaration that 'no party resolution, no government decree can produce art, or transform an agitator into a poet. A party card does not automatically endow a Communist with artistic genius.' Freeman confronted the idea that writers could be compelled to propagandise and produce art of quality, but his stance appears absent from subsequent literary histories.

Perceptions of the propagandist subversion of the novel are only partially rooted in the works themselves. They were also informed by the accounts written in later years. A stream of memoirs[21] and obituaries has assisted a selective amnesia, which makes 'the Thirties' into a historical construct centred on the literary left and at pains to avoid the issue of economic slump. This process started to take shape in works of criticism written while the proletarian controversy was still fresh. For instance, Alfred Kazin's *On Native Grounds* – a measured consideration of the development of modern American letters – loses perspective on the question of 'the Thirties'. Discussing 'the more fashionable kind of hard-boiled writing', he claims that 'the left-wing naturalist surrendered his craft to what seemed ultimate considerations beyond literature. Literature, in the Communist jargon, was a "front" and each militant writer a guerrilla fighting in his own way for a common purpose.'[22]

It is understandable that Kazin – a participant in the 'literary class war' himself – would be partisan, but it is unclear why a contemporary student textbook should adopt the same approach. Thus, *From Puritanism to Postmodernism* shows some objectivity when dealing with individual Communist authors like Michael Gold and Henry Roth, before later tarring them with the brush reserved for left-wing critics. Writing of V.F. Calverton and Granville Hicks, Richard Ruland and Malcolm Bradbury locate 'the sterility of their approach' in a 'limited conception of what is real', before making an imaginative leap unsupported by evidence and claiming that 'the Marxist world of the 1930s' was 'a world preoccupied solely with the play of economic forces; the *only* place for literature in such a world was as a weapon in class warfare'.[23] In another introductory work Gold is quoted urging writers to '"go left", become workers identified with the workers, experience and record and radicalise the proletarian world which provided a writer with "all the primitive material he needs"'.[24] Aside from a synopsis of his novel *Jews Without Money* (1930), there is little to balance this one-dimensional portrait which conflates Gold as agitator with Gold as critic and cultural practitioner. In both examples a part is substituted for the whole, hence the inflation of the two critics into 'the Marxist world of the 1930s'.

In a similar vein, another textbook presents 'the Red Decade: the 1930s' as a time when:

> Mike Gold, who went to the Kharkov in the USSR for the second Congress of Revolutionary Writers, brought back answers: respectively, a more determinedly proletarian art that viewed the world from the worker's perspective, and an artist who subordinated aesthetic objectives to political ones.[25]

Given the role that these texts play – as introductory guides for a general readership – it is clear that the view of literature as propaganda can persist despite the increasing volume of revisionist scholarship.[26] The persistence of these unbalanced formulations in publications intended for a non-specialist audience helps to maintain the purchase of what is, in effect, the hangover of Cold War stereotypes,[27] which insist that novels stressing revolutionary themes were a product of political expediency alone.

In contrast to the mainstream orthodoxy, I would contend that the coincidence of a *literature* of social crisis with a *genuine* social crisis prompted the participation of writers, among others, in organisations that proposed radical solutions to the Depression. Nationally, these ranged from the John Reed Club (Third Period) to the League of American Writers (Popular Front). Instrumentalist views of the incendiary power of literature contributed little to this process.[28] Rather, the 1930s saw a significant body of writers and artists working together in support of common causes. Proletarian literature accompanied these developments, but not sufficiently so as to warrant the central role it is accorded in accounts that developed during the post-1945 period.

Literature with formal origins in the American realist tradition and in mass-produced popular narratives has been systematically misrepresented as an attempt to instigate revolt and/or to create a Communist working-class culture from scratch, usually under Moscow's auspices. Why? Some suggest the limited availability of primary sources, to the extent that 'the caricature of American literature in the thirties presented by most American literary history since Daniel Aaron's *Writers on the Left* could not have remained so long unquestioned had not most of the material it travesties been virtually unavailable for over forty years'.[29] Since this observation was made (in 1985), numerous primary texts have reappeared in print, along with extensive biographies of their authors. Yet the stereotype remains intact.

ORGANISING WRITERS

The assertion that committed authors worked according to a party line can also be tested by considering the organisations that sought to recruit and influence writers. CPUSA officials did attempt to orchestrate campaigns among American writers in the 1930s. However, claims that the key battles were fought over the aesthetics of the novel evade any empirical analysis of the actual conduct of those campaigns. Such analysis tends to suggest that negative perceptions of the 'propaganda novel' were rooted in real conditions, namely CP-controlled writers' organisations, and in the vicious political struggles played out in literary milieux, particularly that against 'Trotskyism'. These ultimately demoralising experiences were sutured together by the often vitriolic literary criticism practised in the pages of the *New Masses*. Taken collectively, these factors constitute the basis for claims that party activity forced proletarian writers to produce propaganda.

Complaints about 'propaganda novels' relate closely to the organisations which novelists were encouraged to join, and to the scores of declarations and public statements that appeared in the political press. The numerous informal networks of fellow travellers – allegedly given to blacklists, nepotism and 'literary gangsterism' – have made cultural organisations a central theme in narrating 'the Thirties' as the age of the propaganda novel. Hence these claims, taken from Malcolm Cowley's memoirs:

The new doctrine called proletcult, which is the telescoped Russian term for proletarian culture, gave them a new vocabulary for attacking established writers. If they lived as respectable citizens, they were 'rotten with bourgeois hypocrisy.' If they flirted at cocktail parties, it was because they 'aped the moral decay of the owning classes.' If they wrote for magazines which tried to earn a profit, they became the 'lackeys and running dogs of capitalism.' If they remained liberals, they were beneath a revolutionist's contempt.[30]

This simplistic account captures some of the phraseology of the period, but its main merit is in reminding us, with reference to 'cocktail parties', of the importance of the milieux which in which writers socialised. Contra Cowley, writers were not animated by moral indignation alone: their political interventions were more often than not underpinned by vibrant, campaigning organisations. In turn, such organisations were part of a wider political subculture, in which authors were far from being the sole participants.[31] Hence my central contention: Stalinist politics did not become entwined with cultural production through a 'political line' imposed on novels, poetry, drama and literary criticism, but in certain writers' negative experiences of a perpetually campaigning peer group. (Many were repelled by the way that the process appeared to culminate in apologies for the Nazi–Soviet Pact, recasting previous activities in a different light.) This pattern exercised a constitutive influence in US Cold War culture, by forming a 'liberal narrative' which relates the dreary tale of 'what happened in the Thirties'.[32]

In opposition to this narrative, Michael Denning has theorised the cultural left of the Depression era and war years – the 'Age of the CIO' – as a social movement with its own particular cultural formation(s). Drawing upon Raymond Williams, Denning interrogates the Cultural Front by emphasising its 'structures of feeling'.[33] Williams developed this category in order to argue that the definitive character of a social formation could be grasped through an examination of routine, everyday practices. Such occurrences were not isolated, but part of an organised and complex whole, shaping belief within an overall framework of class relations.[34] This analysis was later modified to encompass 'lived experience' and past and future aspirations.[35] Accordingly, the Cultural Front is characterised by unionised, second-generation immigrants participating both in social democratic politics and in the popular culture of swing music and Hollywood film, and – significantly – sympathetic to proletarian narrative fictions (in Denning's terminology, the 'ghetto pastoral').

Strategically, this working-class audience was a key constituency in which propaganda campaigns could be conducted. The novel was, however, rarely regarded as the vehicle for such struggles. When the distinct activities of propaganda and literary fiction appeared to overlap, it was in *Daily Worker* book reviews (and, to a lesser extent, in a sprinkling of those in middlebrow magazines like the *Nation* and *New Republic*). Commentators have interpreted reviewers as imposing a political 'line' in literature, when it would be more accurate to say that they attempted to hammer out an aesthetic vision. Such perceptions were certainly reinforced at a rhetorical level, especially given the combative style of literary criticism in the *New Masses*. Rhetoric alone, however, was not sufficient to generate the disillusionment of the 'liberal narrative' that characterised many a postwar literary history: this arose from the cumulative experience of attempts to organise writers as a distinctive social group.

Social milieu also influenced the reception of the novels. Those not directly involved in writing the fiction were often aware of the basic tenets of wider literary debates. Although sales of proletarian novels were almost uniformly low, averaging 2,000 to 3,000 copies, this is an unfair reflection of the influence of such writing during the Depression. Social documentary and egalitarian themes entered the mainstream, competing with (and sometimes complementing) an emphasis on nostalgia and Americana.[36] At a distance, readers of *New Masses*, the *Nation* and the *New Republic* followed the controversy over proletarian narratives. These 'minor' members of the intelligentsia were not writing proletarian novels, nor reviewing them, nor even necessarily reading them, but instead having their perceptions of 'communist culture' shaped by the short stories, book reviews and even advertising that appeared in 'Cultural Front' publications.

As Cary Nelson has argued, journals and little magazines contributed to an 'interactive culture', in which processes such as reading for pleasure connected specific texts to a broader ideological totality.[37] The artwork in a periodical could contribute to the overall effect of the piece it accompanied, while essays and book reviews all informed participants in the 'Cultural Front' of the broad trends unfolding in their milieu. Short stories kept this readership up to speed with the work of various writers and helped to generalise knowledge of *proletcult*. A relatively significant section of the intelligentsia experienced the literary and campaigning faces of the CPUSA simultaneously. One can start to explain the paradox of the 'propaganda novel' by considering the conditions which constituted the body of 'inside' knowledge from which Cold War-era stereotypes could emerge.

Whether an individual was establishing a career in the cultural industries or simply reading radical periodicals, the continuity between such activities – the sense of belonging to a movement – was enhanced by the overlap of cultural and political concerns. In turn, the organisations with which cultural practitioners were associated anchored these arrangements. Organisational affiliations provide the key to explaining the widespread perception that the 'propaganda novel' originated in this febrile atmosphere. Negative personal and political experiences *à la* Malcolm Cowley were often recast as a problem of organisations imposing their will on cultural practitioners and destroying creative autonomy in the process. The key question was not the political content of a work, but the political conduct of a writer.

At the level of manifestos and other campaigning ephemera, it is clear that a sensibility existed which saw cultural production as playing a role in social transformation. Widespread collaboration between intellectuals and the CPUSA originated in prisoners' defence campaigns, well-known examples of which include the International Labor Defense (founded 1925 and 'openly dominated' by the CP until 1927)[38] and the Sacco–Vanzetti campaign. Such activity established a moral imperative for intellectuals to participate in struggles for social justice and, with the crash of 1929, this stance became generalised. Once the Popular Front had recast established or 'bourgeois' writers as potential allies, the ongoing pursuit of 'celebrities' as sponsors and signatories of open letters became a widespread practice. The initial success of this tactic is indicative of the political polarisation catalysed by the Depression, as writers lashed out at a worsening situation.

To many, the possibility of combining literary and political work hinged on the power of reportage. An early contribution to this tradition was John Dos Passos's pamphlet on the Sacco–Vanzetti case.[39] John Spivak's semi-documentary chain-gang story, *Georgia Nigger* (1932), further dramatised such opportunities, replete with photographs of torture and serialised in the *Daily Worker*.[40] Developments of this nature suggested a history-making role for writers, hence 53 prominent writers, artists and critics rallying to the CPUSA for the 1932 presidential election. The organisation was the League of Professional Groups for Foster and Ford; the manifesto was *Culture and the Crisis*.[41] The impact of the slump was such that it seemed to encourage a generation of the best and brightest to adopt an anti-capitalist political outlook.

The League appeared to provide a model of cooperation between Communists and fellow travellers. Its successors inherited a complex legacy of creative practice and internecine combat.[42] For instance, the John Reed Clubs provided support for young writers in the 1930s (only to be disbanded under party instructions). More celebrated in its day was the League of American Writers, which numbered John Steinbeck – a 'New Deal Democrat with a fierce admixture of western individualism and Yankee independence'[43] – and even President Franklin Delano Roosevelt (albeit secretly) among its alumni.[44] (Party activists did much of the League's day-to-day administration; it lost most of its celebrity base in the aftermath of the Nazi–Soviet Pact.) Coeval with these well-known organisations were dozens of local organisations, temporary committees and 'fronts' devoted to specific objectives.

The left's opponents often blurred distinctions between the actual campaigning organisations directed at intellectuals and the imagined efforts of such groups to coerce propagandist fiction out of writers. This trend intensified with the Moscow Trials, which prompted a CP-initiated campaign to ensure ideological homogeneity and a unified response to the frame-ups of the Old Bolsheviks and other alleged saboteurs in Russia. Amid this struggle, the rhetoric of the *New*

Masses became even more venomous than usual, inadvertently supplying the vitriolic quotations which could be recycled in the later myths.[45]

Those further left than the CPUSA were now subjected to a barrage of scurrilous allegations, augmented by the terminology once reserved for 'decadent' writers during *New Masses*' proletcult phase. Thus cartoons depicted Trotsky and Hitler as allies,[46] the *Nation* was accused of abandoning liberalism and becoming 'the organ of a band of counter-revolutionary conspirators and assassins'[47] and John Dewey was denounced as the plaything of 'Trotskyites and fascists'.[48] This process culminated in 'The Moscow Trials: A Statement by American Progressives', predictably signed by Mike Gold and Granville Hicks, but also by Nelson Algren, Dashiell Hammett, Lillian Hellman, Langston Hughes, Albert Maltz and Raphael Soyer, among others, expressing complete confidence in the trials.[49] Tactics and rhetoric of this nature went on to feature strongly in subsequent accounts of 'totalitarianism'. On balance, political pressure was applied in the battles fought among literary figures, rather than in influencing the content of literature itself.

THE 'LITERATURE OF A PARTY'? A CASE STUDY

Perhaps the key test of the arguments over the 'party line in literature' can be found closer to the Party's 'ninth floor' where – Moscow permitting – it was said that the key decisions were made. On the contrary, the incoherence discussed above is still evident even with a 'cultural commissar' like Mike Gold, probably the most popularised 'aesthetician' on the *New Masses*' editorial board.

Gold became a pariah figure in American letters and his influence waned as the Cold War sensibility took hold and established his reputation as a dogmatic literary leftist. Born Itzok Granich to impoverished parents, the young Gold participated in bohemian prewar Greenwich Village, the Provincetown Players theatre company and the *Liberator* magazine. His novel, *Jews Without Money*, is still regarded as a significant document of the 1930s. Gold's forays into literary criticism became synonymous with a boorish authoritarianism, and he has been widely portrayed as insisting that good art should function as propaganda. (Conversely, he is often recalled as condemning any cultural production that privileged aesthetics over politics.) The case for presenting Gold as the primary engineer of the propaganda novel seems watertight, but closer scrutiny indicates a more complex picture.

In his critical blasts at 'bourgeois' writers, Gold appeared to embody all of the negative traits his opponents identified. Alfred Kazin claimed that 'Gold wrote nothing after *Jews Without Money*, which expressed all he had to say, except his *Daily Worker* twaddle.'[50] Gold's major period of cultural production occurred in the 1920s, both in the aforementioned Provincetown Players and as the motive force behind numerous agit-prop plays and processionals, creative activity that culminated in *Jews Without Money*. His critical standards reflected his actual tastes: Gold demanded a simple realism which he also enjoyed in private, such as in the paintings in his home.[51] (It has also been suggested that his limited writing outside the *Daily Worker* was a consequence of his struggles with diabetes and bringing up a young family.)[52]

Did Gold take an instrumentalist view of cultural production, seeing it as capable of fulfilling political goals? When recalling the conflict between the *New Masses* and rival publications, some accounts treat Gold's literary criticism as based on the assumption that creative writing could be the basis for a transformation of working-class consciousness. Thus his vitriolic attack on the plays of Thornton Wilder in the *New Republic* set a precedent, allowing observers to anticipate what Gold's conclusions would be well in advance of their publication. Notoriously, Gold had denounced Wilder as the 'Prophet of the Genteel Christ' and condemned the latter's humanism as irrelevant to the working class.[53] Hart Crane described the review as the 'rape of *The Woman of Andros*', and a furious controversy followed on the *New Republic*'s letters page.[54] Although in content Gold called for a vigorous, realist and popular literature, its scathing, anti-homosexual tenor was taken as the norm for proletarian criticism. (Perhaps this suspicion was reinforced when the article was reprinted in the criticism section of the *Proletarian Literature in the United States* anthology.)

A second common complaint arose in response to *Jews Without Money*. The book is organised as a series of episodes in the life of a family of Jewish immigrants, seen through the eyes of the young son Mikey. Partly autobiographical, its main theme is thwarted ambitions, expressed in the failure of Mikey's father to become a successful businessman. 'A Curse on Columbus!' is heard frequently around the household, as a sequence of intensifying tragedies envelops the family, culminating in the crushing of Mikey's sister under a street car. In organising the novel as a series of sketches concerning ghetto life, Gold confronts the reader with a sequence of powerful scenes. Almost all indict poverty, whether discussing bedbugs or the transformation of childhood friends into petty criminals. In the widely ridiculed climactic last paragraph, Mikey – now a young adult – hears a radical orator on the street corner and decides to commit himself to a life in 'the movement'.

More than any other 1930s novel (with the possible exception of Clara Weatherwax's *Marching, Marching*), Gold's uneven mixture of fiction and autobiography has been interpreted as having a classical 'conversion' ending. Generalising from this and from Gold's influence as *Daily Worker/New Masses* critic, it is alleged that the proletarian novel revolved around an almost religious moment of truth which led to an individual throwing in his lot with the Communist movement. Indeed, the original manuscript to *Jews Without Money* tends to confirm this, as the moment of 'conversion' ending is literally tacked on, appearing in a different typeface.[55] But is this evidence of a propagandist agenda at work?

On the contrary, this flawed and abrupt ending demonstrates the novel's 'mode of production'; it consists of short sketches because that was how it was written, with a view to selling them to magazines (which should not in itself detract from the power of individual scenes in the novel). Where Gold's critics have a point is on the introduction of politics in the closing scene, which typifies Gold's outlook and methods. A radical response to poverty is artificially attached, in a manner jarring to the reader, who finds no prior basis for radicalism to logically develop within the Mikey character. This inevitably arises from an insurmountable gap between propaganda – detailed arguments on the political issues of the day – and the expression in fiction of events, however political, through the eyes and inner voice of an individual.

In political terms, however, it does demonstrate Gold's economism, embodied in the assumption that poverty alone is sufficient to radicalise the working class. Coupled with his appeal to popular prejudice against homosexuals in numerous articles and in passages of *Jews Without Money* (at a time when the police were actively suppressing New York's 'fairy' subculture),[56] it is fair to say that Gold introduced an inadequate political armature into ostensibly literary discussions. Likewise, he interpreted literature as being sufficiently powerful to prompt widespread changes of political allegiance. This was, however, based on an estimation that an exposition of poverty could alter people's political views, rather than an assumption that fiction should change to be propaganda. On balance, he underestimated ideology and ideas, and overestimated the hortatory power of fiction.

The coarse dismissal of writers who did not measure up to his criteria of an orientation towards the workers should not lead us to conclude that there was a 'party line in literature'. It is more that Gold's harsh standards for measuring literary worth stressed the potential contribution that a novel could make to the workers' movement at the expense of other qualities.

DEBATING DEFINITIONS

Gold's polemics influenced the ongoing – sometimes interminable – debate in the *New Masses* over how to define proletarian literature. As discussed above, the key to the 'formula' – a term used here hesitantly – was presented as whether a novel was written by workers, for a working-class readership, or about organised labour and/or the poor. This vague search for adequate categories is not particularly informative in itself, but it does indicate that CPUSA publications provided a forum in which to establish criteria of what constituted worthwhile political creative writing (criteria often undermined by confusion and disagreement). Nevertheless, that such provision occurred remains distinct from imposing a political line.

Finding adequate aesthetic criteria preoccupied many 1930s cultural radicals. During its second year, *Partisan Review* published a substantial article, based on a symposium, entitled 'What is a Proletarian Novel?: Notes Toward a Definition'. Among the discussants was James T. Farrell, whose opening salvo declared that 'too much of revolutionary criticism, both theoretical articles and specific literary criticisms, is tending toward the creation of a kind of revolutionary scholasticism that can only breed sterility. [O]ur critics reveal a crass determinism.'[57] Complaints of this nature were later taken as evidence of the nascent anti-Stalinism of a selection of left-wing writers, but they are also indicative of the wider range of opinions on how to write worthwhile 'committed' fiction.[58] This concern was shared by *Partisan* and the *New Masses* alike, reflecting the importance attached to formulating a precise standard with which to measure a writer's political contribution.

In the absence of an official line, one means of settling such disputes was through the authority of a text from the Marxist 'canon'. Symptomatic of this was Walt Carmon, who contacted Soviet affairs analyst Joshua Kunitz to suggest a translation of Plekhanov's early cultural writings, 'as a sort of guiding line for our own work'.[59] Whereas the frustrated Carmon sought an appropriate textual exegesis to resolve these difficulties, Kunitz himself advocated a clear position by aligning aesthetic value to Soviet 'progress'. Sometimes he was notoriously polemical, but, in a more relaxed atmosphere, he expressed hopes that the decor of a single Russian pavilion could be generalised into an art form worthy of emulation.[60] In Kunitz's eyes, the routine architecture of public spaces could itself become a 'high' cultural form, without recourse to 'propagandist' objectives. Similarly, an anonymous *New Masses* reviewer praised literary critic Carl Van Doren for taking the time to nurture the authors of high culture, 'the masses having been left to Hearst, Macfadden, and Hollywood'.[61] Once again, debates within the Communist party's cultural milieu suggest that, in striving for common standards as to what constituted 'good' art and literature, Kunitz *et al.* had objectives beyond the immediately political.

Such objectives were not confined to the CPUSA. For sections of the literary left, 'high culture' served as a benchmark against which progress could be measured. Positive appraisals of the cultural benefits of western civilisation nestled alongside misguided praise for Stalin's Russia and its perceived economic prowess. This attitude was well expressed by the liberal journalist Matthew Josephson, who excitedly informed Kunitz that John Dos Passos and William Shakespeare were the foreign authors most frequently discussed in Russia. In welcoming this development, he also complained that 'literature and culture etc.' lagged behind social progress there, which he considered to be 'in the bag'.[62] This exchange is instructive, in that it suggests that Josephson – with Kunitz's agreement – hoped that his movement could scale the heights erected by Shakespeare, rather than bypass them entirely. Again, what is missing from such formulations is any emphasis on the direct political utility of texts or cultural practices.

Amid the confusion mainstream critics found themselves blundering into debates over definitions. For instance, when Granville Hicks accused *Hound and Horn* magazine of being anti-social and elitist, given its lukewarm approach to proletarian literature, its editors replied that Hicks was neither working class nor appreciative of the classics.[63] In a similar vein Ernest Boyd demolished the *Proletarian Literature in the United States* anthology by taking its claims to cultural superiority at face value and then stating that it offered slogans in place of authentic – that is literary – engagement, hence failing to match the bombast of the volume's introduction. The book is also ridiculed for claiming an intimate connection with a mass working-class audience, which he asserted was the domain of pulp magazines and Hollywood.[64] Boyd took his political disagreements with the anthology's editors and conflated them with a cursory synopsis of the contributors' shortcomings. This pattern was reproduced in some of the treatment subsequently meted out to proletarian authors, but – unlike in the present day – it did not gain the status of conventional wisdom in the 1930s.

CONCLUSION

Of the key documents from which a 'party line in literature' could be logically expected to emerge, most point instead towards a fragmentary and disjointed approach. Although *New Masses* book reviews often took issue with writers on 'political' rather than 'literary' grounds, this does not prove that the novel was used as a propaganda tool by the CPUSA. So why, at least until the 1980s, was this myth so widely accepted? One explanation would link the conflicts within the literary left – itself part of a historically specific subculture – to the interpretations that developed under subsequent political pressures. In turn, these readings stressed a sinister bid to force novelists to produce propaganda, regardless of real developments in the 1930s.

Ironically, the comprehensive assembly of the propaganda novel myth resembles a 'black propaganda' campaign itself. There is little evidence to suggest a single, centralised conspiracy against proletarian literature, but the different strands of the social formation so central to the continuing assault on 1930s cultural radicalism are worth noting. As is now well known, those 1930s veterans working with the Congress for Cultural Freedom and its US affiliate in the 1950s were contributing to an organisation part-funded by the Central Intelligence Agency.[65] More broadly, we can note the use of book clubs, speaking tours, blacklists and even a Federal Bureau of Investigation 'book review section' to dislodge any residual traces of the Cultural Front in American life. Suffice to say that such tactics, on aggregate, came to resemble the 'literary gangsterism' once viewed as the domain of American Stalinism.

Proletcult was shorthand for the standards by which certain works were sometimes praised or damned in the Communist press in the early 1930s. This scattered pattern of book reviews, confusing 'theoretical' essays and personal disputes between writers cannot support the interpretation that the novel was used as a propagandist tool throughout the decade. Such a view derived its appeal from combining personal memoirs with reflections on a transient trend in Soviet criticism. It was reinforced by recalling the hackneyed tropes of several prominent *New Masses* editors, despite the fact that textual analysis of proletarian novels demonstrates various continuities with established practices in literature and mass entertainment, including hard-boiled crime fiction. These factors were ignored by the 'liberal narrative' that became conventional wisdom in the 1950s.

Thus the imposition of a party line in literature is, in the last instance, a myth. This is despite the authoritarian conduct of the *New Masses*, the CPUSA's main cultural voice. Since myths are, however, not reducible to a collection of the 'wrong ideas', one should consider their origins in real events and conditions. Hence my concern with the conduct of CPUSA campaigns among writers, which was later used as evidence of 'totalitarianism' and a 'party line in literature'. A moral critique of Stalinism and its organisational forms was recast as an attack on instrumentalist uses of fiction and literary criticism. Postwar perceptions of propaganda disguised the literature of a subculture as the literature of a party, to rewrite Rahv's famous phrase.

Notes

1   Thanks are due to John Baxendale, Mark Beachill, Sylvia Harvey, Sara Hinchliffe, Peter Nicholls, Chris Pawling and Alan Wald for their comments on earlier versions of this material. Professor Chas Critcher of the Communication, Media and Communities Research Centre, Sheffield Hallam University secured the funds with which to undertake this research. The staff of the Butler Library, Columbia University (Joshua Kunitz papers), the Franklin D. Roosevelt Library (Presidential Personal File 5259: League of American Writers) and the New York University Rare Books and Manuscripts Collection (*Jews Without Money*, MSS) kindly assisted in the completion of this paper, and thanks are due to them all, especially for permission to excerpt material from these archives. Needless to say, any errors are of my own making.

2   P. Rahv, 'Proletarian Literature: A Political Autopsy', *Southern Review*, 4 (winter 1939), 625. For more on Rahv, see H. Wilford, 'The Agony of the Avant-Garde: Philip Rahv and the New York Intellectuals', in D. Murray (ed.), *American Cultural Critics* (Exeter University Press, 1995), pp. 33–48. A history of the caricature could commence equally validly at Max Eastman's 'Artists in Uniform' (1933), a depiction of the stultifying lives of Soviet writers, published in the *Modern Quarterly* and expanded to a book-length essay the following year.

3   The basis for this distinction was developed in V.I. Lenin's 1901 essay on organisation entitled

'Where to Begin', in V.I. Lenin, *Selected Works* (Moscow, Progress Publishers, 1968, pp. 37–43). An expanded version of these arguments appeared as *What is to be Done?* the following year.

4   This is also how the present author defines propaganda for the purposes of this chapter. On a related terminological issue: where capitalised, Communist/Communism indicate support for the Third Communist International, as opposed to a more general engagement with Marxism and social change per se (which appears in lower case).

5   'On Proletarian Culture', in Lenin, *On Culture and Cultural Revolution* (Moscow, Progress Publishers, 1966), pp. 146–8.

6   M. Hume, 'Was Lenin a Stalinist (or Vice Versa)?', *Confrontation*, 1, no. 5 (summer 1989), 13–26.

7   See L. Trotsky, *The Third International After Lenin* (1936, New York, Pathfinder, 1970 edn).

8   Note the administrative dimension of socialist realism, 'more a set of prescriptive rules for the kind of writing deemed to be desirable by the party and set of yardsticks for criticising "decadent" literature than a literary theory as such'. D. Forgacs, 'Marxist Literary Theories', in A. Jefferson and D. Robey (eds), *Modern Literary Theory: A Comparative Introduction* (London, B.T. Batsford, 1986 ed.), p. 166. Some critics would contend that socialist realism maintained a literary dimension (see n. 15 below).

9   From A.M. Wald's introduction to D. Aaron, *Writers on the Left: Episodes in American Communism* (New York, Columbia University Press Morningside Books edition, 1992), pp. xxiii–xxiv.

10   'Preface' [to fiction section], G. Hicks *et al.* (eds), *Proletarian Literature in the United States: An Anthology* (New York, International Publishers, 1935), p. 33.

11   J.F. Murphy, *The Proletarian Moment: The Controversy Over 'Leftism' in Literature* (Urbana and Chicago, University of Illinois Press, 1991), p. 123.

12   Letter, Michael Gold to Lincoln Kirstein (undated), reprinted in M.B. Hamovitch (ed.), *The Hound and Horn Letters* (Athens, University of Georgia Press, 1982), p. 157.

13   E. Seaver, 'Review and Comment: Socialist Realism', *New Masses* (22/10/1935), pp. 23–4.

14   For an incisive re-reading of this collection, see L.F. Hanley, 'Cultural Work and Class Politics: Re-Reading and Remaking Proletarian Literature in the United States', *Modern Fiction Studies*, 38, (autumn 1992), 715–32.

15   B. Foley, *Radical Representations: Politics and Form in US Proletarian Fiction, 1929–1941* (Durham, NC, Duke University Press, 1993), *passim*, citation from p. 130.

16   See C.V. James, *Soviet Socialist Realism: Origins and Theory* (London, Macmillan, 1973); G. Carleton, 'Genre in Socialist Realism', *Slavonic Review* (winter 1994), *passim*. Carleton parallels socialist realism with medieval English writing, in which convention obliged the reporting of non-existent lions and tigers amid the landscape scene. Stalinism meant that political considerations often over-rode a Soviet writer's commitment to a chosen genre or form, especially when A.A. Zhandov directed cultural policy after 1945.

17   Admittedly, the term propaganda was sometimes deployed in praising works of fiction. Thus Robert Cantwell's *Nation* review of Grace Lumpkin's *To Make My Bread* (1932) used it as shorthand for the novel's persuasive reportage, rather than its political partisanship: Cantwell cited in L. Barnard Gilkes, 'Afterword' to G. Lumpkin, *The Wedding* (1939) (New York, Popular Library, 1977 edn), p. 278. This essay, explaining Lumpkin's place in a 'Lost American Fiction' series of paperbacks, is quick to

attack the 'truly dreadful bunch of bigots and rigid dogmatists she fell in with' (p. 282), thereby contributing to the conventional 'propaganda' narrative.

18   For instance, early editions of *Partisan Review* advanced a sophisticated version of Marxist literary criticism. See A.M. Wald, *The New York Intellectuals: The Rise and Decline of the Anti-Stalinist Left, from the 1930s to the 1980s* (Chapel Hill, University of North Carolina Press, 1987); H. Teres, *Renewing the Left: Politics, Imagination, and the New York Intellectuals* (New York, Oxford University Press, 1996), pp. 38–56.

19   'Introduction', in Hicks *et al.*, *Proletarian Literature in the United States*, p. 9.

20   Hicks *et al.*, *Proletarian Literature in the United States*, p. 12. The 'Man in White' refers to a hypothetical liberal literary critic; the subsequent citation is from p. 11.

21   Space does not permit a discussion of the 'confessional' memoir in the construction of 'the Thirties', so an example should suffice: the late Alfred Kazin established his own position as a sharp contrast to that of his contemporaries among the Depression-era literati: 'I was sick of Communists. I had the deepest contempt for those middle-class and doctrinaire radicals who, after graduating from Harvard or Yale in the Twenties, had made it a matter of personal honour to become Marxists, and who now worried in the *New Masses* whether Proust should be read after the Revolution and why there seemed to be no simple proletarians in the novels of André Malraux.' A similar argument appears in *Making It*, where *Commentary* editor Norman Podhoretz presents *Partisan Review* as 'refusing to accept the Stalinist dogma that experimental poets of a politically conservative bent were to be attacked as decadent while tenth rate proletarian novelists like Jack Conroy were to be promoted as great'. Appearing within a year of each other in the late 1960s, both memoirs employ a stereotype that conflates the Communist party with its literary sympathisers and their cultural activities Alfred Kazin, *Starting Out in the Thirties* (Boston, MA, Little, Brown, 1962), pp. 4–5; Norman Podhoretz, *Making It* (New York, Bantam, 1967), p. 86.

22   A. Kazin, *On Native Grounds: An Interpretation of Modern American Prose Literature* (New York, Reynal & Hitchcock, 1942), p. 387. Perhaps the inclusion of the phrase 'in his own way' is a subtle acknowledgement of the absence of a 'party line' as such.

23   R. Ruland and M. Bradbury, *From Puritanism to Postmodernism: A History of American Literature* (Harmondsworth, Penguin, 1992), p. 361 (my emphasis).

24   M. Bradbury, *The Modern American Novel* (Oxford University Press, 1992), p. 125.

25   D. Tallack, *Twentieth Century America: The Intellectual and Cultural Context* (London, Longman, 1991), pp. 176–8.

26   Space does not permit a full discussion of the many excellent recent works which show the myth of the 'Red Decade' to be untenable. Unfortunately, myths have a capacity to persist despite the facts and logic marshalled against them. Among the significant new studies of the literary left I would include L. Schwartz, *Marxism and Culture: The CPUSA and Aesthetics in the 1930s* (Port Washington, NY, Kennikat Press, 1980); A.M. Wald, *Writing From the Left: New Essays on Radical Culture and Politics* (London, Verso, 1994); and D. Wixson, *Worker-Writer in America: Jack Conroy and the Tradition of Midwestern Literary Radicalism, 1898–1990* (Urbana, University of Illinois Press, 1994).

27   Variations on this theme continue to circulate. For instance, the 1990 Modern Language Association convention was attacked by Roger Kimball (author of *Tenured Radicals*), who claimed that 'one might have been forgiven for believing that the year was 1969 – if not, indeed, 1935': Kimball,

'The Periphery v. the Center: The MLA in Chicago', reprinted in P. Berman (ed.), *Debating PC: The Controversy Over Political Correctness on College Campuses* (New York, Dell, 1992), p. 75. Significantly, the focus of Kimball's attack is Barbara Foley.

28 It is worth noting that this issue resurfaced in the course of HUAC investigations into academic life and in the 1951 *Dennis v. United States* Supreme Court decision. See A. Filreis, 'Words with "All the Effects of Force": Cold-War Interpretation', *American Quarterly*, 39 (summer 1987), 306–12.

29 A.T. Rubenstein, 'Fiction of the Thirties: Josephine Herbst', *Science and Society*, vol. 49, no. 1 (spring 1985), 91.

30 M. Cowley, *The Dream of Golden Mountains: Remembering the 1930s* (New York, Penguin [1965], 1980 edn), p. 146.

31 See M. Denning, *The Cultural Front: The Laboring of American Culture in the Twentieth Century* (London, Verso, 1996), p. 362.

32 The 'liberal narrative' is a key category in T.H. Schaub, *American Fiction and the Cold War* (Madison, University of Wisconsin Press, 1991), esp. pp. 5–7.

33 Denning, *Cultural Front*.

34 See R. Williams, *The Long Revolution* (Harmondsworth, Penguin, 1961), esp. pp. 64–88.

35 R. Williams, *Marxism and Literature* (Oxford University Press, 1977), p. 132. Readers may wish to take issue with any suggestion that this mode of analysis is universally applicable, and history is littered with examples of routine practices that move from being 'taken for granted' to assuming central importance.

36 M. Fearnow, *The American Stage and the Great Depression: A Cultural History of the Grotesque* (Cambridge University Press, 1997), pp. 178–9 n.

37 C. Nelson, *Repression and Recovery: Modern American Poetry and the Politics of Cultural Memory* (Madison, University of Wisconsin Press, 1989), p. 199.

38 See C.H. Martin, 'International Labor Defense', in M.J. Buhle *et al.* (eds), *Encyclopedia of the American Left* (Chicago and London, St James Press 1990), pp. 366–7.

39 J. Dos Passos, *Facing the Chair: The Story of the Americanisation of Two Foreign Born Workingmen* (Boston, MA, Sacco–Vanzetti Defense Committee, 1927).

40 See A. Lichtenstein, 'Chain Gang Blues', *Dissent*, vol. 43, no. 4 (fall 1996).

41 See the appendix to G.W. Barnfield, '"Co-opting Culture": State Intervention in and Party Patronage of Literary and Popular Culture, 1929–1941' (unpublished Ph.D. thesis, Sheffield Hallam University, 1996), pp. v–vii.

42 Among the most detailed of these is J. Kutulas, *The Long War: The Intellectual People's Front and Anti-Stalinism, 1930–1940* (Durham NC, Duke University Press, 1995). Such accounts tend to stress the politics of national cultural-political organisations, rather than their local branches or chapters.

43 J. Parini, *John Steinbeck: A Biography* (New York, Henry Holt, 1995), p. 78. Steinbeck joined the Western Writers Congress in 1936 and the LAW the following year, serving as a vice-president of the latter from 1939 to 1940. As a result, he was subject to FBI surveillance from 1936. F. Folsom, *Days of Anger, Days of Hope* (Niwot, Universities Press of Colorado, 1994), p. 323.

44 For more details see Franklin D. Roosevelt Library, Presidential Personal File 5259: League of American Writers.

45   It was not the first time such campaigns had occurred; the CPUSA hounded *Modern Quarterly* editor V.F. Calverton, among others; see Aaron, *Writers on the Left*, pp. 326–32. The attack on the 'Trotskyites' was unique in its intensity and duration, however. A significant riposte to the Moscow Trials was Philip Rahv's essay 'Trials of the Mind': see Teres, *Renewing the Left*, pp. 85–7.

46   Cary Nelson suggests that, although 'design elements are often not under an author's control, they can have a significant role in giving a book coherent meaning in its own time' (*Repression and Recovery*, p. 192). One could expand this observation to suggest that readers of the *New Masses*, as part of the Cultural Front 'structure of feeling', could be informed by key debates by the wider trappings of their subculture as well as through formal political commentary.

47   Editors, 'The Nation and Trotsky', *New Masses* (10/11/1936), pp. 11–13.

48   'Robert Forsythe' (Kyle Crichton), 'Is John Dewey Honest?', undated *New Masses* clipping, *c.* 1938.

49   *New Masses* (6/5/1938), p. 19.

50   Kazin, *On Native Grounds*, p. 382.

51   A.T. Rubenstein, 'The Cultural World of the Communist Party: An Historical Overview', in M.E. Brown *et al.* (eds), *New Studies in the Politics and Culture of US Communism* (New York, Monthly Review Press, 1993), p. 256.

52   Wald, *Writing From the Left*, p. 33. Perhaps the sharpest account of Gold and his contemporary relevance is J.D. Bloom, *Left Letters: The Culture Wars of Mike Gold and Joseph Freeman* (New York, Columbia University Press, 1992).

53   M. Gold, 'Wilder: Prophet of the Genteel Christ', *New Republic* (22/10/1930), p. 266; see also E. Wilson, 'The Literary Class War', *New Republic* (4/5/1932), p. 319.

54   See M. Goldstein, *The Art of Thornton Wilder* (Lincoln, NA, University of Nebraska Press, 1979), pp. 69–71.

55   M. Gold, *Jews without Money*, MSS, New York University Rare Books and Manuscripts collection.

56   See the penultimate chapter of G. Chaucey, *Gay New York: Gender, Urban Culture and the Making of the Gay Male World, 1890–1940* (New York, Basic, 1994).

57   Seaver *et al.*, 'What is a Proletarian Novel? Notes Toward a Definition', *Partisan Review* (1935), pp. 13–14.

58   It also demonstrates that the first incarnation of *Partisan Review* did not oppose proletarian literature *per se*, but proposed it adopt a more mature approach, becoming capable of integrating the iconoclasm of a high modernist *avant-garde*. In later years the journal insisted that these factors were totally incompatible, as is well known. For a recent example of the *Partisan* mythology, see F.X. Clines, 'The Salad Days Resavored, in a Feast of Fiction', *New York Times* (6/5/1997), Section B4.

59   Butler Library, Columbia University, Joshua Kunitz papers: Walt Carmon to Joshua Kunitz, 5 November 1930.

60   Kunitz, 'Max Eastman's Hot Unnecessary Tears', *New Masses* (September 1933), pp. 12–15; witness also his fierce polemic against *Artists in Uniform*. On his praise for architecture, see 'Creating a People's Art', *Soviet Russia Today* (June 1939), pp. 38, 43. The pavilion art praised includes Andreyev's gigantic stainless steel figure.

61   'Without Malice' (a review of Carl Van Doren's *Three Worlds*), *New Masses* (3/11/1936), p. 24.

62   Kunitz papers: Matthew Josephson to Joshua Kunitz, 30 December 1933. To further illustrate

Kunitz's respect for high culture, it should be noted that he condemned, under a pseudonym, Michael Gold's notorious populist critique of Thornton Wilder.

63 Letter, *Hound and Horn* editors to *New Republic* editors, 9 June 1932 (reprinted in Hamovitch (ed.), *The Hound and Horn Letters*, pp. 156–7). *The Hound and Horn* editorial board consisted of Bernard Bandler, Lincoln Kirstein and A. Hyatt Mayor.

64 E. Boyd, 'Books' (review of *Proletarian Literature in the United States*), *Current Controversy* (November 1935), 32.

65 Teres, *Renewing the Left*, p. 78; H. Wilford, ' "Winning Hearts and Minds": American Cultural Strategies in the Cold War', *Borderlines*, 1, No. 4 (June 1994), *passim*.

Part Six

THE AGE OF
COMMUNICATION
AND PERSUASION

The post-Second World War period has witnessed the largest expansion of media and communications in the history of humanity. The Cold War used these new media in a controlled manner. One could analyse most of the output of the period as propaganda in some sense; but Nicholas Cull argues that one ought to distinguish the output of agencies reflecting a clear and well-defined policy from the more general cultural background which only reflects the world's political polarities. By looking at the production of the United States Information Agency, Cull shows that the projection of Jackie Kennedy's image could convey subtle diplomatic and cultural images for the Kennedy administration abroad and at home. From this world of relatively secure ideological opposites and well-controlled media, we have moved to a more unstable and dynamic situation of a multitude of localised conflicts and the multiplication of media. Philip Taylor shows the part played by positive propagandistic efforts in this new environment. In both these chapters it is important to remind ourselves that propaganda is morally neutral and indeed contributes to peaceful resolution of potential conflicts.

17

PROJECTING JACKIE

KENNEDY ADMINISTRATION FILM PROPAGANDA OVERSEAS IN LEO SELTZER'S *INVITATION TO INDIA*, *INVITATION TO PAKISTAN* AND *JACQUELINE KENNEDY'S ASIAN JOURNEY* (1962)

Nicholas J. Cull

When historians of the Cold War mention film it is usually to repeat the story of how the Hollywood left suffered in the Red scare. Material from film archives and stills collections generally surfaces in documentaries and text books only to illustrate the conventional narratives. We know the clichés: lurching B-movie aliens doubling for communists while well-scrubbed school children demonstrate their 'duck and cover' atomic bomb drill. This approach misses much. Film was more than a battleground for the domestic Cold War and filmic evidence can do more than just spice up the old story of paranoia and conformist peer pressure. Film was a weapon of that conflict, and the images deployed by American propagandists are eloquent in their own right. As an introduction to something of the story still to be told, this is the account of a single film project of the US government's chief Cold War propaganda bureau, the United States Information Agency (USIA), known in the countries in which it operates as the United States Information Service (USIS). This case study will trace that project from its inception in the mind of a Hollywood producer to its release across the non-communist world. In terms of propaganda history, this is an argument for the simplest definition of propaganda and the scholarly agenda that follows from it. Whatever else propaganda may be, it must certainly include the output of those government agencies around the world that exist purely for the purpose of disseminating information. If propaganda is the output of a propaganda agency, then the systematic study of the archives and output of such agencies – in this case the USIA – must necessarily be a prime entry point (and perhaps *the* prime entry point) into propaganda studies. While propaganda may well be more than just the output of a propaganda agency, there is a danger that scholarship can become bogged down in the issue of definitions, and focus on the borderline cases at the expense of the propaganda agencies at the heart of the issue. This tendency and deficiencies in the USIA's archival record have combined to direct scholarship away from the agency that was actually paid to conduct Cold War propaganda.[1]

From its foundation in 1953 to the present day the United States Information Agency has made full use of film and more recently television to project America's image and policy priorities overseas. Agency films were seen by vast audiences in commercial cinemas across the globe, on the developing television networks of Western Europe, Asia and Latin America, and in improvised displays wherever there was road enough for a USIS cinema van. During the Eisenhower years USIA films were stiff, ideologically charged and made under contract by the lowest bidder, which generally meant one of the big newsreel companies. Under the Kennedy administration everything changed. The USIA developed a new type of propaganda film. These films used all the techniques of documentary film to communicate American life and foreign policy to their audience. They were frequently subtle and moving, and soon became a staple of international film festivals. Recognition followed. In 1964 Charles Guggenheim carried off the best documentary short-subject Academy Award for *Nine From Little Rock*, an agency film on the later lives of the black children who broke the colour bar in that city's high school in 1957.[2] USIA film-making had arrived.

This case study charts the story of the films that paved the way for the agency's later successes: Leo Seltzer's account of Jackie Kennedy's tour of South Asia in 1962, released overseas as *Invitation to Pakistan* and *Invitation to India*, and domestically in a combined version as *Jacqueline Kennedy's Asian Journey*. These films stand as fascinating documents of the moment of transition in US film propaganda, and the initiative of the presiding director of Agency motion picture production, George Stevens Jr. Like his contemporaries, Huw Wheldon at the BBC and Tom Daly at the National Film Board of Canada, George Stevens Jr brought an energy and vision to documentary film production in the early 1960s not seen since the pioneering days of John Grierson in the 1930s.[3] The films of Jackie Kennedy in India and Pakistan argued for the propaganda value of the softer documentary approach; no less significantly they reveal the political value of their central subject. To USIA, Jackie Kennedy was more than the apolitical figure that has endured in popular imagination; she was a propaganda weapon of the first order. The films followed accordingly.

THE CONCEPT

The spring of 1961 was not a happy one for America's propagandists. President Kennedy had arrived in style only to fall flat on his face at the Bay of Pigs in April. In May the public relations victories fell to Khrushchev. But June 1961 brought an unexpected success. In a six-day European tour Jacqueline Kennedy captured the public imagination. One British newspaper noted that the last American visitors to draw such a reaction were Douglas Fairbanks and Mary Pickford, back in the 1920s. In France, journalist André de Coizart praised Mrs Kennedy's beauty, facility with European manners and languages, and love of the arts. He declared that: 'The First Lady of the United States has won, in the feminine field, the greatest victory of the century.' In Spain, *La Nación* pointed out that the wives of Communist leaders never looked so good, continuing: 'A new force has appeared in the political arsenal . . . a new "secret weapon" – beauty.' It was a weapon that hit the Communist world on an unprotected flank, for as *La Nación* concluded: ' "To be pretty" presupposes a high grade of social progress, and requires investments in creams, perfumes, lotions and clothing which no Communist country can now manage, nor will conditions for many years in the future allow it.'[4] The publicity value of such a champion was not lost on USIA. When in the autumn of 1961, Jackie Kennedy accepted informal invitations to visit both India and Pakistan in the spring of the following year, the Agency's motion picture branch embraced a plan to record the visit for their own purposes.[5]

In November 1961 the new USIA director, veteran CBS journalist Ed Murrow, set about the task of improving the Agency's film output. He travelled to the West Coast to cajole the leading lights of Hollywood into producing feature films that avoided mere escapism and showed the United States in a good light. 'Movies', Murrow warned a gathering of film-makers on 5 November, 'are doing a lot of harm to America. They convey the notion that America is a country of millionaires and crooks.'[6] He also hoped to find a suitable film-maker to direct the USIA's motion picture programme. This second task proved somewhat easier to accomplish. Just as Murrow began his search for a film coordinator he received a proposal from a young film producer named George Stevens Jr (the son of the legendary director of such classics as *Shane*) and a namesake documentary film producer, Leslie Stevens of Daystar Productions. The two men proposed making a documentary on Jacqueline Kennedy's visit to Pakistan on behalf of the agency. As Stevens recalled thirty-seven years later, his approach to Murrow was motivated by the spirit of the New Frontier. Quite literally he was 'asking what he could do for his country'.[7] Murrow swiftly realised that he had found both his producer and an ideal prestige project in one go. Stevens offered a unique combination of youth, energy and Hollywood connections. January 1962 found Stevens taking the reins of USIA film production in Washington, DC. He pledged to 'improve the quality of USIA films' and 'strengthen' the agency's 'relationships with the film industry'. The project at the top of his agenda remained the Jackie Kennedy film.[8]

From the beginning Stevens envisioned a high quality film. He proposed shooting in colour, with a celebrity narrator (he suggested the poet Carl Sandburg) and a specially commissioned musical score of Pakistani and American themes. Stevens planned to both reflect the democratic spirit of America, and establish the country's interest in a small developing nation by capturing Jackie in action:

> The key, as we see it, is that Mrs. Kennedy comes to *learn* from Pakistan: who its people are, what they hope for, their wants and needs, their culture and

their accomplishments. By virtue of her warm personality and her intense curiosity, Mrs. Kennedy is ideal for such a film . . . a wonderful purpose will be accomplished automatically by her innate *caring* about the people of this smaller country.[9]

Films of overseas visits were standard fare for USIA. The agency filmed more or less every trip abroad made by Eisenhower and Vice-President Nixon, and every major visit by a head of state to the United States. These films usually ran for only ten minutes and were terminally dull. This proposal was different. Stevens wanted to actually show an encounter with the culture of the host country. He even suggested 'particular concentration on the role of women in Pakistan'. The plan raised one immediate problem. The United States could not make a film of the visit to Pakistan without making a parallel film about the visit to India. Given the enmity between Pakistan and India, it was obvious from the outset that the agency would have to make two separate films. Neither country could be given grounds for offence or shown any unreasonable favour.[10] In December 1961 the Indian side of the project received a boost from the ranking American propagandist in India, the USIA's Political Affairs Officer at the New Delhi Embassy, Barry Zorthian. On 5 December Zorthian telegraphed the USIA in Washington proposing a three-reel colour documentary of Jackie Kennedy's visit, 'concentrating on her admiration of Indian cultural achievements, meeting and reacting to Indians as [an] honoured guest, attending Republic Day celebrations'.[11] The road was clear for a two-film project.

Stevens' new job in Washington meant that he could not personally make the films of the South Asian visit; however, he knew what was needed. Here he encountered a major problem. The USIA had minimal film production facilities of its own. When the agency needed a film it commissioned an outside contractor in exactly the same way as the Department of the Interior might commission a contractor to build a bridge. As with bridge building the contract had to go to the lowest bidder, which usually meant one of the newsreel companies, who benefited from economies of scale and their happy freedom from artistic inclinations. Stevens began by ensuring that the agency did more than just 'round up the usual suspects' in its search for a team to film Jacqueline Kennedy in Asia. The film-makers invited to tender for the project included Leo Seltzer, an Oscar-winning documentary film-maker with a reputation for sensitive handling of Third World projects. The day came for the film-makers to tender their bids to Murrow and Stevens. The prospective candidates filed in turn into a boardroom at USIA headquarters. Murrow asked each how they intended to film Mrs Kennedy. Seltzer explained that he hoped to depict the encounter between an interested American and two fascinating cultures, as she 'compared the realities with what she'd read'. Fox and Hearst Metrotone, for their part, answered in purely logistical terms, estimating the numbers of cameras, crewmen and quantity of film stock that they would need. Murrow had no doubt who was the best man for the job. Because the Hearst Metrotone bid was far lower than Seltzer could offer, the contract had to go to that company; fortunately, Stevens persuaded Hearst Metrotone to hire Seltzer as the director and editor of their film. It seemed that the film would be made to Stevens' specifications and Hearst's budget.[12]

THE FILM-MAKER

Leo Seltzer was well qualified for the task of filming Jackie Kennedy's trip. Thirty years' experience in documentary film-making had given him a fine command of the medium. Yet for Seltzer the art of film was secondary to the message it carried. He always considered himself to be a social activist who just happened to use film as his medium. Born in a log cabin in Alberta, Canada, in 1910, within sight of an impoverished American-Indian encampment, and coming of age in Brownsville, Brooklyn, Seltzer was no stranger to either cultural difference or social hardship. He came to film-making almost by accident. In 1931 he found himself in New York with a half-completed education in electrical engineering and an economic crisis all around. He volunteered to help set up darkroom facilities for the radical Film and Photo League in New York, and became interested in their work. He stayed on to learn how to use both still and moving picture cameras to record the demonstrations, riots and repressions of the Great Depression as it unfolded. Seltzer and his colleagues at the Film and Photo League created an alternative visual record of their times, and toured the country, screening their version of events to counter the complacency of the commercial newsreels.[13] Later in the decade he joined the Federal Art Project making documentaries on subjects as diverse as fresco painting for the Metropolitan Museum of Art and public health for the City of New York. During the Second World War Seltzer worked first for the National Film Board of Canada and then served as a first lieutenant in the US Army Signal Corps. He made a number of training films and was the second unit director on John Huston's searing account of veterans' mental disorders, *Let There Be Light*.[14]

After the war Seltzer worked on a succession of films touching on social and medical issues. In 1947 he won an Academy Award for a documentary on a children's hospital, *The First Steps*, made for the United Nations Division of Social Affairs and co-funded by (but not filmed in) India. He began to make films in the developing world, including *The Fate of a Child* (1950), an account of the problem of infant mortality in Latin America made for the United Nations. Given Seltzer's political origins, he was an obvious candidate to run foul of McCarthyism. He had the first inkling of trouble in 1950 when a United Nations official requested that images of peasants using hammers and a sickle be deleted from a film, suggesting that these could be subliminal messages of support for the Soviet Union. Although Seltzer had never been a member of the Communist party, following a trip to Bolivia in 1951 to make a film called *Article 55* for the

UN, the State Department confiscated his passport. They proved happy to hand back the document once Seltzer had signed an affidavit affirming that he 'didn't wish to overthrow the US constitution'. As if to broaden his credentials Seltzer also began working for US corporations, including the Chase Bank.[15]

Seltzer did not make government films during the 1950s. The USIA during the McCarthy years certainly would not have been comfortable for a man with Seltzer's record. The agency was a major target for the junior Senator from Wisconsin and suffered more than its share of forced resignations. By 1962 it was a different story. Murrow made a point of putting the McCarthy era firmly behind the agency. He even rehired the most prominent martyr of that era, Reed Harris, to be his personal assistant. For his part, George Stevens was determined to recruit the best people available to make films for USIA. He was not prepared to be bullied by the security staff at the agency and moved the security clearance process out from behind closed doors, requiring all files and evidence to be produced and considered not in a locked backroom but in the comparative light of the USIA Director's office. Stevens recalled no specific problems around Seltzer's record, but well remembers that security staff took much convincing before they would allow Hollywood liberal José Ferrer to narrate such films as the Spanish language version of Seltzer's later account of President Kennedy's Mexican tour, *Progress Through Freedom*.[16]

Seltzer was delighted to work with the USIA. He shared Murrow's fear that commercial feature films misrepresented the United States overseas. Personal experience bolstered this view. In 1946, as a young signals officer in Germany, Seltzer attempted to negotiate an exchange of propaganda films with a Soviet information officer. His Soviet counterpart insisted that the Russian people had no need of American documentaries as they already knew of American life from the movies of Deanna Durbin, and John Ford's *The Grapes of Wrath*. Seltzer remained eager to show the world something of the value of American life and democracy. His Jackie Kennedy films proved only the first of a series of projects for the agency spanning the rest of the Kennedy and Johnson years, including a filmic essay on the USIA's determination to speak 'truth' in the presence of Communist propaganda: *The American Commitment* (1963).[17]

PREPARATIONS, THE VISIT AND THE CONTROVERSY

In February 1962, four weeks before the arrival of Jackie Kennedy, Seltzer, his cameraman Peasley Bond and the rest of his crew arrived in India to begin the task of shooting background material for the films.[18] Seltzer realised that he would have little chance to capture the feel of places like the Taj Mahal when the circus around the First Lady was in town. He visited every stop on Jackie's projected tour, capturing establishing shots and point-of-view footage to cut into the film of the actual visit. The Indian organisers that he met *en route* were unsure of Seltzer's status and regularly asked him to advise on how they should entertain Mrs

Kennedy. Seltzer soon found himself picking out bedrooms for her in the palaces where she was scheduled to stay. In Jaipur he even suggested that she be offered an elephant ride, and the prospective hosts duly wrote that into her agenda for the day. In anticipation of this episode, Seltzer and his crew also took an elephant ride, and captured some valuable point-of-view shots of the ground as seen from a swaying howdah. These images added a wonderful sense of looking through Jackie Kennedy's eyes when edited into the final film. Similarly, their serene image of the Taj Mahal seen through morning mists quite justified the inconvenience of filming as their equipment sank slowly into a mud bank. Seltzer was gratified to learn that the latter sequence was a personal favourite of Jackie Kennedy herself.[19]

In the last days before the visit, the Public Affairs Officer in New Delhi, Zorthian, wrote a final list of suggestions for the film-makers. Zorthian urged against overemphasis on receptions to which Americans were invited. Mrs Kennedy had come to meet Indians. More significantly, he feared that visits to the ancient Mughal sites 'could well crowd out any interest she may show in contemporary India, ordinary Indians, their problems and their successes'. Zorthian understood that the opportunities to show Jackie with ordinary Indians would be few, yet he also knew that Jackie's every move would be compared with the visit of Queen Elizabeth: 'We don't want Indian audiences to start drawing comparisons and end by saying that, of the two, Queen Elizabeth II is the real democrat – "after all, *she* visited the Aarey Milk Colony" – etc. etc.'[20] Seltzer took these suggestions to heart and, although his final film was anchored in Jackie's approach to the region's heritage, he made sure he included extended sequences of her visits to a children's hospital and the government's prized Cottage Industries Emporium project. Seltzer restricted images of her meetings with Americans to a brief scene of a reception for the Peace Corps, which in any case fitted the broader aim of the film to establish a 'caring' image for the United States. He supplemented Jackie's few meetings with the 'ordinary India' with his own establishing shots of Indian street scenes and a montage of modern Indian faces in close-up.[21] The sort of encounter with India and Pakistan that would inevitably elude the First Lady in person could be created on the editing table. Seltzer felt confident that his film could extend the diplomatic value of the visit and 'reach so many more people' than Mrs Kennedy herself, including those with cynical or sceptical attitudes towards the visit. He hoped that his film would defeat this criticism on her behalf, 're-affirming [the] true aims of the visit, friendship and understanding between two nations'.[22]

The final preparations for Mrs Kennedy's visit to South Asia were fraught with difficulties. Jackie's health required both a postponement of the trip and an alteration to the itinerary. She cancelled her plan to visit East Pakistan, the portion of the country that later won independence as Bangladesh.[23] But on 13 March Mrs Kennedy arrived in India to a rapturous welcome. Between 13 and 20 March, she and her sister, Princess Lee Radziwill, toured India. From 21 to 26 March they visited Pakistan. The tour was a triumph.[24] The US Ambassador in New Delhi, John Kenneth Galbraith, had only one major concern: the apparent obsession of the press corps with Jackie's clothing. With Mrs Kennedy's 'strong concurrence' he took steps on her second day in India to downplay the subject and, as if to emphasise her interest in the higher things in life, Jackie herself requested that the sacred city of Benares be returned to her schedule.[25] The visit to Pakistan was a little less well organised. The press enjoyed Mrs Kennedy's visit to Bashir Ahmed, a Karachi camel driver who had once given a camel ride to Vice-President Johnson. LBJ had responded by inviting Bashir to visit Texas in late 1961. In so doing he briefly transformed the humble camel driver into an international celebrity. Jackie and her sister delivered a letter from Johnson and accepted the obligatory ride on Bashir's camel.[26] USIA measured public reaction to Jackie's visit using the only available comparison, the recent visit of Queen Elizabeth. They found responses roughly comparable, though USIA noted that Jackie's visit had attracted marginally more foreign broadcast coverage. The *Los Angeles Times* summarised the press verdict as 'a propaganda smash at minimum cost'.[27] It now fell to USIA to reproduce the triumph on celluloid. But it was here that Stevens' problems began again.

Stevens' specifications for the project left little room for the savings anticipated by Hearst Metrotone. When the American press revealed that the two films would cost $73,000, Republican constituents deluged the Senate with angry letters. Alluding to another expensive film in the headlines that year, the *New York Daily News* ran a cartoon by Warren King showing the Kennedy family watching a home movie entitled 'My Trip Abroad', with Caroline asking her father, 'Daddy, when does Cleopatra come on?' An associated editorial suggested that the Democratic party should pick up the tab.[28] Senator Hubert Humphrey begged the White House for help in answering such complaints. In reply, the President's Press Secretary, Pierre Salinger, noted that, even with the expense of filming, the trips cost much the same as President Eisenhower's visits had done. Unfortunately, with a TV celebrity at the helm, USIA was now news in its own right. 'It's all that damn Murrow's fault,' Salinger complained.[29] George Stevens was shaken by the wave of criticism and recalled sitting with his head in his hands in Washington DC's Du Pont circle, terrified that his initiative at USIA had done more harm than good.[30] Fortunately, Salinger knew how to pour oil on troubled waters and counter-stories, stressing that the films were excellent value for money, soon appeared in the sympathetic columns of Drew Pearson and Victor Wilson of the *New York Herald Tribune*.[31] It now fell to the films to do the talking.

THE FILMS

Seltzer's films were scrupulous in their balance. Although the Indian film was nearly twice as long as the Pakistani film, both reflected the same priorities. The films include parallel scenes: visits to the grave of Gandhi in one country, Jinnah in the other; the elephant ride in India, the camel ride in Pakistan; and hospital visits in both countries. Above all, Seltzer sought to establish Jackie Kennedy, and by implication her husband's administration, as tolerant, nurturing and culturally sensitive. He was assisted in this task by an able script, written by his then wife Doris Ransohoff.[32] The result was not only a radical departure from the usual USIA visit film, but also contrasted sharply with the Indian government's own depiction of the visit. The Indian film included exactly the sort of scenes of Jackie Kennedy meeting Indian dignitaries, indigenous baby animals and interminable lines of American ex-pats that USIS New Delhi knew would be unhelpful in Seltzer's films.[33]

Seltzer structured both his films so as to emphasise the host countries rather than the visitor. Jackie did not swoop down from the sky into South Asia as though in some latter-day *Triumph of the Will*. Rather, she is shown arriving into worlds that have already been established for the audience. Both films open with sunrise over ancient monuments in the country in question, and set the scene with a discussion of the culture over a soundtrack of indigenous music. To a montage of colourful street scenes, child musicians and architecture, India is described as 'a country as ancient as it is modern' and an 'intricate pattern of civilisation and beauty'. As a crowd of Indians fills the screen we are told that the country is 'the world's largest democracy' and has just held its third national election. Pakistan is introduced with the sound of the call to prayer and scenes of men in various regional costumes, while the commentary describes how 'the age-old articles of faith of the People of Islam have begun to acquire new meaning today in the life of the young nation of Pakistan'.

Both films include shots of Mrs Kennedy's aircraft landing and formal welcomes from Prime Minister Nehru in India and President Ayub in Pakistan. Jackie is described as a 'friend' from a land that, as the commentary takes pains to assert, shares key characteristics with the respective host. In the case of India, this commonality lies in democracy and diversity: Americans are 'also a people of varied backgrounds and customs, of many faiths and races and beliefs'. In the case of Pakistan, the common ground is in the love of independence that is 'close to the hearts of freedom loving people everywhere'.

As George Stevens had originally suggested, both films stress that Jacqueline Kennedy is interested in and respectful of the countries that she is visiting. She is introduced to India as having 'a special interest in the arts and customs old and new'. Her itinerary in both countries includes meetings with artists. Both films also seek to establish Jackie and, by proxy the United States, as nurturing. They include shots of visits to children's hospitals and statements to the effect that: 'As a mother of two young children', she understands, 'the value of a smile, the touch of brightness', to a sick child.[34] In the Indian film Jackie approaches a sick infant in medium-shot, which is then made suddenly intimate by cutting to a closer point-of-view shot of the child smiling back and reaching towards the viewer. The illusion is powerful and it is hard to recall that the image we are seeing is a delighted child reaching for a camera and not a visiting president's wife. The two alleged areas of Jackie Kennedy's interests, children and the arts, come together at the mid-point of *Invitation to India*, when she is seen (with Mrs Gandhi rather ill at ease in the background) presenting 'the children's art carnival' exhibition to the people of India. In tune with the eager search for commonalities in the film, she points out that 'children's art' and 'our feeling for children' are the same 'the world over', and uses this as a springboard for her hopes for peace.

Some of the scenes in India hint at both the government of India's desire to represent itself as a trading power and Jackie's position as the ultimate western consumer. Jackie Kennedy is shown seated like a shopper in a fashion salon, reviewing a 'procession of silks, brocades and muslins for fashions that go round the world'. Indian and European models (the latter being Mrs Galbraith) enter dressed in western and eastern styles. Silks and prints are shown in close-up, and Jackie holds up magnificent gifts of clothing.

In order to support the emphasis on cultural respect within the films, the linking metaphor in *Invitation to India* is a journey into India's past. From the modern architecture and achievements of New Delhi, Mrs Kennedy 'travels back in time' to the splendours of Jaipur, the Taj Mahal and, finally, medieval Udaipur. Each is given a context in Indian and world history. We are told that Jaipur, built in 1728, was 'one of the first planned cities of its day'. Seltzer's pre-visit establishing shots show the sites at their best. Long exquisite takes draw the viewer into the scene. Yet Seltzer refuses to confine these monuments to the past and, in accordance with the wishes of USIS New Delhi, locates the images in India's present. He states that the monuments 'belong to each new day and the people who live it, to priest and scholar, to neighbour, to villager . . . to friend'. His populist point is underscored as the scene changes to the crowds in 'the people's monument' – the sprawling sacred city of Benares – cheering Jackie's boat as it sails past on the Ganges.

The visit to Udaipur is well served by Seltzer's pre-visit 'point of view shots'. We are shown the view from Jackie's bedroom window, opening onto the lake and 'a day of legendary beauty'. The windows close as the sun sets, and we hear Jacqueline Kennedy herself, summing up the visit, speaking over images of successive formal receptions. Musing on a meeting with American Peace Corps volunteers, she remarks: 'going the unknown ways – in my husband's words – requires many gifts of character and a confident vision of the future. I believe that both the people in India and we in our own country share this vision.'

The film ends with Jackie's visit to the grave of Mahatma Gandhi. The commentary links Jackie and, by implication, the Kennedy administration, to Gandhi's life and work. As she lays a wreath, we are told that the Mahatma's true memorial is in 'the hearts of his people and thoughts of those everywhere who seek to maintain freedom and to secure peace'. It is a complex moment. The action at one level aligns Jackie Kennedy with Gandhi's personal commitment to Indian freedom and non-violence, but the associated commentary clearly implies that because of its commitment to freedom and peace (even at the risk of war) the true heir to Gandhi's values was the Kennedy administration.

Invitation to Pakistan posed rather more of a problem for Seltzer as the country had fewer instantly recognisable personalities or places. Ayub's military pageants prevail. Despite Stevens' early hopes, the film does little to address the issue of women in Pakistan beyond including a few in the shots of Jackie meeting female dignitaries and members of the public. Jackie herself shines through in the scene in which she and her sister ride Bashir Ahmed's camel. She seems to have a genuine delight in the experience, takes the reins and flips the camel on its rump enthusiastically. After her ride she laughs with Bashir the camel driver and pets the camel. According to the *Washington Post*, the scene became the surprise hit of the film.[35] Her interaction with the people of Pakistan is shown through her acceptance of gifts, including a magnificent horse and a ritual dagger. The traditional gift of a goat from a Maliq of the Khyber region is shown only beside the giver.

There is no equivalent in *Invitation to Pakistan* to Jackie's visit to the handicraft emporium or silk weavers. If the Indian government constructed Jackie's itinerary to reveal trade items and tourist sites to the world, President Ayub seems to have preferred to conduct his guest and the attendant cameras to locations of immense strategic value, such as the Khyber Pass, and to mount displays of marching bagpipe bands. This was not necessarily a testament to the fact that Pakistan had, as the commentary notes, never before welcomed the wife of a president. President Ayub was well aware that his country's value to the United States was strategic, and the military displays suggested that his country was ready and willing to be a keystone in the defence of the region. As Seltzer recalls: 'he wanted to keep the aid money coming'. Jackie's visit provided the perfect opportunity to show American audiences raised on films like George Stevens Sr's *Gunga Din* that the Khyber Rifles still held the passes against the Russian bear as they had in the days of the British Raj. For good measure, the Pakistanis even arranged to make Mrs Kennedy an honorary member of the regiment, though the gesture, perhaps too redolent of the world of Kipling, is not mentioned in Seltzer's film.[36]

In place of the Taj Mahal, the Pakistan film shows Jackie Kennedy in the Shalimar Gardens. This visit actually took place on the second day of the trip; however, Seltzer uses the visit as his climax, taking the gardens as a metaphor for the emergence of modern Pakistan. The Shalimar Gardens, we are told, belong to the people, not to an elite or the past. They 'now offer repose to anyone who seeks it'. The film concludes with Mrs Kennedy thanking the people of Pakistan for their 'proverbial hospitality' and hoping to return with her husband for a future visit.[37]

During the final phases of production Seltzer worked with the USIA regional experts in Washington, DC. They intervened to change two elements in the film.

First, they asked that scenes showing a snake-charmer in India be cut to avoid causing offence to Indian audiences. Second, they recommended against the inclusion of a particular folksong on the soundtrack. Seltzer had recorded the song in a local language on an Indian railway station and hoped that it might give regional colour to the film – unfortunately, as the USIA expert pointed out, the lyrics were obscene.[38] The final element in each film was the epilogue narrated by Jackie Kennedy herself and recorded at the White House, and an English language narration by Raymond Massey. Mrs Kennedy proved cooperative, and eager to learn the best way to speak her piece, but Massey was awkward. As Seltzer recalled, he was reluctant to follow advice on Indian pronunciation and, as a paid-up Republican, clearly did not regard participation as an honour.[39]

THE RECEPTION

As the unwanted press comment during the making of the films made clear, George Stevens' decision to break with the usual format of USIA films in commissioning *Invitation to India* and *Invitation to Pakistan* carried considerable risk. Fortunately, his gamble paid off handsomely. At home the *Washington Post* called Leo Seltzer's films 'expert and beautiful'.[40] More significantly, as the standard letter sent out to disgruntled American tax-payers pointed out, the films received rave reviews in the South Asian press.[41] The New Delhi *Statesman* wrote of *Invitation to India*:

> The photography can only be described as superb. The monuments, the people, the colours, have all been captured before, but seldom with such exquisite taste, such lovely lighting, and, above all such obvious grace . . . obviously deep research and a natural sympathy for all things Indian have gone into the writing. . . . [This is] one of the finest documentaries on India itself made in many years.

The Pakistan Times was no less impressed by *Invitation to Pakistan*, contrasting the film favourably with the usual propaganda fare:

> documentaries, particularly the ones with a 'PR' purpose, are only too numerous to be looked forward to with any irrepressible enthusiasm. But the Mrs. Kennedy film is something one feels like writing a word about . . . . The director chose to shake himself free of the dates and 'facts' of the trip. He rose above these and knit the photographic record into something of a fantasy. The effect was charming.[42]

That established South Asian critics liked the films is hardly surprising. This was not American cultural imperialism, but rather complicity with the agendas of the indigenous ruling elites, being trade and tourism in the case of India and strategic value in the case of Pakistan. Both the Indian and Pakistani governments had crafted Jackie Kennedy's visit to show the best of their countries, and Seltzer had, in turn, shaped his record to reflect back a yet brighter image of an already polished experience, and to flatter the hosts. Here was a South Asia of magnificent costumes, gleaming new hospitals, breathtaking vistas, smiling people, generous hosts and stable political structures. Like sunlight falling on a series of parabolic mirrors, the reality of life in India and Pakistan – with its extremities of poverty and fundamental uncertainty – here became dazzling. It was at least two steps removed from the truth, but it made a wonderful spectacle.

USIA director Ed Murrow lost no time in informing the once sceptical American public of the 'unprecedented' impact of these films. He hoped that his agency would make 'more like it' and predicted an enthusiastic response to screenings elsewhere in the world.[43] He would not be disappointed. The USIA rushed to release Seltzer's films in seventy-eight countries and twenty-nine different languages for the Indian film (and twenty-two for the Pakistani film). The agency was able to devote three pages of its semi-annual report to the global response. The films drew 20,000 viewers in a single week of screenings at two Beirut cinemas. In Ceylon, USIS noted that audiences were returning for repeat viewings of the English versions, and predicted that Tamil and Sinhalese prints would be a runaway success also. The Pakistani Ambassador to Italy arranged for a gala screening of the American film in Rome, and called the film, 'one of the finest she had ever seen' depicting her country.[44] The USIA, for its part, could draw satisfaction from the level of interest in Jackie Kennedy. As Seltzer's films appeared the USIA arranged the release of the CBS film of her White House tour in those parts of the world beyond the reach of the network's executives, including much of the Third World and even certain countries of the Eastern bloc. Jackie was clearly a major propaganda asset.[45]

President Kennedy himself viewed *Invitation to India* in July 1962 during a lunch meeting with the Indian Ambassador. Seltzer joined the President in the White House screening-room for the occasion and was gratified when, as the film drew to a close, JFK turned and exclaimed: 'wonderful'.[46] With domestic curiosity about both films growing, President Kennedy suggested to Murrow that USIA release both films within the United States.[47] By December Congress had provided the requisite permission.[48] United Artists handled the distribution and released the film in a single thirty-minute edited version entitled *Jacqueline Kennedy's Asian Journey*.[49] Unfortunately, what played well in Peshawar did not necessarily please Peoria. Much about the American version of the film seemed awkward. The film's poster seemed at odds with the message of the film. It showed Jackie, handbag on her arm, standing alone in front of the Taj Mahal. As the poet and critic, Wayne Koestenbaum, has recently noted of an equivalent *Life* magazine photograph, she appears to be both an 'American wife, contemplating her dream house' and a mysterious monument in her own right: 'the Taj Mahal's eerie twin'. The poster added incongruity to this already awkward scene by rendering Jackie in a detached black and white and the Taj Mahal behind her in exotic candy pink. It hardly suggested cultural harmony. True to the manicuring of India inherent in the film, scaffolding on a minaret to Jackie's right had been airbrushed out of the photograph. Evidently Jackie's India was not in need of repair.[50] But there was worse to come. As though to play on the theme of the 'exotic' spectacle, this film opened across New York city on the same bill as the dire Tony Curtis love-among-the-Cossacks costume drama, *Taras Bulba*. The reviews were mixed. Bosley Crowther of the *New York Times* complained of 'endless lines' of Asian monuments and dignitaries on the screen, but quipped that this would at least be 'a nice item in the present First Family's home movie files'. Crowther, however, was never the intended audience of the film.[51] A further sour note came from the film's narrator, Raymond Massey, who protested against the political implications of the domestic release by donating his $300 narrator's fee to the Republican National Committee.[52] Fortunately, the film was good enough to deflect the attention of most of the agency's detractors, and justify the USIA's spending. As *Variety* put it: 'the public can feel confident that their money is being put to good and effective use'. Stevens, Seltzer and USIA film would live to fight another day.[53]

Today Seltzer's films are remembered for the light they cast on the developing image of Jackie Kennedy. As Koestenbaum has noted, they now seem to be a meeting of two exotic spectacles: Asia and Jackie.[54] There is much in Seltzer's agenda to draw forth such a reading. The films always had to tell a double story. Seltzer needed to construct a piece of reportage that would both praise the host countries in their own terms and allow Jacqueline Kennedy's public persona to shine. He intended his films to be a meeting of culture and developing modernity on one side and compassion and tolerance on the other, but he could only add light political freight to powerful pre-existing notions. These films would not have been made had South Asia and Jackie Kennedy not already been exotic spectacles, worth looking at in their own right. The historian may question exactly what the image of Jackie meant to the overseas audiences who saw her bending over a sick child in India, or chatting about the White House furniture in her CBS special. At the very least she gave a human face to an administration which, during those same years, was obliged to stand at the brink of nuclear war. Jacqueline Kennedy also provided a handsome pinnacle for the pyramid of the American way of life. In Seltzer's films she is happy, beautifully dressed, independent, but obviously dutiful to her husband, whose foreign obligations she is sharing. She seems to be proof that the domestic American way can be fulfilling in ways that the models of liberated womanhood then championed by the Communist world could not be. No argument or comparisons are necessary within the script. Jackie makes the point solely by the force of her presence: her star quality.

These films also occupy a unique place in the personal development of Jacqueline Kennedy. The South Asian tour and the associated films were a small part of the learning experience that spanned her years in the White House. Jackie originally hoped that her Asian trip might be a personal encounter with Indian civilisation, and was more than a little disconcerted by the scale of press and public attention. As Galbraith's cables make clear, she proved well able to cope with the transition and understood how to shape her visit to project a politically useful image of America. Twenty months later she proved how much she had learned, introducing telling elements into the coverage of her husband's funeral. Jackie's presence at that event; her insistence on walking behind the coffin; the poignant scene she planned in which her infant son saluted his father's casket; her insistence on a racially integrated guard-of-honour to stress her husband's commitment to Civil Rights, all bear witness to her appreciation for the power of the visual over mere words. Jackie Kennedy had done much to show the world what it had in the Kennedy administration; now she forced them to look full square at what it had lost. These scenes were, of course, captured by USIA cameras for international propaganda purposes.[55]

Despite the strength of Jackie's presence, the films and the First Lady clearly both had their limitations. Leo Seltzer and his team had done a creditable job in breathing new life into the stale genre of the foreign visit film, but the challenges facing the United States at home and overseas required films that ventured to comment explicitly on the great issues of the day while still engaging the audience. In the years that followed, USIA film-makers engaged such subjects as Civil Rights and international development; celebrated the life of President Kennedy and introduced the world to his successor, Lyndon Johnson. Arguably the finest hour of USIA film-making came in 1969, when an agency team led by Stevens' successor as director of motion picture production, Bruce Herschensohn, carried off the documentary short-subject Academy Award for their wordless account of the Soviet invasion of Czechoslovakia: *Czechoslovakia, 1968*.

Yet the glory days of USIA film-making were drawing to an end. By 1968 the agency became deeply divided over the issue of Vietnam and such policies as *détente* with the Soviet Union. Liberal film-makers who, like Seltzer, were eager to project Kennedy administration policies to the world, were less inclined to champion the policies of Richard Nixon. Seltzer redirected his talents to teaching, serving on the faculty of the College of Staten Island, Columbia University and the Philadelphia College of Art before ending his career as Professor of Film at Brooklyn College. Conservative film-makers also found the Nixon administration to be difficult terrain in which to operate. The labyrinthine twists of Henry Kissinger's diplomacy did not lend themselves to representation in film. Finally, the medium of film was itself entering a period of crisis. The agency's old commercial partners, the newsreels, ceased distribution overseas in 1968. The new medium of television required fresh ideas and a quite different approach to visual propaganda, and it was not until the Reagan administration that either the budget or leadership was on hand for the agency to take the initiative once more.[56] Such stories, like Seltzer's films, cast invaluable light on the development of American propaganda and foreign policy as a whole. Until historians systematically engage the history lying undisturbed in the archives of USIA and similar institutions around the world, and in the memories of the propagandists themselves, these stories will remain untold. The historical study of propaganda will be much the poorer.

Notes

1   Like other such high-impact 'p' words as 'pervert' and 'pornography', the term 'propaganda' is more readily enunciated as a term of abuse than it is defined. British propaganda history has been particularly well served by the institutional approach. Such books as Philip Taylor, *The Projection of Britain* (Cambridge University Press, 1979), Ian McLain, *Ministry of Morale* (London, Allen and Unwin, 1979) and Robert Cole, *Britain and the War of Words in Neutral Europe, 1939–1945* (London, Macmillan, 1990) are exemplary and underpinned the author's own approach in Nicholas J. Cull, *Selling War: British Propaganda and American Neutrality in the Second World War* (New York, Oxford University Press, 1995). The best introduction to USIA is written by agency veteran Hans N. Tuch, *Communicating with the World: US Public Diplomacy Overseas* (New York, St Martins Press, 1990). This case study is part of the first full-scale political history of USIA. The author is grateful to Margit Dementi in New York; Catherine Fasbender and Louis Miller in Cambridge, MA; and Bernie and Gloria Kamenske in Washington, DC for their hospitality during the research for this piece; and to George Stevens Jr and Leo Seltzer for sharing their recollections. The author has benefited from discussions with Aileen Tsui of Harvard and Susan Zieger of UC Berkeley on this subject. The research was funded by grants from the John F. Kennedy Library and the University of Leicester.

2   See Richard Dyer MacCann, *The People's Films: A Political History of US Government Motion Pictures* (New York, Hastings House, 1973) and 'Films from Uncle Sam', *Newsweek*, (18/04/1966), p. 109.

3   Interview: George Stevens Jr (10 and 14 April 1998). Stevens recalled that he was keen to develop a sense of documentary film heritage in what soon became an emerging school of young film-makers. To this end he arranged for John Grierson to visit USIA and cast a grandfatherly eye over the heirs to his tradition.

4   John F. Kennedy Library (hereafter JFKL), press translations filed at WHCF, SF, Box 705. Exec., PP5/Kennedy, Jacqueline: *La Nacion* noted that hitherto there had been 'few handsome chiefs of state. The most "elegant" of all, Eden, faded as quickly as a flower.'

5   JFKL Agency Files, USIA, Box 1, Memoranda file one: Guarco to Harris, 15 November 1961. On the background to the visit see National Archives RG59, Central Files, 1960–63, Box 1457, 711.11-KE/3-862, Frederick Dutton (State) to Lindley Beckworth (House of Representatives), 19 March 1962, etc.

6   *Variety* (6/11/1961), 'Murrow furrows H'wood brow – criticizes "image" of US abroad created by films . . .' and (7/11/1961), 'H'wood asks Murrow provide consultant to mirror "image"'.

7   Interview: George Stevens Jr.

8   JFKL Salinger Papers, Box 132, USIA, Wilson to Kennedy, Weekly Report (Secret), 9 January 1961 noted that Stevens' experience included work as a producer on *The Greatest Story Ever Told* and *Diary of Anne Frank*, both directed by his father.

9   JFKL Agency Files, USIA, Box 1, Memoranda file one: Stevens & Stevens to Murrow, 8 November 1961 (emphasis in original).

10   For a sample of Eisenhower era USIA film dealing with this region, see Eisenhower Presidential library, Abilene KS, EL-MP16-157: *Peace and Friendship in Freedom: Eisenhower Visits Pakistan* (1959). The film includes an excruciating description of cricket as 'similar to baseball'. In the event the Indian film was considerably longer than the Pakistani film, reflecting the relative duration of Mrs Kennedy's respective visits. For background, see JFKL Agency Files, USIA, Box 1, Memoranda file one: Guarco to Harris, 15 November 1961.

11   Quoted in Leo Seltzer papers, deeded for deposit in New York Public Library, Zorthian to Rose, 9 March 1962.

12   Interviews: George Stevens Jr and Leo Seltzer (6 April 1998). See also MacCann, *The People's Films*, pp. 184–7.

13   Interview: Leo Seltzer. Five of Seltzer's films from this era are preserved in the Museum of Modern Art, New York: *America Today*; *National Hunger March* (1931); *Hunger: The National Hunger March to Washington* (1932); *Bonus March* (1932); and *Workers' Newsreel: Unemployment Special* (1931). For background, see Russell Campbell, *Cinema Strikes Back: Radical Film Making in the United States, 1930–1942* (UMI Research Press, Ann Arbor, Michigan, 1982).

14   A full filmography for Seltzer may be found in his personality file at the MOMA, Motion Picture Branch. *Let There Be Light* and its medical version *Shades of Gray* may be found at the National Archives as RG 111 M 1241 and RG 111 PMF 5047 respectively.

15   Interview: Leo Seltzer.

16   Interviews: Leo Seltzer and George Stevens Jr. For correspondence on the Reed Harris appointment see JFKL, RFK Attorney General Correspondence, Box 63, USIA, Wilson to RFK, 17 July 1961.

17   For *The American Commitment* (narrated by Howard K. Smith) see NA RG 306 387. The film shows the USIA sending news around the globe of the death of a boy shot while trying to cross the Berlin Wall, and includes scenes of a Public Affairs Officer going about his duties in Central America. He is pictured driving past a wall decorated with the slogan: 'Castro Si, Yankis Non!' Seltzer's other USIA films were: *Progress Through Freedom* (1962) on JFK in Mexico; *Saturn, Space Vehicle* and *Gemini 4* (both 1964) on space; *Poland Abroad* (1964) on a touring exhibition about Polish-American culture; *Day in Malaysia* (1964) on LBJ's visit to that country; *Summit* (1964) on the Punte del Este economic assistance conference; *Sinews of Freedom* (1966) on the economy of Taiwan; and two visit films made as gifts for the leaders featured: *Crown Prince of Laos Visits America* and *A Visit of the President of Tsirinana* (Malagasy Republic) (1968).

18   Interview: Leo Seltzer. Fred Gutman also worked as a cameraman on the India sequences. All shooting used an Ariflex camera with sound recorded on a battery operated portable Nagra recorder. Seltzer claims to be the first American film-maker to import a Nagra recorder from Switzerland.

19   Interview: Leo Seltzer and Leo Seltzer papers, deeded for deposit in New York Public Library, Pam Turnure (White House) to Seltzer, 10 January 1963.

20   Leo Seltzer papers, Zorthian (USIS New Delhi) to Robert Rose (project officer, USIA, Washington DC), 9 March 1962.

21   Leo Seltzer papers, undated script notes by Seltzer note: 'Mrs. K comes to the modern India

as well as to the storybook India. A young Indian workman smiles as he removes the welder's helmet [before the shots of] The airplane in the sky bringing Mrs. K.'

22   A comparison of the Pakistan film and Mrs Kennedy's itinerary also reveals the omission of meetings with American ex-pats. See National Archives RG59, Central Files, 1960-63, Box 1457, 711.11-KE/3-3062, Linebaugh (US Embassy, Karachi) to State, 30 March 1962, 'Mrs. Kennedy's "Magic Week" in Pakistan'.

23   National Archives RG59, Central Files, 1960–63, Box 1457, 711.11-KE/3-762, Galbraith to Rusk, 7 March 1962 (no. 2799).

24   National Archives RG59, Central Files, 1960–63, Box 1457, 711.11-KE/3-1562, Galbraith to JFK (via Rusk), 15 March 1962 (no. 2905).

25   National Archives RG59, Central Files, 1960–63, Box 1457, 711.11-KE/3-1462, Galbraith to JFK (via Rusk), 14 March 1962 (no. 2889).

26   National Archives RG59, Central Files, 1960-63, Box 1457, 711.11-KE/3-3062, Linebaugh (US Embassy, Karachi) to State, 30 March 1962, 'Mrs Kennedy's "Magic Week" in Pakistan'.

27   JFKL Salinger papers, Box 132, USIA, Murrow to Kennedy, Weekly Report, 3 April 1962. Eisenhower's visit of 1959 topped both in terms of words written and broadcasts made but not radiophotos wired. For press comment see JFKL Agency files, USIA Box 2, 'Memos re: film coverage of Mrs Kennedy during visit to Asia', Bennett (Research) to Murrow, 19 April 1962. The New Delhi PAO Zorthian recalled that Jackie Kennedy's visit came at a time when Indian relations with the United States were recovering from a period of considerable strain. The closure of a deal over the Bhopal dam project and India's conflict with China certainly helped matters, but he had no doubt that the visit of so visible and admired a figure as Mrs Kennedy did much to present a positive image of the United States and more than repaid the burden of time and money that it imposed on the Galbraith Embassy. Telephone interview: Barry Zorthian, 29 June 1998.

28   New York Daily News (23/03/1962), p. 41.

29   JFKL WHCF, SF, Box 705, Exec, PP5/Kennedy, J. Salinger to Humphrey, 29 March 1962.

30   Interview: George Stevens Jr.

31   JFKL Salinger papers, Box 132, USIA, Murrow to Kennedy, Weekly Report, 3 April 1962; Agency files, USIA Box 2, 'Memos re: film coverage of Mrs Kennedy during visit to Asia'.

32   The script was, of course, subject to the approval of the USIA. See Seltzer papers, 'India: Technical Specifications', 15 February 1962.

33   Interview: Leo Seltzer. The Indian film – S.C. Desai (prod.), Magic Moments (Films Division, Government of India, 1962) – may be viewed at the Kennedy library. It includes scenes of Indian boys highdiving into a well that were presumably too exotic for Seltzer's account.

34   Invitation to Pakistan renders this: 'The mother of two young children, Mrs. Kennedy knows what it means to bring a smile to the face of a sick child.'

35   'Camel Ride is Hit of Color Movies', Washington Post (28/06/1962).

36   In Lahore Mrs Kennedy was treated to an unscheduled pageant on the evolution of Pakistani women's clothing mounted by the women of Pakistan Arts Council in spite of their government's wishes. The event is not recorded in the film, but is noted in National Archives RG59, Central Files, 1960–63, Box 1457, 711.11-KE/3-3062, Linebaugh (US Embassy, Karachi) to State, 30 March 1962, 'Mrs. Kennedy's "Magic Week" in Pakistan'.

37   Diplomatically, Jackie also expressed the wish to visit East Pakistan, dropped from the visit as originally planned.

38   Interview: Leo Seltzer. The Pakistani film had a more complex soundtrack than the Indian equivalent. While there is virtually no diegetic sound in the Indian film, *Invitation to Pakistan* includes scenes of warriors' dances, marching bands, a dancing camel and a rousing account of the Skye boat song on the bagpipes of the Khyber Rifles, all apparently matched to appropriate recorded sound. The effect is of synchronised sound, with all its attendant immediacy, although, as Seltzer recalls, the only two truly synchronised portions in either film are those in which Jackie herself speaks.

39   Interview: Leo Seltzer. Seltzer recalled that Jackie Kennedy's first reaction to her scripted epilogue was that she 'could not possibly read it in one breath'. He realised that the CBS crew who filmed her White House tour had not coached her on breathing, which accounted for the 'breathy' style of her delivery.

40   *Washington Post* (28/06/1962).

41   JFKL WHCF, Agency files, USIA, Box 1, Memoranda file 1, unsigned draft letter, 17 October 1962.

42   USIA 19th Review of Operations, July 1–December 31 1962 (Washington, DC, 1963), p. 21 (copy in Museum of Modern Art, Dept. of Film, Personality File, Leo Seltzer).

43   'Jackie's Films Draw Raves from Murrow', *New York Daily News* (13/08/1962), p. 27.

44   USIA 19th Review of Operations, July 1–December 31 1962 (Washington, DC, 1963), pp. 21–3.

45   JFKL WHCF, SF, Box 705. Exec., PP5/Kennedy, Jacqueline: Blair Clark (CBS) to Salinger, 4 June 1962 and WHCF, SF, Box 184, Exec., FG 296, Wilson to Salinger, 21 June 1962.

46   Interview: Leo Seltzer.

47   JFKL WHCF, SF, Box 184, Exec., FG 296, Wilson to Salinger, 20 July 1962. Press comment on the film included a sensationalised cover story of *Motion Picture* magazine, July 1962: 'Jackie Kennedy – she's a film star now but you may never be allowed to see the movies she made.'

48   JFKL Agency files, USIA Box 2, 'Memos re: film coverage of Mrs. Kennedy during visit to Asia', Bennett (Research) to Murrow, 19 April 1962, Murrow to Senator Fulbright, 14 August 1962 and Stevens to Murrow, 19 December 1962. According to the acting director of the USIA Donald M. Wilson, the problem over the domestic release of the film was not the restriction on the agency of the Smith Mundt Act but the question of Congressional intent in appropriations. Precedent held that the USIA funds could be spent on overseas publicity only, see JFKL WHCF, SF, Box 705. Exec., PP5/Kennedy, Jacqueline: Wilson to O'Brien (White House) 7 November 1962.

49   The combined version of the film cut out scenes in which the subject matter overlapped (Jackie made only one hospital visit) and included rather more Indian material than Pakistani as a result. It may be viewed at National Archives as RG 306.636. The script for the combined film survives in the Seltzer papers, dated 26 November 1962.

50   A copy of this poster may be viewed as part of the permanent First Lady gallery in the museum of the JFK Library. It appeared in *Variety*, 19 December 1962, p. 14. For Koestenbaum's comments on the photograph, see Wayne Koestenbaum, *Jackie Under My Skin: Interpreting an Icon* (New York, Plume, 1996), p. 102.

51   Bosley Crowther, 'Mrs. Kennedy's Journey' (*sic*), *New York Times*, 5:2 (26/12/1962).

52   *Newsweek* (11/02/1963).

53   JFKL WHCF, Agency files, USIA, Box 1, Memoranda file 1, unsigned draft letter, 17 October 1962.

54   For a retrospective comment on the films' place in the iconography of Jackie Kennedy, see Koestenbaum, *Jackie Under My Skin*, pp. 102–3.

55   The Kennedy funeral was at the centre of the USIA's first feature length production, Bruce Herschensohn (dir.), *John F. Kennedy, Years of Lightening, Day of Drums* (USIA, 1964). On Jackie Kennedy's contribution to the funeral, see book two of William Manchester, *Death of a President* (New York, Harper and Row, 1967) and Koestenbaum, *Jackie Under My Skin*, p. 201.

56   This potted summary of the decline of USIA film is based on interviews with a number of USIA film-makers: Leo Seltzer, Bruce Herschensohn, Charles Guggenheim, Meyer Odes and Jerry Krell; the Hearst Metrotone film-maker Walter DeHoog, and former agency directors, Frank Shakespeare and Charles Z. Wick.

18

THIRD WAVE INFO-PROPAGANDA: PSYCHOLOGICAL OPERATIONS IN THE POST-COLD WAR ERA

Philip Taylor

I t is now quite commonplace to hear our current 'Information Age' described as being in a 'third wave' of societal development whereby nation states, having emerged from their agricultural (first wave) and industrial (second wave) stages, are transforming into post-industrial (or postmodern) 'info-communications' or 'knowledge-based' societies. This model of analysis has also been extended into theories of warfare as part of the so-called 1990s Revolution in Military Affairs (RMA). The common denominator for both frameworks is communications and information technology developed on a national and international scale. In the third wave, it is argued that 'knowledge is now the central resource of destructivity just as it is the central resource of productivity'.[1] Irving Goldstein, head of INTELSAT, has predicted that information will be for the next century:

> what oil and gas were for the beginning of the 20th century. It will fuel economic and political power and give people everywhere more freedom and momentum than the fastest automobile or supersonic jet. Information is no longer the province of the privileged few, nations or individuals, or the economic or power elite. It is the fare of the masses, shaping how they view their lives, their governments, and the world around them. . . . Information will be transmitted in every form we've known and in forms we cannot yet even imagine.[2]

The belief that 'brain power' will in the next millennium lie increasingly at the heart of political, economic, military and individual power opens up exciting – if sometimes quite alarming – new fields of enquiry for propaganda analysts. The current preoccupation in advanced info-societies with such concepts as Information Warfare (IW), Information Operations (IO) and Psychological Operations (PSYOPS) are some examples of this.

These developments reflect the degree to which nation states are seeking to find a new role in a world which no longer enjoys the 'certainties' of an established bi-polar, ideologically based, superpower confrontation. Who is the enemy now? In the information age, it is the computer hacker, the cyberterrorist, the Internet criminal, the info-bomber, defence against whom requires a new breed of warriors: the info-warrior.

The very nature of international competition during the Cold War, itself a global ideological contest in which world public opinion was pivotal and mass communications outlets were widely available, required new and broader concepts of international affairs. It saw the development of a new form of competition, a 'political warfare' which became a function principally of the secret intelligence services. To the British, political warfare meant 'that aspect of intelligence in which information is used aggressively to manipulate opinion or to create special conditions by purely intellectual means'.[3] By the 1950s, it was clear that this was a way of the future, in peace as in war, with its limitations imposed only by technological capacity for the temporal and spatial compression of information. It was conducted both overtly and covertly, the former by ever-growing 'information' machineries such as the United States Information Services or the Propaganda Department of the Politburo, while the latter was part of the war between the CIA and the KGB.

By comparison, however, with the technologies available on the eve of the millennium, the Cold War confrontations, the radio wars and the jamming, the film and television stereotyping of the 'enemy' and the battles for the upper hand in press editorials, seem positively primitive. The end of the Cold War may therefore be said to have marked the end of the second wave of propaganda that began with the coincidence of mass communications and industrialised warfare in the First World War. The 1980s were characterised by massive deregulation and innovation in the field of communications technologies and, whatever contribution those developments may have actually had in first penetrating and then tearing down the Iron Curtain, this has produced a tendency towards 'demassification'. In the fields of both communications and the people who use and receive them, everything is fragmenting. Indeed, as we enter a multi-channel, multi-media, digital, real-time, interactive, free-market universe, it becomes increasingly difficult to talk of mass communications or mass public opinion. As technologies converge, for example, computer-mediated communications provide opportunities for individuals to access the wider world – as observer, participant and even as catalyst – in a way never possible before. From one PC desktop workstation, an individual can access television, video and radio or communicate by fax, phone or e-mail anywhere in the world in an interactive rather than passive manner. No longer solely dependent on the broadcaster for their windows on the world, the individual thus becomes a narrowcaster capable of not just observing the world wherever and whenever he or she chooses but also directly imputing it with whatever information he or she thinks fit – including rumours, conspiracy theories and falsehoods. This even affects the ability of the media as a profession which has evolved over the past century to 'mediate' the doings of the few to the many. The use of a handheld portable camcorder can provide footage from the streets – the infamous footage of the Rodney King beating springs immediately to mind – or the use of a mobile phone can provide eyewitness reports from inside occupied Kuwait. This transforms the relationship between journalism and its audience and indeed blurs traditional distinctions between the press as information providers and the people who consume them. What Walter Lippmann would have made of all this remains open to speculation but one thing is clear: the whole concept of 'public opinion' requires considerable rethought in a world in which the public increasingly have the capacity to map the world out for themselves rather than relying on the cartography of the profession of journalism.

If we accept that, in the second wave, 'urban life developed in a manner that led to strangers being thrust into regular contact with other strangers', a major role of communication was to provide a unifying process as common to education and enlightenment as well as to power and propaganda. Whereas once communications served to turn strangers into friends, or at least acquaintances, now new technology allows strangers to communicate with one another, to gather together in a public sphere that is virtual rather than physical, interactive rather than passive, while retaining their privacy and anonymity and diminishing their reliance upon the traditional media. To survive these developments, the role of the mass media transforms into a provider of entertainment or 'infotainment' rather than as a provider of information. Indeed, the Internet service provider is already cheaper that the annual BBC licence fee or the daily purchase of a newspaper, or even the weekly rental of a couple of videos. In cyberspace, public opinion becomes private opinion, and the concept of the mass – whether it be the public or communications – requires radical rethought: niche communication for niche markets and niche publics gathered together in niche newsgroups.

The Internet, the fastest growing medium of communication the world has ever seen, is an apparently vast and chaotic 'place' in which tens of millions of individuals gather together for a wide variety of purposes. But as the Internet is everywhere and anywhere, perhaps it would be more useful to start thinking of it as a 'space' rather than as a 'place'. It is in that cyberspace that third wave propaganda is most likely to occur. To take a hypothetical but pertinent example, it is more efficient to direct a message via electronic mail than it is to drop millions of leaflets containing the same message. It is simpler, cheaper, more direct, less dangerous and more likely to reach its target. Moreover, the target individual(s) receive the message more safely, more privately and personally. This type of scenario is, of course, only possible with societies that are 'wired-up' to the global information infrastructure. And if you can receive an e-mail, you can also reply to it – unless of course that e-mail contains a virus which destroys your hard disk. If you pick up a leaflet, and are seen to be reading it, then the authorities who wish to prevent this can at least 'delete' you as a person.

This brave new world appears therefore to bring with it a new world information disorder in which information becomes more than ever a commodity rather than as it was once – until relatively recently – perceived, namely as a fundamental human right. Access to that information likewise increasingly becomes a means of measuring power. Instead of talking about class, the next century will perhaps see the world divided into information 'haves' and 'have-nots'. The concept of 'power', itself problematical, need not concern us too much here. Suffice to say that it is widely agreed that power involves 'the ability to exercise control, to get others to do what they might not do were it not for your presence'.[4] This is of course not far removed from definitions of propaganda.[5] Hans Morgenthau defined power as 'man's control over the minds and actions of other men', and as 'a psychological relation between those who exercise it and those over whom it is exercised'.[6] Of course, not all information is propaganda, not all power is propaganda, and nor is all information power since possession of it operates at a variety of levels, from the trivial to the sophisticated. Knowledgeable game show contestants, for example, might win prizes for their ability to answer questions, but does that empower them? Out of the entire American workforce, 60 per cent might well be involved in the 'info-communications' sectors but this covers a broad spectrum, from wordprocessing and debt recovery to public relations and advertising. Information junkies might have access to the Internet, but can they distinguish between fact and fiction? Indeed, the very phrase 'info-communications' neatly encapsulates the distinction between the mere possession of, or access to, information and the ability to disseminate information to niche audiences within the private and the public spheres. And to this can be added the phrase 'info-propaganda' which more clearly identifies the role of information-age persuasion, in peace and in war.

Since the end of the Cold War, there has really been only one conflict of a remotely traditional interstate nature. Even that conflict, the Gulf War of 1991, has been labelled the 'first information war'. This is not to suggest that international crises and conflicts have gone away; indeed, there are more UN peacekeeping forces involved in more trouble spots around the globe now than at any time during the Cold War. These other crises in the 1990s have been more appropriately termed 'conflicts other than war'. It would appear to be a special characteristic of conflict in the 1990s that what we are seeing more of now are intrastate conflicts – or what we used to call civil wars. These are fought out along nationalistic, ethnic or tribal lines within collapsing or ideologically adrift states: Somalia, Bosnia, Rwanda and, most recently, Albania. Such conflicts have been characterised by a particular brutality and confusion, all the more so because they are fought out not just on a traditional battle 'front' that all too often involves civilians, but also on the global 'front' of world public opinion. The warring factions compete for world attention when they need it, and deny media access when they have something to hide.

Thanks to the emergence of international television services such as Cable News Network (CNN) or BBC World Service Television, warfare is no longer confined to traditional battlefields on which soldier fights soldier to determine the eventual outcome. Instead, the involvement of both civilians and the media, especially the medium of live television, transforms the area of conflict again into a global 'battle space' which billions of people can observe in real-time like spectators at an actual (or perhaps 'virtual' would be a better word) football match. For professional soldiers, therefore, their performance – as soldiers fighting an enemy, as blue-helmeted implementers of humanitarian aid or as good old-fashioned peacekeepers – is inevitably now more affected by the roar of the crowd.

Since the Crimean War and the birth of the profession of war correspondent, soldiers have come increasingly to appreciate that their activities could no longer be conducted in the brutal vacuum of battle divorced from public scrutiny. Hence the advent of the war correspondent was accompanied by the birth of military censorship. In wars fought between nation states since then, ever more elaborate censorship and propaganda machineries have evolved to ensure that the public image of battle, win or lose, was such that it did not detract from the distant observing public's willingness to support the continuation of the war. The Somme, Dunkirk, Pearl Harbor, Stalingrad all provide examples of what we would now call 'spin doctoring' in order to ensure that defeats were portrayed as setbacks or as justifications for even greater public support until ultimate victory was assured. Even the Tet Offensive in Vietnam, a military victory for the United States although very much a media/publicly perceived defeat, did not prevent that conflict, that most uncensored of wars, from continuing for as many years as it had already been taking place. But Vietnam was, Korea notwithstanding, the first war in which a mass television audience watched night after night from the increasing discomfort of the living rooms of middle America. It was, from that point of view, a watershed. But television was not the reason for US military defeat. It was, however, the medium through which people could buy tickets to watch a war fought by professional (and, problematically, conscripted) soldiers as a spectacle. It was admittedly a mediated, heavily self-censored, non-live spectacle but it nonetheless provided an unprecedented insight into what human beings were being asked to do to other human beings in the name of patriotism and the nation state. Thereafter, there could be no going back to an age in which images of battle could be sustained in terms of historical traditions of heroism, glorious iconography and remoteness from reality. In this respect, television made the tactics of the soldier's behaviour on the battlefield a matter of strategic significance and concern for the watching civilian public back home. In turn, that watching public's response to what they were seeing affected the conduct of soldiers back in the field. The advent of real-time television since then, which means that civilians watch soldiers' behaviour live at the same time as politicians, the enemy, even the soldiers themselves, has quite simply transformed the media from being an observer of conflict into an actual participant.

Battlefields, in other words, have become increasingly porous 'information environments'. Once, the military could control the flow of information flowing in and out of the battlefield – by censorship, by keeping soldiers apart from civilian perceptions of what they were doing – and the ability to manipulate the media coverage constitutes an important element of the history of warfare in the age of the communications revolution. Within the area of combat itself, increasingly sophisticated methods of targeting information to achieve military objectives gave rise to the use of psychological warfare. From a strictly battlefield point of view, this is perhaps better termed combat or battlefield propaganda. To some extent, this is as old as warfare itself. Information and messages generated by sounds, symbols, gestures – even, in more superstitious times, religious relics and omens – have a long tradition of military deployment in calculated attempts to affect the progress and outcome of battles favourably to one side at the expense of another. Of course, rational theorists have also understood the significance of such techniques in pre-empting the need to resort to war. After all, it was Sun Tzu who wrote in the fourth century BC that 'to subdue the enemy without fighting is the acme of skill'.[7]

Once war breaks out, however, psychological weapons are deployed in an attempt to influence the use of other types of munitions to determine the eventual outcome. Yet because their deployment embraces issues of morale (civilian as well as military, friend as well as enemy) as a factor in determining victory or defeat, there have always been ethical concerns about how this is achieved – by fair means or foul – as well as doctrinal issues about when to use it, and at what level. Most standard histories of warfare still tend to overlook the relevance of this activity,[8] both on the battlefield and beyond, despite the fact that the combined military application of communications and psychology can be identified as far back as biblical times. Although the psychological arsenal available to military commanders has obviously expanded with the twentieth-century explosion in communications technologies, many of the techniques employed nonetheless remain time-honoured. Indeed, Joshua's use of trumpets outside the walls of Jericho had its modern parallel when, during the 1989 US operation in Panama, loud recorded rock music was played through loudspeakers outside General Noriega's compound (including the song by Martha Reeves and the Vandellas, 'Nowhere to Run, Nowhere to Hide'). And just as the British consul in Berne spent a good deal of his time between 1914 and 1918 placing leaflets in bottles to float down the Rhine, so also did PSYOPS officers do likewise in the waters of the Persian Gulf in 1991. In 1991, the PSYOPS teams also sent 'info-bombs' into enemy computers while smart weapons also carried cameras on their noses to transmit pictures of how accurate they were to an astounded global television audience before the screen went blank. The local place for killing had become a global space for watching.

Three examples in particular serve to illustrate how the tactical battlefield has become a strategic battle space. In 1991, uniquely, reporters from enemy countries were permitted to stay in Baghdad. Saddam Hussein hoped to exploit pictures of what he anticipated to be widespread civilian damage, in order to undermine public support for the war in western countries. Accordingly, he permitted western reporters to visit damaged civilian (but, significantly, not military) sites. Yet on the two most famous occasions when this happened – the 'baby milk plant' and the Al Firdos bunker – it failed to shift western public resolve. However, the television pictures enabled the returning coalition pilots to ascertain whether they had in fact hit their intended targets – which mostly, in Baghdad, they did.

The second example involved the Saudi coastal border town of Al Khafji. When a western television camera crew visited the town and pictures were transmitted on CNN showing the town to be empty and undefended, Iraqi troops promptly attacked and occupied the place until a nasty little battle removed them. This was a classic example of why military censors had, since the Crimea, insisted that they must restrict access to the battlefield and vet copy for 'security review' and equally also of how difficult this had become by the early 1990s.

The third example involved media speculation prior to the Ground War as to where the liberation of Kuwait would take place from. Military spokesmen deliberately failed to dampen down speculation that an attack would take place from the sea rather than the left hook from the land which General Schwarzkopf labelled his 'Hail Mary Play'. Indeed, the Marines in the Persian Gulf waters increased their access to journalists during this period in order to reinforce the impression of a sea-borne invasion. That the Iraqis were watching this television coverage is evidenced by the fact that, once coalition forces liberated Kuwait, most Iraqi armour was indeed seen to have been deployed in anticipation of a coastal invasion.

In short, the Gulf War of 1991 was fought out in the transitional period between the second and third waves. How long this transitional period will last, we simply do not know. For its duration, many characteristics of second wave propaganda will remain, especially in conflicts involving second and third wave countries. In such conflicts, the mass media remain important weapons in the struggle for public opinion, all the more so because one axiomatic lesson learned from past struggles is that effective propaganda must also be effective entertainment. The 'dumbing down' of the mass media, especially marked in countries with only a minimum commitment to public service broadcasting like the USA, means that it is especially vulnerable to stunts, spin doctoring and manipulation.

Much recent research has, of course, concentrated upon the reverse process, i.e. the impact of television on policy-makers. As Ed Turner of CNN has argued, 'we continue to collect evidence that television news does have an impact on the conduct of foreign policy, but no one knows how much'.[9] And because CNN is an all-news channel, he defends it as providing fuller coverage than that which the major entertainment networks no longer see fit to provide:

> If we were to take a strong story-line, compress it into a formal documentary, pre-empt the news hours, and run it for say two hours on any night, chances are quite high that very few people would watch. That is the way of the world, rightly or wrongly. But if you take the same information, the news and opinion and build it around a live-from-the-scene reporter or anchor, and inject proper live shots from other aspects of the story, I believe you cannot only attract a sizeable audience but also perform some important and effective services for the viewers.[10]

So, on the one hand we have CNN as a force for increasing popular interest in foreign affairs by making it exciting, while on the other we can argue that this is merely placing undue pressure on politicians to make over-rapid decisions. But however exciting a 'breaking news story' may be, it does not mean that the story is accurate.

Lee Hamilton, Chairman of the US House of Representatives' Foreign Affairs Committee in 1994, felt that:

> Spurred by technological advances ranging from satellites to cellular phones, vivid images of conflict and deprivation are sent instantly to American homes from the world's trouble spots, whether in Haiti or Somalia or Bosnia or the Persian Gulf. These televised images quickly become a central part of the foreign policy debate. They affect which crises we decide to pay attention to and which we ignore. They affect how we think about those crises, and I have little doubt these televised pictures ultimately affect what we do about these problems.[11]

From a propagandist's point of view, it therefore becomes imperative not only to control the 'spin' but actually to shape the media agenda. And in an age when the specialised defence and foreign correspondents are declining in numbers, and when increasing numbers of non-specialised 'hacks' with no military experience are ever more dependent on official spokespersons to explain what is going on, the role of the media as either a cheerleader or a participant in the propaganda wars should surprise no one. It is indeed a characteristic of our times that non-specialist journalists are being confronted increasingly by specialised information officers. These officials understand the pressures of modern journalism only too well, which is why they release information close to publishing or broadcasting deadlines, or why they are only too happy to bypass the traditional mediation/gatekeeping role of journalists by going live and talking directly to a global television audience.

CNN's Ed Turner conceded that journalists faced a further challenge in the age of real-time television, namely, 'will we be smart enough to use the technology wisely? Will we be astute and honest as programmers and as editors of this journalism? It will be expensive and it will be difficult, but given the track record of the free world's journalists, I believe the answer is yes. We are cranky and we are impertinent and not infrequently wrong in this elusive search for truth. But taken as a whole, the answer is yes.'[12] An analysis of the coincidence between the official agenda and the media agenda frequently suggests a different answer, which is why scholars such as Chomsky and Herman talk of 'manufacturing consent', or others such as Jean Beaudrillard argue that 'the Gulf War did not happen'.

The increased use of psychological operations in the 1990s, though barely noticed by scholars, adds a further element into this equation. PSYOPS is about the targeted use of persuasion to achieve national objectives. Traditionally used in combat situations, the changing nature of conflict in the post-Cold War era requires new and imaginative uses – especially given the changing nature of the public sphere, the advent of new communications technologies and the inclusion of non-military (i.e. civilian) personnel as significant actors.

As one would expect from professional propagandists, PSYOPS personnel undeniably package their activity in attractive terms. For example, they argue that if, in dangerous circumstances, attempts are made to encourage enemy soldiers to defect, desert or surrender, thereby saving their lives in the process, then there is a moral case to be made that this is a more acceptable activity than actually killing them. Or, as one officer has put it: 'Our motto is "electrons instead of bullets".'[13] This gains even greater moral authority now that PSYOPS are being applied increasingly to embrace civilians caught up in a conflict. For instance, in planning for a NCEO, or a 'non-combatant evacuation operation', that is the evacuation of civilians from combat situations to a safe haven, it is claimed that PSYOPS 'can reduce interference by the local populace and military forces . . . explain the purpose of the US/allied action to counter confusion and misinformation, and assist in crowd control'.

PSYOPS themes should emphasise that US actions are in accordance with international law and US/allied forces are in the country only to protect the evacuation of US/allied citizens and not to occupy the host nation or take sides with any faction.[14]

Using PSYOPS for such situations is likely to become even more attractive, especially as in June 1996 the International Red Cross was predicting that the number of people around the world fleeing crisis situations was like to double to 50 million within ten years.[15]

This in turn invites a radical rethink about the nature of 'propaganda' as a process of persuasion. Despite the efforts of many scholars to argue that propaganda is a value-neutral process which should more appropriately be judged by reference to the intentions of those undertaking it, it remains a pejorative term in the minds of most people. This certainly hampers the acceptance of the transformation of psychological warfare into psychological operations in the post-Cold War era. Yet scholars of propaganda, as well as practitioners, are only too aware of the legacy of Dr Goebbels and his 'Big Lie'. Indeed, as the western democracies were increasingly forced to engage in propaganda from the First World War onwards, they developed an appreciation of the need to adopt a 'strategy of truth'. This meant that the tradition of democratic propaganda in this century was factually based upon information closely linked to the truth. This is not to suggest that the whole truth was told, but rather that democratic propaganda was rooted in the principle encapsulated by Lord Reith that 'news is the shocktroops of propaganda'. And if accurate news and information form the basis of the historical tradition, it remains a fundamental principle of contemporary democratic propaganda. Perhaps, therefore, 'info-propaganda' is a more appropriate term that helps to distinguish the intent, as well as the content, of contemporary democratic practice from the authoritarian tradition that has sullied the reputation of targeted persuasion techniques.

This would suggest that a clean break with the past is also needed in so far as psychological warfare is concerned. Certainly, in purely military situations, PSYOPS still essentially embraces targeted military information forming an integrated supporting role in command and control warfare (C^2W). More recently, however, the Pentagon's consideration of C^4I planning (command, control, communications, computers and intelligence) has started to attract attention. In the press, there are sensational claims: 'Info warriors hope to transform the way soldiers fight. Their goal: to exploit the technological wonders of the late 20th century to launch rapid, stealthy, widespread and devastating attacks on the military and civilian infrastructure of an enemy.'[16] This involves the full range of communications technology, from flying television stations to the injection of computer viruses into enemy screens and hard discs. 'Modern armies are so dependent on information that it's possible to blind and deafen them in order to achieve victory without fighting in the conventional sense.'[17]

There are, of course, wider implications of this beyond the sheer technology, and these depend upon one's individual perspective. For example, it is possible to argue that because PSYOPS support national objectives it is being used during the 1990s to support American foreign policy objectives based on the premise of consolidating 'victory' over communism in a new world order – although such explicit statements cannot be found in any of the public documents. Instead, they speak of a rededication to fostering 'democratic peace and prosperity'. Is this therefore a new form of ideological activity designed to influence the competitive global political, economic, military and informational environment in a manner favourable to US national objectives? Other nations are beginning to realise that they avoid entering this dimension at their peril,[18] although they call it something else. For these reasons, PSYOPS are increasingly being seen as an additional, and perhaps even indispensable, informational tool to aid not just the old-fashioned concepts of war-fighting and peacekeeping but also newer, more proactive, policies of peacemaking, peacebuilding and peace enforcement – and all at a strategic level.[19]

For this reason, many believe that the UN should embrace PSYOPS as part of its activities:

> With the introduction of non-lethal weaponry, and an increased reluctance on the part of national governments to place their armed forces in harm's way (especially when involved in United Nations operations), psyops has an even more important role to play. This is true in conflict and in the period before conflict begins. The use of psyops in UN peacekeeping as an instrument of UN policy (rather than that of participating countries alone), is overdue. . . . The UN should use psyops as it does diplomacy: as an interlocking tool that, along with other means at its disposal – including force – can be used to limit casualties and assist in achieving aims set by the UN Security Council.[20]

At a tactical or operational level, there are powerful arguments for doing this. The problem, once again, comes at the strategic level.

In the so-called new world order, the American conduct of PSYOPS is less negative in intention than the psywar of the Cold War and other wartime situations in that it tends to be more promotional of the values which helped democracy survive those struggles. It was always thus in a sense but, with a clearly identifiable enemy in the form of the old Soviet Union, it had an ideology to shoot down as well as one to sell: a form of negative advertising. While now being more 'pro' than 'anti' since the demise of communism, the emphasis has also shifted to a global rather than bi-polar environment in which the threat of global nuclear war may have diminished but in which there is a continuing risk of dangerous regional clashes fuelled by the forces of nationalism, or what might be termed the unfinished business of the old imperialistic orders of the past two centuries. Moreover, while supporting notions of prodemocracy, human rights and peacebuilding, there nonetheless also remain several forces which threaten the new emerging order, namely nuclear proliferation, terrorism, drug-trafficking and, where the latter two meet, narco-terrorism. With the most advanced info-communications system in the world, the United States is particularly vulnerable to 'info-bombers' who could disrupt the computerised infrastructure of the economy. So the emphasis of psychological operations is still the business of the targeted use of information to induce results favourable to those undertaking the effort, but the enemies are now identified as transnational threats to a global community rather than ones emanating from a specific regime targeting a specific nation. At the moment, this is used to justify the role of the USA acting as a global policeman on behalf of the majority of nations who share similar values of 'freedom', 'free enterprise' and 'human rights'. States which threaten such 'universal' values will accordingly remain the primary targets of American PSYOPS.

If we survey the use of psychological operations in 1993, one can easily see how the old 'P' word has transformed in nature at the tactical level. For example, a US PSYOPS team supported the UN and the Cambodian Mine Action Centre by producing 'an extensive variety of mine awareness products such as leaflets, posters, bulletins, banners and cards . . . to educate the people about the dangers of unexpended munitions'.[21] Again, in March 1993, when the US Coast Guard towed a refugee ship with over 500 Chinese as part of Operation Provide Refuge to Kwajelein Atoll in the Marshall Islands, PSYOPS personnel were despatched to liaise with the refugees and to produce newsletters and information boards for them.[22] A fifteen-member PSYOPS task force was despatched to Bosnia and was responsible for almost a million leaflets dropped on the night before the first American airdrops of relief supplies, explaining that the aid was impartial and humanitarian in nature, together with safety instructions to keep away from the parachuted food pallets until after they had landed. In Ethiopia, a PSYOPS unit produced ordnance awareness and first-aid handbooks for a joint mine clearance operation with the local forces. In a combined medical readiness and army training exercise in Senegal (MEDFLAG), PSYOPS personnel supplied the American Special Forces teams with 'military information and electronic newsgathering support as well as materials on Senegalese cultural norms' to assist in the 100,000 'informational booklets, posters and pamphlets providing information on personal hygiene, health and sanitation'.[23] PSYOPS Military Information Support Teams (MISTs) were deployed to Barbados, St Lucia and Grenada to work with local committees in order to develop drug awareness campaigns; media ranging from bumper stickers to television commercials were used as part of the fight against narco-terrorism. In Bolivia, the Dominican Republic, Guatemala and Jamaica other MISTs were deployed to work alongside anti-drugs campaigners directing information at schoolchildren through the use of colouring books, videos and other media. In Bolivia, they were said to have helped to decrease the numbers of hectares that were used to cultivate coca. In Belize, cholera prevention materials were supplied. In Venezuela, PSYOPS personnel developed information campaigns supporting 'democratisation, professionalisation of the military, civil-military relations, and counterdrug operations'.[24]

This info-propaganda may ostensibly seem harmless – indeed, it is largely a positive application dressed up so it appears that the principal beneficiary is the target rather than the source, and therefore not propaganda at all. But when we begin to examine the wider implications, alarm bells start to ring. The US Department of Defense defines information warfare as 'actions taken to achieve information superiority by affecting adversary information, information-based processes, information systems and computer-based networks while defending one's own information, information-based processes, information systems and computer-based networks'.[25] In info-war theory, 'nobody is a soldier and everybody is a combatant'.[26] PSYOPS thus becomes a frontline psychological instrument directed at both civilians and combatants within an environment that, thanks to the presence of everything from a mobile phone to a CNN camera crew, has global strategic implications.

The current official American definition of PSYOPS runs as follows:

> Planned operations to convey selected information and indicators to foreign audiences to influence their emotions, motives, objective reasoning, and ultimately the behaviour of foreign governments, organisations, groups and individuals. The purpose of psychological operations is to induce or reinforce foreign attitudes and behaviour favourable to the originator's objectives.[27]

From once being an activity which fuelled uncertainty in the minds of the enemy, psychological operations are now more about indicating intentions and generating information about the presence of military forces. It is those intentions which must remain the object of scrutiny. After all, more than fifty years ago, one propaganda expert wrote that:

> The place of artillery preparation for frontal attack by the infantry in trench warfare will in future be taken by revolutionary propaganda, to break down the enemy psychologically before the armies begin to function at all. How to achieve the moral breakdown of the enemy before the war has started – that is the problem that interests me.[28]

For this author, this was the ultimate object of propaganda. His name was Adolf Hitler. One is ultimately therefore left with a choice. Is it better to persuade people to do something, or to kill them, or to allow them to kill themselves by doing nothing? And, in so far as info-war is concerned, is the command, control and manipulation of information preferable to more lethal means of resolving disputes? The feeling that they are underpins the renewed emphasis on both activities. These are the difficult choices being arrived at in a complex and confusing world, a response to the changing nature of disputes since the end of the Cold War and the political dilemmas they create.

It is important to stress that many of these new applications are still being worked out. As one official warned in 1994:

> There is currently no common understanding of what psychological operations are and what they are not. It appears that we do not clearly understand the difference between the conduct of military PSYOPS as a unique operation and other activities that have a PSYOPS effect whether intended or not. As things now stand, almost anything can be called a psychological operation.[29]

After all, 'PSYOPS is communication and therefore covers the entire field of human action'.[30] This is perhaps going too far. As one authority has pointed out, 'our documents are replete with implications that DoD PSYOPS plays a far greater role in "strategic" PSYOPS than it actually does or will in the near future'.[31] Emerging info-war theory does however threaten this. If we are to see wider applications at a strategic level, the involvement of the media is inevitable. The media will mistrust any information activity designed to manipulate their agenda. For this reason alone, it is essential for PSYOPS to remain within the democratic tradition of the strategy of truth. We are not, of course, talking about the whole truth. But we are talking about the manipulation of information to serve national – and increasingly international – objectives, and this begs important questions for societies whose democratic traditions have evolved since the Enlightenment as they enter the third wave. There are equally implications for the democratic traditions of free journalism as the mediator of information about the doings of the few for the enlightenment of the many. The question whether an increasingly commercialised, competitive and infotainment-oriented media can respond to Ed Turner's challenge about modern technology also applies to postmodern developments in official information management. Indeed, one of the features absent from public pronouncements about C^4I, one suspects, is that what is really meant is C^5I: command, control, communications, computers, intelligence – and CNN!

Notes

1   A. and H. Toffler, *War and Anti-War* (London, Little, Brown & Co., 1993), p. 33.

2   Cited in L. Snyder, Washington, DC, The Annenburg Washington Program in Communications Policy Studies, 1995. http://www.annenburg.uwu.edu/pubs.

3   Ladilas Farago, *War of Wits – the Anatomy of Espionage and Intelligence* (New York, Paperback Library, 1954), p. 241

4   Mark D. Alleyne, *International Power and International Communication* (Oxford, St Anthony's & Macmillan, 1995), p. 4.

5   Philip M. Taylor, *Munitions of the Mind* (Manchester University Press, 1995), p. 6.

6   H. Morgenthau, *Politics Amongst Nations* (New York, Knopf, 1978 edn), p. 30

7   Sun Tzu, *The Art of War* (trans. S.B. Griffiths) (Oxford, Clarendon Press, 1971), pp. 77–8.

8   This tends to explain why John Keegan's *The Face of Battle* (London, Cape, 1976) created such an impact when it was first published.

9   Ed Turner, 'The Power and the Glory', in Christopher Young, *The Role of the Media in International Conflict*, a report on a two-day seminar at the Canadian Institute for International Peace and Security, December 1991.

10   Turner, 'The Power and the Glory'.

11   Turner, 'The Power and the Glory'.

12   Turner, 'The Power and the Glory'.

13   Cited in Capt. Janice M. Morrow, 'Never Seen, Always Heard', *Airman* (02/1993), p. 4.

14   4th Psychological Group (A), Psychological Operations support to Noncombatant Evacuation Operations (Fort Bragg, 1995).

15   *The Times* (29/05/1996).

16   Douglas Waller, 'Onward Cyber Soldiers', *Time* (21/08/1995).

17   Cited in James Adams, 'Dawn of the Cyber Soldiers', *The Sunday Times* (15/10/1995).

18   Since its creation in 1955, the *Bundeswehr* has used PSYOPS units, notably the Fernmelder Battalion 950, a regular battalion of 650 personnel, capable of doubling in size by reservists. It mainly worked to counter East German propaganda during the Cold War but since has been deployed in Somalia. Italy has the Monte Grappa Battalion, about which little is known, while Turkey and Greece also have small units. The British, burned by their experience in Northern Ireland and the Colin Wallace affair, maintain a smaller capability still.

19   See Alfred H. Paddock. ' "No More Tactical Information Detachments": US Military Psychological Operations in Transition', *Low Intensity Conflict and Law Enforcement*, 2 (1993), 195–211.

20   Brian Cloughley, 'Peace in Mind: Will the UN Give PSYOPS a Chance?', *Jane's International Defence Review*, 3 (1996), 59

21   US Special Operations Forces, *Posture Statement 1994*. In author's possession.

22   US Special Operations Forces.

23   US Special Operations Forces.

24   US Special Operations Forces.

25   http://www.atsc-army.org/cgi-bin/atdl.dll/fm/100-

26   Cited in Adams, 'Dawn of the Cyber Soldiers'.

27   US Department of the Army, *Field Manual 33–1: Psychological Operations* (Washington, DC, Government Printing Office, 1992), p. 12. See also US Department of Defense, Joint Chiefs of Staff, *DoD Dictionary of Military and Associated Terms and Abbreviations* (JCS Publication 1–02, republished by Greenhill Books, 1990), p. 291.

28   Cited in Z.A.B. Zeman, *Nazi Propaganda* (Oxford, Oxford University Press, 1973), p. 86.

29   Col. Thomas A. Thimmes, 'Military Psychological Operations in the 1990s', *Special Warfare* (01/1994).

30   William Daugherty for the American Institutes for Research in the Behavioral Sciences, *The Art and Science of Psychological Operations: Case Studies of Military Applications* (2 vols, Washington, 1976), vol. 1, p. 17.

31   Col. Thomas A. Thimmes, 'Military Psychological Operations in the 1990s', *Special Warfare* (01/1994).

19

BIBLIOGRAPHICAL ESSAY

Bertrand Taithe and Tim Thornton

The historiography of the themes touched on in this volume is vast and diverse; as in previous volumes we have not sought to be exhaustive or overly detailed. This further reading will allow further exploration of the themes of propaganda, rhetoric and political communication.

HISTORIOGRAPHICAL TRENDS IN THE SECONDARY LITERATURE

The theme of propaganda has a social history of its own, and it is not insignificant that it enjoyed its uncritical heyday in the 1960s and 1970s Cold War and political tension within western powers. The Arno Press series on International Propaganda and Communications thus reprinted earlier texts such as James Morgan Read, *Atrocity and Propaganda, 1914–1919* (New Haven, Yale University Press, 1941). Also see George G. Bruntz, *Allied Propaganda and the Collapse of the German Empire in 1918*, Hoover War Library Publications – 13 (Stanford University Press, 1938). Both represent earlier instances of academic reflection on propaganda in the wars of the twentieth century and, like Bruntz, conclude on the effectiveness of allied propaganda against German morale (pp. 210–16). See also Daniel Lerner, *Psychological Warfare against Nazi Germany: The Sykewar Campaign, D-Day to VE-Day* (1949; reprinted Cambridge, MA, MIT Press, 1971); Ernst Kris and Hans Speier, *German Radio Propaganda: Report on Home Broadcasts during the War* (London, Oxford University Press, 1944, facsimile by University Microfilms International, Ann Arbor, Michigan, 1979). Recent literature and theory of propaganda is now filling the gaps; the sociologist Ellul led the way to a more theoretically aware approach, albeit dogmatic: Jacques Ellul, *Propaganda: The Formation of Men's Attitudes* (New York, Vintage Books, 1973). Philip M. Taylor who contributes to this volume also represents the most thorough revision of the debate and the development of a technology-driven grand narrative; for an introduction, see Philip M. Taylor, *Munitions of the Mind: A History of Propaganda from the Ancient World to the Present Day* (Manchester University Press, 1995); Philip M. Taylor, *Global Communications, International Affairs and the Media since 1945* (London, Routledge, 1997).

WAR PROPAGANDA

Never is propaganda more active and vital among state services than in time of war. Carl Berger, *Broadsides and Bayonets: The Propaganda War of the American Revolution* (Philadelphia, University of Pennsylvania Press, 1961), documents efforts by the Congress to undermine British morale, subvert its control of German mercenaries and negro slaves, and to promote its own agenda of liberty in England itself. The world wars of the twentieth century saw the rise of sophisticated and often well-equipped propaganda offices. Much has been made of German or Fascist propaganda machines but the more interesting developments in the historiography address the effective manner in which the democratic powers managed their propagandising effort. See Gary S. Messinger, *British Propaganda and the State in the First World War* (Manchester University Press, 1992), a summative account of state-managed propaganda during the first conflict and a prosopography of its key actors; Sally Marks, 'Black Watch on the Rhine: A Study in Propaganda, Prejudice and Prurience', *European Studies Review*, 13 (1983), 297–334; Philip M. Taylor, 'The Foreign Office and British Propaganda during the First World War', *Historical Journal*, 23 (1980), 875–98; Alfred E. Cornebise, *War as Advertised: The Four Minute Men and America's Crusade 1917–1918* (Philadelphia, The American Philosophical Society, 1984); R. Blythe (ed.), *Private Words: Letters and Diaries from the Second World War* (Harmondsworth, Penguin, 1993); P. Fussell, *Wartime: Understanding and Behaviour in the Second World War* (New York, Oxford University Press, 1989); M. Honey, *Creating Rosie the Riveter: Class, Gender and Propaganda during World War II* (Amherst, MA, University of Massachusetts Press, 1984); I. McLaine, *Ministry of Morale: Home Front Morale and the Ministry of Information in World War II* (London, Allen, 1979); L. Rupp, *Mobilizing Women for War: German and American Propaganda 1939–1945* (Princeton University Press, 1978).

IDEOLOGICAL PROPAGANDA

Recasting the mind of defeated enemies has become an urgent priority for the victors in the great ideological conflicts of attrition in the twentieth century. Nazi Germany, more than any other totalitarian regime, called for fully formed and targeted propaganda which aimed at reforming a whole mindset: Arthur L. Smith Jnr, *The War for the German Mind: Re-educating Hitler's Soldiers* (Providence, Berghahn Books, 1996) ends in the false debate on whether it was consumerist materialism or democratic values that won the war for hearts and minds when both could be seen as the sides of the same propagandist coin (e.g. p. 203). Maintaining a propaganda effort in non-combatant nations during the Second World War is the subject of Robert Cole, *Britain and the War of Words in Neutral Europe, 1939–45: The Art of the Possible* (Basingstoke, Macmillan, 1990). Internal propaganda aimed at the population was usually deployed against ideological competition, such as religion. Isabel A Tirado, 'The Revolution, Young Peasants, and the Komsomol's Antireligious Campaigns (1920–1928)', *Canadian-American Slavic Studies*, 26 (1992), 97–117; Fanny Bryan, 'Anti-Islamic Propaganda: Bezbozhnik, 1925–35', *Central Asian Survey*, 5 (1986), 29–47; Peter Kenez, *The Birth of the Propaganda State: Soviet Methods and Mass Mobilization, 1917–29* (Cambridge University Press, 1985).

On subversion see, for instance, Silvia P. Forgus, 'Soviet Subversive Activities in Independent Estonia (1918–1940)', *Journal of Baltic Studies*, 23 (1992), 29–46; Ewa M. Thompson, 'Nationalist Propaganda in the Soviet Russian Press: 1939–1941', *Slavic Review*, 50 (1991), 385–99; Graham Walker, ' "The Irish Dr Goebbels": Frank Gallagher and Irish Republican Propaganda', *Journal of Contemporary History*, 27 (1992), 149–65; Robert J. Bookmiller, 'The Algerian War of Words: Broadcasting and Revolution, 1954–1962', *Maghreb Review*, 14 (1989), 196–213; Wojciech Liponski, 'Anti-American Propaganda in Poland from 1948 to 1954: A Story of Ideological Failure', *American Studies International*, 28 (1990), 80–92; David Wedgwood Benn, *Persuasion and Soviet Politics* (Oxford, B. Blackwell, 1989); Donald S. Birn, 'The War of Words: The British Council and Cultural Propaganda in the 1930s', *Peace & Change*, 14 (1989), 176–90; Ellie Howe, *The Black Game: British Subversive Operations against the Germans during the Second World War* (Lawrence, MA, Michael Joseph, 1983); Mark S. Steinitz, 'The US Propaganda Effort in Czechoslovakia, 1945–48', *Diplomatic History*, 6 (1982), 359–85.

RHETORIC AND HISTORY

On rhetoric see Brian Vickers, *In Defence of Rhetoric* (Oxford, Clarendon Press, 1988); Brian Vickers (ed.), *Rhetoric Revalued: Papers from the International Society for the History of Rhetoric* (Binghampton, New York, Center for Medieval and Early Renaissance Studies, 1982); Takis Poulakos (ed.), *Rethinking the History of Rhetoric: Multidisciplinary Essays on the Rhetorical Tradition* (Boulder, CO, Westview Press, 1993); James J. Murphy, *Rhetoric in the Middle Ages: A History of Rhetorical Theory from Saint Augustine to the Renaissance* (Berkeley, University of California Press, 1974); James J. Murphy (ed.), *Medieval Eloquence: Studies in the Theory and Practice of Medieval Rhetoric* (Berkeley, University of California Press, 1978); James C. McCrosky, *An Introduction to Rhetorical Communication* (1968; 4th edition, Englewood Cliffs, NJ, Prentice-Hall, 1982); Kenneth W. Thompson (ed.), *The History and Philosophy of Rhetoric and Political Discourse* (2 vols, Lanham, MD, University Press of America, 1987); Wilbur Samuel Howell, *Logic and Rhetoric in England, 1500–1700* (Princeton University Press, 1956); Frederick J. McGinness, *Right Thinking and Sacred Oratory in Counter Reformation Rome* (Princeton University Press, 1995); A. E. Chaignet, *La Rhétorique et son histoire* (Paris, Bouillon et Vieweg, 1888); Leo Rockas, *Modes of Rhetoric* (New York, St Martin's Press, 1964), p. ix; Catherine Hobbs Peaden,

'Condillac and the History of Rhetoric', *Rhetorica*, 11 (1993), 135–56; Michael G. Moran (ed.), *Eighteenth-Century British and American Rhetorics and Rhetoricians: Critical Studies and Sources* (Westport, CT, Greenwood Press, 1984); Keith Hamilton, 'The Historical Diplomacy of the Third Republic', in Keith Wilson (ed.), *Forging the Collective Memory: Government and International Historians Through Two World Wars* (Providence, Berghahn Books, 1996); Catherine Ann Cline, 'British Historians and the Treaty of Versailles', *Albion*, 20 (1988), 43–58; Herman J. Wittgens, 'War Guilt Propaganda Conducted by the German Foreign Ministry during the 1920s', *Historical Papers* (1980), 228–47.

PROPAGANDA TECHNIQUES

On early instances of propagands, see Alison Allan, 'Royal Propaganda and the Proclamations of Edward IV', *Bulletin of the Institute of Historical Research*, 59 (1986), 146–54; Elizabeth Skerpan, *The Rhetoric of Politics in the English Revolution, 1642–1660* (Columbia, University of Missouri Press, 1992). On the use of pamphlets to serve an expansionist agenda, see Frederick Merk, *Fruits of Propaganda in the Tyler Administration* (Cambridge, MA, Harvard University Press, 1971); Nicole Pons, *"L'honneur de la couronne de France", quatre libelles contre les Anglais (vers 1418–vers 1429)* (Paris, Librairie C. Klincksieck, 1990); see also Harold D. Lasswell, *Propaganda Technique in World War I* (Cambridge, MA, MIT Press, 1971); on psychological analysis, see Alexandre L. George, *Propaganda Analysis: A Study of Inferences Made from Nazi Propaganda in World War II* (Evanston, IL, Row, Peterson and Co., 1959).

On recent media forms, cinema has taken more than its fair share of the historiography. This interest is multi-faceted but one of its chief attractions is probably the fact that cinema was enjoyed collectively and thus fitted better with mass-control theories than more discreet forms of propaganda. Nicholas Reeves, *Official British Film Propaganda during the First World War* (London, Croom Helm, 1986); S.D. Badsey, 'Battle of the Somme: British War-Propaganda', *Historical Journal of Film, Radio and Television*, 3 (1983), 99–115. Philip M. Taylor, *Britain and the Cinema in the Second World War* (Basingstoke, Macmillan, 1988); Nicholas Pronay and D.W. Spring, *Propaganda, Politics and Film, 1918–45* (Basingstoke, Macmillan Press, 1982); M.L. Sanders, 'British Film Propaganda in Russia, 1916–1918', *Historical Journal of Film, Radio and Television*, 3 (1983), 117–29; Robert E. Herzstein, 'Crisis on the Eastern Front, 1941–42: A Comparative Analysis of German and American Newsreel Coverage', *Film & History*, 13 (1983) (1), 1–11, (2), 34–42; Larry Wayne Ward, *The Motion Picture Goes to War: The US Government Film Effort during World War I* (Ann Arbor, UMI, 1985); R.C. Raack, 'Nazi Film Propaganda and the Horrors of War', *Historical Journal of Film, Radio and Television*, 6 (1986), 189–95; Clayton R. Koppes and Gregory D. Black, *Hollywood Goes to War: How Politics,*

Profits and Propaganda Shaped World War II Movies (New York, The Free Press, 1987); Anthony Aldgate and Jeffrey Richards, *Britain Can Take it: The British Cinema and the Second World War* (Oxford, Basil Blackwell, 1986); Andrew Higson, *Waving the Flag: Constructing a National Cinema in Britain* (Oxford, Clarendon Press, 1995); Rachel Low, *Films and Comment and Persuasion of the 1930s* (London, George Allen and Unwin, 1979); Karen Russell and Benjamin Sandzer-Bell, 'Japanese War Propaganda Films: The Manipulation of National Ethos', *Journal of Asian Culture*, 8 (1984), 61–87; Frans Nieuwenhof, 'Japanese Film Propaganda in World War II: Indonesia and Australia', *Historical Journal of Film, Radio and Television*, 4 (1984), 161–77; Richard S. Geehr and Gerda Geehr, 'Film as Teacher: Goebbels' Speech for the Opening of the Film Project of the Hitler Youth', *Film & History*, 14 (1984), 36–42; Karel Margry, ' "Theresienstadt" (1944–1945): The Nazi Propaganda Film Depicting the Concentration Camp as Paradise', *Historical Journal of Film, Radio and Television*, 12 (1992), 145–62; David Weinberg, 'Approaches to the Study of Film in the Third Reich: A Critical Appraisal', *Journal of Contemporary History*, 19 (1984), 105–26; Nicholas P. Hiley, ' "The British Army Film," "You!" and "For the Empire": Reconstructed Propaganda Films, 1914–1916', *Historical Journal of Film, Radio and Television*, 5 (1985), 165–82. Cf. for radio and music, Horst J.P. Bergmeier and Rainer E. Lotz, *Hitler's Airwaves: The Inside Story of Nazi Radio Broadcasting and Propaganda Swing* (New Haven and London, Yale University Press, 1997), esp. ch. 5; C. Marx, ' "Dear Listeners in South Africa": German Propaganda Broadcasts to South Africa, 1940–1941', *South African Historical Journal*, 27 (1992), 148–72; J.F. Slattery, ' "Oskar Zuversichtlich": A German's Response to British Radio Propaganda During World War II', *Historical Journal of Film, Radio and Television*, 12, (1992), 69–85; also Wendell P. Holbrook, 'British Propaganda and the Mobilization of the Gold Coast War Effort, 1939–1945', *Journal of African History*, 26 (1985), 347–61. On a very sad and recent example, see Mark Thompson, *Forging War: The Media in Serbia, Croatia and Bosnia-Hercegovina* (Bath, Article 19, 1994). Theatre is less well covered but recent scholarly articles have used this material: Eric Robertson, 'Art and Propaganda: Two Dramatic Portrayals of Wartime Alsace', *German Life and Letters*, 45 (1992), 126–39; on earlier understanding of art as propaganda, see Thomas Christensen, 'Music Theory as Scientific Propaganda: The Case of Dalembert's *Éléments de Musique*', *Journal of the History of Ideas*, 50 (1989), 409–27. On other propaganda media, see for instance: Donald Malcolm Reid, 'The Postage Stamp: A Window on Saddam Hussein's Iraq', *Middle East Journal*, 47 (1993), 77–89; Lyman Chaffee, 'Poster Art and Political Propaganda in Argentina', *Studies in Latin American Popular Culture*, 5 (1986), 78–89; buildings can also be construed as the embodiment of state propaganda: James D. Shand, 'The *Reichsautobahn*: Symbol for the Third Reich', *Journal of Contemporary History*, 19 (1984), 189–200.

HISTORY AS PROPAGANDA

The historiography has devoted much time and energy identifying the ways in which historians have shaped national identity (see *War* volume of this series) and helped the propaganda mission of the state. See Gary Ianziti, *Humanistic Historiography under the Sforzas: Politics and Propaganda in Fifteenth-Century Milan* (Oxford, Clarendon Press, 1988); Keith Wilson (ed.), *Forging the Collective Memory: Government and International Historians Through Two World Wars* (Providence, Berghahn Books, 1996). Diplomatic history which deals mostly with foreigners and enemies, and apportions guilt and responsibility for wars is an obvious area of applied propaganda: John J. Murray, *George I, the Baltic and the Whig Split of 1717: a Study in Diplomacy and Propaganda* (London, Routledge and Kegan Paul, 1969) is a detailed instance which could be multiplied, especially for the great twentieth-century conflicts when propaganda and history appeared particularly blurred and borrowed heavily from each other. *J'accuse by a German* is a classic and famous example. The Cold War also invited extreme partisanship and the blurring of categories: Stephen Rosskamm Shalom, *Deaths in China due to Communism: Propaganda versus Reality* (Occasional Papers No. 15, Arizona State University, Center for Asian Studies, 1984). Nancy S. Struever, *The Language of History in the Renaissance: Rhetoric and Historical Consciousness in Florentine Humanism* (Princeton University Press, 1970); Joan Davies, 'History, Biography, Propaganda and Patronage in Early Seventeenth-Century France', *Seventeenth-Century French Studies*, 13 (1991), 5–17.

PROPAGANDA MATERIAL

While it is clear that many elements of our own cultural environment would benefit from being considered critically as propaganda it is interesting to find that propaganda manuals and analyses usually demonstrate clear propaganda aims: John C. Clews, *Communist Propaganda Techniques* (London, Methuen, 1964); Ernst Kris and Hans Speier, *German Radio Propaganda: Report on Home Broadcasts during the War* (Oxford University Press, 1944); Philip M. Taylor, 'Techniques of Persuasion: Basic Ground Rules of British Propaganda during the Second World War', *Historical Journal of Film, Radio and Television*, 1 (1981), 57–66; H.B. Summers, *Radio Censorship, The Reference Shelf* (New York, The H.W. Wilson Co., 1939).

INDEX OF NAMES, PLACES AND THEMES

Index of Authors' Names